Self-Determination
Across the Life Span

Self-Determination Across the Life Span

Independence and Choice for People with Disabilities

edited by

Deanna J. Sands, Ed.D.

and

Michael L. Wehmeyer, Ph.D.

Baltimore • London • Toronto • Sydney

Paul H. Brookes Publishing Co.
Post Office Box 10624
Baltimore, Maryland 21285-0624

Typeset by Brushwood Graphics, Inc., Baltimore, Maryland.
Manufactured in the United States of America by
The Maple Press Co., York, Pennsylvania.

Library of Congress Cataloging-in-Publication Data
Self-determination across the life span : independence and choice for
  people with disabilities / edited by Deanna J. Sands and Michael L.
  Wehmeyer.
     p.   cm.
  Includes bibliographical references and index.
  ISBN 1-55766-238-X
  1. Handicapped—United States.   2. Handicapped—
Education—United States.   3. Autonomy (Psychology).
4. Choice (Psychology)
I. Sands, Deanna J.   II. Wehmeyer, Michael L.
HV1553.S45 1996
362.4'0973—dc20   96-6837
                                                           CIP

British Library Cataloguing-in-Publication data are available from the
British Library.

Contents

Contributors

Brian Abery, Ph.D.
Adjunct Faculty
Coordinator, School-Age Services
Institute on Community Integration
College of Education and Human
  Development
University of Minnesota
150 Pillsbury Drive, S.E.
Minneapolis, MN 55455

Emma Longan Anderson
Project Director
Full Citizenship, Inc.
211 East 8th Street
P.O. Box 447
Lawrence, KS 66044

Martha J. Blue-Banning, M.A.
Research Assistant
The University of Kansas
Beach Center on Families and Disability
3111 Haworth Hall
Lawrence, KS 66044

Mary Jane Brotherson, Ph.D.
Associate Professor
Human Development and Family Studies
Iowa State University
101 Child Development Building
Ames, IA 50011

Christine C. Cook, Ph.D.
Associate Professor
Human Development and Family Studies
Iowa State University
1086 LeBaron Hall
Ames, IA 50011

Patricia A. Dinas, M.A.
Action Planning Facilitator
Full Citizenship, Inc.
211 East 8th Street
P.O. Box 447
Lawrence, KS 66044

Beth Doll, Ph.D.
Associate Professor
Division of Technology and Special
  Services
University of Colorado at Denver
Campus Box 106
P.O. Box 173364
Denver, CO 80217-3364

Brenda Doss
Secretary
The Arc Board of Directors
c/o Route 11, Box 359
Jasper, AL 35501

Sharon Field, Ed.D.
Associate Professor (Research)
College of Education
Wayne State University
469 Education Building
Detroit, MI 48002

Janet Gensert, O.T.
Portland Oregon Public Schools
531 S.E. 14th
Portland, OR 97214

Bess Hatcher
The Arc of Alabama
c/o 873 Delcris Drive
Birmingham, AL 35226

Alan Hoffman, Ed.D.
Associate Professor
College of Education
Wayne State University
339 Education Building
Detroit, MI 48002

Michael J. Kennedy
Training Associate
Center on Human Policy
Syracuse University
805 S. Crouse Avenue
Syracuse, NY 13244-2280

Laura Huber Marshall, M.A.
Professional Research Assistant
University of Colorado at Colorado
  Springs
School of Education
Self-Determination Projects
P.O. Box 7150
Colorado Springs, CO 80933-7150

James E. Martin, Ph.D.
Professor
University of Colorado at Colorado
  Springs
School of Education
Self-Determination Projects
P.O. Box 7150
Colorado Springs, CO 80933-7150

Jeanne Matuszewski
New Hampshire Parent to Parent
Upper Valley Support Group
117 Mascoma Street
Lebanon, NH 03756

Dennis E. Mithaug, Ph.D.
Professor
Teachers College, Columbia University
515 West 120th Street
New York, NY 10027

Inez Mize
Human Development and Family Studies
Iowa State University
101 Child Development Building
Ames, IA 50011

Susan Palmer, Ph.D.
Project Director
Self-Determination Research Project
Department of Research and Program
  Services
The Arc National Headquarters
500 East Border Street, Suite 300
Arlington, TX 76010

Amy Phillips
Granite State Independent Living
  Foundation
P.O. Box 7268
Concord, NH 03301

Laurie E. Powers, Ph.D.
Child Development Resource Center
Oregon Health Sciences University
P.O. Box 574
707 Southwest Gaines
Portland, OR 97207

Claudia Rein
Research Associate
Hood Center
Dartmouth Medical School
Dartmouth-Hitchcock Medical Center
One Medical Center Drive
Lebanon, NH 03756

Deanna J. Sands, Ed.D.
Associate Professor
Division of Technology and Special
  Services
University of Colorado at Denver
Campus Box 106
P.O. Box 173364
Denver, CO 80217-3364

Dona Schumacher, O.T.
Portland Public Schools
531 S.E. 14th
Portland, OR 97214

Kimberly A. Seaton, M.A.
Project Co-Director
Full Citizenship, Inc.
211 East 8th Street
P.O. Box 447
Lawrence, KS 66044

Loretta A. Serna, Ph.D.
Associate Professor
University of New Mexico
Special Education Program
College of Education
Mesa Vista Hall, 3rd Floor
Albuquerque, NM 87131-1261

Roger Stancliffe, Ph.D.
Research Fellow
Institute on Community Integration
College of Education and Human
  Development
University of Minnesota
150 Pillsbury Drive, S.E.
Minneapolis, MN 55455

Ann P. Turnbull, Ed.D.
Professor
The University of Kansas
Beach Center on Families and Disability
3111 Haworth Hall
Lawrence, KS 66045

H. Rutherford Turnbull, III, LL.B., LL.M.
Professor
The University of Kansas
Beach Center on Families and Disability
3111 Haworth Hall
Lawrence, KS 66045

Michael J. Ward, Ph.D.
Bureau Chief
Secondary Education and Transition Services
U.S. Department of Education, Office of
  Special Education Programs
RSA, Room 4624, Switzer Building
400 Maryland Avenue, S.W.
Washington, D.C. 20202

Michael L. Wehmeyer, Ph.D.
Assistant Director
Department of Research and Program
  Services
The Arc National Headquarters
500 East Border Street, Suite 300
Arlington, TX 76010

Cindy Weigel-Garrey, M.S.
Human Development and Family Studies
Iowa State University
101 Child Development Building
Ames, IA 50011

Michael D. West, Ph.D.
Research Associate
Rehabilitation Research and Training
  Center on Supported Employment
Virginia Commonwealth University
P.O. Box 842011
Richmond, VA 23284-2011

Roxanne Wilson
Assistant Director
South East Regional Education Service
  Center
11 Peabody Road
Derry, NH 03038

Robert Zajac
Graduate Student
Institute on Community Integration
College of Education and Human
  Development
University of Minnesota
150 Pillsbury Drive, S.E.
Minneapolis, MN 55455

Foreword

WHY IS SELF-DETERMINATION important to me?

When I moved to New Bedford, I wanted to open a checking account. I went over to the bank and I gave the $10 to open the account and I asked them if there would be a problem. They said no. But, when I went back a couple of days later, they said I could not have an account. I asked them why, and they said they didn't understand my signature. I thought about this and I realized that I had a checking account before I moved, and that had worked fine.

The next morning I put on a suit and a tie and I went down to the main branch. I asked to see the bank president. They told me he was at a meeting. I told them I would wait. I waited for about two minutes and he came out. He brought me into a room and asked me what the problem was. I told him. I also brought my canceled checks and I showed him that I had an account before. He apologized, and I got my checking account.

That is why self-determination is important to me.

Ray Gagne, Chair
National Self-Advocacy Committee
The Arc National Headquarters
Arlington, TX

Foreword

SOCIAL MOVEMENTS ARE always filled with words and word phrases that act as benchmarks and signposts. These buzzwords become the indicators of both best and worst practice. They focus discussion and debate, policy and practice. As new perspectives develop, new words are added to the list, sometimes necessarily and other times, unfortunately, replacing or usurping words that were already there. Our movement is no different. *Quality of life, integration, choice, empowerment, people first, natural supports, person centered, self-advocacy, independent living, supported employment, reasonable accommodation,* and *inclusion* are just words to some but represent fundamental strategies, concepts, outcomes, and values to many others. *Warehousing, segregation, inaccessibility, learned helplessness, institutionalization, dependency, being disconnected,* and *inequality* represent the antithesis of what is acceptable. Still other words—such as *enclave, group home,* and *mainstreaming*—lose favor as they run their course and unanticipated outcomes become apparent. Other words mean such different things to different people that we find ourselves arguing with those with whom we are in complete agreement (e.g., *developmental*). Nonetheless, words are our signposts and are a necessary part of understanding the deeper message of where we've been, where we're going, and what we're all about. *Self-Determination Across the Life Span: Independence and Choice for People with Disabilities* solidifies a place for a very important word on our list and in our movement: *self-determination.* Its place is substantiated by our history, by need, and by a lot of focused theoretical construct and practical application. The book not only reviews these constructs and applications, but also directs and focuses us to understand self-determination in a way that will better ensure its place in our social movement.

Developing buzzword lists is not the only thing we have in common with other great social movements. Most great movements reflect on the needs and rights of marginalized people "to live independently, enjoy self-determination, make choices, contribute to society, pursue meaningful careers and enjoy full inclusion and integration in the economic, political, social, cultural and educational mainstream of American Society" ([Sec. 2 (a)(3)(A-F)] of the 1992 Vocational Rehabilitation Act and Rehabilitation Act Amendments of 1992). Evidence of public policy support for these movements can often be measured by its investment in education. All social movements are supported or thwarted by the adequacy of information exchange. Uneducated people too often have no means of knowing what to ask for and either ask for the wrong things, ask for things in ineffective ways, or don't ask at all. This point is vividly reflected by Pablo Freire (1992) in his book *Pedagogy of the Oppressed.* In reflecting upon his work teaching poor people in South America, he wrote of education becoming a subversive activity. As we learn more of what is possible, we more aggressively and accurately assess and advocate for ourselves and our communities. With improved information exchange and education, the recognition and importance of self-determination has evolved. We are learning to understand self-determination as a means to individually shape, mold, and define the nature of this personal and social experience. Since education has been, and will continue to be, at the heart of this journey, *Self-Determination Across the Life Span* provides us with a basic and essential educational text.

For years, the questions that need to be asked in order to best support the transition of people into community life have been well known. These questions are relatively simple. Where do you want to spend your time living, working, learning, and socializing? What events and activities are important to you in those settings? Who are important people to interact with in these environments and activities? Unfortunately, these questions are not guiding much of our transition efforts. There are many explanations for this. First, bureaucratic requirements too often become obstacles to addressing or even remembering these questions. Our attention to the important questions is diverted rather than focused as a result of compliance procedures, planning documents, forms, and meetings. Second, too many of us still don't know how to ask these questions or to whom we need to direct these questions. Third, too many people with disabilities don't have a way to answer them. Either their experiences have been too limited to facilitate informed choice making or their communication systems have been underdeveloped or ignored. Fourth, many of us don't want to hear the answers. Finally, many of us don't know what to do once we hear them. We tend to try and protect our system or protect the individual; however, as Colleen Wieck (1993) expressed, "We [professionals] thought it was what they wanted, if we are honest, it suited our busy schedules, it was cost effective, issues may have been risky, we did not want them to experience failure, etc., etc., etc." Will you be alarmed when the authors cite research confirming that the vast majority of people with disabilities have had no choice in where they live or work or who they socialize with or who provides them services? *Self-Determination Across the Life Span* not only provides explanations for why these questions and answers are so elusive, but also explains interventions that can attenuate unnecessary barriers. We will promote self determination as we learn to better support asking and answering these questions.

Our ability to focus on the question of *where do you want to spend your time* has been diverted by a **great deception**; that is, we perseverate on believing that the choice people with disabilities should have is whether they want to be integrated or segregated. Integration means there's a place for you and it's with the rest of us. Once that is established as the true normalization statement, choice making will no longer be bipolar. People with disabilities will realize, as others have, that they have an unlimited number of choices regarding where they want to spend their time. We must learn to make community life a more accessible place and, as Robert Perske wrote, a place where we collectively appreciate that

> all human beings possess unique gifts and energies that can enrich a neighborhood. If the interweavings of a truly inclusive neighborhood could be depicted by a colorful piece of fabric, one would find the vivid, colorful threads woven by people with disabilities in that fabric, too. (cited in Amado, Conklin, & Wells, 1990)

Our ability to focus on the question of *what do you want to spend your time doing* has been trivialized by a **great insult**; that is, when you're happy and you know it clap your hands. Skill limitations and challenges too often get equated with treating people with disabilities as irresponsible children who would be happier attending the circus than engaged in adult decisions and activities. We will learn to support meaningful experience and participation in the activities of community life. Participation is not about individual skills and skill limitations. The authors promote viewing personal capacities from a broader perspective, from an environmental context. Experience, trial-and-error, creativity, and persistence allow for the development of likes, dislikes, new abilities, and new opportunities.

Within this context, necessary instruction, accommodation, and skill acquisition all can be considered conditions for success, futures planning, and self-determined behavior. Our ability to focus on the question of *with whom do you want and need to interact* has been minimalized by a **great hoax**; that is, independence is both defined as the goal and is defined narrowly and rigidly. We will learn to value and build richer, sustaining relationships in people's lives that support their involvement in community life. Then, as Heumann (1995) so effectively states it, we will realize that "independent living does not mean doing things yourself. It means having control over what's being done. Very few of us desire moving through out lives alone, doing only for ourselves and not cherishing relationships with others. We are learning to appreciate our social networks and the importance of friendships, mentors, and supports. This circle of relationships becomes a most important tool for gaining advice, direction, back-up, and support for the decisions we each make.

Self-Determination Across the Life Span will help each of us functionally define self-determination. We will find ourselves wrestling with rigid inflexible and alternative definitions. Is it merely choice making and having a voice? Is it being totally independent and in total control? Or is it having primary control and making informed choices that result from experience and a supportive group of people in our lives? At first, answering these questions seems simple until we deal with real people in complex situations. Then these questions cause us to question and clarify our values. Our values will be challenged, and conflict will be unavoidable. When is a dream, or a choice, a bad dream *or* just not ours? When is a goal unrealistic or beyond our ability or willingness to be creative, inconvenienced, engaged, or effective? When is an activity too risky and irresponsible, and when is it a risk worth taking and a necessary part of a person's growth and development? You probably won't find answers to these questions in this book. That would be too easy. This stuff just isn't easy.

This book will, however, help us frame the issues and act more responsibly. We find herein philosophy, definition, research, theoretical constructs, and intervention strategies. It provides us much needed insight, knowledge, and tools. We will undoubtedly become more informed, appreciative, and facilitating of self-determined behavior. Indeed we must.

Ian Pumpian, Ph.D.
Professor and Chair of Special Education
San Diego State University
San Diego, California

REFERENCES

Amado, A.N., Conklin, N., & Wells, J. (1990). *Friends: A manual for connecting persons with disabilities and community members.* St. Paul, MN: Human Services Research and Development Center.

Freire, P. (1992). *Pedagogy of the oppressed.* New York: Continuum Publishing.

Heumann, J. (1995, February). *A conversation with the director.* Presented at the 8th Annual Strategies for Inclusive Education Conference, Denver, CO.

Rehabilitation Act Amendments of 1992, PL 102-569 (October 29, 1992). Title 29, U.S.C. *701 et seq: U.S. Statutes at Large, 100,* 4344–4488.

Wieck, C. (1993, October). *To the far side of interdependence.* Presented at the Annual Seminar by The Bay Conference, San Diego, CA.

Preface

THIS BOOK PROVIDES a comprehensive treatment of self-determination as an educational outcome, from theory to practice. A person reading the chapters from start to finish would learn what led to the emergence of self-determination as a topic of increased interest; be introduced to several frameworks that conceptualize self-determination as an educational outcome; have access to the perspective of several key stakeholders as to the importance of self-determination in their lives; and discover a number of strategies, materials, and procedures to promote this outcome. However, there may be a fundamental question left unanswered in the chapters that follow. Why write a book on self-determination? In our mind, the justification is so fundamental that it may not be clearly articulated. While we could easily compose a response to this question based on issues of educational efficacy and best practice, the truth lies deeper. The fact is that this book emerged as much from a set of shared values, held by both editors and individual contributors, that people with disabilities have the right to experience control in and over their lives, to participate in and make decisions that affect their lives, and to experience the dignity that comes with living self-determined lives. One only has to listen to adults with disabilities to know that this direction is the right direction and that this remains unattainable for far too many people with disabilities today. This book is one way that we have heeded the call of people with disabilities to enable and empower them to take control and make choices.

Which leads to a related issue . . . namely, what this book is not about and what we do not believe. Invariably the topic of self-determination elicits a set of "concerns" that serve to undermine the critical nature of this topic. There exists a mistaken belief on the part of some that by promoting self-determination we are, in fact, elevating individual needs and goals over the needs and goals of a collective family or community. A second misinterpretation is that self-determination means absolute control by the individual. These interpretations are, in our mind, neither fair nor accurate. As to the first, we recognize the tenuous balance that exists between pursuing autonomous, independent behaviors and the need to hold and pursue altruistic and interdependent values and goals. As Michael Kennedy relates in Chapter 3 of this book, self-determination emerged for him on the foundation of trusting relationships with others. This is true time and again for people with disabilities. In many cases that "someone" is a family member, in other cases a friend or professional.

The second misinterpretation, that self-determination is about absolute control, takes the overemphasis on stark individuality to its illogical conclusion. Control is rarely, if ever, absolute, and only the most naïve person assumes that he or she has absolute control over any part of his or her life. In fact, even a cursory examination of the issue of control makes it quite evident that not only do people not have absolute control over many aspects of their lives, they do not want such power! As Wehmeyer and Berkobien (1991) pointed out, while most people want the opportunity to decide if or when they have some necessary surgery, most of the same people will gladly relinquish complete control over the actual operation to the surgeon.

The misrepresentation of self-determination as synonymous with absolute individual control manifests itself in practice in two equally harmful ways: 1) the continued prohibition on the opportunities for people to learn and experience self-determination, and 2) justification for poor or ineffective instructional and programmatic activities. In the first case, when self-determination is equated with absolute control and complete "independence," there is a tendency to criticize self-determination with "what if" scenarios. These "what if" scenarios typically involve a worst-case example. For example: "What if Johnny decides to eat two dozen donuts a day, thereby sending him into a diabetic coma and certain death?" The argument against self-determination progresses through a discussion around whether any other citizen would be allowed to eat himself into a diabetic coma and the general need to protect these helpless citizens and ends with a dismissal of self-determination as unrealistic, dangerous, or naive. Wolfensberger (1995) illustrated such a dire prediction in a review of a book on abuse and disability. He ends the review by stating that

> given the extreme vulnerability of handicapped people that is unendingly revealed in this book, one cannot expect that the current craze of sending these people without personal protection and accompaniment into a predatory, immoral and collapsing society in the name of craze shibboleths, such as self-determination, self-advocacy, and choice, will result in anything but more abuse. (p. 221)

The issues surrounding the topics of medical self-determination, informed consent and decision making, and protection and guardianship for individuals with limited competency are complex and cannot be dismissed as irrelevant. However, to focus on these worst-case scenarios is to ignore the fact that too many people with disabilities continue to hold little if any control over the most seemingly mundane aspects of their lives and are directed and dictated to by others. Until people with disabilities have the opportunity to participate to the greatest degree possible in decisions about where and with whom they live, work, and play and experience the same chances to make choices about what to wear for the day, when to go to the grocery store, or who they want as their personal care attendant as do their peers without disabilities, then it is unfair and unwarranted to inflame the debate about self-determination with horror stories and worst-case scenarios. This book is about enabling people with disabilities to participate fully in their lives. Does promoting self-determination imply a stance that all people with disabilities can independently control all aspects of their lives and should be shuttled out to face the consequences of their actions, no matter how dire? Of course not. Supporting self-determination means that, like their peers without disabilities, people with disabilities have the right to participate in decisions about their lives in a meaningful way and to the greatest degree possible and should be provided the skills and the opportunities to make choices about their lives based on their preferences, beliefs, and values.

This leads to a second topic of contention, that of the role of choice in self-determination. Choice making is the focal point for many advocates and people with disabilities, yet focusing exclusively on choice to the exclusion of other aspects of self-determination is a double-edged sword. Ferleger (1994) gets to the heart of the matter, stating that there "is a current tendency in practice which justifies what I would label deprivation or denial of services, or violation of rights, of people with mental retardation based on invocation of "choice" as a guiding principle" (p. 70). One example we have heard described involved a woman who lived in a group home and spent much of her "leisure" time staring out the front window of the home waiting for a preferred friend to come and pick her up and take her out, even though this friend was not scheduled to visit. The staff at this home justified their lack of intervention in this situation by stating that this was "her choice." This is nothing less than neglect on the part of the staff members, and to ascribe this as honoring that woman's self-determination is absurd. When focusing on choice in isolation from other important characteristics of self-determination (e.g., goal setting, problem solving, self-advocacy), one builds a house of cards that is too easily tumbled. Self-determination is not simply synonymous with choice. However, enabling and empowering people to make choices is an important step toward self-determination and, in many cases, the sensible first step.

There are other reasons that we believe that self-determination is a topic of importance. There is evidence that promoting self-determination enables all individuals to achieve more positive adult outcomes and become self-competent. As we discuss in the final chapter, the self-determination movement is also a necessary component of other reform movements, including school reform and inclusion. Without this key element, we believe that these movements will not fully succeed.

The book is thus divided into two sections. Section I provides an introduction to definitional, theoretical, and policy issues related to self-determination. Chapter 1 provides a historical account and a personal perspective on the self-determination movement and a rationale for why it is important to continue those efforts. Chapter 2 examines the various conceptualizations of self-determination, discusses self-determination as an educational framework, and provides a rationale for the importance of focusing on self-determination as an educational outcome for children, youth, and adults with disabilities. Chapters 3 and 4 provide perspectives on self-determination from key stakeholders in this issue, people with disabilities and parents and family members. After reading their stories, we believe the reader will have a deeper appreciation as to why it is important for people with disabilities, with direct support from their family members, friends, neighbors, teachers, and other service providers, to make a concerted effort to develop and apply the attitudes and skills necessary to act in self-determined ways. Chapter 5 discusses the developmental nature of and course for the capacities and skills associated with self-determination. The chapter identifies ways to maximize instructional efforts to promote self-determination for children and youth with disabilities at the preschool, early and late elementary, and secondary school levels. Chapter 6 focuses on the importance of the interaction between children with disabilities, their families, and the home environment as a means to enhance the acquisition and development of self-determined behavior. Chapter 7 extends the ecological perspective of Chapter 6 through a detailed analysis of the factors that influence both opportunities for personal control and the acquisition of the capacities necessary for self-determination. The last chapter of Section I provides a compelling thesis that self-determination is a right of all people and that there is a collective responsibility for improving the prospects for self-determination among the least advantaged groups. The author argues that the responsibility for improving prospects for self-determination among youth with disabilities is both a moral obligation as well as the fundamental purpose of our special education system.

Section II contains useful information and resources that will help practitioners structure environments and implement assessment, curriculum, instructional, and support practices to facilitate self-determination among their students. We include information specific to early childhood education, school-age programs, and work environments for adults who have disabilities. Chapter 9 outlines important caregiver interactions and parenting styles that are conducive to the development of self-determination. In addition, this chapter identifies guidelines for structuring children's tasks and activities at home and in school to maximize opportunities to develop and express self-determination. Chapter 10 provides a model for school improvement and individualized planning that effectively involves individuals in a collaborative process to create change in their settings. A curriculum that promotes student knowledge, beliefs, and skills that lead to self-determination is described.

Chapter 11 discusses student involvement in the IEP process, and materials are presented that help planners structure and facilitate student leadership of their own IEP process. One school district's attempts to implement a self-determination–oriented transition process is described. Group Action Planning, a person-centered planning process for enhancing self-determination within the transition planning process for adolescents, is the focus of Chapter 12. Case studies are used to provide an overview of the process as well as descriptions of each planning component. Chapter 13 outlines the key conditions necessary to promote self-determination for adolescents with and without disabilities, required shifts in attitudes and practices, and supports necessary to promote the empowerment capacities of parents and professionals. The *Learning with PURPOSE* curriculum is described in Chapter 14. This curriculum focuses on the following skill areas: 1) social relations, 2) self-evaluation, 3) self-direction, 4) networking, 5) collaboration, 6) persistence and risk taking, and 7) stress management. Chapter 15 describes key changes in the Rehabilitation Act that promote choice and self-determination for consumers and ways in which choice and self-determination can be enhanced or abrogated for consumers of vocational rehabilitation. The final chapter provides a framework by which you can examine the values, policies and regulations, organizational structures, and professional behaviors and procedures that are necessary to create contexts that support self-determination as an educational outcome.

REFERENCES

Ferleger, D. (1994). The place of choice. In C. Sundram (Ed.), *Choice and responsibility: Legal and ethical dilemmas in services for persons with mental disabilities* (pp. 69–96). Albany: New York State Commission on Quality of Care for the Mentally Disabled.

Wehmeyer, M.L., & Berkobien, R. (1991). Self-determination and self-advocacy: A case of mistaken identity. *TASH Newsletter, 17*(1), 4.

Wolfensberger, W. (1995). [Review of the book *Violence and abuse in the lives of people with disabilities: An end to silent acceptance?*]. *American Journal on Mental Retardation, 100,* 217–221.

Acknowledgments

WE WOULD LIKE to acknowledge the support and assistance of the editorial and production staff at Paul H. Brookes Publishing Co., particularly our editor, Theresa Donnelly. The level of professionalism and efficiency exhibited at all phases of the production of this book was superb. We are particularly grateful to the contributors to this book for their hard work and tolerance of our seemingly endless stream of requests. To the extent that the book achieves its stated goals, most of the credit goes to these colleagues. The bulk of the chapters were written by researchers and practitioners supported by Department of Education grants to create model demonstration projects and assessment procedures to support self-determination. Michael Ward, Ph.D., bureau chief for the Secondary Education and Transition Services branch of OSEP, and Tom Hanley, Ph.D., project officer for the Self-Determination Assessment projects funded by OSEP's Division on Innovation and Development, deserve credit for providing the leadership to move self-determination from a buzzword to an educational outcome. We have benefited from support and encouragement in our ongoing research into self-determination from colleagues and would be remiss if we were to ignore their support. Thus, we would like to acknowledge Alan Abeson, Ed.D., Sharon Davis, Ph.D., and Richard Berkobien, M.S.W. (M.W.) and Cynthia Rose, M.S., Dennis Corash, Ph.D., Marci Leonard, M.S., and Beth Doll, Ph.D. (D.S.). Finally, we acknowledge the support of our families during this process, particularly Kathy (M.W.) and Gary (D.S.).

This book is dedicated to our children
Taylor Sierra Sands,
Geoffrey Paul Wehmeyer,
and Graham Thomas Wehmeyer
Our hope and dream for them, as they begin their school journeys, is that they have the opportunity to grow up with children with disabilities as friends, classmates, teammates, playmates, and neighbors.

Self-Determination
Across the Life Span

Section I

AN OVERVIEW OF SELF-DETERMINATION

Chapter 1

COMING OF AGE
IN THE AGE OF
SELF-DETERMINATION

A Historical and Personal Perspective

Michael J. Ward

THE HISTORY OF the self-determination movement can be described through the history of related social movements, including the self-advocacy, disability rights, and empowerment movements, all of which contributed to the current emphasis on self-determination. I was born in 1951, before there was an emphasis on self-determination for people with disabilities, and the emergence of my own self-determination has paralleled the emergence of self-determination for all people with disabilities. During the late 1960s, as I was trying to become more independent and autonomous by breaking away from my parents' care, the population with disabilities as a whole was attempting to reverse society's perception that they needed care and protection. The intent of this chapter is to provide a historical account and a personal perspective of the self-determination movement and current self-determination efforts and to explain why it is important to continue these efforts.

A BRIEF HISTORY OF
SELF-DETERMINATION FOR PEOPLE WITH DISABILITIES

History has, too often, not looked favorably upon people with disabilities. Funk (1987) stated that throughout time the inferior economic and social status of people with disabilities has been viewed as the *inevitable* consequence of the physical and mental differences imposed by disability. Gartner and Joe (1987) com-

3

piled several convincing essays on images of disability in literature that illustrate this societal perception. Literature and popular culture have depicted people with disabilities as beggars, heroes, and thieves, including such characters as Tiny Tim, who will always need our pity; Ironside, who has extraordinary investigative abilities *in spite* of a disability; and Captain Hook, who has turned evil because of losing his hand. Most historical accounts of the life of one of the nation's greatest Presidents, Franklin D. Roosevelt, omit and thus deny the existence and implications of his severe disability. The debate continues 50 years after his death (including a controversy over the design of a proposed FDR memorial) as to whether this public cover-up was the result of a conscious attempt to hide the negative image associated with Roosevelt's disability or that the needs of the country were so significant at the time that the image of the President had to be one of strength and ability (R. Harris, personal communication, April 20, 1995; Gallagher, 1985). Whatever the source, these types of images did not portray people with disabilities as being valued, contributing, average, capable, and loving members of society.

Shapiro (1993) pointed out that, throughout most of the history of the United States, there is ample evidence of inhospitable treatment toward people with disabilities. Citizens who experience cognitive, mental, or physical disability have traditionally represented a hidden minority in American society (Percy, 1989). Literally, through institutionalization, and subtly, through negative attitudes and behaviors, people with disabilities have been isolated from the social mainstream and denied the benefits and opportunities available to people without disabilities. Berkowitz (1987) suggested that, from the 1920s to the 1970s, segregation was the theme that predominated in the government's disability programs.

The dehumanization of people with disabilities is further exemplified by the fact that society has treated people with disabilities as if they were incapable and were neither expected nor willing to contribute to society. Thus, services such as rehabilitation too often have been provided in a paternalistic manner that undermines self-initiative and self-respect (Szymanski & Trueba, 1994). Funk (1987) asserted that

> The evolution of disability history and policy in the United States can be described as the increasing humanization of disabled people: humanization is defined as recognition that disabled people have human needs and characteristics, and public policy must be designed to reflect and further this human potential. (p. 8)

The situation began to change in the first half of the present century and built momentum in the second half. A few advocacy groups were established in the late 19th century, particularly for deaf and blind people (Shapiro, 1993). Robert Irwin, who in the 1920s and 1930s presided over the American Foundation of the Blind, promoted self-reliance among blind people. Social policy initiatives established medical and rehabilitation programs to care for veterans disabled during the World Wars and workers injured by accidents. Fortunately, advances made by these programs during the 1940s and 1950s enabled people with disabilities to live longer, especially people with more severe disabilities requiring more specialized and extensive care. Consequently, the increased number of medically stable people with disabilities in the community forced society and policy makers to consider strategies for managing the welfare of these individuals.

Access to Education

The first such strategy was to provide increased opportunities for children with disabilities to receive some form of education. An unintentional result of this strategy was that children and youth who received the benefits from these opportunities grew into young adults who became disenfranchised with their disempowerment through segregation. It has historically been true that, in societies where there were subservient populations, it was forbidden to educate people from lower socioeconomic strata. For example, prior to the Civil War, it was illegal in many southern states to teach slaves how to read and write (Hughes & Meltzer, 1963). At least one reason for this prohibition is that education leads to knowledge, and knowledge leads to power. Such power enables the underclass to make comparisons between what they read about and their actual status and empowers them to advocate for change.

As a disabled advocate, I would like to believe that the lack of educational opportunities for most children and youth with disabilities prior to the 1950s was the result of benign neglect. It would be nice to believe that the reason that children and youth spent their days at home rather than in classrooms was because society just did not realize that the provision of education to individuals with disabilities would have positive benefits. However, this was not entirely the case, and in fact, statutes in many states allowed for the exclusion of students with not only physical and mental disabilities but also those who exhibited behaviors that would make school attendance inadvisable in the viewpoint of school officials (Simon, 1992). Litigation during the early 1970s, including decisions like *Mills v. D.C. Board of Education* (1972) and the *Pennsylvania Association for Retarded Children v. the Commonwealth of Pennsylvania* (1972), were forerunners for the landmark Education for All Handicapped Children Act of 1975 (PL 94-142), which guaranteed all children and youth with disabilities a free, appropriate public education. By the latter part of the decade, thousands of children and youth with disabilities attended public school for the first time under the auspices of PL 94-142.

However, prior to PL 94-142, some children and youth with disabilities, like myself, were receiving an education. From the early 1950s, school districts assumed responsibility for educating an increasing number of children and youth with disabilities, primarily in response to the demands of parents. Still, most districts considered this to be an act of charity. Consequently, many parents became advocates for a better quality of education and an expanded range of educational placements. As children and youth with disabilities began to benefit from better education and better educational opportunities, teachers as well as students also became advocates for education that prepared them for successful postschool outcomes, either college or competitive/sheltered employment.

Disability Rights Movements

The second strategy to reverse societal perceptions and expectations came from the independent living and disability rights movements. The independent living movement began in the 1960s and was strongly influenced by the social and political consciousness of other civil rights movements taking place at the time (Funk, 1987; Percy, 1989; Shapiro, 1993). Lehr and Taylor (1986) suggested that people with disabilities were

> profoundly affected by the social and political upheaval created by the civil rights movement. They identified with the struggles of other disenfranchised groups to achieve integration and meaningful equality of opportunity. For the first time, people with disabilities recognized their own oppression and like other oppressed minorities, they too became angry. They recognized that, as a fractioned minority, people with disabilities had no value, and worse yet, no power. (p. 4)

This lack of value and power led many people with disabilities to realize a common status of marginality with members of racial and ethnic minority groups (Szymanski & Trueba, 1994). People with disabilities also began to respond to society's belief that "the handicapped" were less intelligent, less able to make the right decisions, and therefore, less able to determine their own lives (Berkowitz, 1987).

The concepts of the *right to integration* and *meaningful equality of opportunity* stressed by other civil rights groups, as well as the methods and tactics utilized, were adopted by disability rights efforts. Other trends, such as consumerism, self-help, demedicalization/self-care, and deinstitutionalization, also had an impact on the growth of disability rights. For example, the trend toward consumerism led to the belief that any consumer of disability services "has a right to control what he or she receives, and consequently has a role in the formulation of policy and in the development of quality standards" (Campbell, 1991, p. 68). Each of these movements and trends supported the growing comprehension by people with disabilities that they had rights and could choose, belong, and participate as full and equal members of society.

Ed Roberts, a leader in the disability movement, emphasized the connection between the struggle of other minorities for equality and the marginal status of people with disabilities. Roberts defined independence in terms of the control people with disabilities have over their lives and argued that it should be measured not by the tasks one can perform without assistance but by the quality of one's life with adequate support (Shapiro, 1993). Nosek (1992) defined independent living as "control over one's life based on the choice of acceptable options that minimize reliance on others in making decisions and in performing everyday activities" (p. 103). This includes decisions leading to self-determination and "implies an optimally responsible and productive exercise of the power of choice" (p. 103).

The concepts of self-help and group organizing were key components of the independent living movement (Shapiro, 1993). People with disabilities needed to manage their own care in order to reverse their dependency status and thus focused on self-care skills. Group organizing became important as people with disabilities realized that they would have difficulty making choices in environments built for people without disabilities (Hahn, 1987). They came to the realization that managing their own daily needs was not sufficient for independence as long as environmental and attitudinal barriers limited opportunities for choice making and active participation in the community. Self-care had to mean more than just home care; it had to address the barriers that a person with a disability experienced when attempting to participate in community activities. Thus, a group identity began to grow with a feeling of "one for all and all for one." People with disabilities realized that the barriers they experienced were the same barriers experienced by other people with similar disabilities and by people with other disabilities.

Legislative Mandates Although the disability rights movement became a political force only during the 1960s, it quickly gained some powerful allies in the U.S. Congress. The Architectural Barriers Act of 1968 (PL 90-480) required that all construction supported by federal funds had to be accessible to people with disabilities (Percy, 1989). While the primary intent of this law was to guarantee access to public buildings by people with disabilities, a more significant outcome was that, for the first time, the country stated through law that 1) people with disabilities were indeed an integral part of the public, and 2) accommodations were required to ensure that they had access to public facilities.

Congress also understood that *access* for people with disabilities was not enough to ensure equal opportunity. In 1972, members of Congress attempted to add an amendment to the authorizing vocational rehabilitation legislation requiring that no otherwise qualified person be denied the benefits of federal assistance on the basis of a disability. This simple statement had a profound effect on the growth of the disability rights movement. Because many people with disabilities were outraged at President Nixon's initial veto of this bill, they collectively organized across the country to work, alongside parents and other supporters, for the passage of what became known as Section 504 of the Rehabilitation Act of 1973 (PL 93-112) (Lehr & Taylor, 1986). However, these mandated legislative protections occurred before there was an active disability rights movement (Funk, 1987), evidenced by the fact that it took the executive branch 4 years to begin to issue regulations and another 2–4 years to require implementation. Disabled advocates were not able to mobilize quickly to demand implementation of these newly won protections.

Self-Advocacy Movement   A related, but younger, disability rights movement is the self-advocacy movement. Self-advocacy started as a civil rights movement by people with developmental disabilities who were rebelling against being underestimated, deprived of choices, treated like eternal children, and thought to lead lesser lives (Shapiro, 1993). Self-advocacy began in Sweden when Bengt Nirje, based on his experience with children and adults with mental retardation, came to believe that they could and should have a role in their own choices (Shapiro, 1993). Self-advocacy and self-determination both grew out of Nirje's (1972) normalization principle. This principle stated the importance of "making available to [people with mental retardation] the patterns and conditions of everyday life which are as close as possible to the norms and patterns of the mainstream of society" (Nirje, 1976, p. 363). Normalization (Nirje, 1976) meant having

- Opportunities to have choices, wishes, and desires taken into consideration and respected
- Opportunities to experience a normal rhythm of the day, with daily events, like getting out of bed and eating meals, occurring under similar circumstances and at similar times as the population without disabilities
- Opportunities to experience a normal routine of life, including access to and participation in a similar range of activities (e.g., work, leisure, home) in the same settings used by people without disabilities
- Opportunities to experience the normal rhythm of the year with the celebration of holidays and days of personal or family significance, including the opportunity for vacation and travel
- Opportunities to encounter the normal developmental experiences of the life cycle (For youth with disabilities, this means learning about one's abilities and potential, obtaining an understanding of oneself, and building one's self-confidence. For older youth with disabilities, it is important to move away from home and to live as independently as possible.)

Nirje (1972) extended the normalization principle by teaching self-advocacy skills through adult education coursework. Courses in contemporary society, political science, and parliamentary techniques provided an orientation to the process of decision making, the roles and functions of group members, and financial control. Such skills are necessary for successful self-advocacy groups.

According to Lehr and Taylor (1986), self-advocacy means being able

> to speak for yourself, to make decisions for yourself, to know what your rights are and how to "stick up" for yourself when your rights are being violated or diminished. It also means being able to help others who cannot speak for themselves. (p. 3)

In self-advocacy groups, members learn how to support one another and to help one another become active participants in decisions that affect their lives

(Longhurst, 1994). They advocate for basic civil rights and educate their communities about developmental disabilities in an attempt to dispel prejudice and discrimination.

People First, a self-advocacy organization with chapters in several states, started in Oregon in 1974 with a meeting of self-advocates who came together to discuss housing, business, and equality in society (Lehr & Taylor, 1986). Over time, not only were they successful in helping with deinstitutionalization throughout Oregon, but the number of People First members and chapters, as well as other self-advocacy groups, rapidly spread across the country.

In 1974, there were 16 self-advocacy groups in the United States; by 1984, more than 5,000 people with mental retardation were involved in 152 such groups (Longhurst, 1994). The number of groups increased to 380 in 1990. A 1994 survey identified 505 self-advocacy groups in 43 states and the District of Columbia (Longhurst, 1994). Based on the survey sample, it is estimated that about 11,600 people with disabilities are involved in organized self-advocacy. This survey also found that self-advocacy groups spent their time on 1) individual advocacy (38.2%), 2) social and recreational activities (24.4%), 3) group advocacy (15.1%), and 4) self-help–related topics (14.75%).

A PERSONAL HISTORY

Education, disability rights, the desire for independent living, and instruction in self-advocacy all had a profound effect on the development of my own self-determination skills. I was one of those "unfortunates" who received an education via the charity of the New York City Board of Education. My peers and I continue to debate the value of the education we received. Was it the same as our peers or siblings without disabilities in the range of subjects and challenging curricula? Certainly not! Did it facilitate our intellectual and social development? I tend to equivocate on this one and respond by saying that it depended on what the student and his or her parents were willing to invest in the process. In other words, because my parents and I put a lot into my education, I became educated; however, there were other families who *could not* make this investment and therefore their children did not develop intellectually and socially. Did the school staff do the best that they could to teach us the basic skills and try to motivate us to better ourselves? I will always answer this question with a definite "yes!" They did the best they could because there were no exemplars for doing it better. I must believe that my teachers withheld nothing from me and many of my peers. Whatever we did not get from our education, it was truly the result of benign neglect. However, the fact is that many of us did manage to receive a good education as evidenced by the number of my peers receiving postsecondary degrees and being employed, often in spite of the educational system.

Many of us who did become educated in this happenstance system not only went on to postsecondary education but also joined the initial disability rights movement of the 1970s. I was a founding member, along with Judy Heumann, of New York City's Disabled In Action. At the same time, I was exploring my own independent living options and practicing self-advocacy by being one of the first students with disabilities at a small private college away from the city, and as such was not able to be active in the organization. Yet I did stay connected because I experienced or was aware of many of the issues that the advocates were addressing. Housing was important because I could live in an accessible facility only with help. Transportation was equally important because I did not drive and became tired of relying on others to go places. I knew that employment would become increasingly important because my chances of getting a job were almost negligible. I knew that I needed to be part of the group's identity and identify with the group's issues.

However, receiving an education and being a member of a disability rights group were not enough for me to become self-determined. I believed that my disability made me different and that because I was different, it was all right if society provided me with different, and often unequal, treatment. I was also a follower, meaning that if other people advocated for me as a disabled person, I would gladly partake in the benefits. Probably the reason I was not at the forefront of the movement was that I was too busy thanking people for whatever treatment I did receive! Specifically, I was not willing to risk what I had gained, no matter how unacceptable it was. Was this perception irrational? Certainly, but this kind of thinking was shared by many devalued people and it did lead to my becoming self-determined (see Mithaug, Chapter 8).

By now, you are wondering if the publisher lost any of the pages to this chapter because it is impossible to become self-determined after feeling so inferior and passive. The answer is very simple: Being gracious all the time is hard work, and I became tired of working so hard. The feeling was similar to "been down so long, it looks like up to me." So I became more self-centered and began thinking about and valuing *me*!

My first reaction to my new sense of *self* was to become more independent. When I got tired of receiving inadequate treatment from others, I decided to do it myself rather than demand better service. (Because I still felt different, I felt that I did not have a right to equal service. Therefore, if I demanded better service, I felt that I would be refused and even abandoned.) Although my efforts to become independent did result in learning how to drive and cook, many of my colleagues within the disability rights movement would not have agreed with my approach.

They would have been right. I eventually realized that I did not live in an isolated environment in which I perceived to have total control. The fact is that I could not do everything by myself because of my disability, and trying to do everything alone once again made me very tired. And because I was more "independent," my parents and others who had automatically helped me in the past were no longer around. It took a while for me to understand that I needed help and that I needed good help. It took me even more time to self-advocate for help and then to feel comfortable about asking for and modulating the kind of help I needed. This, in my opinion, is the essence of self-advocacy. It is easy to have knowledge of one's rights under the law, and it is also nonthreatening to work for the common good. Yet it takes high-order skills to apply the general knowledge of the law to a specific situation in which one is directly involved. If this situation is personal, it becomes very threatening to put all one has on the line and take chances. For example, advising other persons with disabilities as to their rights to nondiscriminatory employment opportunities is much easier than advocating for a promotion from your present employer and worrying about repercussions. I kept thinking, "What if I am wrong and don't have a good case, am I doing myself more harm than good?" My needs had to become pervasive before I was willing to self-advocate. However, even now, I have to think that I have a "good case" before I will pursue any self-advocacy.

Once I was forced to take control, I realized that I had the necessary background and skills that I could call upon as needed. Besides having many friends with disabilities who were advocates, I was fortunate that my parents always fought for my participation in programs and activities long before we all realized that I had rights. My parents took an "in-your-face" approach, in that I was always right there and they made people deal with me. If they chose not to deal with me, then they had to deal with my father's Irish temper. Most of the time we would win the argument because who wants to be embarrassed by "a crazy man and his handicapped son"? Sometimes we would lose because his argument was usually based on anger rather than logic or my civil rights. As I became older, my father's adversarial antics would embarrass me, and I decided that I could do a better job if I took a more rational approach in advocating for an equal chance or opportunity to prove myself. (Since this was before the concepts of reasonable accommodation and program accessibility, my initial advocacy attempts focused on securing a chance to at least *try* to participate rather than acquiring the necessary support to participate on an equal basis with others.) So in addition to advocating to be included in various programs and activities, I had to advocate to keep my father in check so I could self-advocate more effectively. Fortunately, he was eager to step back and support me in my new role.

The point of this personal history of self-determination is that it was not enough that I was knowledgeable about disability rights or that I had the skills necessary for self-advocacy. I also needed role models to support me in my initial attempts at becoming self-determined. This personal experience facilitated my involvement in the Office of Special Education and Rehabilitative Services' Initiative on Self-Determination.

OSERS' SELF-DETERMINATION INITIATIVE

The Office of Special Education and Rehabilitative Services (OSERS) began a self-determination initiative in 1988 to focus on systemwide activities that would help people with disabilities have more input in the decisions that affect their own lives (Ward & Kohler, 1996). An OSERS Work Group of staff with disabilities was responsible for administering this initiative. Members of the Work Group were charged with examining self-determination as it related to three levels: 1) internal operation of OSERS, 2) citizens with disabilities, and 3) developing strategies for OSERS' funding and priority setting. The Work Group defined self-determination as "the attitudes and abilities which lead individuals to define goals for themselves and to take the initiative in achieving those goals" (Ward, 1988, p. 2) and focused on concepts such as self-actualization, assertiveness, creativity, and pride.

A major activity of the OSERS' Work Group took place in January 1989, when 60 people with various disabilities and viewpoints were invited to a national conference to recommend activities to promote self-determination at the federal level. This conference provided an opportunity for consumers, parents, and state/local administrators to come together to share ideas, make recommendations, and propose activities. Because these three constituencies are often competing and represent different concerns, this opportunity was truly unique in that it gave everyone an equal chance to share their views and to support one another. A summary of the conference along with the 29 recommendations made by the participants was later published (see University of Minnesota Research and Training Center on Community Living, 1989) and widely disseminated.

In response to one of the recommendations, the Secondary Education and Transitional Services for Youth with Disabilities Program within OSERS supported 26 model demonstration projects to identify and teach skills necessary for self-determination during fiscal years 1990–1993. These projects contained various innovative approaches (Ward & Kohler, 1996), many of which are summarized in later chapters of this volume. Several projects employed a futures planning or person-centered planning process to teach strategies for achieving self-determined futures. Another model project supported youth with disabilities to actualize their dreams. Yet another project for youth with physical disabilities and other health impairments developed a self-determination curriculum that considered some important aspects unique to this population (e.g., managing attendants, leadership through augmented communication). Two projects adapted strategies from the national People First organization for the adolescent population. Another project used training in ethics and self-management skills to promote self-determination among youth with severe emotional/behavioral disorders (SED). Projects focused also on self-determination as a process whereby students become actively involved in setting goals and making decisions. This process was facilitated in many cases through activities such as self-evaluation; goal setting; and, formally, individualized education program (IEP) planning and implementation.

An analysis of activities for 20 of the 26 projects performed by Ward and Kohler (1996) indicated that these projects developed curricula to teach students to

1. Evaluate their skills
2. Recognize their limits
3. Set goals
4. Identify options
5. Accept responsibility
6. Communicate their preferences and needs
7. Monitor and evaluate their progress

Students were taught decision making, goal setting, self-awareness, and self-advocacy skills. To teach these skills, curriculum materials were designed so that teachers, mentors, and parents modeled self-determined behavior; students were involved in role play and simulated situations; student portfolios were developed; and video media were incorporated to instruct and to provide feedback. Furthermore, projects conducted numerous activities in community settings such as business and industrial sites, the public service sector, postsecondary education and training facilities, residential environments, and community art centers. To increase the capacity of others to recognize and promote self-determination, many projects trained teachers, parents, and other significant adults in students' lives. Finally, projects created opportunities for students to exercise their newly developed skills, and, in some cases, formally positioned students as leaders in the IEP process.

Based on my role as the federal official responsible for these 26 demonstration projects, I have learned several obvious lessons. The first is that self-determination *is* important and that it needs to be addressed systematically through a specific curriculum. Preliminary data from these projects (Ward & Kohler, 1996) have indicated that positive outcomes increased when students learned to make decisions, to be assertive, and to self-advocate.

The second lesson is that it is imperative that youth with disabilities receive training in school to develop skills necessary for self-determination and have multiple opportunities to practice these skills (Ward & Kohler, 1996). Because many parents may have difficulty perceiving their youth with disabilities as empowered and self-determined adults, the cycle of dependency for too many of these youth will transfer from parents to teachers, job coaches, and welfare systems.

A third lesson is that self-determination skill training needs to begin with very young children. As projects focused on youth with disabilities who were approximately 14–21 years old, there were reports that for some participants, 14 was far too late to reverse the cycle of dependency, learned helplessness, and feelings of inability. When asked how early self-determination training needed to start, project staff responded that it needed to begin right from infancy.

SUMMARY AND CONCLUSIONS

As of 1995, most studies report that there are between 35 and 43 million people with disabilities in the United States (Shapiro, 1993). They should represent a formidable political force. However, this is not the case as many of these people do not identify themselves as being disabled nor consider the political process to be the answer to their needs. Veterans of the disability rights movement know too well that many different disability groups have often fought against one another rather than moving forward with a cohesive political agenda. This fractionated political force was one of the reasons it took almost 20 years to extend the civil rights protections of Section 504 from only those entities receiving federal assistance to include all public accommodations with the Americans with Disabilities Act of 1990 (PL 101-336).

The reason for the lack of political clout does not lie only with people with disabilities, but, as Shapiro (1994) observed, also in the fact that most people without disabilities just don't get it—the "it" being that disability is a natural condition of life, like being left-handed. Cyndi Jones, publisher of the disability magazine *Mainstream* says, "There's a growing understanding in the disability community that it's all right to be disabled, that it's a natural part of life" (cited in Shapiro, 1994, p. 29). Disability rights leader and Assistant Secretary for the Department of Education, Judith Heumann, explained, "Disability only becomes a tragedy for us when society fails to provide the things we need to lead our lives— job opportunities or barrier-free buildings, for example" (Shapiro, 1994).

Ms. Heumann summarized the status of disability rights for her staff at OSERS. She appealed to her audience that

> As we move into the very last years of the 20th century, we should take a minute to compare where we are today in terms of disability programs, services, and issues, with where this country was as our parents, grandparents, and great-grandparents prepared to enter this century. It's hard to believe that anyone in the year 1894 could have even dreamed of—much less predicted—where we are 100 years later. Compare the status of education of disabled children: warehousing with no expectation of preparation for a meaningful future in the mainstream, vs. guarantees of a free appropriate public education, individually designed and delivered in schools with expectations for every child to learn more and grow up to achieve the goals they set for themselves.
>
> Access to technology that opens doors and promotes independent living. A coordinated effort across the federal government to improve employment outcomes for disabled people. Targeted and strategic efforts to maximize the leadership, empowerment, independence and productivity of people with disabilities. White House leadership to develop coordinated and coherent national disability policy. Higher and higher expectations for each child or adult with disabilities. We approach the 21st century knowing that disabled people want to and can make many more significant contributions than were thought of when we entered the 20th century. (Heumann, 1994)

Ms. Heumann's recognition of the progress made by the disabled community during the 20th century is something we all must appreciate. Children, youth, and adults with and without disabilities need to be aware of the contributions and leadership of the disability rights movement as part of the rich history of American society. However, it is not only the leaders of the movement who have a story. Most disabled people who are living, working, and participating in the community have similar stories about the obstacles that they have overcome to achieve this personal degree of independence. All of our stories need to be heard and appreciated.

If disabled people are ever to attain true independence, the acquisition of self-determination skills is critically important! Disabled people *must* continue to learn from other minorities by taking pride in their own history and culture. This means that youth with disabilities must be given opportunities to learn and practice self-determination skills as well as explore their own assertiveness. They must validate who they are and feel good about being a person with a disability and a disabled person. In that validation, they must realize that they have a right to share the "American Dream" and that they can exercise their rights to ensure the accessibility of their part of this dream. Finally, disabled people themselves must be able to clearly state the equality of these rights to the American public. Disabled people must convince the public that their rights are the *same civil* rights afforded all other minorities.

REFERENCES

Americans with Disabilities Act of 1990 (ADA), PL 101–336. (July 26, 1990). Title 42, U.S.C. 12101 et seq: *U.S. Statutes at Large, 104,* 327–378.

Architectural Barriers Act of 1968, PL 90–480. (August 12, 1968). Title 29, U.S.C. 792 et seq: *U.S. Statutes at Large, 82,* 718.

Berkowitz, E.D. (1987). *Disabled policy: America's policy for the handicapped.* Cambridge, MA: Cambridge University Press.

Campbell, J.F. (1991). The consumer movement and implications for vocational rehabilitation services. *Journal of Vocational Rehabilitation, 1*(3), 67–75.

Education for All Handicapped Children Act of 1975, PL 94-142. (August 23, 1977). Title 20, U.S.C. 1401 et seq: *U.S. Statutes at Large, 100,* 1145–1177.

Funk, R. (1987). Disability rights: From caste to class in the context of civil rights. In A. Gartner & T. Joe (Eds.), *Images of the disabled: Disabling images* (pp. 7–30). New York: Praeger.

Gallagher, H.G. (1985). *FDR's splendid deception.* New York: Dodd, Mead & Co.

Gartner, A., & Joe, T. (Eds.). (1987). *Images of the disabled: Disabling images.* New York: Praeger.

Hahn, H. (1987). Civil rights for disabled Americans: The foundation of a political agenda. In A. Gartner & T. Joe (Eds.), *Images of the disabled: Disabling images* (pp. 181–203). New York: Praeger.

Heumann, J.E. (1994, December 23). Holiday message. *Access to OSERS, 1*(5), 1–2. (Available from the Office of the Assistant Secretary, Office of Special Education and Rehabilitative Services, U.S. Department of Education, 600 Independence Avenue SW, Washington, DC 20202.)

Hughes, L., & Meltzer, M. (1963). *A pictorial history of the Negro in America.* New York: Crown.

Lehr, S., & Taylor, S.J. (1986). *Roots and wings: A manual about self-advocacy.* Boston: Federation for Special Needs.

Longhurst, N.A. (1994). *The self-advocacy movement by people with developmental disabilities: A demographic study and directory of self-advocacy groups in the United States.* Washington, DC: American Association on Mental Retardation.

Mills v. Board of Education of District of Columbia, 348 F. Supp. 866, 880, (D.D.C., 1972).

Nirje, B. (1972). The right to self-determination. In W. Wolfensberger (Ed.), *Normalization* (pp. 176–193). Toronto: National Institute on Mental Retardation.

Nirje, B. (1976). The normalization principle and its human management implications. In M. Rosen, C.R. Clark, & M.S. Kivitz (Eds.), *The history of mental retardation: Collected papers* (Vol. 2, pp. 363–376). Baltimore: University Park Press.

Nosek, M.A. (1992). Independent living. In R.M. Parker & E.M. Szymanski (Eds.), *Rehabilitation counseling: Basics and beyond* (2nd ed., pp. 103–133). Austin, TX: PRO-ED.

Pennsylvania Association for Retarded Children (PARC) v. Commonwealth of Pennsylvania, 343 F. Supp. 279 (E.D. Pa., 1972), Consent Agreement.

Percy, S.L. (1989). *Disability, civil rights, and public policy: The politics of implementation.* Tuscaloosa: University of Alabama Press.

Rehabilitation Act of 1973, PL 93-112. (September 26, 1973). Title 29, U.S.C. 701 et seq: *U.S. Statutes at Large, 87,* 355–394.

Shapiro, J.P. (1993). *No pity: People with disabilities forging a new civil rights movement.* New York: Times Books.

Shapiro, J.P. (1994, November-December). The new civil rights. *Modern Maturity,* 26–35.

Simon, M.Y. (1992). *Education in the least restrictive environment: Implementing integrated programs.* Unpublished manuscript, University of California, Berkeley, and San Francisco State University.

Szymanski, E.M., & Trueba, H.T. (1994). Castification of people with disabilities: Potential disempowering aspects of classification of disability services. *Journal of Rehabilitation, 60*(3), 12–20.

University of Minnesota Research and Training Center on Community Living. (1989). *National conference on self-determination.* Minneapolis: Author. (Available from the Institute on Community Integration, 150 Pillsbury Dr. SE, Minneapolis, MN 55455.)

Ward, M.J. (1988). The many facets of self-determination. *NICHY Transition Summary: National Information Center for Children and Youth with Disabilities, 5,* 2–3.

Ward, M.J., & Kohler, P.D. (1996). Promoting self-determination for individuals with disabilities: Content and process. In L.E. Powers, G.H.S. Singer, & J. Sowers (Eds.), *On the road to autonomy: Promoting self-competence in children and youth with disabilities* (pp. 275–290). Baltimore: Paul H. Brookes Publishing Co.

Chapter

SELF-DETERMINATION AS AN EDUCATIONAL OUTCOME

Why Is It Important to Children, Youth, and Adults with Disabilities?

Michael L. Wehmeyer

ON JUNE 30, 1978, Ruth Sienkiewicz-Mercer, who until that time had lived at the Belchertown State School for most of her life, moved into an apartment in Springfield, Massachusetts. She described the first days of her new life in these words:

> I had never had a place of my own. As a result, I had never worried about buying groceries and planning meals, paying the rent and the phone bill, balancing a checkbook, making appointments, figuring out how to keep the appointments I made—all of the things adults just do. But starting out in society at the age of twenty-eight, after living at a state institution for the mentally retarded for sixteen years, I found these everyday tasks confusing and wonderful and frightening. (Sienkiewicz-Mercer & Kaplan, 1989, p. 202)

Confusing, wonderful, and frightening might be as apt a description of adulthood as any forwarded by academicians or philosophers. Reading Sienkiewicz-Mercer's observations of her new life, perhaps the most noticeable thing is the universality of her experiences. Remove references to disability and these experiences parallel those of most young adults as they venture on their own for the first time. Truth be known, few if any of these young people possessed every skill

Funding for portions of the research reported in this chapter was provided by Grant No. H023J20012 from the U.S. Department of Education, Office of Special Education Programs, Division of Innovation and Development awarded to The Arc (formerly Association for Retarded Citizens of the United States). The contents of this chapter do not necessarily represent the policy of the Department of Education, and no official endorsement by the federal government should be inferred.

they needed to take that step. Yet, step they did . . . sometimes stumbling, other times obtaining solid purchase for their journey. One step followed another until the steps were no longer noticed, only the sights along the way.

Yet there is something that young people who venture into adulthood and succeed have in common. Mithaug (1991) pointed out that

> In every school in this country a few children succeed regardless of the instruction they receive. Teachers identify these students early because they have purpose in their lives. They know what they like, what they can do, what they want and how to get it. (p. ix)

These young people are, Mithaug concluded, self-determined. Appropriately, leaders in the U.S. Department of Education have identified self-determination as a critical outcome for youth with disabilities. Halloran (1993), discussing the transition services requirements of the Individuals with Disabilities Education Act (IDEA) (PL 101-476), identified self-determination as the "ultimate goal of education" (p. 214). Ward (1988) called the acquisition of self-determination "a critical—and often more difficult—goal for people with disabilities" (p. 2).

The education system is not the only system to recognize and emphasize the importance of self-determination for people with disabilities. In PL 102-569, the 1992 Amendments to the Rehabilitation Act, which funds the vocational rehabilitation system, the introduction stated that:

> Disability is a natural part of the human experience and in no way diminishes the rights of individuals to live independently, enjoy self-determination, make choices, contribute to society, pursue meaningful careers and enjoy full inclusion and integration in the economic, political, social, cultural and educational mainstream of American society. [Sec. 2 (a)(3)(A - F)]

That her life experiences ill-prepared her to enter adulthood is not unique to Sienkiewicz-Mercer, nor indeed to people who have lived in institutions. It is the experience of too many people with disabilities whose lives are controlled by others, for whom decisions are made by others, and who experience few opportunities to make choices based on their own interests and abilities (Kishi, Teelucksingh, Zollers, Park-Lee, & Meyer, 1988; Kozleski & Sands, 1992; Stancliffe, 1995; Stancliffe & Wehmeyer, 1995; Wehmeyer & Metzler, 1995). The reason that self-determination should become the ultimate goal of education is that too many people with disabilities remain dependent on caregivers, service providers, and overloaded social systems to do for them what they should, and could, be enabled to do for themselves (Wehmeyer, 1992b). From cradle to grave, people with disabilities are reliant upon dependency-creating systems—educational systems, rehabilitation systems, family systems—to meet their needs. As a result, many people with disabilities fail to reach maximum levels of independence, productivity, inclusion, and self-sufficiency—outcomes that, ironically, are the main objective of most such systems.

The purpose of this chapter is to 1) examine the various conceptualizations of self-determination and their relevance to people with disabilities, 2) provide a definitional framework of self-determination as an educational outcome that will provide an impetus for intervention in this area, and 3) provide a rationale for the importance of focusing on self-determination as an educational outcome.

CONCEPTUAL APPROACHES TO SELF-DETERMINATION

The self-determination initiative funded by the U.S. Department of Education, Office of Special Education and Rehabilitative Services (OSERS), Secondary Education and Transition Services Branch (described by Ward, Chapter 1) brought increased awareness of the importance of this topic to youth with disabilities. Many of the programs and strategies described in later chapters of this book emerged through the auspices of this initiative. However, the author has observed that there are two issues that have the potential to derail efforts to promote self-determination within educational and adult services systems before the movement gets underway.

The first might be referred to as the "Tower of Babel" syndrome. When talking about self-determination, we face the risk of speaking different languages. There are several conceptual approaches that have appropriated the term *self-determination,* and although there are similiarities among these approaches, there are also distinct differences that warrant consideration. Secondly, the term *self-determination* is so rapidly being assimilated into the vocabulary of disability-related services and research that, in the eyes of many, it reflects only the latest "buzzword." A related problem is that self-determination gets too narrowly interpreted as reflecting only choice making or self-advocacy.

To avoid these potential barriers, practitioners and researchers need to clearly articulate the definitional framework within which intervention and policy development regarding self-determination will occur. The following section introduces two of the most influential conceptual approaches to self-determination, as a motivational construct and an empowerment issue, and proposes a third approach, self-determination as an educational outcome, which draws from both of these approaches to address the education and rehabilitation needs of individuals with disabilities.

Self-Determination as Empowerment

The term *self-determination* has historically referred to the right of a nation to self-governance. The term was appropriated by disability rights advocates and people with disabilities to refer to their "right" to have control in their lives (e.g., Nirje, 1972; Williams, 1989). In this context, self-determination and empowerment are often used interchangeably. Empowerment is a term usually associated with a social movement and typically is used, as Rappaport (1981) stated, in reference to actions that "enhance the possibilities for people to control their lives" (p. 15). Ward (Chapter 1) and Kennedy (Chapter 3) eloquently discuss the importance of self-determination as empowerment for individuals with disabilities as well as the advocacy-related historical antecedents to the present emphasis on self-determination.

Self-Determination as a Motivational Construct

A second use of the term has appeared in the literature pertaining to motivation, particularly the work of Deci and colleagues (Deci & Ryan, 1985). In this research, self-determination refers to an internal need contributing to an individual's performance of intrinsically motivated behaviors. According to these theorists, humans are inherently active and internally motivated to engage in activities for which there are no obvious external rewards. Children's propensities to want to learn, undertake challenges, and solve problems are cited by Deci and Ryan as examples of such internally motivated behaviors. Intrinsic motivation, say these authors, is the "energy source that is central to the active nature of the organism" (Deci & Ryan, 1985, p. 11) and is defined as "the innate, natural propensity to engage in one's interests and exercise one's capacities, and in so doing, to seek and conquer optimal challenges" (p. 43). Accordingly, Deci and Ryan (1985) defined self-determination as such:

> Self-determination is the capacity to choose and to have those choices, rather than reinforcement contingencies, drives or any other forces or pressures, be the determinants of one's actions. But self-determination is more than a *capacity*; it is also a *need*. We have posited a basic, innate propensity to be self-determining that leads organisms to engage in interesting behaviors. (p. 38)

The pioneering work of Deci and colleagues has generated considerable attention to the importance of student motivation and interest in learning. Much of the early work of these researchers focused on the putative detrimental effects of external rewards on internal motivation (Deci, 1971; Deci & Ryan, 1985). Subsequent research within this conceptual approach has provided strategies to increase student motivation in the classroom for students with and without disabilities (e.g., Deci & Chandler, 1986; Deci, Hodges, Pierson, & Tomassone, 1992) and, particularly, contributed to an understanding of the impact of teacher control orientation on student motivation and performance (e.g., Boggiano & Katz, 1991; Deci, Spiegel, Ryan, Koestner, & Kauffman, 1982; Flink, Boggiano, & Barrett, 1990).

Limitations of Existing Approaches to Education and Rehabilitation

The U.S. Department of Education's present emphasis on self-determination within special education and rehabilitation owes more, perhaps, to the former emphasis—self-determination as interchangeable with empowerment—than the latter—self-determination as an internal need to perform intrinsically motivated behaviors. Although most of the federally funded projects have been influenced by research on self-determination as a motivational construct and incorporated practices that recognize the importance of enhanced internal motivation for students with disabilities, it was not this approach that appears to have fueled the federal initiative. Instead, the self-determination initiative has emerged as the logical extension of a changing view of disability in our society, the altered role of education and rehabilitation within this conceptualization of disability, and the empowerment of people with disabilities to speak for themselves (Wehmeyer, Kelchner, & Richards, in press).

As Ward (Chapter 1) has documented, the OSERS self-determination initiative is an outcome of the empowering social movements of the preceding decades (e.g., the independent living, disability self-help and self-advocacy, normalization movements). Unfortunately, this heritage has not provided an adequate definitional framework within which to promote self-determination. Advocacy efforts to empower individuals with disabilities necessarily focused on obtaining equal rights and opportunities to be self-determined. Such efforts have spawned legislative and judicial responses, like the Americans with Disabilities Act (ADA), (PL 101-336), that guarantee citizens with disabilities equal rights, equal access to services, and equal treatment in everyday affairs. However, policy initiatives alone do not ensure that people with disabilities will take full advantage of these protections. In addition, people with disabilities must be provided with opportunities to acquire the knowledge and skills necessary to exercise their legal rights. The ADA illustrates the limitations to an empowerment emphasis of self-determination. The act guarantees equal employment protections to individuals with disabilities who are otherwise qualified to perform a job. It does nothing for someone who is not capable of performing the job (Wehmeyer & Ward, 1995). Likewise, access to opportunities to control one's life, make choices, solve problems, make decisions, and set goals are, in and of themselves, useless until the person holds the attitudes and has the abilities he or she needs to take advantage of such circumstances.

Halloran (1993) suggested that actualizing the emphasis on self-determination would "require a major change in the current approach to educating, parenting, or planning for children and youth with disabilities" (p. 214). Many of the chapters in this book outline approaches and strategies to implement such a change. However, we have suggested that to achieve the outcome that children leave school as self-determined individuals, and to provide opportunities for adults with disabilities to become self-determined, there needs to be a definitional framework upon which to build interventions, evaluate the efficacy of strategies and treatments, and conduct research (Wehmeyer, 1992a). This chapter forwards a definitional framework of self-determination as an educational outcome.

DEFINING SELF-DETERMINATION AS AN EDUCATIONAL OUTCOME

Although the current emphasis on self-determination owes much to the empowerment movements of the last few decades and research in motivation, there is a gap between these conceptualizations and the conceptualization of self-determination as an educational outcome. I have proposed elsewhere (Wehmeyer, 1992a, in press) that, for purposes of education and rehabilitation, self-determination is 1) best defined in relationship to characteristics of a person's behavior; 2) viewed as an educational outcome; and 3) achieved through lifelong learning, opportunities, and experiences. Before exploring this definitional framework, it is worth discussing alternative ways in which self-determination could be defined.

Self-Determination as a Set of Behaviors

There is a temptation to define self-determination in terms of specific behaviors like problem solving, assertiveness, or decision making. This temptation is strong because the image of a self-determined person conjured up by most people is that of a successful person using such behaviors. However, after further reflection it becomes evident that the definition of self-determination cannot be restricted to a set of behaviors for two reasons: 1) any behavior can be self-determined, and 2) both the occurrence and nonoccurrence of a behavior can be self-determined.

In the first instance, although there are behaviors that are typically viewed as self-determined (e.g., making choices, problem solving, self-advocacy), when one attempts to compile a list of behaviors that could "define" self-determination, that list will grow exponentially to encompass virtually any behavior in a person's repertoire. For example, speaking up for oneself is generally identified as a self-determined action, and in most cases it is. However, if "speaking up for oneself" is a defining variable of self-determination, then people who cannot speak are, a priori, eliminated from being self-determined. One might then point out that it is not the act of "speaking" itself that is self-determined, but the intention of that act. As such, the list can be expanded to include "speaking up for oneself," "using sign language to communicate one's needs," "using [a specific augmentative communication device] to communicate," and so forth. The list quickly expands to the point of being unwieldy and cumbersome.

One solution to this problem is to broaden the behavior(s) identified as defining self-determination. So, for example, instead of "speaking up for oneself" as the defining variable, this could be rewritten as "communicating for oneself" as the behavior of note. However, this is an unsatisfactory solution for several reasons. First, while some behaviors might be amenable to such summation, others that could clearly be interpreted as self-determined are not. Consider a situation where two consenting adults with disabilities decide to get married. In the aftermath of this decision, they meet heavy resistance from friends, family members, and professionals who predict disaster and threaten to prohibit the marriage. In response to this, the couple elopes to Nevada and they are married the next week. Is, then, "getting married" a behavior we should add to our definition? Obviously not, as many people choose to remain single or live together without getting married. What, then, is the broader behavior to be identified? In essence, the couple was acting on a decision, exerting control over their lives and acting on preferences and dreams. Alone, none of these adequately describe why the act was self-determined, and several (e.g., exert control, act on dreams) would hardly be described as "behaviors." We are left with the unsatisfactory option of listing, ad infinitum, behaviors like "getting married" alongside of mutually exclusive behaviors like "not getting married."

This illustrates the second barrier to defining self-determination by behaviors. In most cases one can identify acts that are intuitively self-determined, but mutually exclusive! The example of getting married or staying single is one such situation. Returning to the previous example of a self-determined behavior, speaking up for oneself, there are situations where doing so is not a wise course of action and the preferred option might be to remain silent. So, for example, if a person knows that speaking up for his or her rights might unduly harm someone else, that person might choose to sit quietly. As such, one can describe situations where the behaviors of "speaking up for one's rights" and "not speaking up for one's rights" are both self-determined actions. Finally, defining self-determination solely as a set of behaviors fails to take into account cultural and regional differences. A common example of such differences is that although looking someone directly in the eyes when speaking to that person is a self-determined action in many cases, in some Native American cultures it is a sign of disrespect and would not be viewed as self-determined.

Self-Determination as an Individual Trait or Personal Characteristic

A second option is to define self-determination as a characteristic or trait of an individual. This is, perhaps, more satisfactory than defining it by behaviors, but there are problems that remain with this approach. Positing that human behavior is motivated by needs, drives, traits, or impulses has been criticized as inherently circular. Bandura (1977) pointed out that in such theories, "inner determinants often were inferred from the behavior they supposedly caused, resulting in description in the guise of explanation" (p. 2). Self-determination as a trait or personal characteristic could only be inferred from the presence of behaviors (e.g., problem solving, choice making, goal setting) the trait or characteristic presumably caused. Furthermore, theories proposing the existence of drives, traits, impulses, or needs have not overcome the criticism that they fail to account for the marked variability in human behavior across time and environmental conditions. As Bandura (1977) has argued, it is not the presence of motivated behavior that is questioned, but whether it is useful to ascribe such behaviors to drives, traits, needs, or impulses. It is almost impossible to describe self-determination as a characteristic of a person without entering this morass.

As well as attributing self-determination to personal characteristics, there is also a tendency to attribute the description "self-determined" only to successful people who act in successful ways. This, however, is an inaccurate characterization of self-determination. Research in the area of goal setting and achievement emphasizes that goal-oriented behavior can have 1) the desired outcomes, 2) unintended outcomes, or 3) no outcome, and each of these outcomes may or may not be beneficial. So too, self-determined behavior may have multiple outcomes. Returning to the example of the couple who eloped to be married, this may have been a reasonable or unreasonable action based on the circumstances, and, independent of the reasonableness of the action, the marriage may succeed or fail.

Self-Determination as a Characteristic of Actions or Events

To circumvent the problems associated with defining self-determination as either a set of behaviors or as a characteristic of an individual, this author and his colleagues have defined this construct according to characteristics of actions or events. Self-determination refers to "acting as the primary causal agent in one's life and making choices and decisions regarding one's quality of life free from undue external influence or interference" (Wehmeyer, 1992a, 1996). Causal agency implies that an outcome was purposeful and the action was performed to achieve that end. A causal agent is someone who makes or causes things to happen in his or her life (Wehmeyer, Kelchner, & Richards, in press). As Deci and Ryan (1985) emphasized, the focus on causing things to happen in (rather than controlling) one's life is an important distinction because there are times when even the most self-determined person chooses to relinquish actual control over actions. We have suggested before that if a person is having his or her gall bladder removed, he or she may want to have control over the decision to undergo this procedure and choose the surgeon to perform the procedure, but if that person is wise he or she will certainly relinquish control over the procedure itself to the surgeon (Wehmeyer & Berkobien, 1991).

Essential Characteristics of Self-Determined Behavior An act or event is self-determined if the individual's action(s) reflects four essential characteristics: 1) the individual acted autonomously, 2) the behaviors were self-regulated, 3) the person initiated and responded to event(s) in a "psychologically empowered" manner, and 4) the person acted in a self-realizing manner (Wehmeyer, in press; Wehmeyer, Kelchner, & Richards, in press). As the description *essential* suggests, we (Wehmeyer et al., in press) have proposed that self-determined behavior reflects all four of these characteristics, as depicted graphically in Figure 1. They represent a set of attitudes (psychological empowerment and self-realization) and abilities (behavioral autonomy and self-regulation) that must be present if a person is to be self-determined. To the degree that a person consistently (not to be confused with unfailingly) exhibits self-determined actions, he or she can be construed as being self-determined. The following sections describe these essential characteristics in greater detail.

Behavioral Autonomy Sigafoos, Feinstein, Damond, and Reiss (1988) stated that "human development involves a progression from dependence on

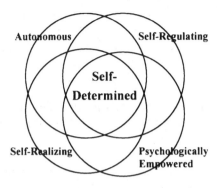

Figure 1. Graphic depiction of essential characteristics of self-determination.

others for care and guidance to self-care and self-direction" (p. 432). The outcome of this progression is autonomous functioning or, when describing the actions of individuals achieving this outcome, behavioral autonomy. Lewis and Taymans (1992) defined autonomy as

> a complex concept which involves emotional separation from parents, the development of a sense of personal control over one's life, the establishment of a personal value system and the ability to execute behavioral tasks which are needed in the adult world. (p. 37)

The word *autonomy* derives from the Greek words *autos* (meaning self) and "nomos" (meaning rule) and refers to the condition of living according to laws set by oneself (Haworth, 1986). Within the definitional framework for self-determined behavior, a behavior is autonomous if the person acts 1) according to his or her own preferences, interests, and/or abilities and 2) independently, free from undue external influence or interference.

Sigafoos et al. (1988) operationalized the concept of behavioral autonomy, identifying four behavioral categories: 1) self- and family care activities, 2) self-management activities, 3) recreational activities, and 4) social and vocational activities. Self- and family care activities involve daily activities, including routine personal care and family-oriented functions such as meal preparation, care of possessions, performing household chores, shopping, and home repairs. Self-management activities involve the degree to which a person independently handles interactions with the environment. These activities include the use of community resources and the fulfillment of personal obligations and responsibilities. Recreational activities reflecting behavioral autonomy are not specific actions per se but rather the degree to which an individual uses personal preferences and interests to choose to engage in such activities. Likewise, social and vocational activities comprise social involvement, vocational activities, and the degree to which personal preference and interests are applied in these areas.

Self-Regulated Behavior   Whitman (1990) defined self-regulation as

> a complex response system that enables individuals to examine their environ-
> ments and their repertoires of responses for coping with those environments to
> make decisions about how to act, to act, to evaluate the desirability of the out-
> comes of the action, and to revise their plans as necessary. (p. 373)

Self-regulated behaviors include self-management strategies, (including self-
monitoring, self-instruction, self-evaluation and self-reinforcement), goal setting
and attainment behaviors, problem-solving behaviors and observational learning
strategies (Agran, in press). Individuals with disabilities need to become the
causal agents in their lives (Agran, in press; Wehmeyer, in press).

Acting in a Psychologically Empowered Manner   Psychological empowerment is a term referring to the multiple dimensions of perceived control,
including the cognitive (personal efficacy), personality-driven (locus of control),
and motivational domains (Zimmerman, 1990). Essentially, people acting in a
psychologically empowered manner do so on the basis of a belief that 1) they
have control over circumstances that are important to them (internal locus of
control); 2) they possess the requisite skills to achieve desired outcomes (self-
efficacy); and 3) if they choose to apply those skills, the identified outcomes will
result (outcome expectations).

A number of researchers in self-determination have stressed that acting in a
self-determined manner requires a combination of abilities and attitudes (Ward,
1988; Wehmeyer, 1992a). Most people can readily identify someone who possesses one but not the other. A person who knows an effective decision-making
strategy (ability), but who does not believe that if he or she applies that strategy
the desired outcomes will be achieved (attitude), is not likely to make decisions.
In the same situation, someone who believes that he or she is effective and can
influence outcomes by acting, but who lacks the requisite decision-making skills,
may be more likely to act but no more likely to come to a satisfactory outcome
from that action.

The inclusion of psychological empowerment as a defining variable for self-
determined behavior illustrates the importance of both cognitive and behavioral
contributions to this framework. Bandura (1977) argued that a "theory of human
behavior cannot afford to neglect symbolic activities" (p. 13). Agran (in press)
noted the importance of cognitive behaviors in achieving self-regulation, including the use of metacognition, self-instruction, self-reinforcement, and observational learning strategies. Such "cognitive" aspects of self-determined behavior
are not easily observed, but, in our view, are essential if someone is to be self-
determined.

Self-Realization   Finally, self-determined people are self-realizing in that
they use a comprehensive, and reasonably accurate, knowledge of themselves
and their strengths and limitations to act in such a manner as to capitalize on this
knowledge. This self-knowledge and self-understanding forms through experience

with and interpretation of one's environment and is influenced by evaluations of significant others, reinforcements, and attributions of one's own behavior (Wehmeyer, in press).

Empirical Support for the Definitional Framework   To test the validity of the definitional framework, we interviewed more than 400 adults with mental retardation and developmental disabilities (Wehmeyer et al., in press), using self-report measures of each of the essential characteristics. Scores from measures of each of the four essential characteristics differed signficantly based on whether or not individuals exhibited behaviors typically identified as reflecting self-determination. In each case, individuals who were in the high self-determination group held more positive beliefs or exhibited more adaptive behaviors. Measures of behavioral autonomy and self-regulation were particularly potent predictors of self-determination status.

Component Elements of Self-Determined Behavior

We have suggested elsewhere that there are a number of component elements whose development are integral to the emergence of the four essential characteristics of self-determination (Wehmeyer, in press). As previously discussed, these component elements cannot be used to define self-determination, but the acquisition of each is necessary, if not sufficient, for the expression of self-determined behavior. Doll, Sands, Wehmeyer, and Palmer (Chapter 5) describe the unique development of each of these component elements. It is at this level that instructional efforts to promote self-determination will be focused. Although not intended as an exhaustive taxonomy, the following component elements seem particularly important to the emergence of self-determined behavior:

- Choice making
- Decision making
- Problem solving
- Goal setting and attainment
- Self-observation, evaluation, and reinforcement
- Internal locus of control
- Positive attributions of efficacy and outcome expectancy
- Self-awareness
- Self-knowledge

A comprehensive review of the literature related to these component elements and children, youth, and adults with disabilities is beyond the scope of the current chapter. However, this literature, as reviewed by Wehmeyer (in press), has provided evidence that 1) people with disabilities have too few opportunities to learn the skills they need to acquire these component elements; 2) people with disabilities have limited access to experiences in which to apply these skills; 3) others' expectations and perceptions of people with disabilities significantly limit such opportunities; and 4) when provided adequate learning opportunities and the chance to apply this learning, people with disabilities can acquire the component elements.

Many efforts to promote self-determination focus on activities aimed at the individual him- or herself, such as teaching the person specific skills (Wehmeyer, Martin, & Sands, in press). While this is important, it is but one direction in which efforts to promote self-determination must head. Napoleon Bonaparte said that ability is of little account without opportunity, and much that remains to be accomplished to enable people with disabilities to be self-determined must focus on changing environments as well as changing others' expectations (Brotherson, Cook, Cunconan-Lahr, & Wehmeyer, 1995). These component elements provide a starting point for instructional emphasis and direct efforts to alter the environment to provide individuals with disabilities the opportunities to experience choice and control and to change others' perceptions and expectations.

WHY SELF-DETERMINATION IS IMPORTANT TO AND FOR PEOPLE WITH DISABILITIES

People with disabilities have made it clear that self-determination is an outcome that is important to them. Williams (1989) stated "We want it [self-determination as a complete way of life] not just for ourselves but for all people with disabilities. Indeed, we want it for all people—period. And, we want it now" (p. 16). Kennedy (1993) said that "what people need to realize is that self-determination can be different things to different people. All people should have the opportunity to be self-determining, based on what that means for them" (p. 11). It is not difficult to understand that when a person has limited control and choice in his or her life, the reclamation of such control and choice becomes an issue of importance. What most of us may not recognize is the intensity of those feelings. Pearl Buck said that people who have always been free cannot understand the power of the hope of freedom to those who are not free.

In the opinion of this author and his colleagues, the call for self-determination by people with disabilities is, in and of itself, sufficient justification for focusing on this outcome. However, there are other reasons that it is important to focus limited resources, including time, personnel, and money, to achieve self-determination for individuals with disabilities. These reasons include the importance of self-determination to experience an enhanced quality of life and integration into one's community and recent findings concerning adult outcomes for people with disabilities (see later section, "Adult Outcomes for People with Disabilities").

Self-Determination and Quality of Life

We have opted to frame causal agency within the concept of quality of life because we believe that, along with its historical ties to the empowerment movement, self-determination is associated with quality-of-life issues. Schalock (1990) provided six fundamental quality-of-life principles:

1. Quality-of-life for persons with disabilities is composed of those same factors and relationships that are important to persons without disabilities.
2. Quality-of-life is experienced when a person's basic needs are met and when he or she has the same opportunity as anyone else to pursue and achieve goals in the major life settings of home, community, and work.
3. Quality-of-life factors vary over the life span of a person.
4. Quality-of-life is based on a set of values that emphasize consumer and family strengths.
5. Quality-of-life is determined by the congruence of public values and behavior.
6. Quality-of-life is a concept that can be consensually validated by a wide range of persons representing a variety of viewpoints of consumers and their families, advocates, professionals and providers.

Like self-determination, quality of life focuses attention on both subjective and objective indicators. Dalkey (1972) stated that

> Quality of life is related not just to the environment and to the external circumstances of an individual's life, but whether these factors constitute a major share of an individual's well being, or whether they are dominated by factors such as a sense of achievement, love and affection, perceived freedom and so on. (p. 9)

An individual's quality of life is determined across settings, environments, and opportunities. Causal agency is a critical element contributing to an individual's enhanced quality of life; virtually all choices and decisions contribute at varying degrees to some aspect of quality of life, be it physical, psychological, or social. Conceptualizing self-determination as contributing to an enhanced quality of life reflects the importance of both major decisions that occur infrequently (buying a house, medical decisions) and daily choices that are less consequential but more frequent, such as what to wear or eat or how to spend one's free time.

The measurement of both quality of life and self-determination share considerable overlap. Both examine issues of choice and access to various activities and emphasize individual perceptions about and self-reports of experiences and expectations. Research into the former suggests that people with disabilities experience fewer choices and have more limited access to desired activities than peers without disabilities. For example, Stancliffe and Wehmeyer (1995) reviewed the literature related to choice making by people with mental retardation and developmental disabilities. They concluded that, despite evidence that they could make effective choices, people with mental retardation and developmental disabilities too infrequently had such opportunities. Wehmeyer and Metzler (1995) found that 66% of nearly 5,000 people with mental retardation and developmental disabilities did not choose where they were currently living, 88% did not choose their current staff person, 77% did not choose their present roommate, and 56% did not choose their current job or day activity.

Similarly, Wehmeyer, Kelchner, and Richards (1995) found that even in a sample of more than 400 members of self-advocacy groups, composed of people with mental retardation who are most likely to be self-determined, a large percentage did not have choices in their lives. For example, while 30% of the group indicated they did not choose where they lived, only 15% indicated they had selected where they live unassisted. Comparatively, Kozleski and Sands (1992) used the same survey with adults without disabilities and found that only 10% indicated they had no choice in where they lived and 13% had no choice in their roommate.

Although we have focused most of our research efforts toward examining self-determination of people with mental retardation, these experiences are not unique to people with cognitive disabilities. Jaskulski, Metzler, and Zierman (1990) surveyed more than 13,000 people with developmental disabilities to determine the degree to which they were integrated into their communities, functioned independently, and led productive lives. Of this sample, 41% had a physical disability, 10% experienced a sensory disability, 6% had an emotional disability, and 42% were identified as having mental retardation. Thus, 57% of the sample did not have a cognitive disability. From this group (respondents without mental retardation), 41% indicated they had no choice in their current living arrangement. Sands and Kozleski (1994) analyzed differences between adults with disabilities and adults without disabilities on multiple indicators of quality of life. They concluded that

> Most importantly, the degree of choice which individuals with disabilities were able to exercise was significantly limited when compared to adults without disabilities. This lack of opportunity to make choices extended from relatively innocuous activities such as decorating a bedroom to such fundamental choices as to who shares that bedroom. (p. 98)

There is an intuitively evident link between increased opportunities to make choices and decisions and take more control over one's life and an enhanced quality of life. The research literatures on quality of life for people with disabilities and the self-determination of people with disabilities send the same, clear message—people with disabilities lack the opportunity to experience control and choice in their lives, and their lives would be more fulfilling and satisfying if this were not the case.

Adult Outcomes for People with Disabilities

Another variable influencing the emphasis on self-determination and justifying the commitment of resources to this end is adult outcomes for people with disabilities. In the early 1990s, the first generation of youth with special learning needs who had access to special education services for the duration of their educational career has graduated from public schools. The transition of these youth to adulthood provided an opportunity for a pulse-check for the education system, and a number of follow-up or follow-along studies have emerged examining how these graduates fared as young adults (e.g., Affleck, Edgar, Levine, & Kortering, 1990; Haring & Lovett, 1990; Mithaug, Horiuchi, & Fanning, 1985; Neel, Meadows, Levine, & Edgar, 1988; Scuccimarra & Speece, 1990). These studies have provided impetus for changes in transition and vocational service delivery (Johnson & Rusch, 1993), including the focus on self-determination as an educational outcome (Wehmeyer & Ward, 1995).

Chadsey-Rusch, Rusch, and O'Reilly (1991) reviewed many of these studies and concluded that across multiple areas, including employment, residential, and social integration, preferred outcomes are not being realized among youth with disabilities. Their review suggested that few students, across multiple disability categories, enter employment after school and that as they age, these ex-students are even less likely to become employed, live independently, and participate in their community. The bottom line was that, although the two decades since the implementation of the Education for All Handicapped Children Act (PL 94-142) had witnessed numerous gains in such outcomes for youth with disabilities, there was still much to achieve. Nor has this gone unnoticed by people with disabilities themselves. Schriner, Roessler, and Berkobien (1993) found that between 30% and 50% of adults with mental retardation employed were dissatisfied with choices available to them in working hours, promotion opportunities, and access to paid vacation and sick leave benefits. Thus, it was as these findings emerged that policy makers and researchers began to search for additional areas of instructional emphasis, and self-determination came more to the forefront.

Inclusion, Normalization, and Community Integration

The Rehabilitation Act amendments discussed earlier illustrate the changing perceptions of disability, and the role of people with disabilities, in our society. This act stated that "disability is a natural part of the human experience" [Sec. 2 (a)(3)(A - F)]. This perspective of disability places all human abilities and experiences on a continuum and views disability as a part of, not outside of, that continuum. As contrasted with historical disease or deficit models, I have described this perspective as a competency model of disability, pointing out that

> Within such a conceptualization, disability is seen not as aberrant, outside the norm, or pathological, but as a part of the human experience. People with disabilities are not viewed as sick, diseased, or broken, but valued for their uniqueness. While deficit and disease models of disability led to the labeling of people with disabilities in dehumanizing terms like "cripple," "quad," "trainable," or "retardate," conceptualizing disability within the continuum of human abilities and experiences allows us to apply new labels to people with disabilities: neighbor, colleague, home owner, card collector, football fan, parent, dancer, dog owner, spouse, leader, role model, friend. Not all people with disabilities will actually own a home. Not all people without disabilities own homes. Some people with disabilities will not be good leaders. Some people without disabilities are poor

leaders. The central principle of the competency model is that people with disabilities are people first, and have the right be valued and experience dignity and respect independent of any qualifier or label others might place on them. (Wehmeyer, in press).

The outcome of such a changing perspective also is reflected in the 1992 Rehabilitation Act Amendments:

[The presence of a disability] in no way diminishes the rights of individuals to live independently, enjoy self-determination, make choices, contribute to society, pursue meaningful careers and enjoy full inclusion and integration in the economic, political, social, cultural and educational mainstream of American society. [Sec. 2.(a)(3)(A - F)]

Like the intuitive link between quality of life and self-determination, it seems self-evident that until people with disabilities are enabled to be self-determined, they will remain dependent upon systems and other people. Despite the best intentions of such entities, they will continue to fall short of the goal expressed in the Rehabilitation Act of "full inclusion and integration in the economic, political, social, cultural and educational mainstream of American society" [Sec. 2 (a)(3)(A - F)].

Ray Gagne, a leader in the self-advocacy movement in the United States, related this situation more eloquently. Writing about his experiences as a person with a significant disability, he titled the section describing the years he lived at an institution as "A Life of No Power: Eighteen Years in an Institution" (Gagne, 1994, p. 328). He titled the subsequent section, which described his movement back into the community, "Twenty Years in the Real World: A Struggle for Power" (Gagne, 1994, p. 332). It is telling that Gagne viewed his efforts to be self-sufficient and self-supporting as a struggle not for independence, integration, inclusion, productivity, or any other descriptor familiar to professionals, but as a struggle for power. For Gagne, the term *struggle* is not simply hyperbole. When he moved from the state school to an apartment that he shared with two other men with disabilities, he still worked in the sheltered workshop at the institution and, according to his words, lacked many of the basic daily living skills he needed to become independent.

Gagne's efforts to obtain power and control over his life extended over many years, even though he lived in increasingly more independent settings. He had to acquire the skills he needed to be self-sufficient, and perhaps more importantly, he needed to believe that he could be in control of his life. What propelled him in that direction were his commitment to become self-determined; the occasional support of a professional, friend, family member, or employer who listened to him and enabled him to achieve what he wanted; and opportunities to be involved in advocating on his own behalf. With the latter came increased skills in self-advocacy, communication, and consumer advocacy.

Gagne described the incremental steps to empowerment in his autobiographical chapter. He stated

I learned about Section 504 of the Rehabilitation Act and helped found an advocacy group named the Massachusetts Coalition of Citizens with Disabilities. I learned the skills of leadership, advocacy, consumer organization and assertiveness by watching people, participating in meetings and asking questions. My ability to communicate my ideas to facilitate work toward changing the status quo developed over time. (Gagne, 1994, p. 333)

"After four years," Gagne writes, "I moved twice more. I continued to learn new skills and became more involved in self-advocacy and consumer advocacy" (p. 33). Regarding a new job he had obtained at a chapter of The Arc, he said

Unlike the staff at the institution, the human services professionals I met at this job treated me with respect. They gave me a chance to contribute my input and feedback and believed in many of my ideas. My colleagues also adapted the working environment to help me communicate with them. (Gagne, 1994, p. 333)

SUMMARY

The movement to support and promote self-determination is about treating people with dignity and respect. It is about enabling people with disabilities to achieve independence, integration, and inclusion to the greatest extent possible by providing them the opportunities to learn the skills they need and the chance to put those skills into action. It is about empowerment, choice, and control. One critical aspect of empowerment is the equitable distribution of valued, and often scarce, resources such as jobs, financial security, and health care. People with disabilities continue to experience social isolation, segregation, un- and under-employment, and discrimination. It is critical to provide greater opportunities for inclusion and choice, employment, home ownership, and social integration. A key factor in realizing these goals is achieving the outcome that individuals with disabilities are self-determined. Gagne (1994) makes the same point when he summarized his life experiences:

I wrote this story to let people know what it was like growing up in an institution from the 1950s through the 1970s. The total lack of power in making decisions about my life made me angry, and I was treated as an outcast. The staff's abuse, neglect, and insensitivity kept me from being educated and learning the other basic skills that many children learn from caring adults. When I got into the real world, I wasn't sure what my role was. Nobody ever talked to me or taught me how to be successful. I learned to survive mostly on my own and with the help of a few good people. I feel that what happened to me should never happen again. (p. 334)

In this chapter, I have forwarded a definitional framework of self-determination as an educational outcome that can guide practice in education and rehabilitation. Subsequent chapters in this book describe programmatic efforts to achieve self-determination for youth and adults with disabilities. It is critically important that educators, adult services providers, parents and family members, and people with disabilities work together to ensure that the momentum to provide such programming does not disappear and that self-determination does not become yesterday's buzzword. I have had the valuable opportunity to work with Ray Gagne and I must echo his call—what happened to Ray must never happen again. Moreover, to paraphrase former President John F. Kennedy, it is our profound loss as individuals and as a society if we fail to enable individuals like Ray Gagne to become self-determined, independent, and productive citizens.

REFERENCES

Affleck, J.Q., Edgar, E., Levine, P., & Kortering, L. (1990). Postschool status of students classified as mildly mentally retarded, learning disabled, or nonhandicapped: Does it get better with time? *Education and Training in Mental Retardation, 25*, 315–324.

Agran, M. (in press). *Student-directed learning: A handbook on self-management.* Pacific Grove, CA: Brooks/Cole.

Americans with Disabilities Act of 1990 (ADA), PL 101-336. (July 26, 1990). Title 42, U.S.C. 12101 et seq: *U.S. Statutes at Large, 104*, 327–378.

Bandura, A. (1977). *Social learning theory.* Englewood Cliffs, NJ: Prentice Hall.

Boggiano, A.K., & Katz, P. (1991). Maladaptive achievement patterns in students: The role of teachers' controlling strategies. *Journal of Social Issues, 47*(4), 35–51.

Brotherson, M.J., Cook, C., Cunconan-Lahr, R., & Wehmeyer, M.L. (1995). Policy supporting choice and self-determination in the environments of persons with severe disabilities across the lifespan. *Education and Training in Mental Retardation and Developmental Disabilities, 30*, 3–14

Chadsey-Rusch, J., Rusch, F., & O'Reilly, M.F. (1991). Transition from school to integrated communities. *Remedial and Special Education, 12*, 23–33.

Dalkey, N.C. (1972). *Studies in the quality of life: Delphi and decision-making.* Lexington, MA: Lexington Books.

Deci, E.L. (1971). Effects of externally mediated rewards on intrinsic motivation. *Journal of Personality and Social Psychology, 18*, 105–115.

Deci, E.L., & Chandler, C.L. (1986). The importance of motivation for the future of the LD field. *Journal of Learning Disabilities, 19*, 587–594.

Deci, E.L., Hodges, R., Pierson, L., & Tomassone, J. (1992). Autonomy and competence as motivational factors in students with learning disabilities and emotional handicaps. *Journal of Learning Disabilities, 25*, 457–471.

Deci, E.L., & Ryan, R.M. (1985). *Intrinsic motivation and self-determination in human behavior.* New York: Plenum.

Deci, E.L., Spiegel, N.H., Ryan, R.M., Koestner, R., & Kauffman, M. (1982). Effects of performance standards on teaching styles: Behavior of controlling teachers. *Journal of Educational Psychology, 74*, 852–859.

Education for All Handicapped Children Act of 1975, PL 94-142. (August 23, 1977). Title 20, U.S.C. 1400 et seq: *U.S. Statutes at Large, 89*, 773–796.

Flink, C., Boggiano, A.K., & Barrett, M. (1990). Controlling teaching strategies: Undermining children's self-determination and performance. *Journal of Personality and Social Psychology, 59*, 916–924.

Gagne, R. (1994). A self-made man. In V.J. Bradley, J.W. Ashbaugh, & B. Blaney (Eds.), *Creating individual supports for people with developmental disabilities: A mandate for change at many levels* (pp. 327–334). Baltimore: Paul H. Brookes Publishing Co.

Halloran, W.D. (1993). Transition services requirement: Issues, implications, challenge. In R.C. Eaves & P.J. McLaughlin (Eds.), *Recent advances in special education and rehabilitation* (pp. 210–224). Boston: Andover Medical Publishers.

Haring, K., & Lovett, D. (1990). A study of the social and vocational adjustment of young adults with mental retardation. *Education and Training in Mental Retardation, 25,* 52–61.

Haworth, L. (1986). *Autonomy: An essay in philosophical psychology and ethics.* New Haven, CT: Yale University Press.

Individuals with Disabilities Education Act of 1990 (IDEA), PL 101-476. (October 30, 1990). Title 20, U.S.C. 1400 et seq: *U.S. Statutes at Large, 104,* 1103–1151.

Jaskulski, T., Metzler, C., & Zierman, S.A. (1990). *Forging a new era: The 1990 report on people with developmental disabilities.* Washington, DC: National Association of Developmental Disabilities Councils.

Johnson, J.R., & Rusch, F.R. (1993). Secondary special education and transition services: Identification and recommendations for future research and demonstration. *Career Development of Exceptional Individuals, 16,* 1–18.

Kennedy, M. (1993). Self-determination. *TASH Newsletter, 19*(9), 11.

Kishi, G., Teelucksingh, B., Zollers, N., Park-Lee, S., & Meyer, L. (1988). Daily decision-making in community residences: A social comparison of adults with and without mental retardation. *American Journal on Mental Retardation, 92,* 430–435.

Kozleski, E.B., & Sands, D.J. (1992). The yardstick of social validity: Evaluating quality of life as perceived by adults without disabilities. *Education and Training in Mental Retardation, 27,* 119–131.

Lewis, K., & Taymans, J.M. (1992). An examination of autonomous functioning skills of adolescents with learning disabilities. *Career Development for Exceptional Individuals, 15,* 37–46.

Mithaug, D.E. (1991). *Self-determined kids.* Lexington, MA: Lexington Books.

Mithaug, D.E., Horiuchi, C.N., & Fanning, P.N. (1985). A report on the Colorado statewide follow-up survey of special education students. *Exceptional Children, 51,* 397–404.

Neel, R.S., Meadows, N., Levine, P., & Edgar, E.B. (1988). What happens after special education: A statewide follow-up study of secondary students who have behavioral disorders. *Behavioral Disorders, 13,* 209–216.

Nirje, B. (1972). The right to self-determination. In W. Wolfensberger (Ed.), *Normalization* (pp. 176–193). Toronto: National Institute on Mental Retardation.

Rappaport, J. (1981). In praise of a paradox: A social policy of empowerment over prevention. *American Journal of Community Psychology, 9,* 1–25.

Rehabilitation Act Amendments of 1992, PL 102-569. (October 29, 1992). Title 29, U.S.C. 701 et seq: *U.S. Statutes at Large, 100,* 4344–4488.

Sands, D.J., & Kozleski, E. (1994). Quality of life differences between adults with and without disabilities. *Education and Training in Mental Retardation and Developmental Disabilities, 29,* 90–101.

Schalock, R.L. (1990). Attempts to conceptualize and measure quality of life. In R.L. Schalock (Ed.), *Quality of life: Perspectives and issues* (pp. 141–148). Washington, DC: American Association on Mental Retardation.

Schriner, K., Roessler, R., & Berkobien, R. (1993). Employment concerns of people with mental retardation. *Journal of Job Placement, 9,* 12–13.

Scuccimarra, D.J., & Speece, D.L. (1990). Employment outcomes and social integration of students with mild handicaps: The quality of life two years after high school. *Journal of Learning Disabilities, 23,* 213–219.

Sienkiewicz-Mercer, R., & Kaplan, S.B. (1989). *I raise my eyes to say yes: A memoir.* Boston: Houghton Mifflin.

Sigafoos, A.D., Feinstein, C.B., Damond, M., & Reiss, D. (1988). The measurement of behavioral autonomy in adolescence: The autonomous functioning checklist. In C.B. Feinstein, A. Esman, J. Looney, G. Orvin, J. Schimel, A. Schwartzberg, A. Sorsky, & M. Sugar (Eds.), *Adolescent psychiatry* (Vol. 15, pp. 432–462). Chicago: University of Chicago Press.

Stancliffe, R. (1995). Assessing opportunities for choice-making: A comparison of self- and staff reports. *American Journal on Mental Retardation, 99*, 418–429.

Stancliffe, R., & Wehmeyer, M.L. (1995). Variability in the availability of choice to adults with mental retardation. *Journal of Vocational Rehabilitation, 5*, 319–328.

Ward, M.J. (1988). The many facets of self-determination. *NICHCY Transition Summary: National Information Center for Children and Youth with Disabilities, 5*, 2–3.

Wehmeyer, M.L. (1992a). Self-determination and the education of students with mental retardation. *Education and Training in Mental Retardation, 27*, 302–314.

Wehmeyer, M.L. (1992b). Self-determination: Critical skills for outcome-oriented transition services. *The Journal for Vocational Special Needs Education, 39*, 153–163.

Wehmeyer, M.L. (in press). Self-directed learning and self-determination. In M. Agran (Ed.), *Student-directed learning: A handbook on self-management*. Pacific Grove, CA: Brooks/Cole.

Wehmeyer, M.L. (1996). Self-determination in youth with severe cognitive disabilities: From theory to practice. In L. Powers, G.H.S. Singer, & J. Sowers (Eds.), *On the road to autonomy: Promoting self-competence in children and youth with disabilities* (pp. 115–133). Baltimore: Paul H. Brookes Publishing Co.

Wehmeyer, M.L., & Berkobien, R. (1991). Self-determination and self-advocacy: A case of mistaken identity. *TASH Newsletter, 17*(7), 4.

Wehmeyer, M.L., Kelchner, K., & Richards, S. (1995). Individual and environmental factors related to the self-determination of adults with mental retardation. *Journal of Vocational Rehabilitation, 5*, 291–305.

Wehmeyer, M.L., Kelchner, K., & Richards, S. (in press). Essential characteristics of self-determined behavior of individuals with mental retardation. *American Journal on Mental Retardation*.

Wehmeyer, M.L., Martin, J.E., & Sands, D.J. (in press). Self-determination for children and youth with developmental disabilities. In A. Hilton, D. Finn, & R. Ringlaben (Eds.), *Best and effective practices in educating students with developmental disabilities*. Austin, TX: PRO-ED.

Wehmeyer, M.L., & Metzler, C.A. (1995). How self-determined are people with mental retardation? The National Consumer Survey. *Mental Retardation, 33*, 111–119.

Wehmeyer, M.L., & Ward, M.J. (1995). Student involvement in transition planning: Fulfilling the intent of IDEA. *Journal of Vocational Special Needs Education, 17*, 108–111.

Whitman, T.L. (1990). Self-regulation and mental retardation. *American Journal on Mental Retardation, 94*, 347–362.

Williams, R.R. (1989). Creating a new world of opportunity: Expanding choice and self-determination in lives of Americans with severe disability by 1992 and beyond. In R. Perske (Ed.), *Proceedings from the National Conference on Self-Determination* (pp. 16–17). Minneapolis: Institute on Community Integration.

Zimmerman, M.A. (1990). Toward a theory of learned hopefulness: A structural model analysis of participation and empowerment. *Journal of Research in Personality, 24*, 71–86.

Chapter 3

SELF-DETERMINATION AND TRUST

My Experiences and Thoughts

Michael J. Kennedy

SELF-DETERMINATION HAS set the direction for my life in spite of what my disability limits me in doing. I always knew that I wanted to be treated equally, and I feel like I have always strived to be more self-determining, even though I had never heard of the word and was always told that I had to let other people make the decisions about my life. In this chapter, I discuss how I define self-determination, how important trusting relationships are in self-determination, and how the service system can support it. I use many examples from my own life because that is what I know the best. I got some of my ideas from talking to other people, and many of them are from my own experiences. At the end of the chapter, I give suggestions about how the service system can support self-determination for everyone.

MY DEFINITION OF SELF-DETERMINATION

First, I'd like to talk about how I define self-determination for myself. I think it is different for each person, depending on the person's circumstances and what his or her disabilities are. In my case, I need physical assistance in almost every area, such as getting up out of bed, taking a shower, washing my hair, getting dressed, using the bathroom, combing my hair, brushing my teeth, preparing meals, and

Preparation of this chapter was supported in part by the U.S. Department of Education, Office of Special Education and Rehabilitative Services, National Institute on Disability and Rehabilitation Research, through Cooperative Agreement No. H133B00003-90 and Contract No. H133B80048. The opinions expressed herein are those of the author, and no official endorsement from the U.S. Department of Education should be inferred. This chapter was dictated to and edited by Bonnie Shoultz. The author also thanks the following people for their ideas and suggestions: Kathy Hulgin, Pam Walker, and Bonnie Shoultz.

so on. For me, self-determination is not physical independence. It's more about my knowing what I need and being able to explain this to my personal care assistants so that they can help me with my daily living.

Also, self-determination for me is knowing that there are resources out there that I can use to educate myself about things that will enhance my growth or independence. I don't always know how to meet all of my needs, and things change, so it helps to know that I can find and use other resources to improve my situation. For me, that is true self-determination. It doesn't just help my growth, it helps my personal care assistants grow, too. We learn together. It is great when I have assistants who are willing to learn, both from me and from the other resources that are out there.

I believe that self-determination is a process. You keep learning how to be more self-determining. Each year you grow more, and things keep changing, so it is an ongoing process. You keep learning how better to ask for help, and who can best help you with a specific area or problem. You keep learning more about when to take risks and when not to, and about when and how to speak up. The other people around you keep learning, too.

For example, it may be self-determining to speak up when you are upset about something. But the first time you may scream it out and then think, "Oh, God, I made a fool of myself." Or you say something to the person you are upset with when there are other people around and find out that this made you look bad and made the other person upset with you. Later, you would learn to take the person aside and tell him or her what you need in a calm voice, and hopefully you would be able to come to an agreement and still get your needs met at the same time. Later on, you might learn even better ways of speaking up, or you might realize that you need to call in an outside mediator to help both parties come to an agreement. All of this could be called self-determination, but it shows how the growth process might go. It affects all the parties involved, not just the person with a disability.

I believe that self-determination means different things for different people. In my case, because I need my personal care assistants, it is a matter of teamwork. I am not trying to become independent of my assistants, even in the sense of me being the one who knows everything that needs to be done. I am their employer, but we work together hand in hand and respect each other's ideas and opinions. If we disagree on something that has to do with my care, my assistant knows that I have the final say. He might say, "I wouldn't do it this way, but you know your body and your life," and I might say, "I am probably taking a risk, but I have to take the risk and if I make a mistake I will learn from it." If I ever feel—and this doesn't happen often—that he is overstepping his bounds, I will take him aside and tell him that. He might get hurt, but he will think about it and come back to me later and say, "Michael, you were right. I have to remember that it's your life and you are my boss. Even if I don't think it's the easiest way to do it, I need to remember to do it your way."

Here's an example of how we work things out. I have two assistants, but one is only part time. The assistant who is full time has worked with and for me for 9 years. He is the one who usually helps me write my checks. My mother always told me, "If you have the money in the bank, pay your bills and get them out of the way. Why let them sit around?" So that's basically what I do. My assistant sometimes says, "You don't have to pay this bill right now," but I would just as soon do it and get it out of the way. He realizes that I have my own ways of doing things, and he goes along with me. He used to try to change my mind about things like this, but now he knows that I want to do things my own way, and he respects me for it. As you can imagine, issues like this can come up all the time because there are two people working together who each have their own opinions about things.

For other people, physical assistance might not be an issue, but they might need assistance in other ways. One person might need help in budgeting his money, or even in spending his money. Another person might need help in preparing the right kind of meals, or in eating a balanced diet. Someone else might need help in becoming more responsible in most of the aspects of her daily life. I have lived with many people who have difficulty communicating their needs and wishes. If someone has a way of communicating his or her choices, that way should be used to understand what the person wants and needs. But if someone has very severe disabilities, it takes a while to get to know the person. Some people don't know what their choices are, or they just leave it up to professionals to make their decisions. But people do let others know what they don't want. Maybe they can't express it in words, but they do express it in their actions.

There are many considerations to make when someone doesn't communicate choices in an understandable way. Rather than giving people drugs to quiet them down, we need to get other people into their lives, people who have a personal investment in getting to know them well. There are ways to do this, but it can be hard to put that kind of real support in place. When someone has had limited or no experiences, risk taking is a big issue. It may take a long time for the person to learn to make good choices, so the support he or she receives needs to be flexible. It is important to start with the assumption that people *can* make choices and express preferences. It may be that a communication system is needed before other decisions can be made. And whenever anyone is assisting someone to make choices, it is always going to be limited by the helper's beliefs and expectations. People need to be very aware of this, but they shouldn't assume that the person who is helping someone wasn't chosen by the person in need of help or that the support person has ulterior motives. It can be a fine line, and we have to accept that. At the end of this chapter, I will give some suggestions for how the system can help people to make choices for themselves.

IMPORTANCE OF TRUSTING RELATIONSHIPS

In my experience, real self-determination will happen best when the person has a trusting relationship with someone, or with several people. I can't emphasize enough how important this is. With a trusting relationship, self-determination can grow. For example, if the person with the disability wants to do things that might hurt him or her, he or she might be given the opportunity to make mistakes, within reason. The person he or she trusts can try to show the consequences of these mistakes and how to make better decisions about things. It takes a lot of faith to trust another person to care enough to help someone understand what is best for him or her.

To me, teamwork and equality are the keys to a trusting relationship. There is a big difference between that and just giving an order, such as, "No, you're not going to eat this," or "No, you can't buy that." Put yourself in the place of the person with a disability. The person you trust can help you understand the reasons behind things, and because he or she does it out of caring for you as a person, you may go along with it even if you don't fully understand. Instead of the support person overpowering you, there is a sharing of the responsibility, and each of the people in the relationship can grow to make things work for both of you. Neither of you pretends to have all the answers.

However, you can trust someone too much, and become dependent on them, and that's not self-determination. If you become dependent on someone, and leave everything for the support person to do, you have stopped growing. You have allowed the other person to take over, and you have stopped working on things yourself. What happens if the support person can't be there some day, or gets another job and leaves? You won't know how to teach another person what you want done, or how you need it done, because it's always been done without your involvement. Also, you can trust someone so much that they could be taking advantage of you without your knowing about it. If you aren't involved, and if you don't keep checking to make sure the person is doing what you want them to do, you might get ripped off, or important things might not get done. It is not enough just to have a good relationship with the support person. You still have to take responsibility for what they are supposed to do, and you may have to put your friendship to the side and be businesslike. I have learned these things the hard way. I did get ripped off once by someone who presented himself as a warm, friendly person who cared about me. I hired him without getting enough background on him, and trusted him because he acted like a nice guy.

In my case, trust continues to grow between me and my full-time personal care assistant. I was married a year ago and got a new apartment. Now, my wife and I have given my assistant a key to our apartment, and he can come and go even when we are not there. We know he is very honest, and we trust him with our things. We have learned to take steps like this slowly, but to go ahead if it seems reasonable. My wife and I help each other with this, and we also get help from our assistants. If we are hiring a new person, we all tell each other our feelings about the person. Sometimes our assistants will know something about a person that we don't know and will give us feedback on whether they think the person will work out for us. We are getting good at telling whether a person will work out, and we can usually tell this now within the first week of someone working with us.

The other thing I want to mention is that I have had to learn ways of dealing with my assistants positively. In the past, people walked all over me because they had the power. Now that I have the power to hire and fire people, I have to figure out ways of working with my assistants so they will do what I want. I use humor, and there is a lot of give and take and mutual respect. I try not to be heavy-handed, unless I feel I need to be. We have bucked heads at times, but we have never had a battle that we couldn't work through. To work it through, everyone involved has to be levelheaded. To me, all of these issues have to do with self-determination.

Finding Someone to Listen

Self-determination developed for me over many years, as I learned to speak up for myself and found people who would listen to me. I wasn't always able to be as independent as I am today, but I always wanted to be. I wanted to be in control of my own life. One way I started to work toward this goal was to use my voice. Even though I didn't know much about how to become independent, I was a persistent person. From ages 5 to 22, I lived in three New York State institutions. The first one was a nursing home for children. The other two were state schools (now they are called developmental centers). I didn't like the institutions, but my family had no choice but to put me there. At that time, there were no supports in the community. When I was 22, I moved into the community.

When I was in the institutions, I spoke up when abuse or neglect happened to me or other people. I got to a point where I couldn't handle seeing these things happen and decided that, even if I would get punished, I was going to voice my opinion or my concerns about things that were going on. At first I couldn't find anyone to listen to me, and I got a lot of abuse for speaking up. I went without meals sometimes for 2 days in a row, I got drugged to keep me quiet even though I wasn't on medication, and once I got put in a cold shower and then the staff went out and got a huge bucket of snow and put it on me. I caught pneumonia and almost died because of that, and I was only a teenager.

Even with all the abuse, I always kept it in my mind that there had to be somebody out there who would have the heart and compassion to listen. I didn't find very many, but there were three key people who did. The first one, who was maybe the most helpful, was my physical therapist. We hit it off right from the beginning when I met her, and she noticed that I was a very bitter individual. She asked me why, and I opened up to her. She told me, "Michael, stop it. You have more going for you than you give yourself credit for." She made me see that I am somebody, in all kinds of ways. I still call her my adopted big sister. There was also a staff member who had a son with a slight disability, and a volunteer who used to come on a weekly basis. I became really good friends with these two people, and once I felt comfortable enough, I began to tell them about the conditions. The staff person worked in another building, but I had gotten to know her through some institution picnics. My volunteer worked with me specifically for a half hour once a week and would help me write letters to my other friend. I would tell them about what was going on, and they would encourage me to make changes in my life, like advocating for myself to get out of the institution. It took a couple of years of them preparing me before I could act on it.

What made me start trying to get out was watching two of my friends die because of the abuse. As a resident, I was not told how or why they died but I believe one died because he was denied food and the other one got another resident to help him hang himself. I started speaking up more within the institution. One day, when there was an inspection, I pointed out abuse to the inspector. I begged my friends to help me write a letter to the paper, and they would take me down to the administration offices so I could complain. My friend who was a staff person got so she didn't care about keeping her job because she couldn't stand seeing what was going on. I was trying to get the abuse stopped, but then I realized that if I was going to do anybody any real good I had to get out of the institution. I was scared to death, but I felt I had to write the letters and complain about the things that weren't right.

To this day, I don't know or remember how it happened, but the staff of a community agency heard about me and came to the institution and told me about a Medicaid-funded apartment program (an intermediate care facility [ICF]) they were opening for people with cerebral palsy. I don't know for sure who was advocating for me to get out. The apartment program had some good policies, like allowing us to be involved in the hiring of the staff. We would have meetings with the apartment managers even before the apartments opened up. Once I moved in, my ability to be in charge of my life improved. The program would bend some of the Medicaid rules based on what we wanted.

LIFE CHANGES CAN SUPPORT SELF-DETERMINATION

My empowerment came both from the support of others and from inside myself. I had some trusting relationships that helped me, with people who would frame things so it made me think. In the institution I had developed an arrogant attitude and I took that into the community. There, I noticed that it turned people off. I thought about it and realized there was a better way, but I had to work on changing my attitude and the way I perceived people in the service system. I realized I wasn't going to go anywhere without the support I needed, so I worked on myself. That's self-determination, especially because I realized this myself, not from anyone else forcing me to change. Yes, people made comments about it, but I realized it. For example, one of my good friends pointed out that I needed to listen to myself and see how people responded; I did, and I picked it up. This friend was able to be very up front about things I was doing, and I appreciated that.

My empowerment also meant that I had the chance to tell other people how I wanted things done, and how my disability affects me. This was hard at first because the service agency system wasn't set up to do things this way, maybe because they did not think I had the capability to direct my own care. I felt the system was molding me into what it wanted and had lost sight of the feelings and wants and needs I had as a human being and not just a person with a disability. They wanted to do things their way—that made it easier for them—and told me that I couldn't do things on my own. When that happens you start to believe what they tell you, and that stays with you even when you move into a place where there is more encouragement.

Nevertheless, there is something about just living in the community that supports self-determination. In the community, you learn how things are done. You can experiment with solving things yourself without calling staff people to help you out, but you can also learn when to call for help. There is a different atmosphere around you than in an institution, and you have exposure to so many different things in the community. You begin to realize what you like and what you want, and you are also teaching other people that you have something to offer. You learn to be more self-determining because you have more to choose from, and more support to make choices. You start hearing about what is possible and what is not.

A Place of My Own

I've already told some of the story of how I left the apartment program to be in a place that was more my own, and how I have changed since then (Kennedy, 1993a, 1993b). I have also written a little about how the Center on Human Policy at Syracuse University empowered me (Kennedy, 1990). At the Center, I learned about the philosophy of self-determination. They believed that people with disabilities should be able to live like everyone else and be involved in how their services are run. I learned that it is possible for people with disabilities to live a quality life. People at work and in the community encouraged me to think about what was right for myself and supported me even when I made decisions that did not work out for me. My opinions were valued, and I realized that I and other people with disabilities have something to offer to the world.

There were many times when I felt like a failure and like throwing in the towel. These feelings just built up in me even when I was putting on a good front. Often I was stuck in the old institutional mode and didn't say anything to my friends and co-workers about how I was feeling. I felt that they were busy and that I shouldn't be a burden to them by dropping all this on them. I know now that it can take years to overcome the old way of thinking about your rights and choices and abilities. For example, it took me 2 months after I moved into my own apartment—I moved in with two friends who did my personal care—to stop asking if I could use the phone or anything else in the house. I was in the habit of asking for permission, and I felt like I didn't have the right to use my own things. I didn't know how people would react if I tried to do things on my own. At work, I felt like I wasn't living up to what I should be doing, but I didn't say anything. It got bad enough that I decided to move to Georgia and try to make a new life for myself. The good thing about this move was that people supported me even if they didn't think it was a good decision. My boss told me that my job would be open if I ever decided to come back, but he supported my decision to leave.

Really Learning to Trust Others

My move to Georgia didn't work out, but I learned from it. I learned that the services here in Syracuse are much better than they are in the part of Georgia I lived in. Back here, where you have more access to services, people in the service system knew me well. I learned that I had a wide range of supports in Syracuse, even though at the time I didn't see it. I found out I had people here who cared enough about me to be there for me when I came back. They told me that it was okay to ask for help if I needed it, and that they valued me as a person, not just as someone with a disability. I found out that if I told people when I was feeling bad or needed something, I was happier. They would respond, or at least they would listen. Now I know that I can't carry the load by myself, and that I can get the support when I need it. When I came back it was like having a whole different light on things. I felt really different inside, after being gone for a year and a half. After I had been gone for a while, I felt like I was out of touch, like I was in seclusion, and that's what told me I missed Syracuse. Coming back is when I really learned about trusting people.

I feel I should point out that I still have times when I get down on myself. I get frustrated when I can't do things to help my wife in the apartment, or when I need something and I can't get it and nobody is around. A perfect example is when I have to use the bathroom and nobody is around to help me, or when my wife needs help lifting something or getting something. Then I have to step back and look at the qualities I do have and learn to deal with what I cannot do. I am still working on this, and this is one way my empowerment comes from inside as well as from other people. What I am realizing, and I think it is ongoing, is that I am competent. I can direct someone on how to do things, even though I can't do it myself. Many times the things I need done can injure someone if they do it the wrong way, and I know the steps they need to take so they won't get injured. I am realizing that I've got the knowledge to figure out how to do things. I've also found that if people ignore me when I tell them how to do things, they are sorry.

I have changed a lot myself because of my self-determination goals, and I believe that other people will, too. I have much better control, and I don't get upset as much or as often. Like Nancy Ward (1989) says, I have learned to direct my feelings in a positive way instead of blowing up or keeping them to myself. I have found that if I do this, people are more likely to listen and do something about what I am complaining about. Even if they can't do anything about it, talking helps to release the tension. Before, I thought I had to keep everything to myself, and then it would build up to the point where I would blow up. No one wants to hear that, when it's that bad! I had to get some honest feedback, and I had to change myself, but I also needed those people who would listen to me.

When I advocate for other people, and when I give talks to people about taking charge of their own lives, it encourages me to keep going with my own life. I point out to other people with disabilities that no matter how severe their disabilities are, they can be as independent as possible. As long as they know what they want, they can work with their service system to be included in the decision making about their lives. Because I tell other people these things, I have to live it myself. I have to be an example for myself and for other people, and I use my own experiences to teach others. The best way that I can point these things out is to tell my own personal story, even when it hurts. I think that doing this means that I have to look inside myself and believe in myself, so I will have the determination to go after what I want.

CREATING SERVICE SYSTEMS
THAT SUPPORT SELF-DETERMINATION

The way service systems operate now, they create a lot of barriers to self-determination. For example, the providers often create a set of services and expect the person to fit into what exists instead of taking people as individuals and creating what they need. For example, a person may be offered either an ICF/MR or a group home, and each of these will have a set of services that are built in, like service plans that everyone has to have whether they want them or not. At the same time, some of what a person really wants in life is not available in these situations. A person might really want to learn about things but not to have them written down, with verbal prompts; or a person might want to choose who is going to work with him or her each day. Someone else may really want to live on his or her own but cannot because the system isn't set up to assist them to permit that. Too often, the person with the disability is not included in the process of developing the services he or she is going to get. I have a radical proposal for how those barriers can be eliminated.

I know that people with disabilities need help from agencies, but I believe we need to figure out how to free up the money that goes with our services so that it goes into our hands. That way we could pay for our own services, maybe by contracting with agencies, and if we didn't like the services we were getting, we could go elsewhere. For example, someone who is now living in a group home could work with someone they trust, like a friend or family member, to decide where he or she wants to live, what services the person needs, what involvement he or she wants others to have, and the person could then buy those services. If the person didn't know how to go about it, he or she could ask for support in getting started and finding out what is available. If the person was given a number of options and didn't really know which option to choose, he or she could ask for support in making those decisions. Choosing services should be based on the individual needs people have, and this process would be easier if the money could go directly to the person seeking services, and if the support could be made available to help the person learn what options could meet his or her individual needs. The agency could be there for support in terms of helping the individual figure out the best way of spending the money so that all of his or her needs are met.

Right now the system is not set up in most places to work in the way that I have described. The money doesn't come to us, but goes directly to the agencies that are set up to serve us. The problem with this is that the agencies have most of the control. If you need a service, even if you know what your needs are, the agency will develop services that *they* think you need rather than coming to you to find out what your needs are and what it would take to support you. Oftentimes it is set up as a medical model. The other thing the system does is to keep threatening to take away money and services. If you are trying to become more independent and self-sufficient, you are penalized and can lose some of the important services you now have. For example, right now I am being told that Medicaid will no longer pay for my personal assistance services because my wife and I make too much money. However, we don't make enough between us to cover the services I need, let alone our monthly bills for food, housing, and so on. Both of these ways of dealing with people with disabilities undercut self-determination. The system can make us reluctant to be more self-determining because it creates fear that we will be punished in some way.

For real self-determination, people with disabilities need to be moved from the bottom to the top of the decision-making pyramid. Changing how the money flows would help this, but we also need to change the way the system is structured so that people with disabilities have the control as well as the supports they need. This can mean changing the attitudes about people with disabilities so that we are viewed as valued assets to our communities, and taking the system apart in such a way that it gives more power and more flexibility. I don't have the answer, but we need to come up with a creative way to do this. People need to get together to figure out how to free up the money and resources and create some different ways of doing things. I know there are some people who are experimenting with this kind of approach. I think these projects should be studied to see how it works.

SUGGESTIONS REGARDING SELF-DETERMINATION

The system (and the people in it) need to be willing to try a lot of different things to help a person learn to become more self-determining because at first no one can know what will work. For example, a person could make a list of things he or she wants to learn how to do, even though he or she isn't sure what will actually work. With this list, everyone involved with the person can try different things until they find something that does work. There should be an agreement that the person can let his or her helpers know if someone is overstepping the bounds and doing things for the individual that he or she could do independently. Even if the person makes mistakes, the person needs to do so in order to learn.

I think the service system is getting better in terms of trying to work with people, though they have a long way to go. I still get scared about the situation where there are people who can't communicate well. I think about how many things I had to learn and all the struggles I have had, and I wonder how these others can make it. I think the system has even more responsibility when people can't communicate well because they can't do as much for themselves as others can. Direct service workers, service coordinators, and administrators need to be in tune with these people to help them become more in control of what happens to them and to become more aware of what is out there for them. The need to develop trusting relationships is even more important with people who can't communicate well because their lives are in the system's hands. If they don't have people they can trust and who really know them, their lives can be in a shambles. Their supports can fall apart, and they can end up not getting what they need to survive or live a good life. However, I do believe the system is changing, slowly, in this direction. Compared to when I was a child, it is easier to find caring people who are doing their best on somebody's behalf. It is still hard for people with disabilities who cannot easily communicate their needs, but I do see a significant amount of difference.

The system could help people find support people they can trust to help them become more self-determining in several ways:

- Not moving people who care about a person out of his or her life
- Encouraging people who care about a person to build networks with other people who know him or her, so they will be connected with each other and can work together to help the person
- Allowing and supporting these networks to be built
- Trusting the people who are closest to the person when they express things for the person, rather than discounting what they say (for example, not discounting them because they are gay, or because they are not as well-educated, or are in other ways different from the professionals)
- Encouraging the professionals to look at themselves if they start distrusting others

The system can also encourage people with disabilities and their helpers to learn about the resources that are available to them and to realize that the learning is going to go on and on. It needs to support the idea of teamwork and power sharing between people and their helpers. The system also needs to support the idea that people should be able to live how they want to, even if the professionals would live differently. The system is there to assist, offering guidance but not threatening us if we don't take the advice. This always means listening to us, really listening, and giving us feedback that is honest but respectful.

I think service providers, family, and friends will find that if they both listen closely and give honest feedback to people, which can include being clear about what their own limits are, that people will learn better ways of communicating what they need in such a way that together they can act on it. It goes back to the trust issue. If you talk calmly to someone who is upset, the person is more apt to stop and think about what he or she is doing and take a different approach. Then you have a better chance of getting to the root of the problem and making the changes that need to be made.

For staff people and others who don't have disabilities, as well as for people with disabilities, power sharing is what is needed. It's not that there is an outcome where the person with the disability now has some or all of the power, but that there is an ongoing process involved. At every part of the day, there are decisions that have to do with power. The question is, who makes the decision? Where does it start and where does it end? The person with a disability needs to have the final say as to what will happen, even if it's a decision that is made jointly with other people. If a decision is made jointly, the responsibility (including the risk) for the decision needs to be joint, too. The power-sharing process doesn't stay the same all the time. It changes as the people involved grow and learn from each other.

The final suggestion I have is that we have to find ways of getting the money directly in the hands of the people who need it. This will take a lot of thought and planning by all kinds of people, but it needs to be done.

SUMMARY

Self-determination is what life is all about. Without it, you might be alive, but you wouldn't be living—you would just be existing. That's why it is so important for everyone to learn about self-determination and be in charge of their own lives. It's about trust and power sharing and communication. It's about systems change, putting the person with the disability at the top, and supporting that person to live a full life. To me, it's a combination of all these things and more.

REFERENCES

Kennedy, M. (1990). Caring people working to make a change. *TASH Newsletter, 16*(2), 4.

Kennedy, M. (1993a). Out of my old life and into my new one. In B. Shoultz (Ed.), *Community living for adults* (pp. 3–4). Syracuse, NY: Center on Human Policy.

Kennedy, M. (1993b). Turning the pages of life. In J.A. Racino, P. Walker, S. O'Connor, & S.J. Taylor (Eds.), *Housing, support, and community: Choices and strategies for adults with disabilities* (pp. 205–216). Baltimore: Paul H. Brookes Publishing Co.

Ward, N. (1989). Self-determination. In R. Perske (Ed.), *National conference on self-determination: 29 recommendations*. Minneapolis: Institute on Community Integration, University of Minnesota.

Chapter 4

SELF-DETERMINATION AS A FAMILY AFFAIR

Parents' Perspectives on Self-Determination

Brenda Doss and Bess Hatcher

THE GOAL OF most parents who have a son or daughter with a disability is to raise their child to be as independent as possible. Parents want a safe and caring atmosphere, but because of our desire to protect our children from harm or displeasure, we are often overprotective. People learn from experiences in life, and as parents we sometimes prevent our children from having learning experiences because we are afraid they may get hurt or fail.

As parents of two children with disabilities, we firmly believe that self-determination has to start as a family affair. Families must insist that skills of independence be learned early in life. They must be willing to allow their children with disabilities to take risks and let them fail from time to time. Families must permit their children to be different and to develop their own unique personalities. Finally, parents must often take a back seat when their goals for their child come in conflict with that child's goals. Individuals with disabilities have the right to be respected for their own abilities, values, and desires and should be encouraged to pursue their personal dreams.

Long before the term *self-determination* was expressed as a critical goal for people with disabilities (Ward, 1988), we knew it was important to raise our children to be self-determined adults. Our family stories, which follow, demonstrate how, as parents, we arranged for our children with disabilities to have as many opportunities as possible to live their lives similar to other children in the community. We have both struggled with their transition to adulthood, and this chapter shares our concerns as well as our pride in their steps toward independence.

ROBIN'S PATH TO SELF-DETERMINATION (BRENDA DOSS)

When Robin was born, she was given only 1 year to live, and the doctors predicted she would spend most of that year in the hospital. She was hospitalized only once during that year (with congenital heart failure) and will be celebrating her 26th birthday soon. She certainly is self-determined—not only determined to live, but determined to become a productive member of our family and community as well.

I remember so well, even now after 25 years, the happiness tinged with pain in my husband Bill's face as he told me that our daughter had Down syndrome. After two boys, he was happy we finally had that little girl he wanted so badly— he wanted six children if they could all be girls, believing that little girls just loved their daddies more! Not really knowing anything about Down syndrome, he could not immediately realize the full implications of her disability. But as a special education teacher I could, and I had hysterics, imagining what I thought was the worst—severe mental retardation.

Bill had been unsure how to break the news to me, so he had asked our closest friends to be with him. It took all three to hold me on the bed as I came to grips with the news, while we all cried together. Later in the night, after Jim and Margaret had gone home, I asked to see my baby. A compassionate nurse brought her to the room, and breaking all hospital rules in 1969, she let Bill stay in the room with us. We held her so closely, examining every inch of her little body as we gently kissed her fingers, toes, and cheeks. She was so fragile, with all the tell-tale signs of Down syndrome, but she had a smile in her eyes, and we fell instantly in love with a little girl who was to change not only our lives, but the lives of so many others.

Self-Determination Begins at Home

When Robin was born I was finishing the last semester of my master's degree in special education, with certification in mental retardation. During the course of earning that degree, I had worked on a practicum at Alabama's only institution for people with mental retardation (Partlow) and had been appalled at some of the living conditions there. Thus I was determined that Robin would never live in an institution. I think I started teaching her to be independent and self-determined the very day we brought her home from the hospital. If I felt she could do something for herself, I would not let anyone help her, often making her daddy leave the house while she tried repeatedly to achieve a small task. His patience often gave out! And that went double for her grandparents—they kept declaring, "She's going to outgrow this yet."

Robin's brothers became my allies and insisted that she learn chores and take care of herself, especially Gary, who was only 3 years older. He never allowed her to get by with anything. Gary and Robin developed a true sibling rivalry, but he was also the one who would take her to the neighborhood mall to play the pinball machines. Billy, 5 years older, was more tolerant and much more protective. Still, both were eager to include her in their activities and never hesitated to invite their friends to our house. She attended ballgames, band concerts, and school plays to cheer for her brothers, and they in turn encouraged her participation in neighborhood and school activities. They were as proud of her as she was of them. Although her developmental skills were somewhat delayed, Robin took ballet lessons with the neighborhood kids, performing right on cue during recitals. It was those first ballet lessons that gave her a love for dancing and she now square dances, clogs, and line dances. Along with bowling in a unified league, music and dancing are probably her biggest loves.

Robin's School Experiences

Robin started school in 1972 at the age of 3, before the Education for All Handicapped Children Act of 1975 (PL 94-142) was passed. She attended a general education preschool with other children in the small town in Alabama where we were living at the time. She learned her colors, numbers 1–10, and some important social skills—to share, to take turns, and to defend herself. During that year her language increased, her articulation improved, and she overcame much of her shyness.

The following year (1973) I enrolled her in a special school in Birmingham, quitting my own job to transport her 35 miles from home. She attended this school for a year and a half before we moved to Jasper. Here she attended another special school for a little over a year, while I taught in a different school system. The class I was teaching was on a regular school campus, and we were mainstreaming our students. I came to believe that this was the educational program I wanted for Robin, and at the start of the next school year I enrolled her in a more inclusive setting. She learned her academics; interacted with "regular" classmates; and developed a sweet, friendly personality and an even, easygoing temperament. She loved school, and she set herself several goals: 1) to go to high school, 2) to go to the prom, and 3) to graduate! It was here that we ran into our first major problem. That "progressive" school system was not quite ready to allow students labeled "trainable mentally retarded" to go to the local high schools. They were afraid the students would be laughed at, might not be safe, couldn't keep up, and wouldn't fit in—all the old excuses!

So, like many other mothers, I joined (in fact, I spearheaded) a class action suit against the Alabama State Department of Education and my own school system—the system that paid my salary! Only a few parents who also wanted their children in more age-appropriate settings with same-age peers agreed with my cause. At the time I was in a supervisory position in the school, and all the teachers and aides working under my direction adamantly disagreed with me. Needless to say, that was a very difficult year for me personally; still, we persisted. In the end, even though the Office of Civil Rights (OCR) ruled in our favor, the district judge ruled against us because we had not gone through proper due process before filing the suit.

However, that did not stop our efforts. I simply called the principal at the high school and asked if he would give the class a room if I came with them as the teacher. He immediately said yes. He had the room painted over the summer and 16 eager students diagnosed with moderate to severe mental retardation attended the first day of classes—their first day in high school and the first students with that level of mental retardation to enroll in a high school in the system. Talk about being proud! I learned that many things can be achieved without a court's intervention and with a lot less stress.

Robin's senior year truly lived up to her expectations. She made new friends, rooted for her home team as she attended football and basketball games, joined a social club, and took a home economics class. The year passed much too quickly. She and a longtime friend, James, attended the prom. He arrived to pick her up in his tuxedo, carrying a corsage of baby pink roses that just matched her beautiful pink formal gown. And like all the other couples that night, they went out to eat at a local restaurant (just to show off) and found their seats right in the middle of all the other seniors. Since James had no driving license, his aunt chauffeured them in her big Lincoln Continental (close to a limousine). At the prom they danced the night away, refusing to leave until the lights went out—certainly a night to remember.

Then came Class Night. In planning for this event, the seniors of Cordova High school really showed their love and acceptance for the six students with mental retardation who were graduating with them. Traditionally, each senior would start the program by introducing him- or herself and his or her parents and then would share his or her plans immediately following graduation. This class got together and decided they would not talk about their plans for the future because they reasoned that those six students would not be going to college, joining the army, or getting a job, and they did not want them to be embarrassed. The principal overruled their decision and declared that they had to follow the previous format. The class officers stood their ground and continued to refuse. After all, the class president reminded the principal, "most of us lie anyway," and they won the battle. Those six students learned their lines of introduction as well as the class songs and again made the whole school proud of them. They were not the stars of the show, but they certainly were a part.

Then it was time for graduation—all too soon. Dressed in blue robes and matching mortarboards, my daughter and her five friends finally realized a lifelong dream. Her name, Robin Doss, was called. She marched up, shook hands with the principal, accepted her Certificate of Completion, moved her tassel from the right to the left, flashed an "I did it" smile at the audience, and proudly walked back to her seat—the first student with Down syndrome to ever walk across that stage! Fifty-five other students, including five with severe disabilities, did the same. Then came the moment to toss that cap—they were graduates! Robin's graduation day was probably one of the happiest days of our lives.

Robin's Life After School

Immediately following graduation, in 1990, Robin started work at the sheltered workshop operated by the Association for Retarded Citizens (now The Arc). This was the only option available to her at that time. She stayed there about a year before moving into their supported employment program and going to work at a Wendy's fast-food restaurant. She was the second person from this program to be placed in a community job and the first in our county with Down syndrome to actually work at a "real" job, although there are several others doing so now.

Nine months into the job at Wendy's, Robin announced that she hated the job, and she quit. Later, working at Wal-Mart, she was laid off due to a reduction in employees. She went back to the sheltered workshop, but was very insistent that she did not like that at all. It did not allow her enough independence. After volunteering for a summer program for young children with disabilities, she was asked by the teacher to come and work in her class during the regular school year. Here she has found her niche. She really loves working with small children and hopes to continue for several years. She has also worked with the 2 year olds in church for several years.

Robin loves to stay home alone and expresses some interest in moving into an apartment, a goal I share with her. I want her to learn to drive, but she absolutely refuses to try—an example of self-determination! She is determined about her clothes, especially her shoes, wearing one old pair of tennis shoes that I would love to throw away. She is becoming much more assertive as a result of participating in Partners in Policymaking of Alabama this year and through her membership in the self-advocacy group People First for the last 7 years. She has served the local People First group as Secretary and has served on the Alabama People First Board of Directors. She loves to travel with the group and represented Alabama at the 1994 Celebration of the ADA in Washington, D.C., attending the President's reception on the White House lawn.

Allow Your Child to Fly

As I reflect over the last 25 years I remember the many experiences—joyful and painful—we have shared with Robin. I remember watching as she took her first wobbly steps at the age of 15 months; her bouncy steps down the aisle at the age of 4 as flower girl in her babysitter's wedding; and later, at the age of 20, her graceful walk as she served her future sister-in-law as bridesmaid. I remember her often saying to me, "Well, just forget it!" after I had asked her for the third time to repeat something I had not understood; I soon learned to listen closely! I remember the week of sleepless nights when she first went to summer camp at the age of 8, the first day I went to work leaving her alone at the age of 14, and the first day we put her in a cab alone to go to her job at Wendy's (I confess to allowing them to get out of sight before following that taxi in my car—just to make sure she got there safely!), and I still remember anxiously watching the clock for 5 hours while waiting for her to call me to come get her on that first day of "real" work. I remember all the doubts, frustrations, anxiety, and fears that we, as a family, have had to conquer in allowing Robin to reach her goals. And I remember the many friends who have helped us along the way, especially the friends who also have family members with disabilities.

Last week (May, 1995) Robin and I went back to her alma mater for graduation exercises. Tears welled up in my eyes as 83 students, including 8 with mental retardation, paraded across the football field to receive diplomas. One of the eight had lived for several years in the state institution in which I taught before Robin was born, and another was recognized as an honor student, having maintained a 3.5 grade point average in her prescribed course of study for 4 years—the first student with mental retardation at the school to be so honored. I have to believe that their graduation was made possible by Robin's ambitions and determination 5 years earlier; she and her classmates had opened those doors for many others to have an inclusive, typical high school education.

In my current role as director of an agency providing service coordination to persons with mental retardation and developmental disabilities, I can understand the anguish in the eyes of parents who come into our office, wondering where to go for help after learning that their child has been diagnosed with a disability. I can smile with them later when they learn to enjoy that child—disability and all. My advice to those families is to cry a little but laugh a lot; insist on full access to services but always accept and fulfill their own responsibilities as a parent; and, above all, turn loose and allow the child to fly—to fail, surely, at some tasks but to soar, with self-assurance and self-determination, into full adulthood.

STEVE'S PATH TO SELF-DETERMINATION (BESS HATCHER)

Our son, Stephen Hale Hatcher, was born May 14, 1961, with Down syndrome. He has a brother, Jay, who is only 14 months older. As a parent, Jay was my model for development, even though he did everything early, and Steve was late sitting up, crawling, and walking. Steve had to be taught many things that Jay picked up easily. I will never forget how guilty I felt when I fussed at Steve for not picking up his toys in the back yard. He cried and asked pitifully, "What is the front yard and what is the back yard?"

Steve was the youngest of the five boys who lived in our neighborhood, but he went everywhere with them. They liked to play and camp out in the woods near our house. All the boys loved to go with my dad to his place in the country. Steve loved to ride Honey, his black pony, but he did not like to fish or hunt. He loved playing pool and ping-pong in our basement, where all the neighborhood children gathered.

As Jay and Steve grew up, Jay was the one who insisted Steve could run his own bath water, bathe himself, and wash his hair. Since I was involved in many meetings and wasn't always at home, Steve was taught to make up his bed; get his snack after school; make a peanut butter and jelly sandwich; and later, how to use the microwave and washing machine.

Steve's School Experiences

The only school in Birmingham that would take Steve was the Opportunity Center School, a private school for 250 children with mental retardation. It was owned and operated by the Association for Retarded Citizens (ARC; now The Arc). I put Steve's name on a waiting list and prayed he would be accepted. In 1966, when Steve was 5 years old, we were told he would be one of 10 children to attend the school's first preschool class. Steve attended the Opportunity Center School for 4 years.

The preschool teacher, who had become my good friend, encouraged me to have Steve tested. If he scored in an IQ range considered to be "educable" (which he did), he could go into special education classes in the public school. After a year in public school, the special education class was moved to another public school within the same system. In all, Steve attended three different grammar schools.

Many people in ARC, especially those of us who attended national conferences, wanted all children with mental retardation to have the right to attend public school. Many other ARC members strongly opposed this concept. I was elected president of our local chapter of the ARC and conducted negotiations with the Alabama board of education. The room was full of parents the night the board of education voted to accept children with mental retardation as full-time students of the public school. Many parents were excited, but after the meeting lots of angry parents who had been my friends were screaming at me as I got on the elevator and quickly closed the door. The Opportunity Center School was closed.

Jay was in his second year of high school when Steve's teacher asked if I intended to leave Steve in a grammar school setting until he reached age 21. I went to visit a high school that had special education classes. The head teacher took me around the school and assured me they would be glad for "our children" to attend their classes. I happened to mention that my son had Down syndrome. The teacher took three steps back and told me she was sorry, but there was no way Steve could go to their school. Steve's teacher and I sat down and wrote a letter to the Board of Education requesting the establishment of a special education class at our local high school. Our request was honored.

Jay was afraid the high school students would make fun of Steve or that he would get lost. I was afraid to send my little boy to this big school, but I knew it was the right thing for Steve. Jay had a car, so he and Steve went to high school together. Steve knew where his homeroom was located, and he had already met his teacher. I was so nervous the first day of school that I could hardly wait until 3:00 P.M. for them to come home. That afternoon Steve came bounding in the house with his eyes sparkling and a big smile on his face. He loved going to high school.

Steve was in high school 1 year before I was requested to attend a meeting after school with the special education central office staff. They did not tell me what the meeting was about, but Steve's teacher told me they were planning to transfer the "lower functioning" students to another school across town. She said Steve had dropped to a "trainable" level on the IQ test he was given before he left grammar school.

When my husband and I arrived at school, several other parents were already there. They did not know either why they were asked to come to the meeting. I began to feel more and more uncomfortable as parents were called in one by one. We were the last to go in. I was surprised to see 8–10 people from the board of education sitting around a huge table. We were introduced to the Director of Special Education. Our fears were confirmed. After what seemed like several hours of intimidating discussion and arguing, I would not agree to let Steve be transferred to another school. We said we would get a lawyer and go to court.

For several months I was on the phone almost every night talking to my friends about due process. When I met again with the Director of Special Education to tell him I was ready to go to due process, he leaned across his desk and told me he did not have time to fight with me. He also told me how awful I was and how I was hurting other children by insisting Steve stay at our local high school. But Steve stayed at the school. After that, Steve attended several general education classes, and he rode the school bus with other students to receive training at the vocational school. It was the first year special education students were allowed to attend classes in vocational education.

When Steve was a senior he was assigned to a regular homeroom. I often wondered if he sat in the back of the room by himself or if he talked to the other students. I got my answer in May on Steve's birthday when he came home from school with a big card wishing him "Happy birthday from the whole damn crew," and signed by everyone in his homeroom. Our family sat in the stadium with tears running down our faces when Steve walked across the stage to shake hands with the principal and receive his high school diploma. He looked so handsome and proud in his cap and gown.

Steve's Life After School

Steve was about 16 years old when I attended a conference where Dr. Marc Gold talked about how he taught a man who had a low IQ score to drive. I decided right then, one day Steve would drive a car. Steve took driver's education in high school and passed with a C grade. While my husband was at work at night, Steve and I would go out and he would drive around in large parking lots. We drove around a grocery store so many times on one of our midnight drives that the store manager called the police! When my husband found out Steve was learning to drive the car, he gave me 100 good reasons why he should not drive. The first 50 reasons were about insurance. I had two better reasons why he should drive. Steve wanted to drive, and I thought he was capable. After three attempts, Steve passed the test for his driver's permit and, months later on the second try, passed the test for his driver's license.

Steve had a hard time learning to use money. If he had a dollar and something cost 75 cents, he wasn't sure he had enough money. He quickly learned that if he drove the car he had to be responsible to pay for the gas he used. I taught him how to read the gas pump and told him he had to have enough money to pay for the gas. For the first time he was learning to manage money.

A fellow Toastmaster's club member with a new nephew with Down syndrome helped Steve obtain a job in food service at the Baptist Hospital. Thanks to the teaching skills of a caring and patient supervisor, Steve has worked there for 10 years. He was a permanent part-time worker for several years. Then, one day his supervisor called and said she wanted Steve to apply for a full-time position that had become available. He would have to compete with other hospital workers who applied for the job. I coached Steve all weekend. However, when he went to the interview he did not tell the director the things I had him practice. Instead, he told the director he should get the job because he was better qualified than anyone else and that he already knew how to do the job because he had worked that position when the person had a day off. Steve was hired full time.

While I had learned all about assisted living arrangements at ARC conventions, I couldn't really imagine Steve living anywhere without me. However, because some members of Steve's church group lived in a group home, I asked him if he would like to live there. He said no and asked me why I thought he would like to live in a group home. Still, I continued to believe that Steve should have the opportunity to choose where he wanted to live and about a year later asked him if he would like to have his own apartment. He immediately said yes. Steve told his grandmother and several of his friends he was going to move into his own apartment. We often talked about the apartment, but I never really made a serious search for one. I did not know one other person with Down syndrome who lived independently.

Finally, I was pushed into action when a friend made a donation to the ARC to buy a condominium for Steve to rent! Steve and I decided on something with two bedrooms, so Steve could share the condo with another person. We also decided that it needed to be located on the bus line. Finally, we found a condominium to buy. I kept asking myself if I was doing the right thing for Steve. My husband thought this was the most ridiculous thing I had ever done. He could not understand why it would be good for Steve to leave a place where he had no expenses. Up until then he had put most of his paycheck straight into his bank account. Now he would be in a situation where it would take most of his money every month just to buy groceries and pay rent and utility bills. However, when the day arrived his dad helped Steve move his belongings and get settled.

Steve lived alone in his condo for 1 year while we searched for someone to live with him. We asked friends, and I called the schools for recommendations. I talked to lots of parents, but no one was willing to let their son leave home. I finally met a mother whose son was not happy living in a group home. He and Steve liked each other, and we were all excited when the two moved in together. They have shared the condo now for 6 years.

There have been problems to solve because Steve lives independently. He deposits his paycheck into his account at the bank where I also have an account. One day the bank teller called and said Steve had not made a deposit lately, and his account was overdrawn. A man who worked with Steve was going with him to cash his check. He told Steve his sick mother needed medicine and he was "borrowing" most of Steve's paycheck. Steve now has his paycheck directly deposited into his bank account by his employer.

Another time Steve told me he was going to sell calculators, books, and steak knives! Sure enough, a salesman had convinced Steve he could buy these things, resell them, and make a nice profit. He gave the salesman a check for $500. We called the bank, and of course, the check had been cashed and the company was not listed with the telephone company. But we put our heads together and worked out of that jam. A friend of Steve's dad had a bookstore, so he bought all the books. Steve's sister-in-law sold most of the calculators to people where she works. Several relatives bought calculators, and everybody we know got steak knives for Christmas!

Because Steve realizes he has a hard time saying no to people, he decided to leave his checkbook at our house in a drawer that contains some of his things. He has a key to our house so he can come get a check to pay his rent and utility bills, buy groceries, or get some cash.

Steve has a very active social life. He met and fell in love with Rebecca, who also has Down syndrome, at a People First convention. Because Rebecca lived 80 miles from Steve, he learned to drive by himself on the interstate and cope with car troubles. Steve and Rebecca dated for several years and they are still friends. I hope one day Steve will meet someone he wants to marry.

Steve loves sports and attends the local high school football games. I called him one Saturday, and he and his roommate were going to a University of Alabama football game that was to be played in Birmingham. I panicked and gave him many reasons why he should not go—the traffic is terrible; the stadium location is terrible; they didn't have a ticket; and I would worry about them. They went and had a wonderful time at the football game. They bought tickets from a man on a motorcycle for $10 each and sat on the 50-yard line, and Alabama won the football game.

Church is also a big part of Steve's life. He prefers to attend a Sunday School class for people with developmental disabilities where he has made many friends. He occasionally attends socials with the singles class. He helps with lighting and sound for Sunday and Wednesday night church services. He sings in a church choir for people with disabilities that sings at churches all over Alabama.

Steve played baseball on one of the seven teams from the church but decided he would rather play in the baseball and basketball league for people with developmental disabilities. He enjoys going to the church gym to lift weights and work out. He and several friends go once a month to dinner and a social for people with disabilities at another church. He goes to dances sponsored by Parent Advocates for Down Syndrome (PADS), and he goes with me to the PADS meetings. Parents tell me Steve is their role model.

Steve has been with me to the ARC's Governmental Affairs meetings in Washington, D.C., where we discuss concerns of people with developmental disabilities with our members of Congress. He tells them if he voted for them in the last election. He is a member of People First. He has never missed a meeting, and he especially enjoys the state conventions, and particularly going to Nashville and Canada for International People First conferences. Steve is also on the state Department of Education's team on transition from school to work.

It has been extremely difficult for my husband and me to give up control over our son. But, in the end, we know it is what we must do. Steve continues to need some assistance, but we believe that he has the right and the capabilities to make decisions that affect his life. He would never have developed these capabilities if he had not been allowed to experience both failures and successes in life. In turn, my husband and I cannot believe how independent Steve has become! We never in our wildest dreams thought our baby with Down syndrome would accomplish so much and in such a positive way affect the lives of so many people who have come in contact with him.

HELPING PARENTS PROMOTE SELF-DETERMINATION

We firmly believe that parents play a critical role in fostering self-determination in their sons and daughters. As we reflect on our approaches to raising our children, we can identify some of the actions that led to each of them now being very self-determined adults. We insisted on Robin and Steve being given opportunities, beginning when they were very young, to have the same experiences growing up as their siblings did. We included them in all the family activities and encouraged their involvement in a variety of community activities. We tried not to overprotect them and allowed them to take risks to apply skills related to self-determination. We also held expectations and perceptions of them as capable of being self-determined and tried not to limit their opportunities and experiences by our worries and fears.

In advising other families, we think that the 10 steps for promoting independence and self-determination proposed by The Arc (Davis & Wehmeyer, 1991) provide a useful beginning:

1. Walk the tightrope between protection and independence. Allow your son or daughter to explore his or her world. This may mean biting your lip and watching from the kitchen window when your child first meets the neighbor's kids, instead of running out to supervise. While there are obvious limits to this, all parents have to "let go" and it is never easy.

2. Children need to learn that what they say or do is important and can influence others. This involves allowing risk taking and exploration. Encourage your child to ask questions and express opinions. Involvement in family discussions and decision-making sessions is one way of providing this opportunity to learn.

3. Self-worth and self-confidence are critical factors in the development of self-determination. Model your own sense of positive self-esteem to your child. Tell your child he is important by spending time with him. Again, involve him in family activities and in family decisions.

4. Don't run away from questions from your child about differences related to her disability. That does not mean, however, focusing on the negative side of the condition. Stress that everyone is individual, encourage your child's unique abilities, and help him or her accept unavoidable limitations.

5. Recognize the process of reaching goals, don't just emphasize outcomes. Children need to learn to work toward goals. For older children, encourage skills like organization and goal-setting by modeling these behaviors. Make lists or hang a marker board which shows the daily schedule for each family member. Talk about the steps you are going to use to complete a task and involve them in tasks leading to family goals, such as planning for a vacation.

6. Schedule opportunities for interactions with children of different ages and backgrounds. This could be in child care centers, schools, churches and when playing in the neighborhood. Start early in finding chances for your son or daughter to participate in activities that help all children realize that everyone is unique.

7. Set realistic but ambitious expectations. Take an active role in your child's educational experience. Be familiar with his or her reading ability and identify books that provide enough challenge to move to the next reading level. Be sure you don't just force activities which lead to frustration, but don't assume that all of the progress should occur at school.

8. Allow your child to take responsibility for his own actions—successes and failures. Provide valid reasons for doing things, instead of simply saying "because I said so!" Providing explanations provides the opportunity for the child to make an activity his own.

9. Don't leave choice-making opportunities to chance. Take every opportunity to allow your child to make choices; what she wears, what is served for dinner, or where the family goes for vacation. And, although this is not always practical or possible, make sure that these choice opportunities are meaningful. Also, when offering choices, make sure the child's decision is honored.

10. Provide honest, positive feedback. Focus on the behavior or task that needs to be changed. Don't make your child feel like a failure. We all learn from our mistakes, but only if they are structured so that they do not lead us to believe that the problem is within us.

Finally, as we look back on what influenced us in promoting our own children's self-determination, we both believe we benefited tremendously by being active in parent organizations. We attended meetings where we learned from other parents. We also learned about the latest research and philosophies influencing services and supports for people with mental retardation by attending state and national conventions of The Arc. We learned about the accomplishments of many adults with mental retardation who were provided opportunities to participate fully in the community—living, working, and socializing. We heard their stories of satisfaction with their lives in having real jobs, of having their own apartments, in participating in self-advocacy groups, and in having social and leisure activities of their choice. After learning about what others with disabilities chose for themselves, we wanted our children to have similar opportunities to choose for themselves how they would like to live their adult lives. We believe we provided Robin and Steve a firm foundation on which they can continue to build their futures.

REFERENCES

Davis, S., & Wehmeyer, M.L. (1991). *Ten steps to self-determination*. Arlington, TX: The Arc National Headquarters.

Education for All Handicapped Children Act of 1975, PL 94-142. (August 23, 1977). Title 20, U.S.C. 1400 et seq: *U.S. Statutes at Large, 89,* 773–796.

Ward, M.J. (1988). The many facets of self-determination. *NICHCY Transition Summary: National Information Center for Children and Youth with Disabilities, 5,* 2–3.

Chapter 5

PROMOTING THE DEVELOPMENT AND ACQUISITION OF SELF-DETERMINED BEHAVIOR

Beth Doll, Deanna J. Sands, Michael L. Wehmeyer, and Susan Palmer

NEWBORNS DO NOT enter the world self-determined but instead become self-determined through learning across multiple environments and through developing within multiple domains. It is unfortunate, then, that most efforts to understand and support self-determination have dealt solely with adolescents and adults, overlooking and sometimes excluding a developmental perspective on the emergence of this outcome (Sands & Doll, 1994). There is little empirical evidence to document age- or experience-related differences in the capacity of students with disabilities to behave in self-determined ways. Consequently, we have a limited understanding of the ways in which early precursors to self-determined behavior might be enhanced or impeded by the daily practices of schools, families, or communities. Efforts to foster self-determined behavior as it emerges during a student's elementary and middle school years have been hampered by this narrow perspective. Although research is not available to describe the development of self-determination, per se, the present chapter describes a developmental course for self-determination that has been extrapolated from existing literature describing the development of related competencies. Subsequently, this understanding is applied to a description of students' abilities and limitations for engaging in self-determined behaviors at each educational level, and ways to maximize instructional efforts to promote self-determination for children and youth with disabilities are offered.

Wehmeyer (Chapter 2) defined self-determination according to characteristics of actions or events: Self-determination referred to "acting as the primary causal agent in one's life and making choices and decisions regarding one's quality of life free from undue external influence or interference." Self-determined actions reflected four essential characteristics: 1) the individual acted autonomously, 2) the behaviors were self-regulated, 3) the person initiated and responded to event(s) in a "psychologically empowered" manner, and 4) the person acted in a self-realizing manner (Wehmeyer, 1996; Wehmeyer, Kelchner, & Richards, in press). Satisfying these characteristics requires that a person be competent in a number of related skills that Wehmeyer calls "component elements." These include such skills as choice making; decision making; problem solving; goal setting and task performance; self-observation, evaluation, and reinforcement; internal locus of control; positive attributions of efficacy and outcome expectancy; self-awareness; and self-knowledge. These component elements are prerequisite to the appearance of self-determined behaviors and appear as foci of most interventions that promote this outcome (Wehmeyer et al., 1995, in press). Our construction of a developmental course of self-determination is extrapolated from research on the development of these elements.

The term *development* engenders strong debate as researchers argue the existence of progressive development and whether developmental paths are uniform across all children in all contexts (Hodapp, Burack, & Zigler, 1990). In addition, theories from differing orientations debate the presence of quantitative and qualitative differences in children's cognitive development (Thomas & Patton, 1994). Developmental psychologists reserve the term *development* for describing qualitative changes, while referring to quantitative changes as *growth* or *maturation*.

Werner and Kaplan (1984) described such a qualitative change as being the movement from a globally undefined organism to one consisting of clearly defined and articulated components. This is nicely illustrated by an example from the physical development of human beings, where development proceeds through the stages of fertilized egg to embryo and, finally, to neonate. Differences between the stages are qualitative, not merely quantitative. At one stage the fetus does not have a hand, at the next stage there is a visible hand with clearly articulated fingers. Then, the fingers evolve into a functional hand. From that point on, little additional development occurs relative to the hand. Instead, as the child ages, the hand will become larger and stronger—changes that are called *maturation* and *growth* because they are essentially *quantitative* and not *qualitative* in nature. The qualitative changes that development comprises can be gradual and continuous, as in fine and gross motor development, or relatively sudden, as is the case when children acquire a conceptual understanding of conservation of mass. Both kinds of changes will be evident in the development of component elements of self-determination.

When children grow or demonstrate skills at a rate that is different from expected developmental paths, alternative explanations are posed to explain the source of those differences. For example, researchers attempting to understand the basis of learning disabilities have attributed these students' differing development to 1) central nervous system dysfunction or neurological problems; 2) genetic causes; 3) developmental lags or different rates by which mental processes mature; 4) environmental causes such as poor educational experiences; and 5) interactional influences between personal and sociological factors such as motivation, health, socioeconomic status, and ethnicity (Turnbull, Turnbull, Shank, & Leal, 1995). Too often, when children and youth with disabilities demonstrate qualitative or quantitative differences in their learning, they are viewed as deviant, and responses to their problems tend to be punitive, remedial, and segregating interventions (Turnbull et al., 1995). In fact, a developmental approach to teaching some skills has resulted in cases where adolescents, particularly individuals with more severe cognitive disabilities, spend their day involved in childlike activities associated to their mental rather than their chronological age. We are not advocating for the use of chronological age–inappropriate activities to define the curriculum and content of instruction for students with disabilities.

We adopt the position that there are universal principles of development that can inform our work with people with disabilities (Giaia, 1993; Hodapp et al., 1990; Weisz & Zigler, 1979). An understanding of these principles can guide practice by 1) identifying the critical elements that emerge and thus the targets of instruction; 2) identifying the likely sequence of skills and thus the scope and sequence of instructional activities; and 3) describing the early indications of the successful emergence or likely nonemergence of self-determination, thus providing early warning signs that a student requires more comprehensive support around self-determination goals. Furthermore, we believe that the absence or delay in the emergence of a developmental milestone need not be synonymous with developmental lag as, in many cases, there are other ways for a person to manifest the essential capacity represented by a milestone. For example, tying one's own shoes is frequently used as a developmental milestone, not because shoe tying is essential, but because it represents the emergence of important cognitive and fine motor skills and releases the child from dependence on adults for basic grooming. It may be possible to provide accommodations that permit a child who cannot tie shoes to achieve independence in grooming skills nevertheless. In this way, the child's essential cognitive and fine motor capacities might be manifested despite a shoe-tying delay.

When students with disabilities vary in their attainment of identified developmental milestones, adaptive means can be used to achieve those milestones. For example, some children with mental retardation develop language later than what is described in typical child development, due in part to problems associated with low muscle tone in speech mechanisms, difficulties with hearing impairments, or delayed cognitive development (Thomas & Patton, 1994). However, with the use of alternative or augmentative means of communicating, like rudimentary sign language, many children are able to express their wants and needs much earlier than they can through oral language. Intentional communication is achieved through another pathway, but it is achieved nonetheless.

Finally, we view development as occurring within a sociocultural context that can serve to impede or facilitate both the maturation and expression of developmental capacities. Aspects of the sociocultural contexts for self-determination are covered in other areas of this volume (e.g., see Chapters 4 and 6–8). We propose that understanding the development of component elements of self-determination, in conjunction with an understanding of individual needs, can be a springboard for articulating age-appropriate activities that are useful for promoting self-determination.

DEVELOPMENT OF COMPONENT ELEMENTS OF SELF-DETERMINATION

The thesis of this chapter is that 1) self-determination emerges as children, youth, and adults develop and acquire the component elements of self-determination; and 2) limited opportunities to practice skills necessary for self-determination at early ages can unduly constrain adolescent expression of self-determined behaviors. Although it is difficult to conceptualize qualitative transformations that characterize development within self-determination, where changes are not easily measured or viewed, prior research has described common developmental courses for children's acquisition of each of the component elements. An understanding of each element's development, and of the degree to which each complements and supports the development of the other component elements, is essential if schools are to promote self-determination for students with disabilities.

Because explanations of the development of certain component elements overlap to a large extent with those of other components, we have collapsed Wehmeyer's nine component elements into five distinct topics: 1) self-awareness and self-knowledge, 2) self-evaluation and attributions of efficacy, 3) choice making and decision making, 4) metarepresentation, and 5) goal setting and task performance. In some cases, the qualitative changes of a given element typically occur at very early ages. For example, the developmental components of choice making (indicating preferences, communicating preferences, understanding options) are established through typical child development as early as 18 months of age; most subsequent changes reflect maturational growth (i.e., quantitative changes) due to children's accumulated opportunities to learn from successes and failures in choice-making experiences. Consequently, several of these developmental explanations will focus on very early ages.

As a tool to make these developmental progressions more explicit and easier to interpret, Table 1 describes the most important developmental steps in an age-by-competency matrix. By reading across the rows in Table 1, it is possible to follow the developmental progression of each component element from the preschool years through adolescence. By reading down the columns, one can find the primary developmental markers for all component elements within a discrete age group. To emphasize the relevance of this knowledge base for the promotion

Table 1. Developmental progression of nine antecedent abilities of self-determined behavior

Early childhood (2–5 years)	Early elementary (6–8 years)	Late elementary (9–11 years)	Secondary (12–18 years)
Self-Awareness and Self-Knowledge			
Have a sense of self as being separate from caregivers	Accurately label the feelings of happy, sad, afraid, and angry	Actively seek information about task performance in order to fine-tune approach	
Can understand their own feeling states and recognize them in a pictured person	Understand how different dispositional states might be expressed in different situations		
Understand that people have characteristic features (dispositional states)	Selected approaches to tasks reflect accurate understanding of personal competencies		
Tend not to self-reflect on their own thinking			
Self-Evaluation and Attributions of Efficacy			
Self-descriptions of abilities are strikingly inaccurate and capricious	Self-estimates of ability become stable and global across tasks	More adept at comparing performance to a peer group and less likely to inflate achievement	Emotional turbulence accompanies negative self-evaluations
Typically overestimate the quality of their performance relative to others	Begin to understand that task abilities can be compared among children	Use self-evaluations as the basis for appropriate decisions to request help	Vulnerable to negative overgeneralizations of global negative self-attribution
Can accurately judge the quality of their work compared to models or templates	Understand ability as a place on a peer continuum of task performance	Distinguish between luck and effort, and understand that games of chance cannot be improved with effort or ability	
Attribute success or failure to effort rather than ability or luck	Believe that practice can improve their performance on games of chance		
Choice Making and Decision Making			
Routinely express preferences, verbally or nonverbally	Can decide what kind of instructional support is required	Understand what is required to state a preference regarding medical treatment	Can systematically evaluate solutions, their consequences, and credibility of information underlying medical decisions
Language comes to replace nonverbal gestures as the primary mode of expressing preferences		Capable of identifying the risks and benefits of psychotherapy	Capable of providing informed consent for treatment
Choices tend to reflect instantaneous whims			

(continued)

Table 1. (continued)

Early childhood (2–5 years)	Early elementary (6–8 years)	Late elementary (9–11 years)	Secondary (12–18 years)
Metarepresentation			
Can identify others' emotional states of happiness and sadness	Realize that other people see, hear, and think differently than themselves	Anticipate how others are likely to respond	Can accurately predict a person's differing thoughts and affect, and decipher purposes for another's behavior
Assume naively that someone else will see what they see, think what they think, and respond just as they would	Can take above into account in planning ways to interact with others	Monitor problem solving and systematically modify their approach in the face of evidence that it isn't working	
Have a simple understanding of intention, memories, feelings, and images	Can use language-based rules to mediate problem solving		
Can think of solutions to social problems similar to those of older children, although fewer in number and less detailed	Able to describe 50% more solutions to social problems than younger children		
Goal Setting and Attainment			
Play reflects children's preconceptions about their future lives	Set goals that set them up to learn information	Can set goals to increase skills and abilities—they take risks, set moderately difficult goals, and cope with failure	
	With teacher praise for incremental increases, can gradually increase a personal work goal	Differentiate between goals for ability, effort, and performance	

of self-determined behavior, a more comprehensive description of the developmental path for each component element is provided on the following pages. Then, the final section of the chapter presents the implications these paths hold for self-determined behavior within each age group and for policies and practices that foster self-determined behavior and its early precursors.

Self-Awareness and Self-Knowledge

If they are to act in self-determined ways, people must possess a basic understanding of their individual strengths, weaknesses, abilities, and limitations (i.e., self-awareness) and know how to use these unique attributes to enhance their quality of life (i.e., self-knowledge) (Wehmeyer, 1996). The development of both self-awareness and self-knowledge require the acquisition of a *categorical sense of self*, that is, an understanding of one's uniqueness and separateness from others (Damon, 1983). In subsequent years, self-awareness and self-knowledge require an accurate sense of the cognitive self, that is, an understanding of one's own thinking and reasoning acts and the capacity to deliberately manipulate these to suit one's purposes.

Until recently, most researchers agreed that infants fail to recognize themselves as distinct beings from their caregivers until they are between 8 and 12 months of age (Lewis & Brooks-Gunn, 1979). Newer studies of infant behavior, using technologically advanced measures and sophisticated experimental designs, suggest instead that infants experience a sense of an emergent self beginning at birth, with no confusion between self and other at any point during infancy (DeCasper & Spence, 1986; Stern, 1985). In either case, at as early as 3 months of age infants begin to display an interest in and act intentionally toward caregivers and other social objects. This intentional behavior is the catalyst for the growing recognition that they are distinct beings from their caregivers (at 8–12 months) and that they can control or cause specific outcomes through their own actions. Most children have a fully developed categorical sense of self by the age of 15–18 months (Lewis & Brooks-Gunn, 1979), providing a foundation upon which future self-awareness and self-knowledge can be built.

The emergence of self-awareness and self-knowledge that are both positive and realistic requires an understanding of emotions, feelings, and other within-person states that are common to all individuals. Children have a rudimentary understanding of their own internal states by no later than 3 years of age and can begin to understand that others experience these as well at roughly the same age (Bretherton & Beeghly, 1982; Eder, 1989). For example, 3-year-olds are able to decide when a pictured person is happy, while 4-year-olds can determine both happy and sad (Moore, 1979; Shantz, 1975). By 6 or 7, children can accurately label four emotional states: happy, sad, afraid, and angry (Shantz, 1975). With age and experience, children's understanding of affective states becomes more differentiated and they become more accurate in predicting the affect of other persons (Selman, 1980).

Dispositional states are frequent, enduring tendencies that are used to characterize people. Unlike internal states, dispositional states are not shared by all persons but may represent important differences among them. For example, where some children tend to be thoughtful and reflective when facing a problem, others tend to be agitated and impulsive. Understanding these dispositional states occurs somewhat later in children, emerging in its most simple form around 3½ years of age (Eder, 1990). At that age, most children understand that people familiar to them have characteristic ways of being that are stable over time. By ages 7 or 8, children have developed a more complex understanding of these dispositional characteristics, with a sense of how such characteristics might or might not be expressed across different situations or events (Rholes & Ruble, 1984). It is not until ages 9–10, however, that children begin to use these dispositional characteristics to predict the behavior of others (Rholes & Ruble, 1984).

Metacognitive self-knowledge refers to children's ability to reflect upon their own mental processes and is evidenced when children take increasing control over the cognitive processes that they use. There is ample evidence that the accuracy of children's metacognitive knowledge increases with age, as does children's propensity to use that understanding to actively direct and control their cognitive processes (Belmont, 1989; Chi, 1981; Fabricius & Hagen, 1984; Garner, 1987). Preschoolers and kindergartners do not attend to their own thinking, do not always notice when they are being either ineffective or effective, and so tend not to revise or fine-tune their cognitive approaches to tasks even when these are unsuccessful (Forrest & Walker, 1980; Ghatala, 1986; Paris & Lindauer, 1982). Early elementary students do a better job of matching their strategies to the problem than kindergartners and are more likely to plan ways to approach a task that takes advantage of their own competencies (Forrest & Waller, 1980; Paris & Lindauer, 1982). By sixth grade, students actively seek information so that they can judge their task success and adjust their task approach as necessary (Ruble & Flett, 1988). The impact of metacognitive self-knowledge on task performance can be seen in a set of studies showing that the performance of young children can equal that of adolescents if they are directed to pay attention to metacognitive information. The young children in these studies were provided with training in the use of appropriate strategies, feedback regarding the usefulness of the strategy in enhancing task performance, and frequent and very directive reminders to use the strategies in subsequent problem-solving tasks (Cornoldi, 1987; Cornoldi, Gobbo, & Mazzoni, 1991; Ghatala, 1986).

Clearly, self-awareness and self-knowledge develop in unison with self-efficacy and one's personal locus of control; an individual builds realistic and positive self-awareness and self-knowledge on the foundational beliefs that he or she is a competent person who possesses the capacity to act successfully and has control over areas that are important to him or her. These result in expectations of success and competence. The development of self-evaluation and attributions of efficacy are discussed subsequently as they relate to self-awareness and self-knowledge.

Self-Evaluation and Attributions of Efficacy

An inherent tension exists between the self-determined person's need to perceive the self as competent and powerful and the need for that self-perception to be accurate and undistorted. It is essential to self-determined behavior that the person act in a psychologically empowered manner. That is, self-determined actions convey the individual's belief that he or she has control over circumstances that are important to him or her (internal locus of control); 2) he or she possesses the requisite skills to achieve desired outcomes (self-efficacy); and 3) if he or she chooses to apply those skills, the identified outcomes will result (outcome expectations) (see Wehmeyer, Chapter 2).

Acting in a psychologically empowered manner also requires that self-determined people recognize their own actions and their outcomes clearly and without bias (self-evaluation). Through self-evaluation, individuals may confront personal weaknesses or incompetencies that conflict with their ideals and challenge their vision of the self as essentially capable. Resolving this tension so that one's self-evaluation is both accurate and empowering is one of the key challenges to the development of self-determination. Moreover, candid self-evaluation of personal strengths, weaknesses, and needs is an affectively loaded task that becomes singularly difficult for individuals with limited self-efficacy or pronounced insecurity about their acceptance by significant others. In this respect, because children tend to become less self-confident and less secure in their relationships with age, self-evaluation becomes affectively more difficult for older children. Consequently, unlike other developmental tasks, resolving the conflict between accurate self-evaluation and empowering self-efficacy is a task one faces relatively late in the developmental sequence underlying self-determination.

Rudimentary self-evaluation has been observed in preschool children as they predict whether they might succeed at a task (Butler, 1990). These early self-descriptions are strikingly inaccurate and capricious and are often highly inconsistent from one task or situation to another (Frey & Ruble, 1987). However, they represent an emerging understanding by the preschooler that specified kinds or levels of performance are valued by others and merit the effort required to achieve them (Higgins, 1989). It is not until the early elementary grades that children's estimates of their own ability become stable and global across tasks (Dweck & Elliott, 1983; Rholes & Ruble, 1984). About the same time, by the age of 6 or 7 years, children begin to understand that such task abilities might be the basis for comparisons among children or skill domains (Higgins, 1989; Nicholls & Miller, 1984; Renick & Harter, 1989; Ruble, 1983), even though they are unlikely to use normative comparisons spontaneously until the age of 10 years (Nicholls, 1978; Ruble, Boggiano, Feldman, & Loebl, 1980). By the middle elementary school grades, students' spontaneous self-evaluations are stable across time and settings, are relatively accurate, and could become appropriate foundations for student self-advocacy.

Judging one's performance against a normative standard is a more complex cognitive task than comparison with mastery standards. In one study, preschoolers struggled to describe their own competence when asked to use normative standards that ranked their performance against those of their peers (Butler, 1990), but were as accurate as fifth graders when judging their task performance against fixed mastery standards exemplified in models or templates (Stowitschek, Ghezzi, & Safely, 1987). Similarly, preschool children were adept at judging the degree to which their copy of a drawing matched the original, but overestimated their performance when asked whether theirs was the best copy in their group (Butler, 1990). It is not until the early elementary grades that students begin to understand their own ability as a point on a peer continuum of task performance. By third grade, students became more adept at comparing their performance to that of a normative group and were less likely to inflate their achievements (Butler, 1990). Only after fifth grade were students likely to use these self-evaluations as the basis for appropriate decisions to request instructional assistance or utilize cognitive strategies (Ghatala, 1986; Nelson-Le Gall, Kratzer, Jones, & DeCooke, 1990).

With increasing age and experience, children's self-evaluations become less optimistic and more congruent with their actual task performance. The renowned over-optimism that characterizes preschool self-evaluations has led some theorists to suggest these self-evaluations represent wishful thinking rather than actual expectations of success (Butler, 1990; Eccles, Midgeley, & Adler, 1984; Frey & Ruble, 1987). They attribute age-linked declines in children's estimates of their own competence to an increasing ability to overcome an emotional press to "congratulate oneself." Alternatively, Butler (1990) points to parallels between these erroneous self-assessments of preschoolers and the similar overestimates of adults who are provided with insufficient information about their performance or information that is difficult to organize and understand. She suggests instead that the cognitive complexity of self-evaluation biases children toward overestimating their likelihood of success.

Concurrent with their increasingly accurate self-evaluations, children's development of perceptions of control and efficacy contribute to their acquired understanding of causality, including an understanding of contingency relationships (x caused y) and the different roles that effort, ability, and luck play in determining outcomes (Skinner, 1990). In children's earliest understandings of causality (ages 5–6), they attribute excessive importance to effort for producing success and preventing failure, ignoring the contributions of ability and chance (Skinner, 1990). Even at 8 and 9 years of age, children fail to differentiate between successes they could control and those that they could not, believing that practice could improve their chances of winning a game of chance (Weisz, 1980). Not surprisingly, children's internal perceptions of control at this age appear unrelated to their achievement (Findley & Cooper, 1983). By the age of 10 years, children begin to distinguish between effort and luck, understanding that a game of chance is noncontingent and uncontrollable, whereas effort can improve one's performance only on tasks one can control (Weisz, 1980). It is then that the relationship between children's internal perception of control and their academic achievement begins to emerge (Findley & Cooper, 1983). An understanding of the contribution of ability to task success is late to develop; until the age of 11, children believe that if they try hard they will succeed and view other children as smart when they devote extensive effort or practice to a task as well as when they have exceptional ability (Frey & Ruble, 1987; Weisz, 1980).

The affective implications of self-evaluation and self-efficacy have been carefully elucidated by Higgins' (1989) model of self-discrepancy. Higgins postulated that children experience disturbing sadness when their actual self (representing candid self-estimates of their task performance) is discrepant in important ways from their ideal self (representing standards of task performance that they would like to achieve). Alternatively, when their actual self is discrepant with the standards of performance that significant others set for them, students become edgy, worried, or fearful. Because the salience of self–other discrepancies do not fully emerge until the late elementary grades (Harter, 1983; Higgins, 1989), the emotional turbulence that can accompany self-evaluation gains in significance between the middle childhood years and adolescence (Higgins, 1989; Renick & Harter, 1989). Moreover, adolescents' expanding capacity for higher order reasoning leaves them especially vulnerable to negative overgeneralizations or global negative self-attributions, abstractions that are particularly difficult to defend against.

Choice Making and Decision Making

Self-determination requires that individuals be adept at choice making, defined elsewhere as an uncoerced selection from two or more alternatives (Brigham, 1979). Developmental aspects of choice making focus on children's capacities to identify and communicate preferences. Once a child develops these capacities, the maturation of choice-making ability relies on children's opportunities to make selections and experience the consequences of these choices. Even later, children acquire the capacity for systematic decision making, which includes the following two components in addition to recognizing and making selections: 1) having rational reasons for the selection and 2) understanding the risks and benefits of the alternatives (Herek, Janis, & Huth, 1987; Janis & Mann, 1977; Mann, Beswick, Allouache, & Ivey, 1989; Meisel, Roth, & Lidz, 1977).

The capacity for indicating preferences is present at birth; newborns discriminate between various objects and people in their environment and show evidence of preferences for some of these over others (Fantz, 1961; Haith, 1980; Stern, 1985). For example, neonates prefer round objects with facial features rather than similar sized square or triangular objects or even circular objects without facial features (Bower, 1977). Other preferences emerge based on infants' interactions with individuals, objects, and the environment.

Making a selection requires that the child designate a specific option from between two or more choices, an act that requires the emergence of intentional communication. The cry of an infant, the emergence of a social smile, and the use of eye gaze represent forms of communication available to infants by 4–5 months of age, whereas motor skills like reaching, pointing, and moving toward an object are usually in place by 10 months of age. Very young children will select by pointing, reaching, or smiling but initially do so without a fully developed understanding that they can elicit a desired response. Once children learn that these communicative efforts can elicit the outcome they desire, they begin to use communication purposefully and intentionally. Thus, the cry of a 1-year-old when she is hungry becomes not only a notice of an internal state (hunger) but also an attempt to get someone else to meet her need. Independent of how a child communicates, most children develop the necessary skills for indicating preferences and making a selection from options by 12 months of age. When the child's first words emerge, as early as 12 months of age, they are combined with gestures to make the communication of selections and preferences more effective. As children develop more advanced verbal skills at age 3, language typically replaces visual and motor activities as the primary source of information about preferences.

The organization of preferences and choice making into systematic decision making and problem solving takes more time. In fact, research on competent decision making in children and adolescents is scant, in part because it has been assumed that formal operational thinking would be necessary for an individual to appreciate the nature and consequences of alternatives and thus reach reasonable decisions. To the contrary, as early as third grade, students can decide what kind of instructional support they require after assessing their own task performance (Nelson-Le Gall et al., 1990). Students at the elementary and middle school levels are capable of making autonomous decisions regarding scholastic interventions (Bandura, 1982; Deci, Schwartz, Sheinman, & Ryan, 1981; Garner, 1987), and, in another study, 10-year-olds were as capable as 20-year-olds in identifying the risks and benefits of psychotherapy (Kaser-Boyd, Adelman, & Taylor, 1985). The capacity of 14-year-olds to provide competent, informed consent for and refusal of medical and psychological treatment was comparable to that of 18- and 21-year-olds in most respects. Even though 9-year-olds appeared less competent, they understood what was required to state a preference regarding treatment, expressed clear, sensible treatment preferences similar to adults, and appropriately considered most salient factors in decision making (Weithorn & Campbell, 1982).

While older adolescents generally are superior to younger adolescents in 1) their strategies to generate options, 2) their anticipation of the consequences of decisions, and 3) their evaluation of the credibility of information, these skills are emerging in the younger adolescents (Ormond, Luszcz, Mann, & Beswick, 1991). As decision-making skills continue to develop during adolescence, individual differences appear to be determined by students' social–emotional adjustment as much as their age and maturity (Ormond et al., 1991).

Metarepresentation

Because self-determination usually occurs within a social context, and with reference to others, it follows that a self-determined person must be able to think about others and their actions if they are to create effective social interactions within which to advocate for social, vocational, or instructional choices. Flavell (1985) has termed this understanding of others' actions, intentions, and perspectives *metarepresentation* because it describes thinking about another's representation of the external world. It is metarepresentation that permits a self-determined person to acquire a diverse array of effective social behaviors with which to meet any conceivable situation that he or she might encounter as well as the social cognitive skills that permit the individual to accurately assess social events and select the correct behavior to use (Kendall, 1984; Moore, 1979; Wojnilower & Gross, 1988).

Much of the investigation of young children's metarepresentation has been conducted within the sphere of children's pretend play; and, like other areas of development, young children are probably much more sophisticated in this area than previously predicted. For example, the early work of Selman (1980) suggested that prior to ages 5–7 years, children used the "same situation = same viewpoint" rule, naively assuming that someone else will respond just as they would. Only after ages 5–9 does Selman's theory suggest that children understand and take into account the differing perspectives of other persons. However, Joseph Perner (Perner, Frith, Leslie, & Leekham, 1989; Perner & Wimmer, 1985, 1988) has noted evidence of a simple understanding of intentions, memories, feelings, and images in the play of children as early as 3 or 4 years of age.

By age 7, children realize that other people see, hear, and think differently from themselves (Moore, 1979) and can take this into account to plan ways to interact with another person (Selman, 1980). Judging the intentions underlying another's behavior develops later. Thus, while 4-year-olds make judgments about whether another's actions were "on purpose," and 5-year-olds consider intentionality when weighing blame (Shantz, 1975), sophisticated abilities to decipher purposes for behaviors are not clearly established until late adolescence (Leadbeater, Hellner, Allen, & Aber, 1989; Selman, 1980). In each case, children's social understanding originates in self-understanding; they construct hypotheses about another person's intentions using personal knowledge of why they themselves might act in the same way (Stein & Goldman, 1979). Consequently, perspective taking develops first for tasks familiar to the child and for people most like the child (Cairns, 1986; Selman & Byrne, 1974).

Metarepresentation skills are closely linked to childrens' and adolescents' capacity for interpersonal social problem solving (Wehmeyer & Kelchner, 1994). As originally conceptualized by Spivack, Platt, and Shure (1976), social problem solving incorporates the component skills of seeing cause–effect relationships between discrete social events, recognizing the consequences of social actions, acknowledging multiple alternative solutions to social problems, and choosing solutions most likely to be successful. In particular, Wehmeyer and Kelchner (1994) identified this as an area of concern for promoting self-determination for individuals with mental retardation. Even preschoolers differ in the number of solutions they can pose for a social problem, and more effective problem solvers generate more solutions (Spivack et al., 1976). In one study, for example, 7-year-olds were able to describe half again as many solutions as 5-year-olds, and their increased ability to use language increased the number of rules they used for solving problems (Scarr, Weinberg, & Levine, 1986).

Social problem-solving situations typically involve complex interactions with other people, introducing multiple processing demands and numerous possible solutions. Thus, mature social problem solving emerges from a person's font of social knowledge, including knowledge of various social behaviors, their likely causes and consequences, and their effective utilization. Moore (1979) argued that, like knowledge of the physical world, social knowledge is acquired through children's active experimentation with different ways of approaching others. However, because society never reaches absolute consensus about which social behaviors are appropriate, social knowledge remains arbitrary and difficult to discern, and children struggle more in its acquisition (Moore, 1979; Piaget, 1959). Thus, social problem solving continues to develop as children move into adolescence and early adulthood, with the associated growth in abstract social knowledge acquired during those periods.

Goal Setting and Task Performance

By definition, self-determined behavior is purposeful; that is, it is intentional and planned to meet some preselected objective. Goals define the objective or what the person is trying to accomplish through action (Locke, Shaw, Saari, & Latham, 1981). Investigations of goal setting are necessarily intermingled with abilities to plan for and evaluate the consequences of actions, as people who are goal-directed plan to act in ways that they believe likely to further progress toward their attainment of goals.

This causal link between goals and the actions taken to achieve set goals is not easily detected by children younger than four. Even young children as old as 4 require more information about the situation before they can recognize the goal plan illustrated by a series of pictured events (Trabasso, Stein, Rodkin, Park, & Baughn, 1992). By the age of 5, most children can link goals and actions to achieve this understanding. However, their personal goals for a task are likely to be goals to acquire information rather than to increase their skills and abilities (Nicholls & Miller, 1984; Woolfolk, 1990). Moreover, they require ongoing teacher support, in the form of praise for incremental increases in performance and attention to measures of current performance, to set specific goals to work on each day (Price & O'Leary, 1974, as cited in Woolfolk, 1990). At about the age of 11 or 12, children begin to set different goals for effort, ability, and performance on a given task. Mastery-oriented students at this age set goals to increase skills and abilities in cognitive activities—they take risks, set moderately difficult goals, and cope with failure. Failure-avoiding students of the same age set performance goals that are exceedingly low or so high as to be unattainable, take fewer risks, make feeble efforts, or procrastinate (Woolfolk, 1990).

Once children begin to set and work toward personal goals, they are open to the elation that accompanies success and the disappointment that accompanies failure (Nicholls & Miller, 1984; Stipek, Recchia, & McClintic, 1992). Although toddlers as young as 21 months of age show an interest in being recognized for their achievements during free play, goal-failure disappointment is rarely evident in children under 2 years (Stipek et al., 1992). Stipek and colleagues (1992) suggested that either children this young did not have the attention span to keep a goal in their memory for any length of time or that their self-knowledge was not at the point that they were able to compare their performance with that of others. Older children begin to match their performance with that of others, feel disappointment when a stated goal is not attained, and really do not enjoy losing a contest or competition.

In many cases, the goals that children set and work toward involve comparisons with a standard that is set by others and that may not have practical merit (Nicholls & Miller, 1984). Infants and toddlers younger than 24 months of age differ considerably in this respect from older children. An infant is developing universal competencies that do not require social feedback, such as grasping and releasing objects or walking (Stipek et al., 1992). By 18–24 months, after gaining a categorical sense of self, children begin to appreciate the positive implications of praise and to strive to attain a mastery of task performance that is culturally defined. As they become more self-aware, they are influenced by standards of achievement and their own ability to attain these standards.

SELF-DETERMINATION ACROSS THE LIFE SPAN

The preceeding synthesis of developmental research provides a framework of the development of self-determination that practitioners and family members can use to understand both the outcome they want their child to achieve and the path that is usually followed to reach that outcome. From there, a course of intervention can be charted that can keep the child on that path, speed him or her along at times, and find shortcuts and other paths when necessary. Practices that families and professionals can use to foster self-determination are identified throughout this volume. In the final section of this chapter, the preceeding synthesis is applied to describe elements of this developmental path toward self-determination. Examination of the sequence of skills preceeding self-determination is especially important, as efforts to teach certain skills may prove to be detrimental if the child is not developmentally capable of succeeding in this area. For example, the decision-making process involves both choice-making and problem-solving abilities. Children who have not acquired these prerequisite skills will not be able to demonstrate decision-making skills. To clarify and extend recommendations embedded within this discussion, interventions that foster self-determination are listed by age level in Table 2. Each new age grouping of interventions in Table 2 is cumulative so that, as students get older, interventions for their own current age group, as well as previously listed interventions for younger children, would be appropriate to implement.

Table 2. School and family-based interventions to support the development of self-determination

Early Childhood (Ages 2–5)

Provide opportunities to make structured choices, such as, "Do you want to wear the blue shirt or the red shirt?" Extend choices across food, clothing, activity, and other choices.

Provide opportunities to generate choices that are both positive and negative, such as, "We have 10 more minutes. What could we do?" and "You spilled your milk. What could you do to clean it up?"

Provide formative and constructive feedback on the consequences of choices made in the recent past, such as, "When you pushed hard on the pencil it broke. What might you want to do the next time?" and "When you used an angry voice, I didn't do what you wanted. What could you do differently?"

Provide opportunities for planning activities that are pending, such as, "You need to choose a dress to wear to the wedding," or "Decide what kind of sandwich you want to take for lunch tomorrow."

Provide opportunities to self-evaluate task performance by comparing their work to a model. Point out what they've done that's like the model, such as, "Look, you used nice colors too, just like this one," and "Do you see that you both drew the man from the side?"

Ask directive questions so that the child compares his or her performance to a model, such as, "Are all of your toys in the basket, too?" or "I'll know you're ready for the story when you are sitting on your mat with your legs crossed, your hands on your knees, and your eyes on me."

Early Elementary (Ages 6–8)

Provide opportunities to choose from among several different strategies for a task, such as, "Will you remember your spelling words better if you write them out, say them to yourself, or test yourself?" or "What is the easiest way for you to figure out what this word means?"

Ask children to reconsider choices they've made in the recent past, in light of those choices subsequent consequences, such as, "This morning you decided to spend your lunch money on the comic. Now it's lunchtime and you're hungry. What decision do you wish you'd made?" or "I remember when you decided to leave your coat in your locker. What happened because you made that decision?"

Encourage children to "think aloud" with you, saying the steps that they are taking to complete a task or solve a problem, such as, "Tell me what you're thinking in your head while you try to figure out what the word means," or "You've lost your house key. What are you thinking to yourself while you decide what to do?"

Provide opportunities for students to talk about how they learn, such as, "Is it easier for you to tell me what you want by saying it or by writing it down?" or "Do you remember better if you study for a test all at once or a little bit on several different days?" Help students test out their answers.

Provide opportunities for students to systematically evaluate their work, such as, "Here's a very neat paper, and here's your paper. Is your paper as neat as this one? What are the differences between this paper and yours? How are they alike?"

Help students set simple goals for themselves and check to see whether they are reaching them, such as, "You said you want to read two books this week. How much of a book have you read so far? Let's color in your goal sheet so you can see how much you've done."

(continued)

Table 2. (*continued*)

Late Elementary (Ages 9–11)

Provide guidance in systematic analyses of decisions: writing the problem at the top of a sheet of paper, listing all possible choices, and sketching out the benefits and cost of each choice.

Use the same systematic structure to analyze past decisions now that their consequences are evident, such as, "You were angry at Jo for teasing you, and so you punched her in the cheek. Now you have to sit out at recess for a week. What are some other things that you could have done instead? What might have happened then?"

Provide opportunities for students to commit to personal or academic goals: writing the goal down and storing it in a safe place, revisiting the goal periodically to reflect on progress toward it, listing optional steps to take toward the goal, and trying out the steps and reflecting on their success.

Provide opportunities to systematically analyze adult perspectives, such as the point of view of the volleyball coach when a student is late to every game or the perspective of the librarian when a student returns a book that is dirty and torn. Help the student guess what the adult is thinking and feeling and what might be done as a result.

Provide opportunities for students to evaluate task performance in affectively "safe" ways: identifying weaknesses and strengths in performance, reflecting on ways to improve performance, trying out some new ways, and reevaluating performance to check for improvement. For example, "You got a lower grade than you wanted on your research paper. What steps did you take to make it a really strong paper? What steps did you leave out? What might you do now to make it even better?"

Secondary (Ages 12–18)

Provide opportunities for students to make decisions that have important impact on their day-to-day activities, such as academic goals, careers to explore, schedules to keep, diet and sleep habits, and others.

Make it easy for students to see the link between goals they set for themselves and the daily decisions that they make, such as, "You made a point of going to bed early last night, and now I see you earned a 95 on today's quiz. Going to bed on time seems to be helping you meet your goal of higher grades this semester," or "You've set aside half of every paycheck, and now you have $625 in the bank. It won't be long before you have enough to buy the computer you want."

Provide guidance in breaking students' long-term goals into a number of short-term objectives. Lead students through planning activities to determine steps to take to progress toward these goals. For example, help a student break the goal of a higher math grade into smaller objectives of rechecking math homework before handing it in, practicing the math problems on nights before the test, asking questions whenever something isn't clear.

Assist the student in realistically recognizing and accepting weaknesses in key skills. You might say, for example, "It's hard for you to do your math problems without making mistakes in your math facts. What are some parts of math that you're good at? What could you do to get around the reality that you don't remember math facts well?"

Assist students in requesting academic and social supports from teachers. Say, for example, "You'd like Mrs. Green to let you have some extra time to complete the weekly quiz. How will you ask her for that?" or "You think you'd do better work if your boss would let you use a note pad to jot down the orders. What can you do to ask for that?"

Self-Determination in Early
Childhood Years (Ages 2–5)

Even preschool children evidence some rudimentary elements of self-determined behavior. They are able to recognize their own personal preferences; can express these clearly and unequivocally when provided an opportunity; and are typically aware of some, albeit not all, of the alternative options in a decision. Preschoolers' choice making is largely dependent on the quality of their caregiver relationships, where control over the process is retained by caregivers, and freedom to engage in the process is dependent upon the level of trust that exists between child and caregiver. Additionally, preschool children's growing mastery of language appears essential to choice making, increasing the ease with which 1) choices can be offered and described to them, and 2) they can identify preferences. What preschoolers appear to lack are linkages to connect the choices and preferences they indicate to personal goals that describe what, ultimately, they might want to achieve. In large part, this may be because preschool children do not yet reflect purposefully on personal goals or aspirations, although their imaginary play does reflect a fascination with being "grown-up" along with some preconceptions about what that might entail. Thus, their choices appear to reflect their present wants, unencumbered by the need to achieve some future goal or objectives.

However, even if preschoolers could voice their goals, it is unlikely that they would systematically shape their actions to achieve them. This is because inaccurate and overoptimistic estimates of their own abilities limit their capacity to direct their own purposeful efforts. Additionally, their egocentric social perspective precludes the skilled direction of the behavior of others. Although aware of their own uniqueness, and sensitive to their own differing affect, they tend not to reflect on these features in others. Moreover, even within the limits of a single task, preschool children do not spontaneously or systematically refine or revise their choice of action depending upon their success or failure.

Adults can support elements of self-determination emergent in the preschool child by providing ample chances for them to exercise the choice-making and choice-recognition capacities they possess. Necessary supports might include 1) offering choices to the child wherever possible, 2) assisting the child to recognize alternative choices, and 3) restricting the child from making choices that are detrimental to his or her future opportunities. Adults can encourage a preschooler's emergent understanding of the links between choices and later opportunities by revisiting the choices that the child has made in the very recent past, helping them identify the consequences of those choices, and discuss plans for similar choices in the future. Linkages between choices they have made and later opportunities can also be fostered by encouraging preschoolers to be planful about their daily activities. Adults can encourage early perspective taking by asking preschoolers to reflect on how other people might be feeling or thinking in a given situation. Finally, adults can provide preschoolers with practice evaluating their own performance by presenting them with models of good performance and helping them compare what they have done with the model.

Self-Determination in Early
Elementary Years (Ages 6–8)

By the early elementary years, students more actively direct their own thinking and reasoning, a necessary step toward self-determined behavior. They identify increasingly varied solutions to problems that they encounter. Compared to preschoolers, they are more likely to implement the solutions that they generate and, because they are better judges of their own strengths and weaknesses, are more likely to select strategies, solutions, and options, that complement their abilities. Their concrete–operational reasoning allows them to recognize generic rules that explain problems and their solutions—rules that can be generalized to new, but similar, problems in the future. Moreover, their improved perspective taking makes it possible for these students to shape the ways that others behave toward them, granting them some control over their social context as well.

Still, once they have chosen a path or a plan, early elementary students are slow to abandon it, persisting with their original approach even when faced with little or no success. Despite their initial responsiveness, they do not purposefully redirect their efforts in response to information about their plan's results. Although first graders can set goals and work to achieve them over brief intervals of time, they need the support of an adult to point out their incremental improvements and praise them liberally for these successes. Without such adult direction, early elementary–age students do not spontaneously engage in goal-governed actions.

Adult support for self-determination in the early elementary years should reinforce a student's identification of multiple strategies and options for choice and decision making. Such support should assist students to articulate and make explicit the match between the strategies that they select and their own unique abilities. More important, adults can assist the student to revisit previously made decisions and choices once information on their impact is available, reconsider the choices available to them when making those decisions, and examine the possible consequences of each choice and shift their task approach as necessary. Part of this process should include an analysis of others' contributions to their choice successes or failures. In addition, early elementary students can benefit from frequent and systematic evaluation of their own performance and a consideration of the factors that enhanced or impeded their work. They should be encouraged to practice their newly emerging understanding of rule-based decision making. Where rules exist that can guide decision making and problem solving, they should be encouraged to say the rule aloud, apply it to the problem, and decide whether or not the rule points to the best choice. Finally, adults should guide early elementary students in setting, monitoring, and adjusting simple goals for familiar tasks that they complete.

Self-Determination in Late Elementary Years (Ages 9–11)

It is during the late elementary years when the first real evidence emerges that students spontaneously set personal goals that shape their subsequent actions. In part, this is because late elementary–age students have acquired the capacity to systematically alter their behavior in response to information they have acquired. They can recognize when their problem-solving approach is and is not working and adopt a new strategy more likely to be successful. They are able to recognize when they need assistance and ask for this assistance. They also recognize when additional effort is likely to improve their performance on a task. Moreover, they can anticipate the response that their behavior is likely to elicit from other people and select actions with those social consequences in mind. With these essential tools, students in late elementary–school grades are able to selectively shape their actions so that these support, rather than subvert, their aspirations. It is not surprising, then, to find that late elementary school students can make medical treatment decisions that approximate those of adults, even though they cannot systematically analyze the consequences of the various choices, and their preferences still reflect the most salient consequences of a choice.

What late elementary–age students lack is the structure for systematic analysis of the consequences of the various options from which they choose. Therefore, it is not always possible for them to verbalize a clear rationale for the decisions that they make, even though they are able to make decisions very similar to adults. Moreover, these students are likely to disregard less salient or striking options of a decision, especially when a problem is new or unfamiliar.

Late elementary–age students can benefit from adult support in structuring their decision-making activities, assisting them through the process of listing options, explicitly describing their consequences, and weighing the respective costs and benefits of each. Structuring activities helps them to arrange their list of decision options in a manner that is easier to compare systematically. Adults can assist students in systematically revisiting past decisions to recognize the impact that these have on their present lives and make the cost–benefit decisions more concrete. Next, late elementary–age students can be assisted to generalize their decision-making skills to setting specific and achievable goals for their own personal and academic lives, determining whether current decisions advance or conflict with those goals, and monitoring their progress towards them. Most late elementary–age students will require adult guidance if they are to formulate evaluations of their own strengths and weaknesses that are both accurate (so that they advance students' abilities to plan for future goals that are realistic) and accepting (so that students' acknowledgment of skill deficits and limitations does not disrupt their sense of personal confidence and self-worth). Finally, and because so many of their activities continue to be adult governed, late elementary–age students will benefit from learning how and when to approach adults with specific requests for assistance or resources.

Self-Determination in Secondary Years (Ages 12–18)

Secondary-age students demonstrate a capacity for systematic decision making that is similar in most respects to that of adults. Their decisions incorporate an analysis of the consequences of each choice as well as a determination of the credibility of the information that they use. Similarly, their approach to task completion and problem solving is spontaneously strategic, and they systematically analyze and revise their strategies in the face of successful or unsuccessful experiences. They easily generalize successful problem-solving strategies from one task to other tasks. Moreover, their sophisticated perspective taking makes it possible for them to exert accurate and effective control over the social ecology that determines their destiny. Informed consent by adolescents approximates that of adults. In fact, the primary barrier to self-determined behaviors of the adolescent tends to be their emotionality; individual differences in their perceptions of self-control have more to do with their emotional turbulence, and their prior learning experiences, than with their developmental potential.

Because most of the precursors to self-determination are intact in the typical adolescent, the primary emphasis of adult support for students at this level is the provision of frequent and varied opportunities to practice self-determination behaviors. So that adults do not inadvertently limit students' decision-making opportunities or unnecessarily protect students from the consequences of those decisions, it is often useful to plan in advance for ways to extend students' self-determination opportunities with the students and with other adults who support those students. Secondary students also continue to need assistance to analyze their decisions systematically and to critically evaluate the source of knowledge they use to make decisions. Finally, adults can assist secondary students with the emotional demands that self-examination requires by providing emotional support to assist the students to recognize their strengths and weaknesses without obscuring the reality of their life decisions.

Social Context of Self-Determination

Inadequate opportunities may suppress or hinder the development of self-determination and, for many people with disabilities, the lack of such opportunities may result in the eventuality that an individual is not self-determined. This issue of opportunity presents a special puzzle for the study of self-determination in children and adolescents, whether or not they have a disability. This is because children, like people with disabilities of all ages, have not traditionally been thought of as individuals who require or should be granted freedom from undue interference by those entrusted with their care. Consequently, it is very difficult to tell whether limitations in children's abilities to act as their own causal agent are due to biologically determined limits on their competence as self-sufficient persons or to culturally induced practices that discourage them from exercising self-determination. Concurrently, due to these cultural constraints, it is too easy to deny children and adolescents the opportunity to be self-determined. Many of the studies cited in this developmental chapter were completed within a social context that, in many respects, discouraged the expression of skills in children and youth, especially if they had disabilities. It will be necessary, then, to use caution in interpreting developmental progressions emerging from research on the prerequisite skills for self-determination.

SUMMARY

This chapter reviewed the developmental components of self-determination as these are described by research on the development of capacities that are necessary for self-determined behavior to occur. Our analysis has revealed that these prerequisite skills and capacities are often intact by the early elementary years and are certainly present by the emergence of adolescence. Consequently, it was argued that the capacity for self-determined behaviors are developmentally typical in the secondary grades, suggesting that when self-determination does not emerge, it may be due to limited opportunities to engage in self-determination during adolescence or limited opportunities to engage in the skills prerequisite to self-determination earlier in life. Finally, instructional and parenting practices were described that can support the emergence of self-determination and its precursors; these most often demand a teacher–learner relationship that is embedded in learning, coaching, and facilitation that is co-directed by both learners and teachers.

REFERENCES

Bandura, A. (1982). Self-efficacy mechanism in human agency. *American Psychologist, 37*, 122–147.

Belmont, J.M. (1989). Cognitive strategies and strategic learning: The socio-instructional approach. *American Psychologist, 44*, 142–148.

Bower, T.G.R. (1977). *The perceptual world of the child.* London: Fontana Press.

Bretherton, I., & Beeghly, M. (1982). Talking about internal states: The acquisition of an explicit theory of mind. *Developmental Psychology, 18*, 906–921.

Brigham, T. (1979). Some effects of choice on academic performance. In L. Perlmuter & R. Monty (Eds.), *Choice and perceived control* (pp. 131–142). Hillsdale, NJ: Lawrence Erlbaum Associates.

Butler, R. (1990). The effects of mastery and competitive conditions on self-assessment at different ages. *Child Development, 61*, 201–210.

Cairns, R.B. (1986). A contemporary perspective on social development. In P.S. Strain, M.J. Guralnick, & H.M. Walker (Eds.), *Children's social behavior: Development, assessment and modification* (pp. 3–91). Orlando, FL: Academic Press.

Chi, M. (1981). Knowledge development and memory performance. In M. Friedman, J. Das, & N. O'Connor (Eds.), *Intelligence and learning* (pp. 34–62). New York: Plenum.

Cornoldi, C. (1987). Origins of intentional strategic memory in the child. In B. Inhelder, D. De Caprona, & A. Cornu-Wells (Eds.), *Piaget today* (pp. 183–201). Hillsdale, NJ: Lawrence Erlbaum Associates.

Cornoldi, C., Gobbo, C., & Mazzoni, G. (1991). On metamemory–memory relationship: Strategy availability and training. *International Journal of Behavior Development, 14,* 101–121.

Damon, W. (1983). *Social and personality development.* New York: Norton.

DeCasper, A.J., & Spence, M.J. (1986). Prenatal maternal speech influences newborns' perception of speech sounds. *Infant Behavior and Development, 9,* 133–150.

Deci, E.L., Schwartz, A.J., Sheinman, L., & Ryan, R.M. (1981). An instrument to assess adults' orientations toward control versus autonomy with children: Reflections on intrinsic motivation and perceived competence. *Journal of Educational Psychology, 73,* 642–650.

Dweck, C.S., & Elliott, E.S. (1983). Achievement motivation. In E.M. Hetherington (Ed.) & P.H. Mussen (Series Ed.), *Handbook of child psychology: Vol. 3. Socialization, personality and social development* (4th ed., pp. 643–691). New York: John Wiley & Sons.

Eccles, J., Midgeley, C., & Adler, T.F. (1984). Age-related changes in the school environment: Effects on achievement motivation. In J.H. Nicholls (Ed.), *The development of achievement motivation* (pp. 57–90). Greenwich, CT: JAI Press.

Eder, R. (1989). The emergent personologist: The structure and content of 3½-, 5½-, and 7½-year-olds' concepts of themselves and other persons. *Child Development, 60,* 1218–1228.

Eder, R. (1990). Uncovering young children's psychological selves: Individual and developmental differences. *Child Development, 61,* 849–863.

Fabricius, W., & Hagen, J. (1984). Use of causal attributions about recall performance to assess metamemory and predict strategic memory behavior in young children. *Developmental Psychology, 20,* 975–987.

Fantz, R. (1961). The origin of form perception. *Scientific American, 204,* 66–72.

Findley, M.J., & Cooper, H.M. (1983). Locus of control and academic achievement: A literature review. *Journal of Personality and Social Psychology, 44,* 419–427.

Flavell, J.H. (1985). *Cognitive development* (2nd ed.). Englewood Cliffs, NJ: Prentice Hall.

Forrest, D.L., & Walker, T.G. (1980, April). *What do children know about their reading and study skills?* Paper presented at the annual meeting of the American Educational Research Association, Boston.

Frey, K.S., & Ruble, D.N. (1987). What children say about classroom performance: Sex and grade differences in perceived competence. *Child Development, 58,* 1066–1078.

Garner, R. (1987). *Metacognition and reading comprehension.* Norwood, NJ: Ablex.

Ghatala, E.S. (1986). Strategy-monitoring training enables young learners to select effective strategies. *Educational Psychologist, 21,* 43–54.

Giaia, G.A. (1993). Development and mental retardation. In R. Smith (Ed.), *Children with mental retardation: A parents' guide* (pp. 51–87). Rockville, MD: Woodbine House.

Haith, M. (1980). *Rules that babies look by: The organization of newborn visual activity.* Hillsdale, NJ: Lawrence Erlbaum Associates.

Harter, S. (1983). The perceived competence scale for children. *Child Development, 53*, 87–97.

Herek, G., Janis, I.L., & Huth, P. (1987). Decision making during international crises: Is quality of process related to outcome? *Journal of Conflict Resolution, 31*, 203–226.

Higgins, E.T. (1989). Continuities and discontinuities in self-regulatory and self-evaluative processes: A developmental theory relating self and affect. *Journal of Personality, 57*, 407–444.

Hodapp, R.M., Burack, J.A., & Zigler, E. (1990). The developmental perspective in the field of mental retardation. In R.M. Hodapp, J.A. Burack, & E. Zigler (Eds.), *Issues in the developmental approach to mental retardation* (pp. 3–26). New York: Cambridge University Press.

Janis, I., & Mann, L. (1977). *Decision making: A psychological analysis of conflict, choice and commitment.* New York: Free Press.

Kaser-Boyd, N., Adelman, H., & Taylor, L. (1985). Minors' ability to identify risks and benefits of therapy. *Professional Psychology: Research and Practice, 16*, 411–417.

Kendall, P.C. (1984). Social cognition and problem-solving: A developmental and child-clinical interface. In B. Gholson & T.L. Rosenthal (Eds.), *Applications of cognitive developmental theory* (pp. 115–147). New York: Academic Press.

Leadbeater, B.J., Hellner, I., Allen, J.P., & Aber, J.L. (1989). Assessment of interpersonal negotiation strategies in youth engaged in problem behaviors. *Developmental Psychology, 25*, 465–472.

Lewis, M., & Brooks-Gunn, J. (1979). *Social cognition and the acquisition of the self.* New York: Plenum.

Locke, E.A., Shaw, K.M., Saari, L.M., & Latham, G.P. (1981). Goal setting and task performance: 1969–1980. *Psychological Bulletin, 90*, 125–152.

Mann, L., Beswick, G., Allouache, P., & Ivey, M. (1989). Decision workshops for the improvement of decision-making skills and confidence. *Journal of Counseling and Development, 67*, 478–481.

Meisel, A., Roth, L.H., & Lidz, C.W. (1977). Toward a model of the legal doctrine of informed consent. *American Journal of Psychiatry, 134*, 285–289.

Moore, S.G. (1979). Social cognition: Knowing about others. *Young Children, 34*, 54–61.

Nelson-Le Gall, S., Kratzer, L., Jones, E., & DeCooke, P. (1990). Children's self-assessment of performance and task-related help seeking. *Journal of Experimental Child Psychology, 49*, 245–263.

Nicholls, J.G. (1978). The development of the concepts of effort and ability, perception of academic attainment, and the understanding that difficult tasks require more ability. *Child Development, 49*, 800–814.

Nicholls, J.G., & Miller, A. (1984). Conceptions of ability and achievement motivation. In R. Ames & C. Ames (Eds.), *Research on motivation in education: Vol. 1. Student motivation* (pp. 39–73). New York: Academic Press.

Ormond, C., Luszcz, M.A., Mann, L., & Beswick, G. (1991). A metacognitive analysis of decision making in adolescence. *Journal of Adolescence, 14*, 275–291.

Paris, S.G., & Lindauer, B.K. (1982). The development of cognitive skills during childhood. In B. Wolman (Ed.), *Handbook of developmental psychology* (pp. 333–349). Englewood Cliffs, NJ: Prentice Hall.

Perner, J., Frith, U., Leslie, A.M., & Leekham, S. (1989). Exploration of the autistic child's theory of mind: Knowledge, belief and communication. *Child Development, 60*, 689–700.

Perner, J., & Wimmer, H. (1985). John thinks that Mary thinks that . . . Attribution of second-order beliefs by 5- to 10-year-old children. *Journal of Experimental Child Psychology, 39*, 437–471.

Perner, J., & Wimmer, H. (1988). Misinformation and unexpected change: Testing the development of epistemic-state attribution. *Psychological Research, 50*, 191–197.

Piaget, J. (1959). *The language and thought of the child.* London: Routledge and Kegan Pauls. (Original work published in 1923.)

Renick, M.J., & Harter, S. (1989). Impact of social comparisons on the developing self-perceptions of learning disabled students. *Journal of Educational Psychology, 81*, 631–638.

Rholes, W.S., & Ruble, D.N. (1984). Children's understanding of dispositional characteristics of others. *Child Development, 55*, 550–560.

Ruble, D.N. (1983). The development of social comparison processes and their role in achievement-related self-socialization. In E.T. Higgins, W.W. Hartup, & D.N. Ruble (Eds.), *Social cognition and social development: A sociocultural perspective* (pp. 134–157.) New York: Cambridge University Press.

Ruble, D.N., Boggiano, A.K., Feldman, N.S., & Loebl, J.M. (1980). A developmental analysis of the role of social comparison in self-evaluation. *Developmental Psychology, 16*, 105–115.

Ruble, D.N., & Flett, G.L. (1988). Conflicting goals in self-evaluative information seeking: Developmental and ability level analyses. *Child Development, 59*, 97–106.

Sands, D.J., & Doll, B. (in press). Fostering self-determination is a developmental task. *Journal of Special Education.*

Scarr, S., Weinberg, R.A., & Levine, A. (1986). *Understanding development.* San Diego: Harcourt Brace Jovanovich.

Selman, R.L. (1980). *The growth of interpersonal understanding.* New York: Academic Press.

Selman, R., & Byrne, D.F. (1974). A structural-developmental analysis of levels of role taking in middle childhood. *Child Development, 45*, 803–806.

Shantz, C.U. (1975). The development of social cognition. In E.M. Hetherington (Ed.), *Review of child development research* (Vol. 5, pp. 257–323). Chicago: University of Chicago Press.

Skinner, E.A. (1990). Age differences in the dimensions of perceived control during middle childhood: Implications for developmental conceptualizations and research. *Child Development, 61*, 1882–1890.

Spivack, G., Platt, V.V., & Shure, M.B. (1976). *The problem-solving approach to adjustment.* San Francisco: Jossey-Bass.

Stein, N.L., & Goldman, S. (1979). *Children's knowledge about social situations: From causes to consequences.* (Technical Report No. 147 of the Center for the Study of Reading.) Champaign, IL: University of Illinois at Urbana Champaign.

Stern, D. (1985). *The interpersonal world of the infant.* New York: Basic Books.

Stipek, D., Recchia, S., & McClintic, S. (1992). Self-evaluation in young children. *Monographs of the Society for Research in Child Development, 57,* 70–79.

Stowitschek, J.J., Ghezzi, P.M., & Safely, K.N. (1987). "I'd rather do it myself": Self-evaluation and correction of handwriting. *Education and Treatment of Children, 10*, 209–224.

Thomas, C.H., & Patton, J.R. (1994). Characteristics of individuals with milder forms of retardation. In M. Beirne-Smith, J.R. Patton, & R. Ittenbach (Eds.), *Mental retardation* (4th ed., pp. 204–240). New York: Macmillan.

Turnbull, A.P., Turnbull, H.R., Shank, M., & Leal, D. (1995). *Exceptional lives: Special education in today's schools.* Englewood Cliffs, NJ: Prentice Hall.

Trabasso, T., Stein, N., Rodkin, P., Park, M., & Baughn, C. (1992). Knowledge of goals and plans in the on-line narration of events. *Cognitive Development, 7*, 133–170.

Wehmeyer, M.L. (1996). Self-determination for youth with severe cognitive disabilities: From theory to practice. In L. Powers, G. Singer, & J.A. Sowers (Eds.), *On the road to autonomy: Promoting self-competence in children and youth with disabilities* (pp. 115–133). Baltimore: Paul H. Brookes Publishing Co.

Wehmeyer, M.L., & Kelchner, K. (1994). Interpersonal cognitive problem-solving skills of individuals with mental retardation. *Education and Training in Mental Retardation and Developmental Disability, 29,* 265–278.

Wehmeyer, M.L., Kelchner, K., & Richards, S. (1995). Individual and environmental factors related to the self-determination of adults with mental retardation. *Journal of Vocational Rehabilitation, 5,* 291–305.

Wehmeyer, M.L., Kelchner, K., & Richards, S. (in press). Essential characteristics of self-determined behavior of individuals with mental retardation and developmental disabilities. *American Journal on Mental Retardation.*

Weisz, J.R. (1980). Developmental change in perceived control: Recognizing noncontingency in the laboratory and perceiving it in the world. *Developmental Psychology, 16,* 385–390.

Weisz, J., & Zigler, E. (1979). Cognitive development in retarded and non-retarded persons: Piagetian tests of the similar sequence hypothesis. *Psychological Bulletin, 86,* 831–853.

Weithorn, L.A., & Campbell, S.B. (1982). The competency of children and adolescents to make informed treatment decisions. *Child Development, 53,* 1589–1598.

Werner, H., & Kaplan, B. (1984). *Symbol formation.* Hillsdale, NJ: Lawrence Erlbaum Associates.

Wojnilower, D.A., & Gross, A.M. (1988). Knowledge, perception and performance of assertive behavior in children with learning disabilities. *Journal of Learning Disabilities, 21,* 109–117.

Woolfolk, A.E. (1990). *Educational psychology* (4th ed.). Englewood Cliffs, NJ: Prentice Hall.

Chapter 6

HOMES TO SUPPORT
THE SELF-DETERMINATION OF CHILDREN

Christine C. Cook, Mary Jane Brotherson,
Cindy Weigel-Garrey, and Inez Mize

THE HOME ENVIRONMENT offers children their earliest opportunities to
make choices, experience control, and exhibit competence. Children's family
members are an important source of feedback as children act on the environment
and observe the consequences of those actions (Wohlwill & Heft, 1987). Daily
activities unrestricted by the physical environment are the underlying fabric of
self-determination, enhancing children's self-esteem and providing them with responsibility and opportunities for independence. Experiencing a mastery over the
environment can help children to feel that their life is under their own control
(Hendershott, 1989).

Home is both a physical place and a cognitive concept (Tognoli, 1987).
Viewed as a physical place, the home environment is a complex system of rooms
and spaces, furnishings and equipment, storage areas and displays, and the connections among these. The actual physical features of the dwelling, however, account for only a small portion of the definition of home. As a cognitive concept,
the home is viewed as the center of experiential space, "a place of comfort and
security, of care, concern, and commitment, and a place in which the personal
meanings of home become tied to the individual's conception of self" (Feldman,
1990, p. 184). Viewed in this way the home can meet sociopsychological needs
for identity and territory, nurturance, privacy, socialization, manipulation, and
stimulation (Miller, 1986).

Little research has focused on the home environments of children with disabilities and their families. Although much of the literature in the field of early
childhood special education focuses on family-centered intervention strategies,
surprisingly little attention has been paid to the homes in which these strategies

are implemented. In this chapter, the focus is on the importance of the interaction between children with disabilities, their families, and the home environment as a means to enhance their growth and development. We review the literature that supports the role of the home environment in providing opportunities to develop skills leading to self-determination.

In addition, we discuss our investigation of the home environments of children with disabilities and their families. Although still in its earliest stages, this research examines the extent of access to spaces within the home and the modifications made to the homes of children with disabilities. A protocol being developed will allow us to consider the attitudes families hold regarding self-determination and choice for children in the home. The goal of our research is to better understand how the home environments of children with disabilities can be arranged to meet their sociopsychological needs and thereby encourage the development of self-determination skills.

ROLE OF HOME ENVIRONMENTS IN THE LIVES OF CHILDREN

Early research on home environments focused primarily on the social environment, specifically dyadic interactions with caregivers (Wachs, 1986; Wohlwill & Heft, 1987). The setting for these interactions, the physical environment, was frequently neglected (David & Weinstein, 1987). More recently, however, an interactional theory of environment and behavior has evolved in which the person, the environment, and the interaction between the two is emphasized (Moore, 1986). Previous biases toward the behavior of individuals as the sole focus of intervention is being replaced by consideration of people within the contexts of the social and physical settings of which they are part and which influence them (Bronfenbrenner, 1979; Orford, 1992; Wachs, 1990). This research has contributed to an understanding of the importance of the home environment and its manipulation (Orford, 1992; Stokols & Altman, 1987).

From childhood through adulthood, the physical environment sets parameters for available choices (Altman & Wohlwill, 1978; Lang & Sullivan, 1986; Lawton, 1975; Lewis, 1986; Miller, 1986) and influences activity by facilitating certain actions and limiting others (Barker, 1968; Barker & Associates, 1978). "The home can be a restrictive, inappropriate environment for young children" if it obstructs play and movement (Johnson, 1987, p. 143), as play is the primary means through which children acquire social, cognitive, and physical skills (Hanline & Fox, 1993). In the home, however, children frequently engage in activities that place the fewest demands on the household environment—quiet, passive play routines rather than noisy, active, or potentially messy types of play (Gaunt, 1980). Both physical limitations of the home environment (e.g., entry ways too narrow to accommodate a wheelchair or walker) and the expected uses of the home (e.g., quiet rather than noisy activities) may be detrimental to the development of children with or without disabilities.

Arrangement of the Physical Environment

The arrangement of the physical environment (bedrooms, bathrooms, kitchen, and living areas), play equipment, and assistive devices (e.g., communication board, wheelchair, prosthesis) should be considered an opportunity to plan, initiate, and direct activity, such as the freedom to enter the kitchen and bathroom as needed, to select toys and games from a shelf or drawer, to turn lights on and off, to be a part of family discussions and meals, to move from room to room within the dwelling. The circulation paths between and among spaces and activities have significance for increasing the range and extent of access within the home that, in turn, can increase the autonomy and self-determination of young children (Brotherson, Cook, Mise, & Weigel-Garrey, 1994). Wachs (1986) reported that seven dimensions of the physical environment have been consistently related to various cognitive parameters in typically developing children. Positively related were 1) availability of stimulus materials, 2) variety of stimulus materials, 3) responsivity of the physical environment, and 4) regularity of scheduling. Negatively related dimensions included 1) ambient background noise, 2) overcrowding, and 3) physical restraints upon exploration. Although untested, it seems likely that these dimensions of the environment are important to children with disabilities as well.

Sociopsychological Impact of the Home Environment

Place identity is the term used to describe the physical world socialization of children (Proshansky & Fabian, 1987). Place identity theory is derived from the literature on the formation of self-identity but proposes that the description of the relationships between children and other people (part of the evolution of self-identity) has neglected the role of children's experiences with the physical or material world in defining *self*. Certain spaces, places, and objects are "owned," that is, identified as one's own, for example, one's family, one's siblings, or belonging to others outside the household. Rooms, clothing, playthings, and an entire assortment of objects and spaces can be controlled, thus satisfying and maintaining a child's sense of self. As Doll, Sands, Wehmeyer, and Palmer (Chapter 5) point out, among the earliest experiences children have is that of distinguishing themselves from others and objects and identifying spaces over which they can exercise choice and control.

"The home plays a very important role in the development of a clear, stable definition, and a positive evaluation of the self for children" (Miller, 1986, p. 57). Identity and personalization go hand-in-hand. Personalization involves using the material, physical world to reflect ourselves. Personalization supports and enhances our ideas of self. Throughout the home there are opportunities to send "environmental messages" that reinforce and contribute to the feeling that the child with a disability is a part of the family and is worthwhile (Becker, 1977). Photographs of the family and child, the child's art work hung at his or her eye level, and a mirror that allows a child to see his or her whole body contribute to the formation of positive identity (Dodge, Koralek, & Pizzolongo, 1989). When children can participate in the selection of toys, furnishings, equipment, or color schemes for their room or play spaces, autonomy and feelings of self-worth and confidence can be enhanced.

A number of sociopsychological dimensions have been identified as significant in the evaluation of the home environment and in the formation of a positive self-identity; these include territory, nurturance, privacy, socialization, manipulation, and stimulation (Miller, 1986). The importance of each of these concepts to children's development and some of the ways in which the physical environment may provide for these sociopsychological needs are described below.

Territory Territorial behavior is defined as claiming control over a particular area (Sebba & Churchman, 1983). While children have a strong desire to own, control, and occupy space, research suggests that territory is often a scarce resource for them (Miller, 1986). Children sometimes control a bedroom, or a portion of a shared bedroom, or out-of-the-way places such as attics, storage areas, garages, and corners. For children with disabilities, the concept of the control center or nest to achieve a personalized territory might be borrowed from the literature on the elderly (Lawton, 1989). The control nest is delineated by a chair or space on the floor from which a child can see much of the activity of the home, has a view of the outside, and can reach favorite toys or regulate stimulation such as a television, videocassette recorder, or stereo.

Toys, play equipment, or assistive devices may be prohibited in or "cleaned up" from living areas of the home at times during the day because safe, adequate, or accessible storage is not available in the living areas of the home. Small activity pockets, like those used in child care environments, may be an effective way to encourage varied play within a home setting for a child with disabilities. These activity pockets also could be arranged to encourage play with siblings or neighborhood friends.

Nurturance Places that children call warm, comfortable, protected, snug, and cozy are "soft" nurturing settings (Miller, 1986; Phyfe-Perkins, 1980). Indicators of "softness" include 1) adult/child furniture such as rockers, couches, or large pillows; 2) plush rugs or carpeting; 3) tactile sensory materials such as grass, sand, dirt, play dough, finger paint, or water; 4) animals to hold and cuddle; 5) single sling swings; and 6) laps upon which to sit (Prescott, 1978). Light, temperature, color, texture, room arrangement, and furniture selection and placement can lead to feelings of being safe and secure. For example, one's own chair in the living or family room, displays of family photographs and children's artwork, the proximity of parents' and siblings' bedrooms to the child, and a designated place at the dining room table promote feelings of security within the home.

Most young children want to play within visual and acoustic range of adults. The kitchen in many homes is a center of family activity and is a convenient setting for a number of children's activities including food preparation, painting, and play dough or water play. Many of the skills needed for independent living are related to food preparation and cleanup. While counters and appliances may not be accessible to young children, work areas can be devised and simple assistive devises (e.g., raised platforms, grabbers, Dycem) used to expand the opportunities available to children in the kitchen such as counting, measuring, mixing, preparing, and washing. Items put on low shelves and in low cabinets and the use of a microwave oven can provide a child experiences in selecting and/or preparing snacks and contributing to meal preparation.

Privacy Children, both with and without disabilities, need some defined space of their own that can be regulated to ensure privacy (Proshansky & Fabian, 1987). Although the way that privacy is achieved is culturally determined, it is perhaps the most important dimension in the development of self-identity and autonomy because it involves setting up and controlling boundaries between oneself and others (Laufer & Wolfe, 1977). Children, however, often are subject to intrusion because they are defined as dependents (Proshansky & Fabian, 1987). Depending on the situation, control over privacy may be related to preventing or limiting distractions, interruptions, or observations of their activities.

Control over access to a child's defined space might take the form of a closed or locked door; a private drawer; one's own chair or one's own room; a small, quiet area away from family activity; or headphones for a cassette recorder (Dodge et al., 1989). In child care settings, quiet places are often provided by a small tent; a low cabinet with the door removed; sheets and pillows; or large, carpeted blocks. Similar kinds of spaces and materials can be used in the home.

Sociability The contribution of the family to social interaction and friendship formation among children with disabilities has been paid less attention than children's socialization in classroom settings (e.g., Buysse, 1993; Levitt & Weber, 1989; Peterson & McConnell, 1993). Research is only beginning to examine friendships in school; almost no research exists on strategies to help families with children with disabilities to facilitate the child's friendships through activities in the home (Staub, Salisbury, Gallucci, & Peck, 1994). Many social interaction skills are learned at home by inviting friends over to play and by sharing living quarters and activities with family members (Miller, 1986). Children enjoy separate spaces to share with their own friends. In school settings, friendship formation among preschoolers with disabilities is stimulated by 1) time spent together and 2) the way in which classroom materials and activities are arranged (Buysse, 1993). Barriers and enclosures can enhance social interactions in child care settings (Levitt & Weber, 1989). At home, the arrangement of furnishings and the provision of indoor and outdoor spaces for activities stimulates children's cooperative play. Spaces away from family activities that include toys, games, and comfortable seating can signal to neighborhood children that children with disabilities are ready and willing playmates.

Stimulation and Manipulation Everything about the home environment provides stimulation, from windows, decor, plants, pets, books, and wall displays to the auditory stimulation of the television, stereo, and radio. The degree to which this stimulation can be accessed and controlled represents the manipulation capability of these elements. "Children derive satisfaction from actively manipulating and changing the environment" (Miller, 1986, p. 55). Some research has indicated that often children's home environments do not have specific areas set aside for their different play activities (Clarke-Stewart, 1986). More different kinds of "adult decorations" that are "off-limits" to children have been observed than different kinds of toys and educational materials for children (Clarke-Stewart, 1986, p. 35). Children with and without disabilities need to have a variety of materials and opportunities available for stimulation and manipulation. Self-selected opportunities to look out a window, for example, can provide environmental access and control.

A room-by-room appraisal can identify opportunities for modifying home environments. The scale and positioning of various fixtures in the home, the height of shelves, clothes racks, door knobs, mirrors, towel racks, and light switches can be planned in accordance with children's needs. A 5-year-old, for example, with limited mobility can vacuum with the use of a scooter board and a hand-held vacuum cleaner (Bigge, 1991). Children can be encouraged to select their own clothing or dress themselves by stacking clothing on the floor of the closet, lowering the clothes bar, or taking the door off the closet. Clothes in a lower drawer of a dresser can be accessible if the pull and the weight of the drawer are considered. Parents are sometimes reluctant to allow a wheelchair or walker into the home because of space limitations and/or perceived hazards or damage to walls and furnishings. Inexpensive plastic piping or tubing can be laid on the floor against the walls to minimize damage and allow for greater mobility.

Particularly in home settings, efforts should be made to clear enough open space to allow for movement and for construction activities. There is increasing interest in indoor play equipment—slides, cushions and blocks, large balls, tube tunnels—that will encourage young children to participate in a variety of physical activities (Johnson, 1987). Active play is important to children's development. Children with visual, physical, and developmental impairments often have limited ability to explore objects and toys and, consequently, to receive an appropriate quantity and quality of sensory feedback (Langley, 1985); and environments should be adapted to support such activities.

FAMILY ATTITUDES AND HOME MODIFICATIONS

Parents have sometimes been reluctant to adapt environments for their children with disabilities (Hovey, 1993; Johnson, 1987; Lang & Sullivan, 1986; Lewis,

1986). Hovey's (1993) study of home modification for children with disabilities included a housing accessibility survey. The survey examined the home in great detail, including entrances; interior passage ways; bathrooms; kitchen; bedrooms; living or family rooms; and overall space, floor coverings, and controls in the home. She interviewed 23 families with children with physical disabilities and varying levels of cognitive disabilities.

Although the availability of financial resources was a critical variable that enabled or inhibited families in making home modifications, several other factors were found to be equally important. First, a family's perception of how easy it was to make home modifications influenced their modification decisions. Families that believed an alteration would be difficult were less likely to modify their home. Second, some families would not make home modifications because of the perceived stigma associated with the change. Wheelchair ramps, for example, were viewed "as a neon sign saying I have a kid with a problem" (Hovey, 1993, p. 50). Third, the age of onset of the child's disability was also an important factor in whether or not a family made alterations. If the onset of the disability was at a later age, the family was more likely to make alterations to maintain the child's independence. Lastly, the gender of the child was associated with modifications; if the child was a female almost no home modifications had been made that would either ease caregiving or increase accessibility. If the child was a male, modifications allowing greater independence were more likely to be made.

Lewis (1986) also found a reluctance among parents raising children with severe mobility problems to remove architectural barriers from the home. The research focused on the "stigmatized home" and explored the notion that the home functions as an extension of self. Furthermore, Lewis (1986) found that families resisted altering the external appearance of their home in ways that would call attention to themselves as being significantly different from others. In addition, results from in-depth interviews with families indicated that none of the professionals that had worked with them ever inquired about barriers in the home. Lewis (1986) concluded that professionals need to be more aware of parents' feelings and attitudes toward the home and all that it symbolizes.

Behavioral expectations are conveyed and attitudes are formed by the architectural design of homes (Orford, 1992; Stokols & Altman, 1987). In fact, some architectural determinists argue that the designed environment dictates behavioral responses (Broady, 1972). A home that is physically receptive to children with and without disabilities promotes social exchange and begins to remove attitudinal barriers. Thus, over time the perceptions of children without disabilities are altered, becoming more familiar and accepting of children with disabilities because they "fit" into the physical environment. The perceptions of children with disabilities can also be altered because they see themselves as "fitting" into the environment. Thus, the psychological environment can be affected by changes in the physical milieu (Gump, 1987).

EXAMINING THE HOME ENVIRONMENTS
OF CHILDREN WITH DISABILITIES: A PILOT STUDY

A review of the literature on children and environments shows that little research has investigated the extent to which families manipulate the home environment to promote the development of skills leading to self-determination among children with disabilities. It is not at all clear from the literature whether the supports needed to provide these opportunities for their children are available to families. Research is needed to identify and evaluate the most successful strategies to give families to renovate home environments. Furthermore, families' attitudes toward self-determination have not been examined. These attitudes and other family resources may enhance or impede the development of self-determination among children with disabilities.

To begin to analyze some of these issues, we have conducted a pilot study of the home environments of children with disabilities, drawing heavily upon the literature described previously. This study is described in detail on the following pages.

Study Format and Protocols

The study involved an examination of family attitudes toward self-determination and choice for children and a rigorous assessment of the physical environment in which children with disabilities live. Family views were elicited through face-to-face family interviews and a parent attitude survey. A room-by-room analysis of the home environment examined indicators that children's sociopsychological needs were or were not being met. The pilot study was designed to assist in the development of protocols and instruments to help us answer these questions:

1. What is the home's role in and capacity for promoting the development of self-determination skills?
2. How are children given opportunities for choice, control, and decision making in their home environments?
3. In what ways have families modified or adjusted their home environments to promote the development of skills of self-determination for their child with a disability?

We conducted in-depth interviews with 12 families of children with disabilities (ages 5–10). All of the children had physical disabilities and varying levels of cognitive development. The children's disabling conditions included cerebral palsy, spina bifida, dwarfism, brain injury, genetic muscle disease, and multiple disabilities. Four of the children had no cognitive impairment, and eight children experienced a range of cognitive disabilities. Eight of the children used a wheelchair, and only three children had no limitations in the area of mobility.

Each interview took from approximately 90 minutes to 2 hours. At least two investigators were present at the interview. One investigator interviewed family members, most often mothers. The second investigator moved through the home, examining inside and outside the home. The interview was taped and later transcribed. A photographic record of the home, composed of slides, prints, and sometimes videocassette recording, was obtained as well.

Interviews with Families

The data collection instruments we have used continue to evolve. In the first six interviews, for example, all information was gathered in the interview and the direct room-by-room observation. More recently, we have recast a portion of the interview as a survey, mailed out a week before the interview is scheduled. Through this survey, we collect information about the child's disability, the family members' attitudes, some accessibility information, and a checklist of activities in which the child regularly engages. The first 20–30 minutes with the family is devoted to reviewing the mail survey so that both the interviewer and the observer are better informed about the child and family before beginning.

The attitude survey (see Figure 1) examines families' attitudes toward self-determination and independence and children's roles and responsibilities in the home. In the interview, parents are asked to describe their child's routine. Parents are asked, for example, whether their children routinely or regularly help with selecting and preparing food and selecting clothing, have privacy in the toilet, visit other children with or without disabilities, use the telephone, or play outside unattended.

Room-by-Room Observation

Figure 2 illustrates the room-by-room survey. The development of the observation protocol borrowed heavily from needs assessments of typically developing children. Two sources, Miller (1986) and Johnson (1987), were especially instructive in the preparation of this instrument.

When the family interview is scheduled, participants are notified of our interest in examining each of the rooms in the home. The families are told at that time that photographs will be taken throughout the home, both inside and outside. They are given the opportunity to define areas that are "off limits" or to deny access altogether. When the study team arrives, they visit with the family before one or two members of the team leave to complete the observation. Although the room-by-room observation seems invasive, families to date have been very cooperative. Although participating children have sometimes accompanied observers, adult members of the family are engaged in the interview when the observation is taking place.

The observation of the home and the photographic essay are integral parts of the understanding of the physical environment of children with disabilities. We continue to refine the observation protocol as we visit family homes so that the survey systematically captures what we observe and so that the data are recorded in a meaningful way.

Family # —————————

The following statements are about your view of children with or without disabilities. Please tell us which best describes how you feel.

	Strongly agree	Agree	Disagree	Strongly disagree
1. Children with disabilities require almost constant supervision.	1	2	3	4
2. Children should have lots of opportunities to play with their peers.	1	2	3	4
3. Independence is a high priority for children with disabilities.	1	2	3	4
4. Independence and risk taking are higher priorities for children with disabilities than for children without disabilities.	1	2	3	4
5. Independence and risk taking are higher priorities for children than is protection from challenges.	1	2	3	4
6. Children with disabilities are unable to participate in most family decisions.	1	2	3	4
7. It is impractical for children with disabilities to have their own bedrooms.	1	2	3	4
8. Children cannot go outdoors unsupervised.	1	2	3	4
9. Children with disabilities cannot go outdoors unsupervised.	1	2	3	4
10. Children with disabilities are more vulnerable and need protection compared to children without disabilities.	1	2	3	4
11. Children with disabilities have unique abilities.	1	2	3	4
12. Development of self-worth and self-confidence are high priorities for children with disabilities.	1	2	3	4
13. Private time in the bathroom is important to children.	1	2	3	4
14. Children with disabilities cannot have private time on the toilet or in bathtub because they are at risk.	1	2	3	4
15. Children need almost constant supervision.	1	2	3	4
16. Children with disabilities need more overall supervision than do children without disabilities.	1	2	3	4
17. Children with disabilities should have a variety of opportunities to interact with peers without disabilities.	1	2	3	4
18. Children with disabilities need to work on goals at home as well as at school.	1	2	3	4
19. Children with disabilities should be allowed to explore, unsupervised, most places in the home.	1	2	3	4
20. Young children with disabilities need some private time to be alone.	1	2	3	4
21. Children with disabilities are able to make most decisions and choices for themselves.	1	2	3	4

(continued)

Figure 1. Parent attitude survey.

Figure 1 *(continued)*

	Strongly agree	Agree	Disagree	Strongly disagree
22. Children are most likely to learn about decision making, assertiveness, and self-advocacy in school.	1	2	3	4
23. Children with disabilities are unable to participate in most family, recreation, and outdoor activities.	1	2	3	4
24. Most children of 5 years can dress themselves unassisted.	1	2	3	4
25. It is important for children with disabilities to learn about and accept differences related to their disability.	1	2	3	4
26. It is impractical to make physical adaptations to the home for children with disabilities.	1	2	3	4
27. Toys and activities for children should be confined to their bedroom or a playroom.	1	2	3	4
28. Without supervision, most rooms in the home are "off limits" to children with disabilities.	1	2	3	4

Results

Preliminary results indicated that parents view self-determination as a long-range goal for their children. There is a high level of agreement with statements that relate to the provision of choice and independence. Table 1 shows a summary of selected findings from both the interview with families and from direct observation. Toys and children's beds were quite accessible items to children with disabilities. Toys were permitted in many areas of the home and were usually on the floor, on low shelves, or in low storage boxes. One family had converted the low shelves of a china hutch to toy storage. This allowed toys to be out of sight when necessary but meant play was very much in the midst of the visual and acoustic range of adults (Johnson, 1987). Several of the families had made the bed accessible by placing the mattress directly on the floor or taking the box spring off the bed frame, leaving only the mattress. Only one child slept in the upper bed of bunkbeds. This child's parents had put a railing up to prevent falls and found it easier to lift him in and out of bed than to have a mattress on the floor.

Children had very limited access to their clothing and very little choice about clothing selection. Clothes were typically hung too high for children to reach, and when clothing was in drawers, the weight of the drawers or the drawer pull made access difficult. Few of the children chose their own clothes, and none of the homes had been modified to permit children to select their clothes (e.g., clothes stacked on the floor, lowered clothes bar, door removed from closet).

Most families had photographic displays that included the child with a disability. Some families did not have any photographs displayed, nor was any of the child's artwork posted. As with many homes, children's artwork was often confined to the refrigerator and some in the child's room. Other kinds of displays

Dimension of Psychological Needs
Observations of the Physical Environment

Room: _____

Nurturance: Children feel nurtured when the environment is secure, safe, protected, content, warm, comfortable, snug, and cozy. Observe room temperature (including warmth from sunlight), atmosphere, bright colors and designs, natural content, furnishings, size of room (too large/small), and how area is personalized.

| 1 | 2 | 3 | 4 | 5 |
| no evidence | | some evidence | | a lot of evidence |

_____ Mirror provided
_____ Family photographs displayed
_____ Children's art displayed
_____ Child-sized furnishings provided

Comments:

Territory: Children have a strong desire to own, control, and occupy space. Observe how the area is defined by child's bed, chairs, floor coverings, toys, pillows, blankets, sheets, bookcases, pictures, and so on.

| 1 | 2 | 3 | 4 | 5 |
| no evidence | | some evidence | | a lot of evidence |

_____ Play area evident
_____ Opportunities to regulate sound (e.g., TV, stereo)
_____ Opportunities to regulate lighting
_____ Wheelchair/special equipment use allowed

Comments:

Identity: The home plays a very important role in the development of a clear, stable definition and a positive evaluation of the self for children. Choice and autonomy are critical issues here. Observe how the space allows child to express identity through the personalization of space; through distinctive furnishings, toys/equipment, individual and family displays, and room or area differentiation; and through opportunities for making choices.

| 1 | 2 | 3 | 4 | 5 |
| no evidence | | some evidence | | a lot of evidence |

_____ Adapted toys/equipment
_____ Accessible full-length mirror
_____ Personal space for child (e.g., behind couch, in closet, tent)
_____ Child's art display
_____ Photo of child

Comments:

(continued)

Figure 2.   Room-by-room observation form.

Figure 2 *(continued)*

Stimulation: Children need home environments that provide opportunities for external stimulation.
Observe views from windows and porches; colors of room (bright?); amount of sunshine; variety of embellishments and decorations; amount of room to explore (nooks, crannies, closets, passages); banisters or stairs to slide down; a variety of textures, sounds, tastes, and smells—modalities other than the visual sense.

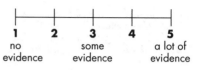

1	2	3	4	5
no evidence		some evidence		a lot of evidence

_____ Visual access to the outside
_____ Large motor skill opportunities
_____ Adaptive toys and switches
_____ Provision for learning skills appropriate for the room (e.g., cooking, setting the table in the kitchen, sorting laundry in the laundry room)
_____ Variety of sights, sounds, textures, aromas
_____ Pets part of the home

Comments:

Environmental manipulation: Children derive satisfaction from actively manipulating and changing the environment.
Observe the degree to which the area can be changed or modified by the child. Observe movable furnishings or materials and closets or storage areas that the child uses as play spaces.

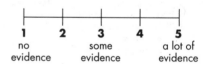

1	2	3	4	5
no evidence		some evidence		a lot of evidence

_____ Toys modified
_____ Low shelves, drawers, cupboards, and so on used to make toys, clothes, materials, equipment accessible
_____ Steep stairs and other hazards safe
_____ Modifications for wheelchairs/special equipment

Comments:

(continued)

Figure 2 (continued)

Privacy: Children need to be able to physically withdraw as well as have psychological distancing to obtain privacy. Observe how space can be regulated to ensure privacy for the child (private bedroom, bathroom, play and reading spaces, tents, cubbies, etc.).

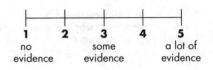

_____ Bedroom not shared
_____ Tent available (blanket over chairs, table, etc.)
_____ Toilet that can be used without assistance
_____ Shower curtain for bath time
_____ Stereo/radio headphones for private listening

Comments:

Sociability: The home is a setting in which children satisfy social needs by participating in a cohesive family unit, by inviting friends to take part in a variety of activities, and by sharing living quarters with siblings. Observe interaction spaces or activities (room to share meals, play games, watch movies and TV, have conversations, etc.).

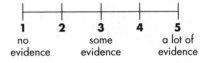

_____ Safe outdoor play space evident
_____ Indoor play space that accommodates child with disabilities and other children
_____ Mobility provided for child with disabilities to move throughout the room and from room to room.

Comments:

in the children's rooms were placed very high on the wall; sometimes children's awards were hung in their rooms.

Only a few children had access to mirrors in which they could see themselves completely. Full-length mirrors in a child's room were unusual. In some homes, the only mirror was over the bathroom sink. One family, however, had modified their child's bedroom by placing the mattress on the floor and a mirror horizontally alongside it.

Of the families whose children used a wheelchair or walker at school, only one child used it regularly at home. In this home, remodeling had been done with

Table 1. Summary of findings related to independence and dimensions of self-identity

Access to shelves for toys	Access to clothes	Access to bed	Artwork displays	Pictures/photograph displays	Access to mirror
Generally, children are provided access to toys, primarily available on the floor. Some toys throughout the house, low shelves, and storage boxes.	Almost no access to clothes, clothes hanging too high to reach. Where clothing is accessible, however, mom usually selects.	Lowering the bed, mattress on the floor, lower bed frames provide most children access to their bed. Several parents chose, instead, to lift child in and out of bed.	Children's artwork displays are surprisingly limited, mostly on the refrigerator and some in the child's room. Four families displayed no children's artwork at all.	Displays of family photographs were observed throughout most homes. In homes where there were no photographs, there were also no children's artwork displays.	Only three children had access to mirrors in which they could see themselves entirely. Placement of mirrors tends to be out of reach or in mirror sizes that allow only facial views or partial views.

Access to special equipment indoors	Access to equipment outdoors	Participates in cooking	Access to kitchen equipment, dishes, etc.	Privacy	Visual access to outside
Only one of the children who used a wheelchair used it regularly at home. Six children with wheelchairs and walkers were rarely permitted to use them inside the home.	Two children had motorized toys; another had an adapted tricycle. Swingsets and toys were found outside, but accessibility was questionable.	Parents' concerns about hazards prevent most children from participating in cooking or food preparation tasks.	About half the children had access to kitchen spaces, with some children allowed to get treats. Generally, parents were reluctant to allow children use of the kitchen.	Toileting independently was especially difficult to achieve. Children sometimes bathed alone, but parents perceived safety risks. Children achieved time alone by being out of view.	Low windows and ceiling-to-floor windows provide most children with access to outdoors. Several children had limited or no view of outside.

wheelchair accessibility in mind. Several of the parents simply did not permit the use of this equipment in the home. Space limitations and perceived hazards or damage to walls and furnishings were usually cited as reasons for this decision. One mother indicated, however, that the one wheelchair they could afford had to be kept at school because it was too difficult (heavy and cumbersome) to bring back and forth on a daily basis.

We are reluctant to make recommendations based on the results of a pilot study. However, we have heard repeatedly from families that they want, but get, very little advice on home modifications, safety, toy selection, and ways to better accommodate their children. Adaptations or modifications in the home might be identified as outcomes by some families during the individualized planning process (e.g., individualized family service plans, individualized education programs). Actual strategies and printed materials about accommodating home environments, including low-tech and inexpensive assistive technology, could serve families well. The pilot study raises questions such as, how prevalent is the observation that children have restricted use of wheelchairs and walkers in the home. The ability to move freely through the home seems a basic requirement of promoting skills of self-determination.

PLANNING FOR THE FUTURE

The expansion of opportunities for children with disabilities to make choices and have control in their environments is a dominant theme in disability literature (Brown, Belz, Corsi, & Wenig, 1993; Newton, Horner, & Lund, 1991; Schloss, Alper, & Jayne, 1993; Shevin & Klein, 1984; Wehmeyer, 1992a, 1992b). Because the home is such a meaningful part of the human experience, it is important to understand both its physical and cognitive role for children with disabilities. Learning to make one's own decisions and care for oneself and others are not skills that an individual begins to develop or exercise easily in adulthood (Brotherson, Backus, Summers, & Turnbull, 1986). The skills of self-determination, like self-confidence, choice, and decision making, are acquired through lifelong experiences that begin in childhood and continue through adulthood. In childhood, choices begin with daily opportunities in the home to make decisions about where and when to engage in everyday activities, such as eating and dressing, or participation in family and neighborhood activities.

Over the last decade, the accessibility of the physical environment for persons with disabilities has been increasingly emphasized. The intent of recent legislation, most notably the Americans with Disability Act (ADA) (PL 101-336), is the integration of individuals with disabilities into the mainstream of American life. Furthermore, current research in the area of adult services suggests expanding the delivery of residential options for adults with disabilities to include owning their own homes (O'Brien, 1994; Racino, Walker, O'Connor, & Taylor, 1993). This research argues that home ownership can improve quality of life by the development of a sense of place, control over selecting a place to live and with whom to live, and the security of place that comes from an increased sense of stability and personal security. Recognized as legitimate tenants, individuals with disabilities can make choices about caregivers, support services, and the house and neighborhood in which they reside. The movement toward home ownership is gaining momentum. It should be clear that decisions as significant as those involved in home ownership require the development of skills and a positive self-identify that begin early in childhood at home.

Children are dependent on their parents and families to provide shelter and learn early the cultural meaning and family values ascribed to rooms and objects within the home (Morris & Winter, 1978). Families are in the best position to offer suggestions and alternatives on how to accommodate to the individual needs of their children. As managers of the home environment, parents' attitudes toward self-determination and toward behaviors leading to self-determination are important. Because the home is the private sanctuary of families, however, intervention in this arena has often been limited. Early intervention can help parents develop a set of expectations for integrated community life and provide home environments that promote the development of self-determination and a positive self-identity. Parents need information to understand the importance of making adaptations in the home environment and support for making those adaptations in the home.

There are a number of home modifications suggested in the literature that are not necessarily costly to families in terms of time and money. Some communities are beginning to organize toy and equipment showrooms and lending libraries for families with children with disabilities to see available items and get information from families in similar circumstances. Each family has a finite amount of time, money, physical home space, and support network for making home modifications. Families will want to examine their own priorities, balance needs, and define the most important quality of life outcomes for them. Professionals can provide information and assist with family problem solving and decision making to help families set home environment goals.

In our view, the home is a learning environment. Research on the home environment of children with disabilities has been limited. Two important questions remain unanswered. First, how can self-determination in the home be measured and defined? Second, once defined, do homes arranged to provide more control and self-management help prepare children with disabilities for the choices they will make in the future? It seems likely that research efforts to answer these fundamental questions will, on the one hand, require tools and protocol to systematically assess the home environment, and on the other, require longitudinal investigations. Furthermore, research of this type must begin from the premise that there is no social environment that is not also a physical environment (Gump, 1987). Both components—social and physical—are available to manipulate on behalf of children with disabilities.

If the arrangement of the home environment is actually to work to the advantage of children with disabilities, their family members all must benefit as well. A child with a disability who becomes more self-sufficient, who has more joy in her or his life circumstances can turn that around to the benefit of all family members. Working in concert, educators, advocates, families, and children with disabilities themselves, can promote opportunities that allow children to make choices in schools, at home, and in the communities in which they ultimately will reside.

REFERENCES

Americans with Disabilities Act of 1990 (ADA), PL 101-336. (July 26, 1990). Title 42, U.S.C. 12101 et seq: *U.S. Statutes at Large, 104*, 327–378.

Altman, I., & Wohlwill, J.F. (Eds.). (1978). *Children and the environment.* New York: Plenum.

Barker, R. (1968). *Ecological psychology: Concepts and methods for studying the environment of human behavior.* Stanford, CA: Stanford University Press.

Barker, R., & Associates, Inc. (1978). *Habitats, environments and human behavior.* San Francisco: Jossey-Bass.

Becker, F.D. (1977). *Housing messages.* Stroudsburg, PA: Dowden, Hutchinson and Ross.

Bigge, J.L. (1991). *Teaching individuals with physical and multiple disabilities.* New York: Macmillan.

Broady, M. (1972). Social theory in architectural design. In R. Gutman (Ed.), *People and buildings* (pp. 170–188). New York: Basic Books.

Bronfenbrenner, U. (1979). *The ecology of human development.* Cambridge, MA: Harvard University Press.

Brotherson, M.J., Backus, L.H., Summers, J.A., & Turnbull, A.P. (1986). Transition to adulthood. In J.A. Summers (Ed.), *The right to grow up: An introduction to adults with developmental disabilities* (pp. 17–44). Baltimore: Paul H. Brookes Publishing Co.

Brotherson, M.J., Cook, C.C., Mise, I., & Weigel-Garrey, C. (1994, April). *Homes to support children with disabilities.* Paper presented at the meeting of the Division of Early Childhood, Council of Exceptional Children, St. Louis.

Brown, F., Belz, P., Corsi, L., & Wenig, B. (1993). Choice diversity for people with severe disabilities. *Education and Training in Mental Retardation, 28*, 318–326.

Buysse, V. (1993). Friendships of preschoolers with disabilities in community-based child care settings. *Journal of Early Intervention, 17*, 380–395.

Clarke-Stewart, A. (1986). Family day care: A home away from home? *Children's Environments Quarterly, 3*(1), 34–46.

David, T., & Weinstein, C. (1987). The built environment and children's development. In C. Weinstein & T. David (Eds.), *Spaces for children* (pp. 3–20). New York: Plenum.

Dodge, D.T., Koralek, D.G., & Pizzolongo, P.J. (1989). *Caring for preschool children* (Vol. 1). Washington, DC: Teaching Strategies.

Feldman, R.M. (1990). Settlement-identity: Psychological bonds with home places in a mobile society. *Environment and Behavior, 22*(2), 183–229.

Gaunt, L. (1980). Can children play at home? In P.F. Wilkinson (Ed.), *Innovation in play environments* (pp. 194–205). London: Croom Helm.

Gump, P.V. (1987). School and classroom environments. In D. Stokols & I. Altman (Eds.), *Handbook of environmental psychology* (pp. 692–732). New York: John Wiley & Sons.

Hanline, M.F., & Fox, L. (1993). Learning within the context of play: Providing typical early childhood experiences for children with severe disabilities. *Journal of The Association for Persons with Severe Handicaps, 18,* 121–129.

Hendershott, A.B. (1989). Residential mobility, social support, and adolescent self-concept. *Adolescence, 24,* 217–232.

Hovey, D.L. (1993). *Factors influencing home modifications in families who have children with physical disabilities.* Unpublished master's thesis, University of Minnesota, St. Paul.

Johnson, L.C. (1987). The developmental implications of home environments. In C.S. Weinstein & T.G. David (Eds.), *Spaces for children* (pp. 139–158). New York: Plenum.

Lang, M., & Sullivan, C. (1986). Adapting home environments for visually impaired and blind children. *Children's Environments Quarterly, 3*(1), 50–54.

Langley, M.B. (1985). Selecting, adapting, and applying toys as learning tools for handicapped children. *Topics in Early Childhood Special Education, 5*(3), 101–118.

Laufer, R.S., & Wolfe, M. (1977). Privacy as a concept and social issue: A multidimensional developmental theory. *Journal of Social Issues, 33*(3), 22–42.

Lawton, M.P. (1975). *Planning and managing housing for the elderly.* New York: John Wiley & Sons.

Lawton, M.P. (1989). Environmental proactivity in older people. In V.L. Bengtson & K.W. Schaie (Eds.), *The course of later life* (pp. 15–24). New York: Springer-Verlag.

Levitt, M.J., & Weber, R.A. (1989). Social involvement with peers in 2½-year-old toddlers: Environmental influences. *Environment and Behavior, 21*(1), 82–98.

Lewis, B.E. (1986). The stigmatized home: Why parents delay removing architectural barriers. *Children's Environments Quarterly, 3*(1), 63–67.

Miller, S. (1986). Designing the home for children: A need-based approach. *Children's Environments Quarterly, 3*(1), 55–62.

Moore, G.T. (1986). Effects of the spatial definition of behavior settings on children's behavior: A quasi-experimental field study. *Journal of Environmental Psychology, 6,* 205–231.

Morris, E.W., & Winter, M. (1978). *Housing, family, and society.* New York: John Wiley & Sons.

Newton, J.S., Horner, R.H., & Lund, L. (1991). Honoring activity preferences in individualized plan development: A descriptive analysis. *Journal of The Association for the Severely Handicapped, 16,* 207–212.

O'Brien, J. (1994). Down stairs that are never your own: Supporting people with developmental disabilities in their own homes. *Mental Retardation, 32,* 1–6.

Orford, J. (1992). *Community psychology: Theory and practice.* West Sussex, England: John Wiley & Sons.

Peterson, C.A., & McConnell, S.R. (1993). Factors affecting the impact of social interaction skills interventions in early childhood special education. *Topics in Early Childhood Special Education, 13*(1), 38–56.

Phyfe-Perkins, E. (1980). Children's behavior in preschool settings—A review of research concerning the influence of the physical environment. In L.G. Katz (Ed.), *Current topics in early childhood education* (Vol. 3, pp. 91–125). Norwood, NJ: Ablex.

Prescott, E. (1978). Is day care as good as home? *Young Children, 33*(2), 13–19.

Proshansky, H.M., & Fabian, A.K. (1987). The development of place identity in the child. In C.S. Weinstein & T.G. David (Eds.), *Spaces for children* (pp. 21–40). New York: Plenum.

Racino, J.A., Walker, P., O'Connor, S., & Taylor, S.J. (Eds.). (1993). *Housing, support, and community: Choices and strategies for adults with disabilities.* Baltimore: Paul H. Brookes Publishing Co.

Schloss, P.J., Alper, S., & Jayne, D. (1993). Self-determination for persons with disabilities: Choice, risk, and dignity. *Exceptional Children*, *60*, 215–225.

Sebba, R., & Churchman, A. (1983). Territories and territoriality in the home. *Environment and Behavior*, *15*(2), 191–210.

Shevin, M., & Klein, N.K. (1984). The importance of choice-making skills for students with severe disabilities. *Journal of The Association for the Severely Handicapped*, *9*(3), 159–166.

Staub, D., Salisbury, I.S., Gallucci, C., & Peck, C.A. (1994). Four portraits of friendship at an inclusive school. *Journal of The Association for Persons with Severe Handicaps*, *19*, 314–325.

Stokols, D., & Altman, I. (1987). *Handbook of environmental psychology*. New York: John Wiley & Sons.

Tognoli, J. (1987). Residential environments. In D. Stokols & I. Altman (Eds.), *Handbook of environmental psychology* (pp. 655–690). New York: John Wiley & Sons.

Wachs, T.D. (1986). Noise in the nursery: Ambient background noise and early development. *Children's Environments Quarterly*, *3*(1), 23–33.

Wachs, T.D. (1990). Must the physical environment be mediated by the social environment to influence development: A further test. *Journal of Applied Developmental Psychology*, *11*, 163–170.

Wehmeyer, M.L. (1992a). Self-determination: Critical skills for outcome-oriented transition services. *The Journal for Vocational Special Needs Education*, *15*, 3–7.

Wehmeyer, M.L. (1992b). Self-determination and the education of students with mental retardation. *Education and Training in Mental Retardation*, *27*, 302–311.

Wohlwill, J.F., & Heft, H. (1987). The physical environment and the development of the child. In D. Stokols & I. Altman (Eds.), *Handbook of environmental psychology* (pp. 281–328). New York: John Wiley & Sons.

Chapter 7

THE ECOLOGY OF SELF-DETERMINATION

Brian Abery and Roger Stancliffe

RICHARD IS AN assertive young man who has well-developed choice-making, problem-solving, and personal advocacy skills. He has repeatedly expressed a desire to take greater control over his life and has joined a self-advocacy group to further improve his capabilities within this area. His residence, the job he holds, and the activities in which he engages in his leisure time, however, are all based upon decisions made by others on his behalf.

Erin is an extroverted senior high school student who always attends her transition and educational planning meetings. Her teacher meets with her prior to every meeting and reviews the topics that will be discussed and the decisions to be made. During planning sessions, she is given numerous opportunities to voice her opinions and contribute to program development. Erin has great difficulty, however, articulating her personal vision for the future and rarely contributes to the formulation of the goals and objectives for her educational program.

At age 35, Angela is at a point in her life during which most individuals cherish the personal control they exercise. She has many friends and an active social life, but, when she finds herself in choice-making situations, she typically refuses to make decisions, seemingly wanting staff to take charge.

At the present time, Richard, Erin, and Angela have little control over their lives. Although it might at first appear that their lack of self-determination is due to a variety of factors, the basic problem confronting each of these individuals is quite similar. The environment(s) in which they developed or currently reside do

Preparation of this chapter was supported by a research project funded through the U.S. Department of Education, Office of Special Education Programs, Grant No. H023J2001 and by a cooperative agreement between the National Institute on Disability and Rehabilitation Research (NIDRR) and the Research and Training Center on Residential Services and Community Living at the University of Minnesota, College of Education and Human Development, located within the Institute on Community Integration. The opinions expressed herein are those of the authors, and no official endorsement by cooperating agencies should be inferred.

not adequately support their self-determination. Richard's difficulties revolve around significant others in his current environment failing to provide him with sufficient opportunities to make his own decisions. Erin's situation during her childhood was quite similar to Richard's current predicament. Rarely was she allowed to make choices by family members or the educational staff with whom she worked. Predictably, Erin failed to acquire and refine many of the capacities necessary for self-determination. Angela has lived within a moderately large residential facility for the past 14 years. Observations of social interactions within the residence suggest that her attempts to exercise self-determination are typically ignored or punished by staff.

Many professionals would conclude that the lack of personal control exercised by Richard, Erin, and Angela is a result of their lacking the competencies necessary for self-determination. Conceptual models of self-determination developed by Wehmeyer (1992), Field and Hoffman (1994), and Mithaug (1991) quite comprehensively delineate the most critical individual capacities necessary for self-determination. Self-determination, however, is more than a collection or composite of skills, knowledge, or beliefs. Rather, it is a result of a dynamic interaction between individuals and the environments in which they live (Abery, 1994).

This chapter explores the self-determination process from an ecological perspective—a framework that recognizes the contributions of the individual and the environment and the synergistic relationship that exists between the two. First, an argument is made for the necessity of taking an ecological approach to understanding self-determination. Second, an ecological framework for self-determination is presented, and the manner in which ecological factors influence both opportunities for personal control and the acquisition of the capacities necessary for self-determination is explored. Third, the implications of current work on the ecological antecedents of self-determination for research, theory, and practice are discussed.

NEED FOR AN ECOLOGICAL PERSPECTIVE

What is self-determination? The current research literature is far from complete. It does appear clear, however, that it is a complex *process*. This process can be viewed as driven by the intrinsic motivation of each of us to be the primary determiner of our thoughts, feelings, and behavior (Abery, 1994). Although there is currently no generally accepted definition of self-determination, most professionals view the construct from a perspective that stresses the internal attributes of the individual. Various conceptual frameworks have identified goal setting, choice making, problem solving, self-regulation, personal advocacy skills, knowledge of self and the external environment, and a host of motivational factors (e.g., locus of control, sense of self-efficacy) as necessary for the exercise of personal control (Abery, 1994; Field & Hoffman, 1994; Mithaug, 1991; Wehmeyer 1992). As Ward (1994) has cautioned, however, one can possess self-advocacy skills and not advocate for oneself and have sufficient decision-making skills and not make choices.

By focusing primarily on the individual, many models have not adequately acknowledged the important role of environmental factors in the self-determination process. Self-determination does not occur within a vacuum. The capacities necessary for the exercise of personal control are acquired, refined, and utilized within a variety of contexts. These environments, which change on a moment-to-moment, daily, and long-term basis, are likely to have a profound influence on the degree of control an individual exercises. Some environmental factors may facilitate self-determination, others are likely to serve as barriers to enhanced personal control. Rather than ignoring the impact of environmental factors, it is time to acknowledge the significant role that such variables play in the individual's quest for self-determination.

RECOGNITION OF ENVIRONMENTAL INFLUENCES ON BEHAVIOR

As examined by Cook, Brotherson, Weigel-Garrey and Mize (Chapter 6), recognition of the important influence of the environment on behavior is not a recent phenomenon. For many years, it has been widely accepted that a person's actions are at least partially determined by contextual stimuli. At one end of the spectrum, the behavioral/operant learning tradition (e.g., Skinner, 1953; Watson, 1925) focused almost exclusively on the manner in which external stimuli exert control over behavior. Closely related to this notion of environmental determinism is the idea of the situational specificity of behavior (Mischel, 1968). This belief in environmental determinism has been supplanted in recent years by a characterization of behavior as resulting from a continuous, reciprocal interaction between the individual and his or her environment (Bandura, 1977). Within this framework, the environment is conceptualized as affecting the individual while at the same time the individual's behavior is thought to affect the environment.

Recognition of the impact of the environment upon behavior has, over the past several decades, led to numerous changes in legislation and basic assumptions underlying the manner in which individuals with disabilities are served. Service delivery principles have, at least philosophically, begun to stress rights and freedom, personal choice, and individual decision making. Legislation has been passed in some states giving individuals with disabilities considerably greater authority over decisions directly affecting their lives.

Although professionals have begun to accept that the potential for self-determination exists within all people with disabilities regardless of age, level of severity, or type of disability, recent research demonstrates that this potential often remains unrealized (Abery & Eggebeen, 1993; Baker, Seltzer, & Seltzer, 1974, 1977; Barlow & Kirby, 1991; Colorado Division for Developmental Disabilities, 1992; Kishi, Teelucksingh, Zollers, Park-Lee, & Meyer, 1988; Parmenter, Briggs, & Sullivan, 1991; Sands & Kozleski, 1994). At the same time, however, available investigations offer hope for the enhanced self-determination of people with disabilities. Recent findings suggest that some people with disabilities exercise relatively high levels of self-determination (Stancliffe, 1995). In addition, programs designed to enhance the self-determination opportunities of people with disabilities (e.g., Abery, Rudrud, Arndt, Schauben, & Eggebeen, 1995; Hoffman & Field, 1995; Serna & Lau-Smith, 1995; Wehmeyer, 1995) have shown considerable promise. Such findings demonstrate that low levels of self-determination are not inevitable outcomes for people with disabilities. Rather, they suggest that if individuals are provided with environments that effectively support self-determination they will be more likely to acquire and effectively use strategies that will allow them to take greater control over their lives.

If, as is also discussed by Wehmeyer (Chapter 2), it is accepted that self-determination does not "lie within the person" but rather is a product of an interaction between the individual and the environment, then it becomes critical to examine those aspects of the ecology that serve to either support or act as barriers to the exercise of personal control. One conceptual framework that holds great promise for enhancing understanding of the multiple environmental factors related to self-determination is the ecological perspective.

AN ECOLOGICAL FRAMEWORK FOR SELF-DETERMINATION

Viewed from an ecological perspective, self-determination can be conceptualized as a product of an ongoing interaction between individuals and the multiple environments within which they function. Based upon this assumption, Abery (1994) has proposed an ecological theory of self-determination drawing on the work of Bronfenbrenner (1977) and Garbarino (1982). The ecological approach does not eschew the importance of personal characteristics in the individual's quest for self-determination. There are a multitude of factors at the individual level that have an impact upon self-determination, many of which have been previously reviewed (see Abery, 1994; Field & Hoffman, 1994; Mithaug, 1991; Tymchuk, 1985; Wehmeyer, 1994). What an ecological framework contributes is the placement of these personal capacities within a broader perspective—a perspective that views the individual within an environmental context. The units of analysis for the study of self-determination therefore begin with the person but also extend outward to the individual's ecosystem. This ecosystem can be viewed as consisting of four different levels, ranging from the smallest to the largest:

1. Microsystem
2. Mesosystem
3. Exosystem
4. Macrosystem

Consistent with an ecological approach, one would expect a variety of environmental factors to be associated with the exercise of self-determination and the availability of opportunities for personal control. At the current time, however, there is an enormous gap in our knowledge of the manner in which the environment influences self-determination. In addition, much of the research that has been conducted within this area takes an oversimplified approach to evaluating the influence on self-determination of isolated environmental variables. Although limited, this research base does provide a starting point for beginning to understand the complex relationship between the person and the environment as it relates to self-determination. In the following sections of this chapter, an overview of available research pertaining to environmental influences on self-determination is provided as conceptualized through an ecological framework (Abery, 1994). This body of studies draws from a number of sources and includes research results based upon work with people with a variety of disabilities ranging in age from early childhood to the adult years.

Microsystem Influences on Self-Determination

The immediate settings in which individuals develop and spend their daily lives are referred to as their *microsystem* (Garbarino, 1982). This construct embodies not just a physical setting but also the pattern of activities, roles, and interpersonal relations experienced by the individual within these contexts (Bronfenbrenner, 1979). The relevant features of the microsystem include not only the objective properties of specific settings but also the manner in which these properties are subjectively perceived and interpreted by the individuals who populate each setting.

The typical microsystem settings within which self-determination is acquired and exercised include the family or other residential setting, school, and/or work context. Face-to-face interactions that occur between individuals within each of these settings have a profound influence upon both the acquisition and behavioral manifestation of self-determination (Abery, 1994). These microsystem contexts are discussed below.

Family Context As described by Cook and colleagues in Chapter 6, the initial setting within which most people function is the family, and it is therefore the first context within which self-determination is learned and refined. As individuals with disabilities reach adulthood and leave their family for independent living situations or community residential settings, spouses, roommates, staff, and/or fellow residents assume the roles previously played by family members. Through direct instruction and observational learning within the family/residential environment, individuals acquire the skills, knowledge, and attitudes necessary for self-determination.

The opportunity to exercise choice, engage in decision making, and regulate one's behavior within the framework of family relationships provides children the chance to practice skills and develop the belief systems that will eventually allow them to exert control over their lives as adults. Developmental outcomes as diverse as achievement motivation, independence, autonomy, and responsibility have all been linked to family interaction and parenting styles that allow children personal choice (Baumrind, 1967, 1977).

As early as the first few days after birth, the seminal underpinnings of self-determination begin to develop (see Doll, Sands, Wehmeyer, & Palmer, Chapter 5). Through their vocalizations, crying, and nonverbal behavior, infants quickly exert a controlling influence on their environment. This control is, at first, mediated through parents (Ainsworth, 1979; Perry, 1980). Attachment theorists (e.g., Egeland & Farber, 1984; Sroufe, Fox, & Pancake, 1983) stress the importance of caregivers becoming attuned and responding to such "infant communication" because they are the child's first attempts to gain some rudimentary degree of control over the environment. If parents and other family members ignore a child's attempts to exercise control, become highly skilled at recognizing and responding to unspoken preferences, provide few opportunities for choice making, or fail to allow a child to experience the consequences of choices, the end result may be a person who rarely expresses preferences, has a difficult time making decisions, and cannot effectively problem-solve. Although such an environment may alleviate short-term distress, it is often at odds with the desire of most families to eventually facilitate their child experiencing a high level of inclusion within the community.

Despite the obvious importance of the family in the development of self-determination, relatively little research has been conducted within this area. The large majority of published work has focused, not on children and youth, but on adults with developmental disabilities who have remained living at home. The results of this research suggest that, whether they live with biological or foster families, adults with mental retardation find that opportunities for the exercise of self-determination are quite low. In general, it appears that when youth and adults with developmental disabilities live at home, parents exercise a large degree of control and protection, providing low levels of autonomy in all but the most basic aspects of life (Cattermole, Jahoda, & Markova, 1988). The autonomy of adults with mental retardation living in foster homes has also been found to be considerably less than that of people who reside in nonfamily-based settings (Baker et al., 1974, 1977). In fact, evidence suggests that consumer satisfaction with levels of autonomy allowed within various community residential contexts is lowest among individuals living with their own (or with foster) families (Burchard, Hasazi, Gordon, & Yoe, 1991; Gollay, Freedman, Wyngaarden, & Kurtz, 1978; Seltzer & Seltzer, 1978). This may be related to less importance being placed on the assumption of personal responsibility and self-determination by parents as compared to staff (Bartnik & Winkler, 1981).

Other research on family influences on self-determination has focused on characteristics of the relationships that exist between parents and their adult children with disabilities. Zetlin, Turner, and Winik (1987) classified the relationships between parents and their adult children with disabilities as supportive (35%), dependent (22%), or conflict-ridden (13%). The remaining 30% were older and coped without the support of their parents. A central dimension of such relationships was independence in decision making. Supportive parents, while providing ongoing social–emotional support, had ceased making decisions for their adult child. Parents who maintained dependent relationships had adult children who deferred to them with respect to most decisions. Conflict-ridden relationships were characterized by parent–child disputes over the amount of support considered necessary and expectations concerning autonomy.

In the 1990s, research has been initiated on the family's influence on the self-determination of children and youth with disabilities. Abery and Eggebeen (1993) examined family-based opportunities for the exercise of self-determination among young adults with mental retardation or physical disabilities with no cognitive impairment and a comparison group of peers without disabilities. Young adults with mental retardation were found to exercise less self-determination than their peers without disabilities or with physical disabilities only. Of importance to this discussion was the finding that the exercise of self-determination within the home could not be fully explained/predicted on the basis of personal characteristics alone (e.g., disability type, IQ, level of self-determination skills). Although individual competencies were related to levels of personal control, the extent to which children were allowed opportunities for control within the context of the family also contributed significantly to the degree of self-determination exercised. Additional investigations conducted by this research group (Abery, McGrew, & Smith, 1995) have expanded these results to include younger children and those with other disabilities, including learning disabilities, behavior disorders, autism, deaf-blindness, and mental retardation that requires significant support. More specifically, in a sample of over 250 students with disabilities and a comparison group of peers without disabilities ranging in age from 5 to 21 years, predictions of the levels of self-determination exercised by students within the home and community were significantly improved when the environmental variable, *family opportunities for personal control*, was taken into consideration.

Some children, regardless of whether or not they have disabilities, have substantially greater opportunities than others for self-determination within the home. Not surprisingly, the chance to exercise self-determination appears closely linked with the degree of personal control children and youth actually have over their lives. It is not yet clear which specific family factors underlie the differences between families with respect to this phenomenon. The degree to which children and youth are given the occasion to take an age-appropriate degree of control over their lives may be related to parenting methods (Baumrind, 1967, 1977), family interaction style (Olson, 1993), cultural and religious beliefs, socioeconomic status, and a host of other factors. What does appear clear is that if researchers are to develop effective programs to enhance self-determination, greater attention needs to be paid to the manner in which the family environment supports the development of self-determination.

Community Living Settings   Adults without disabilities typically have control over most aspects of their lives including where they reside, with whom they live, and in what type of work they engage (Kozleski & Sands, 1992; Sands & Kozleski, 1994). Unfortunately, this often is not the case for people with disabilities. Many research studies have reported levels of self-determination among adults with moderate to severe disabilities living in community settings that are obviously far more restrictive than is typical for adults in our society (Baker et al., 1974, 1977; Barlow & Kirby, 1991; Colorado Division for Developmental Disabilities, 1992; Kishi et al., 1988; Parmenter et al., 1991; Raynes, Johnson, Sumpton, & Thorp, 1987; Sands & Kozleski, 1994; Seltzer & Seltzer, 1978; Wehmeyer & Metzler, 1995).

Simply living in a community setting by no means ensures access even to the most routine opportunities for self-determination. Although two recent studies (Stancliffe, 1995; Stancliffe & Wehmeyer, 1995) reported higher levels of choice availability among adults with mental retardation living in noninstitutional settings, one common feature of both of these research efforts was that they included substantial numbers of people who lived independently or semi-independently. Does this style of living provide more opportunities for self-determination? Many people with mental retardation think that the answer to this question is yes. As one man explained, "I want my own apartment. I want to be on my own and go out when I want, come home [when I want] you know. . . ."

Do research findings support this man's expectation that living semi-independently in his own apartment will provide more opportunities for self-determination? Group home residents do have significantly less access to self-determination than individuals living semi-independently or independently (Burchard et al., 1991; Colorado Division for Developmental Disabilities, 1992; Schalock, Keith, & Hoffman, 1990; Seltzer & Seltzer, 1978; Stancliffe, 1994b; Stancliffe & Wehmeyer, 1995). Some would argue that these differences are simply due to variations in the characteristics of people with disabilities residing in these types of residential settings. Individuals with cognitive disabilities who require low levels of support tend to be overrepresented in semi-independent living programs (Harner & Heal, 1993; Hill, Lakin, & Bruininks, 1988). Intellectual functioning and adaptive behavior are also known to be related to self-determination (Abery & Eggebeen, 1993; Colorado Division for Developmental Disabilities, 1992; Kishi et al., 1988; Schalock, 1994; Schalock et al., 1990; Stancliffe & Wehmeyer, 1995). The greater personal capacities of people living semi-independently could account for their elevated opportunities for self-determination. Recent studies, however, have shown that this is not the case. Using statistical methods to hold constant the influence of level of ability, Stancliffe (1994b) and Stancliffe and Wehmeyer (1995) have demonstrated that differences in opportunities for and the exercise of self-determination among people living in different community settings remain substantial. Individuals living independently and semi-independently still appear to have the most opportunities for personal control over their lives, compared with those living with family, in group homes, or in institutions.

What are the factors associated with residential programs that appear to inhibit self-determination? The work of Stancliffe (1994b) identified two of the variables that need to be considered: 1) staff presence and 2) the number of individuals served. More specifically, the fewer hours staff spend within a community residence and the smaller the number of people for whom they are responsible, the greater the opportunities for self-determination. These effects appear to hold true even after the influence of level of ability and decision-making skills are taken into account. Related findings have been reported in qualitative studies of residential programs concerning the effects of group living on self-determination (Bennett, Shaddock, & Guggenheimer, 1992; Stancliffe, 1991). The very presence of staff can apparently serve as a barrier to residents assuming personal control. Residents may be reluctant to voice or act on their true preferences in the presence of staff, deferring instead to staff opinion. They may also feel a need to seek out staff approval prior to engaging in a course of action. Clearly, it would be simplistic to suggest that enhancing self-determination is merely a matter of reducing or eliminating staff support. Rather, these findings are a reminder that opportunities for self-determination are mostly likely to be available in the absence of authority figures, and that exercising control in these circumstances is an important criterion for achieving self-determination.

School and Work Environments   A third context within which self-determination develops and is exercised is the school, an environment that is replaced during adulthood by the work setting. The classes students select, the manner in which they complete their assignments, their extracurricular activities, and the people with whom they associate are all aspects of self-determination exercised by most children and youth during the school years. Upon completing their education, the majority of individuals choose an occupation and select the specific employment opportunities they will pursue. While the flexibility available in specific occupations varies greatly, most people are also able to exert at least some control over the hours they work, when they will take breaks, the manner in which they complete assigned job-related tasks, and the time periods during which they will take vacations.

The importance of providing a school environment that facilitates self-determination has been pointed out by a number of researchers. Instruction within the areas of choice making, problem solving, self-advocacy, and self-regulation have developed into stand-alone curricula or incorporated into special education programs developed by a number of educators (e.g., Abery, Rudrud, et al., 1995, Hoffman & Field, 1995; Martin & Marshall, 1995; Wehmeyer, 1995). At the present time, however, such instruction is included in only a small number of educational programs. Additionally, the results of research efforts indicate that the typical special education classroom may serve more as a barrier than a catalyst to self-determination.

Orlansky (1979) described educational programs for students with severe disabilities as "too controlling" and "overprogrammed." Other researchers (e.g., Guess, Benson, & Siegel-Causey, 1985; Guess & Siegel-Causey, 1985; Peck, 1985) have focused on the negative effects of highly programmed classroom routines that often feature strong adult control over student behavior. The results of these studies revealed high levels of teacher directiveness and few opportunities for student control across both teachers and task situations. In addition, teachers and paraprofessionals have been found to respond infrequently to student expressions of preference and choice, with the majority of the few choices offered restricted to highly structured, programmed activities (Houghton, Bronicki, & Guess,1987).

The lack of opportunities for students with a much wider variety of types and levels of disability to exercise personal control within the context of the school has recently been documented. Abery and Eggebeen (1993) have reported that transition-age students with either mental retardation or physical but no cognitive disabilities have few opportunities for self-determination during the typical school day. Extending their work to students with other disabilities and ages, the findings of this research group also indicate that across all age and disability conditions, students with disabilities have little opportunity to exercise control over their educational environments (Abery, McGrew, et al., 1995). Experiences of this type would be likely to lead any individual, with or without a disability, to eventually conclude that he or she cannot exercise personal control, his or her preferences are irrelevant, and adults are the decision makers.

Although research indicates that children and youth with disabilities have few opportunities for self-determination within the context of the school, it might be hoped that, upon reaching adulthood, these individuals would assume greater control within the context of their employment. Unfortunately, existing data demonstrate that this is not typically the case. Low levels of choice with respect to deciding one's place of employment have been reported by a number of researchers (e.g., Jenkinson, Copeland, Drivas, Scoon, & Yap, 1992; Kishi et al., 1988; Parmenter et al., 1991; Stancliffe, 1995; Stancliffe & Wehmeyer, 1995; Wehmeyer & Metzler, 1995). In addition, those opportunities for personal control that are available at work often appear to be quite banal, focusing on "here and now" matters requiring a yes/no response or choice between two concrete alternatives presented by supervisors (Shaddock, 1993).

Despite the findings of much of the research in this area, a lack of environmental support for self-determination is not characteristic of all work environments. Investigations suggest that greater opportunities for personal control are typically available to individuals who take part in programs that stress normalization or inclusion. People with disabilities taking part in community-based programs, for example, make significantly more choices than their counterparts working in sheltered workshops and small businesses employing primarily people with disabilities (Shaddock, 1993). Increased opportunities for personal control are apparently appreciated, as people with mental retardation who work in competitive employment programs have been found to report greater satisfaction about their freedom to make decisions at work than their peers who are employed in sheltered workshops (Jiranek & Kirby, 1990).

Individual Planning Just as people with disabilities may have limited opportunities to exercise personal control on a daily basis, it is also quite unusual for them to be actively involved in the development of their individual service plans. Although existing data are quite limited, it appears that, at the current time, most people with disabilities have little input into the development, implementation, and evaluation of their individual plans (Abery & Eggebeen, 1993; Shaddock & Bramston, 1991). Although innovative efforts are currently under way to develop a process for consumer-directed program planning (see, e.g., Martin & Marshall, 1995; Mount, 1987; O'Brien, 1987; Vandercook, York, & Forest, 1989), through the mid-1990s most service providers continue to use traditional staff-centered methods for program development.

Based upon the results of the extant research, there seems to be little doubt that adults with disabilities, especially those with significant support needs, experience low levels of self-determination with respect to the specific residential, employment, or day programs they attend (Jenkinson et al., 1992; Kishi et al., 1988; Parmenter et al., 1991; Shaddock & Bramston, 1991; Stancliffe, 1995; Stancliffe & Wehmeyer, 1995; Wehmeyer & Metzler, 1995). Research findings concerning job choice by consumers, especially with respect to more recently developed employment alternatives such as supported employment, reveal a somewhat more encouraging situation, but one with considerable room for improvement (Parent, 1993).

In summary, just as people with disabilities may have limited opportunities for self-determination within the context of family and residential settings, an analogous situation exists within school and employment/day programs. Despite recent mandates, it is quite unusual for such people to be actively involved in moment-to-moment decision making or in the development of individualized service and habilitation plans. Participation in goal setting and service planning decisions is, at best, something the service providers do in cooperation with parents and guardians. All too often, decisions regarding educational programs, job training opportunities, employment, and residential placements reflect the preferences and choices of well-meaning parents and staff. The individual most affected by such decisions is often given little voice in determining his or her future.

Enhancing Self-Determination: Microsystem Interventions

Few efforts have been directed at enhancing self-determination through changing the environment. The majority of intervention/program development work has focused instead on strengthening the various skills postulated to be related to self-determination. Outcome data from projects funded by the OSERS self-determination initiative (see Ward, Chapter 1) generally suggest that relatively short-term instructional programs have the potential to enhance many of the skills necessary for self-determination (Abery, Rudrud, et al., 1995; Hoffman & Field, 1995; Ludi & Martin, 1995; Martin & Marshall, 1995; Serna & Lau-Smith, 1995; Wehmeyer, 1995). Outcomes with respect to increases in the actual exercise of self-determination in everyday life were less clear. Other successful skill-based intervention programs involving adults (Foxx, Faw, Taylor, Davis, & Fulia, 1993; Heller, 1978; Reese, 1986; Tymchuk, Andron, & Rahbar, 1988) and preschoolers (Rietveld, 1983) are also available. Unfortunately, a number of these studies also suffer from an absence of data about the real-life application of the newly acquired self-determination skills.

Two published studies have specifically evaluated the effectiveness of increasing environmental support for self-determination. Working with educational staff serving students diagnosed with autism and mental retardation, Peck (1985) taught teachers and aides to change their interaction style with the students they served. This entailed staff increasing their responsiveness to and compliance with student-initiated communicative behavior, as well as providing more opportunities for choice making, student initiation, and student control of social interactions. This environmental intervention was successful in increasing student choice and control. Targeted student behaviors increased immediately following staff training while remaining at baseline levels for students served by staff not involved in training procedures. The immediate postintervention changes in student behavior strongly suggested that these children already had the skills needed to make more choices and that the crucial difference was a classroom environment that had previously made few opportunities available to exercise control.

Focusing on the family environment, Abery, Rudrud, et al. (1995) developed and field-tested an education and support program for families of young adults with disabilities with the goal of facilitating greater opportunities for self-determination at home. Those families taking part in the program met with instructors over a 9-month period and learned a variety of skills for supporting the exercise of self-determination. Following this intervention, students with disabilities were assessed as having increased opportunities for control within the context of the family, community, and with respect to a variety of personal health care issues. Increases in opportunities for control were accompanied by enhanced self-determination. This result was true even of those students whose self-determination *skills* (e.g., choice-making, personal advocacy, problem-solving skills) had not improved significantly during the intervention period. Once again, these findings point to the crucial role of environmental change for the exercise of greater personal control.

Some individuals with multiple disabilities and pervasive support needs do not currently possess the skills to effectively communicate their preferences. For these individuals, self-determination may most often be exercised through care-givers determining and responding to the person's preferences. Traditionally, preferences have been determined according to caregivers' judgments of the individual's desires because of the difficulty of obtaining reliable indications of preference directly from such individuals. Procedures have now been developed to directly assess preferences by presenting tangible items in repeated, structured preference assessment trials and carefully observing the person interacting with those items (Dattilo & Mirenda, 1987; Green et al., 1988; Mithaug & Mar, 1980; Pace, Ivancic, Edwards, Iwata, & Page, 1985; Parsons & Reid, 1990; Parsons, Reid, Reynolds, & Bumgarner, 1990; Realon, Favell, & Lowerre, 1990). Parsons and Reid (1990) and Parsons, McCarn, and Reid (1993) are among the researchers to have shown that regular staff could be trained to reliably undertake this type of choice assessment. Successful demonstrations of these procedures have occurred within experimental settings. They have not, however, been widely incorporated into day-to-day service provision within programs serving individuals with disabilities (see Parsons et al., 1993).

Environmental interventions of the type described may be contrasted with approaches that focus solely on the development of self-determination skills on the part of individuals with disabilities. It is difficult to envision how, given the substantial cognitive and linguistic requirements of many skill-based interventions, they would be applicable to people with serious disabilities. Total reliance on the skills of the individual with a disability implies that self-determination remains unavailable until specific competencies are developed. This appears difficult to justify when simple and effective environmental interventions are available to better meet the preferences of these people.

Mesosystem Influences on Self-Determination

The vast majority of all educational, psychological, and developmental research has focused on single settings or groupings of individuals. A typical person, however, functions within multiple settings on any given day. It is therefore necessary to take into account the *linkages* that exist between the multiple settings in which a person participates. These connections have been referred to as the *mesosystem* (Bronfenbrenner, 1989; Garbarino, 1982). The existence, strength, and valence of the linkages that exist between settings is likely to have a profound impact upon an individual's self-determination. In the absence of research, current conceptualizations with respect to the manner in which the mesosystem influences self-determination are primarily theoretically based, extrapolated from existing studies focusing on other developmental outcomes. The results of these investigations, however, make a powerful case for the importance of these linkages if one's goal is to enhance the self-determination of people with disabilities.

School–Family Linkages Since the mid-1980s, considerable attention has been given to the study of the extent to which school–family linkages have an impact on student outcomes. Parent participation, involvement, and communication with the school have all been linked to student achievement. School–family collaboration has been associated with gains in reading and math performance as well as improvements in student behavior (Becher, 1984; Dornbusch, 1986; Epstein, 1986, 1987, 1988; Henderson, 1988). Strong, positive linkages between family and school have also been related to the development of positive attitudes toward education by both parents and children including student attitudes toward work, homework routines, and school in general (Christenson, Rounds, & Gorney, 1992; Henderson, 1988).

Despite ample research to suggest that family–school collaboration has a positive effect on student outcomes, it is often the case that the linkages that exist between family and school are tenuous at best. Numerous studies have found low levels of parent involvement in schools and poor communication between parents and educators. This tendency has been shown to be especially true of parents of students with disabilities (Davies, 1987; Epstein, 1986; Goldstein, Strickland, & Turnbull, 1980; Vaughn, Bos, Harrell, & Laskey, 1988). Barriers to increased collaboration have been found to include teacher attitudes and stereotypes, such as resistance to viewing parents as collaborators in the education process and a desire to keep them out of decision-making processes (Christenson, Rounds, & Gorney, 1992; Epstein, 1987).

Given the multiple outcomes with which family–school collaboration has been associated, little inference is necessary to conclude that these same linkages are likely to be crucial to self-determination. First, strong, positive connections between families and service providers will reinforce in one context learning that occurs in others, thus encouraging the generalization of skills. Second, ongoing information exchange is likely to ensure that attempts to exercise self-determination are supported in a similar manner across environments. Third, strong linkages between settings provide people with disabilities with opportunities to observe the degree to which specific behaviors are valued by individuals within different contexts. A student attending an individualized education planning meeting, for example, may have the opportunity to observe parents and other family members actively contributing to the process, their comments valued by service personnel and incorporated into the final educational plan.

Strong connections between the family and school are but one example of the necessity for the family to be closely linked to each of the environments within which the individual functions. As young adults leave school and home for community employment and residential programs, family–service provider connections remain critical.

Interagency Collaboration If one's goal is to enhance the self-determination of individuals with disabilities, collaboration must occur between the different agencies providing the individual with services. Consistency in the manner in which 1) program planning is handled, 2) staff respond to specific behaviors associated with self-determination, and 3) opportunities for personal control are provided is critical if individuals with disabilities are to develop and exercise those capacities necessary for self-determination. In the mid-1990s, however, it would appear that interagency collaboration is more the exception than the rule.

In spite of the current state of affairs, there are signs of improvement in the linkages between service systems, especially as this relates to the process of young adults transitioning from the school to the community. With the encouragement of the Office of Special Education Programs (OSEP) within the U.S. Department of Education, many states have developed local interagency committees that have the specific task of fostering interagency collaboration. These committees function to bring together professionals, families, and people with disabilities to ensure that service provision is a cooperative effort between school districts and their surrounding communities. Innovative service planning and delivery structures in the process of being evaluated, or in the planning stage, include 1) unitary service coordination across agencies; 2) the use of technology to better share information; 3) new referral processes for students needing to access community resources; and 4) the development of formal interagency agreements among schools, county social services, vocational rehabilitation agencies, and other community resources (Hunt, 1995). Although many of these approaches hold great promise and could be applied to the delivery of services to children as well as adults, in many states, coordinated services for people with disabilities remain a haphazard proposition at best.

Enhancing Self-Determination: Mesosystem Interventions

Conceptualizing a mesosystem as consisting of the relationships that exist between two or more settings, intervention at this level of the ecosystem needs to focus on enhancing the number, strength, positive valence, and diversity of these linkages. Since the mid-1980s, a number of programs have been developed aimed at enhancing family–school and interagency collaboration (see Christenson, Rounds, & Franklin, 1992; Johnson, Wallace, & Krawetz, 1994; Kagan, 1984). Although none of these projects have specifically reported on the extent to which enhanced relationships between settings influence self-determination, there is much to be learned from these efforts.

The results of a large number of school–family involvement studies have made it abundantly clear that if strong, positive multiple linkages are to be established between the family and service providers, families and professionals alike must view consumer learning and development as a shared responsibility and believe that their collaboration is directly linked to desired outcomes. The basic elements of such collaborative relationships include mutual respect for skills and knowledge, honest and clear communication, two-way sharing of information, mutually agreed upon goals, and shared planning and decision making (Christenson, Rounds, & Franklin, 1992). How do these recommendations translate into interventions that have the potential to enhance self-determination? Epstein (1987) offers a classification of types of school–family involvement that is both well-researched and likely to prove useful in developing strategies to increase collaboration. These classifications are discussed below

Providing Basic Support Providing basic support for individuals with disabilities is the first type of service provider–family linkage in Epstein's typology. As it relates to self-determination, this basic support might entail service providers providing information to families on parenting styles/skills, age-appropriate expectations, and strategies to build positive home learning conditions that will facilitate the acquisition of competencies for and the exercise of self-determination. Indirect service activities used to accomplish this goal might include distributing to parents printed material and videotapes relevant to self-determination and self-advocacy, establishing a self-advocacy lending library, organizing parent support programs, and offering workshops on self-determination. Although little information is currently available within this area, Abery et al. (1994) have developed and field-tested a family education and support program that provides information to family members of people with disabilities on the importance of self-determination as well as strategies that can be used to effectively support young adults with disabilities taking greater personal control over their lives. Direct service activities could include making home visits and counseling parents about specific ways to provide greater opportunities for self-determination within the home and community.

Improving Family–Service Provider Connections and Communication A second set of activities within the Epstein (1987) framework focuses on strengthening family–service provider connections through improved communication. Efforts to enhance self-determination within this area might include the development of frequent, efficient forms of communication between parents and staff that increase family members' awareness of the progress a student/client is making with respect to taking greater personal control as well as areas of needed improvement. It is important that these communications be used not only as an avenue through which to problem-solve about difficulties but also to focus on recognizing and celebrating accomplishments. Family service provider conferences provide another avenue through which to foster clear communication among parents, students/clients, and professionals. These meetings can be used not only to provide information to the family about observed progress but may serve as an opportunity for the adults involved to model self-determined behavior and for individuals with disabilities to practice and refine their capacities within this area.

Stimulating Family Involvement Stimulating family involvement at the school, residence, or place of employment is a third means through which to enhance self-determination. Within any type of service setting, the development of family volunteer programs provides parents and staff with an excellent occasion to gauge the consistency that exists across environments with respect to an individual's opportunities for choice and control. Ongoing involvement within service settings also allows both professionals and parents to model and observe the behaviors each has successfully used in stimulating enhanced self-determination.

Achieving Consistency Across Settings Consistency across settings is crucial to the development of those behaviors necessary for the exercise of personal control. To achieve this consistency, staff will need to master a variety of skills to prepare them to work effectively with parents and other family members. Providing staff with pre- and in-service training that prepares them to work effectively with families to establish home learning environments conducive to self-determination is therefore a fourth strategy to ensure the development of positive linkages between service providers and families. Furnishing family members with information and support to implement specific activities that will reinforce the competencies necessary for self-determination as well as providing them with the means to monitor the effectiveness of interventions used at home and in the community will greatly enhance the efficacy of the interventions employed.

   Encouraging Family Advocacy   A fifth type of family–service provider involvement entails encouraging families to take part in program decision making, governance, and advocacy. In some cases, service providers will need to recruit family members to fill existing roles, in others, participatory roles will need to be created. To accomplish this, staff need to train parent representatives in decision-making skills, collaboration, and ways to communicate with other parents about program issues. Family members can then become involved in the development of program policy and the creation or revision of the program's mission and vision such that it is supportive of self-determination.

Exosystem Influences on Self-Determination

The self-determination of people with disabilities is influenced not only by those settings in which they directly participate, but also by decisions and actions that occur within contexts that do not include them as an active participant. At this level of analysis, referred to as the *exosystem*, one considers the impact on more immediate settings of the external contexts within which they are imbedded (Bronfenbrenner, 1979). Events occurring at this level may affect the individual in both a direct and indirect manner.

   To date, there have been few attempts to explore the specific impact of exosystem level variables on personal growth. This does not imply, however, that less importance should be attributed to these variables. The manner in which an organization decides to develop, implement, and evaluate educational/service programs and the training staff receive, for example, are both likely to have a significant impact on the frequency with which opportunities for choice are allowed, the support provided to enhance decision making, and indirectly, the degree of control that consumers exercise. What are some of the factors at the exosystem level that have an impact on self-determination? One important influence is the manner in which providers develop service plans for the individuals whom they serve.

   Since the mid-1980s, a number of educational, residential, and employment service providers have become dissatisfied with traditional methods used in service planning. The typical individualized education program (IEP), individualized service plan (ISP), and individualized habilitation plan (IHP) meetings place decision-making power clearly in the hands of the professionals, and people with disabilities and their families take a back seat. It was in reaction to this state of affairs that a number of person-centered planning processes have been developed with the goal of empowering people with disabilities within the context of program planning. Making Action Plans (MAPS; formerly the McGill Action Planning System) (Forest & Lusthaus, 1987; Vandercook et al., 1989), Personal Futures Planning (Mount, 1987; Mount & Zwernik, 1988), LifeStyle Planning (O'Brien, 1987), and Planning Alternative Tomorrows with Hope (PATH) (Pearpoint, O'Brien, & Forest, 1993) are variants of these processes. The MAPS process has been used extensively by Forest and her colleagues to develop and implement inclusive educational programs for children and youth with disabilities. Personal Futures Planning (PFP), LifeStyle Planning (LSP), and variants of the two have been used with adults with developmental disabilities to facilitate the generation of service plans that more adequately meet their needs and foster a higher quality of life (Beare, Severson, Lynch, & Schneider, 1992; Malette et al., 1992; Newton, Horner, & Lund, 1991).

The decision on the part of a service provider to relinquish traditional service planning procedures in exchange for person-centered planning is a choice at the exosystem level that has the potential to significantly enhance opportunities and environmental support for self-determination. The commitment to service planning of this type, however, requires staff to develop a new way of thinking. This alternative mind-set must entail a focus on capabilities rather than disabilities, available resources rather than barriers, and the unique dreams of each person served as opposed to the desires of others.

Program Structure and Content Programmatic factors, including the degree of structure inherent in a program as well as the specific experiences to which people with disabilities are exposed are also likely to strongly influence the exercise of self-determination (Guess et al., 1985; Peck, 1985; Peck & Schuler, 1983). Program structure and content have a direct impact on self-determination at the microsystem level (i.e., the immediate behavioral context). However, because decisions regarding these factors are typically made at administrative and managerial levels in the absence of input from consumers and family, they must also be understood as exosystem factors.

Decisions made at the exosystem level also determine, in large part, program content. Some types of experiences/content are likely to facilitate decision-making and problem-solving capacities while others may not. Programming that 1) provides ongoing opportunities for people with disabilities to make and experience the consequences of decisions within community-based settings and 2) furnishes instructional experiences that foster the acquisition and refinement of the competencies necessary for personal control are likely to facilitate the development of self-determined individuals (Levine & Langness, 1985). The absence of these experiences will serve as a significant barrier to enhanced personal control.

Staff Autonomy and Self-Determination One aspect of the work setting that has been linked to self-determination is the degree of freedom staff have available in carrying out their day-to-day jobs. In at least one study (Packer & Wright, 1983), levels of direct service staff autonomy have been found to be strongly associated with levels of resident autonomy. The greater the autonomy allowed to direct service staff by residential management, the higher the level of personal control residents had over their own lives. In fact, the predictive power of levels of staff autonomy outstripped a wide variety of other factors often associated with personal control. The importance of staff autonomy as a factor related to self-determination was also suggested in a qualitative study designed to identify barriers to self-determination (Abery, Eggebeen, Rudrud, & Sharpe, 1991). Numerous educators commented on the difficulty they had providing students with opportunities and support for self-determination when they felt that they were rigidly "locked in" to specific curricula and procedures mandated by their schools or supervisors.

These results support the existence of a relationship between staff autonomy and self-determination. This connection, although needing to be confirmed by further research, clearly demonstrates the manner in which environmental factors play an indirect role in the personal control people with disabilities exercise over their lives. It suggests that decisions made at administrative levels that affect the atmosphere of the workplace and on staff roles must be taken into consideration in efforts to enhance self-determination.

Enhancing Self-Determination: Exosystem Interventions

In discussing strategies of restructuring and reform, Fullan (1993) argued that, "people underestimate the complexity of how systems operate" (p. 124) and suggested that change requires new skills and behaviors, but most of all new beliefs (Fullan, 1993). Whether one is attempting to enhance self-determination via reducing the structure of a program, providing staff with greater autonomy, or developing new strategies for program planning, some degree of change at the exosystem level is likely to be required. In addition, fundamental modifications may need to take place in the manner in which staff perceive and interact with the people whom they serve and in how staff view their roles as professionals. Specific strategies for facilitating the necessary changes within organizations to increase self-determination for people with disabilities have yet to be directly researched. Much can be learned, however, from an examination of the available systems change literature.

A review of various theories of organizational change (Anderson, 1993; Fullan, 1993; O'Neil, 1993; Wagner, 1993) indicates that if all parties involved do not support the process of change, it is unlikely the desired results will be achieved. One of the most productive ways to encourage necessary collaboration is to work initially at creating a shared vision of the desirable future among staff (Ysseldyke, Christenson, & Thurlow, 1993). Second, an organizational change program must identify priorities for change, the strategies that will be used to work toward desired outcomes, and the structures necessary to create and maintain change (Fullan, 1993). Third, an individualized program must be generated that not only educates staff and administrators but provides them with concrete strategies for achieving desired goals. A fourth and final consideration is the development and implementation of an evaluation program that allows those within the organization to track progress toward desired outcomes. A more detailed presentation of this organizational change process as it related to enhancing self-determination can be found in Table 1.

Person-Centered Program Planning   The preceding discussion focused upon a generic organizational change process. An example of a specific organizational change that has the potential to enhance self-determination is conversion from traditional models of program planning to those that are *person centered* in their focus. As described earlier in this chapter, personal futures planning and its variants have been used in an attempt to increase the control people with disabilities have over their lives. Although research efforts specifically designed to determine the extent to which these alternative planning processes actually increase consumer control is still quite rare, available results present an encouraging picture. Malette et al. (1992), for example, described the application of a person-centered procedure called the *lifestyle development process* (LDP). LDP is a five-step process through which individuals with disabilities, their families, direct care staff, and others 1) develop a vision of quality life in the community for the target individual; 2) assess and remediate service delivery and other barriers that interfere with the target individual's ability to participate in the community; 3) develop daily and weekly schedules that facilitate the individual working toward their preferred vision; 4) generate and implement consumer programs and staff training to promote the individual's behavioral, communication, and other skills; and 5) evaluate the effectiveness of these efforts in assisting the individual to attain their vision. In each of four studies Malette and colleagues reported, large increases (200% or greater in most cases) were evident in the number of preferred, integrated activities in which individuals engaged following the use of this process. Examining programs that used systems for developing and monitoring IHPs that included detailed methods for determining each person's preference for and participation in a wide variety of activities, Newton et al. (1991) found that a high proportion of participants' IHP objectives involved preferred activities. Although these studies were nonexperimental in nature, they do illustrate the potential influence of person-centered planning on the ability of individuals to control one important aspect of their lives—participation in preferred activities.

Restructuring Services to Emphasize Individual Choice   A number of more wide-ranging exosystem interventions have been implemented as a means of fostering enhanced self-determination. Brown, Bayer, and Brown (1992) provided a range of evidence on the positive outcomes of restructuring rehabilitation services for a large group of people with mental retardation. A

Table 1. Steps in systems change process

1. *Examination of programmatic strengths and weaknesses.* An examination of the strengths and weaknesses of participating programs is first undertaken to provide staff with feedback about structural and organization features of their service that enhance or inhibit self-determination experienced by persons with disabilities.

2. *Development of a unifying vision.* The development of a unifying vision of what programs that serve persons with disabilities should be like is a second step in the systems change process. Without the creation of a consensual vision that is broadly understood and easily translated into criteria for assessing results, organizational change efforts will quickly bog down.

3. *Generation of a coherent vision of service provision.* Through conducting consensus-building activities, participating service staff are encouraged to come to agreement on a core body of knowledge, skills, and capacities for the persons with disabilities whom they serve and on goals for organizational change.

4. *Identification of priorities and strategies for systems change.* Different organizations will evolve different priorities for change depending upon what they perceive as their most urgent needs. The identification of two or three priorities and strategies for systems change that will enhance the opportunities for self-determination available to persons with disabilities serves as the fourth step.

5. *Identification of structures necessary for desired change.* Only after goals, priorities, and steps for change have been defined can an intelligent discussion occur about new structures that will support and maintain desired changes. Working with small groups including both administrative and direct-service personnel from participating services, the manner in which individuals desire to work together, and *what they need* to get the job accomplished is explored.

6. *Identification of skills and resources necessary for change.* At this stage of the organizational change process, staff are encouraged to explicitly define the specific types of training and technical assistance they need to enhance the self-determination of those whom they serve. Based upon feedback from staff, programs to provide the necessary skill development need to be identified or created and implemented.

7. *Development of assessment processes to support enhanced self-determination.* For systems change to occur, all aspects of an organization must move forward. In this stage, personnel from service agencies develop and implement strategies to ensure that those within the system can adequately track organizational change and the impact of this change upon the self-determination of those individuals whom they serve.

fundamental feature of the style of service developed was that a person-centered approach was used to assist consumers in attaining self-selected personal goals. Beare and colleagues (1992) described the organizational change process they used to convert a small employment agency from a model in which many clients worked within sheltered workshops to community-based employment with a strong emphasis on individual choice of jobs. A "housing and support" approach to community living characterized by greater choice and increased options for community living beyond those traditionally offered has also been delineated (Racino, Walker, O'Connor, & Taylor, 1993); the experiences of some agencies that have implemented this approach are described in Shoultz (1993). The approaches to change described are currently more the exception than the rule. They do, however, offer hope that changes can be made within the current service system that will significantly enhance the self-determination of individuals with disabilities.

Macrosystem Influences on Self-Determination

Within any given culture, there is a degree of consistency in the belief systems, attitudes, and values held by its members. These beliefs and values, which affect and are altered by the overarching institutional and ideological patterns of the society, are referred to as the *macrosystem* for development (Garbarino, 1982). Individual development takes place over an extended period of time within the context of an everchanging macrosystem. As the environment changes, so do the belief systems, attitudes, and values held by members of the society and thereby the microsystems, mesosystems, and exosystems within which growth and daily functioning take place (Bronfenbrenner, 1979).

Few attempts have been made to explore the influence of the macrosystem on development in general, or on self-determination. Nevertheless, occurrences at this level do appear to influence the exercise of personal control. Since the mid-1970s, macrosystem changes of particular significance to self-determination include the movement toward the deinstitutionalization of adults with developmental disabilities, the passage of the Education for All Handicapped Children Act of 1975 (PL 94-142) and its later reauthorization as the Individuals with Disabilities Education Act of 1990 (IDEA) (PL 101-476), the movement toward educational inclusion, and the passage of the Americans with Disabilities Act (ADA) (PL 101-336). These changes are discussed on the following pages. There remain, however, numerous examples within the law, as well as in the attitudes and beliefs held by members of the society, that suggest that it will continue to be difficult for individuals with disabilities to exercise personal control over their lives.

Deinstitutionalization It is well established that few opportunities for self-determination are available to people living within institutions and that individuals residing within community settings exhibit higher levels of personal control (Baker et al., 1977; Barlow & Kirby, 1991; Colorado Division for Developmental Disabilities, 1992; Seltzer & Seltzer, 1978). Deinstitutionalization, however, appears to be a necessary but not sufficient condition for high levels of self-determination. Although individuals with disabilities who reside within the community exercise greater self-determination than their counterparts in institutions, there is consistent evidence that they are substantially less self-determined than their peers without disabilities (Kishi et al., 1988; Parsons et al., 1993; Sands & Kozleski, 1994; Wehmeyer & Metzler, 1995).

Much work remains to be undertaken if community residential settings are to be conducive to self-determination. There is consistent evidence that those community living programs providing the most normalized environments (e.g., semi-independent and independent living programs) have the most satisfied and self-determined consumers (Baker et al., 1977; Burchard et al., 1991; Gollay et al., 1978; Halpern, Close, & Nelson, 1986; Stancliffe, 1994b, 1995; Stancliffe & Wehmeyer, 1995). If high levels of self-determination are to be achieved by people with disabilities, a change in both values and policy will be required away from today's highly regulated and intensely supervised community group living toward more individualized alternatives. Commentators such as Brown et al. (1992) and Racino and Taylor (1993) have argued that community living services need to be radically restructured if individual control is to be significantly enhanced. These public policy issues are unlikely to be advanced by a research and service delivery agenda that focuses solely on attempting to enhance the self-determination capacities of people with disabilities and overlooks the restrictions on opportunities to use these capacities that are inherent in many service settings where people with mental retardation are educated, live, and work.

Individuals with Disabilities Education Act   The enactment in 1977 of the Education for All Handicapped Children Act (PL 94-142) brought society into an era in which access to public education became a basic right of all children with disabilities. This legislation, reauthorized in 1990 as the Individuals with Disabilities Education Act (IDEA), possesses the potential to ensure that all students with disabilities are provided with the supports they need to become self-determined adults. Through mandating that schools educate students within the least restrictive environment, IDEA and its predecessor have increased opportunities for students with disabilities to be educated in general education classrooms alongside of students without disabilities. The higher level of student-directed activity found in such environments is considerably more conducive to self-determination than that in the traditional, highly structured special education setting while also providing students with access to peers without disabilities.

The 1990 reauthorization of IDEA reflects that, to the greatest extent possible, educational planning for older students with disabilities should be student driven. Until recently, parents and professionals have been the primary decision makers. IDEA presses school districts to provide transition-age students with opportunities to actively take part in planning their educational goals and mandates that the services with which they are provided take into account their preferences and interests. If this participation mandate is to be successfully followed, however, schools, from an early age on, will need to provide students with disabilities with instruction that will encourage meaningful involvement in educational decision making (Abery, Rudrud, et al., 1995; Martin & Marshall, 1995). As of 1995, few of these changes have been realized within most school systems.

Americans with Disabilities Act   Upon its passage into law in 1990, the Americans with Disabilities Act (ADA) (PL 101-336) was hailed as landmark legislation that would guarantee the civil rights of people with disabilities for years to come. The mandates of this legislation should greatly increase the options from which people with disabilities can choose within all aspects of community life. The extent to which the ADA will live up to its potential, however, is currently unknown. Although many in the community appear to have embraced basic tenets of the act, there still appears to be a rather large segment of the population that either does not adequately understand the legislation or views it as a hinderance to continuing to undertake business as usual. In the end, the impact of the ADA on the self-determination of people with disabilities will be determined not by legislators, attorneys, and litigation, but rather by members of the general population developing value systems and behavior that support equal rights for all members of society.

Guardianship and Conservatorship Societal assumptions about people with disabilities are reflected in the legal doctrines applied to this group. Viewed, in a legal sense, as "vulnerable" in the same manner as children and the elderly, people with disabilities are often denied the right to make decisions because they are believed to be legally incapable of making informed and competent choices.

There remains in United States legal practice a widespread presumption that people with cognitive disabilities who have reached majority age are incapable of making their own decisions, even when the evidence for this conclusion arises from a lack of capacity within a single area, such as financial management (Flower, 1994; Stancliffe, 1994a). This results in the widespread imposition of plenary (i.e., all-encompassing) guardianship orders that are lifelong in duration and remove all legal decision-making authority from the individual. The civil rights people with disabilities lose as a result of such orders may include the right to vote, marry, hold a driver's license, or make independent decisions regarding health care, residential, employment, and support services. Despite evidence that many people with disabilities have the competencies necessary to make decisions with respect to their own lives (Lindsey, 1994), plenary guardianship orders remain the norm in many parts of the United States.

Views regarding the legal decision-making capacities of individuals with disabilities appear to be considerably more flexible in other cultures and countries. Guardianship orders in several Australian states, for example, are tailored according to the decision-making capacities of each individual. In addition, a person's civil rights remain unaffected by guardianship status and, when such orders are necessary, they are rarely plenary in nature. These differences in the legal systems of the United States and Australia have clear implications for the self-determination of people with disabilities.

Societal Values and Beliefs Regarding Self-Determination The recent legislation discussed has helped to ensure the basic rights of individuals with disabilities. Just as important to self-determination are the societal beliefs and values upon which this legislation is based. Unfortunately, there exist within today's society many individuals and institutions that neither value nor are concerned with the welfare of people belonging to this group. In spite of the progress that has been made in recent years, many attitudinal barriers with respect to the self-determination of individuals with disabilities still exist. Although society has become more "tolerant" of people with disabilities, this does not mean that we have come to accept such individuals as equals. Why might this be the case?

Mercer (1973) developed a social systems perspective on disability that may help explain this process. Examined from this perspective, disabilities can be understood as socially prescribed roles. Throughout our lives each of us fill a num- ber of such roles (e.g., student, parent) and each of these carries with it culturally- specified behavioral expectations. When an individual fails to meet these expec- tations, he or she is assigned an alternative role. In the case of individuals with disabilities, they are labeled mentally retarded or learning disabled or assigned one of a wide variety of other stigmatizing designations. This role, and the person to whom it is assigned, are devalued by members of the community, initiating a series of events that often lead to a loss of basic human rights. Unless this societal process is ended, it is likely that individuals with disabilities will continue to lack the support and opportunities needed to take their rightful places as self-deter- mined members of the community.

Enhancing Self-Determination: Macrosystem Level Interventions

Development, from birth to adulthood, is influenced by the cultural and political context (Garbarino, 1982). A society that places high value on material goods is likely to produce children who also hold such beliefs. A culture that stresses the importance of the individual giving something back to his or her community in- creases the probability that the next generation will hold such behavior in high regard. At the present time, the values and structure of American society stress the importance of independence and autonomy. Interdependency—needing the support of others—is viewed as a character flaw and an inherent sign of weak- ness. This macrosystem affect permeates all aspects of our lives.

How is the notion of interdependence related to self-determination? Doesn't the construct itself imply that independence and autonomy are goals toward which all should strive? In response to this question, one must consider that self- determination is of little importance if it does not facilitate a high quality of life. Who leads the highest quality of life—the isolated loner in complete control, or the person who is integrated into a supportive social network? If one examines the lives of individuals with and without disabilities, it becomes abundantly clear that those people with the highest quality of life are those with high levels of *in- terdependency*—people who both contribute to and receive from others. Interde- pendence is especially important if one's goal is to support people with disabili- ties to exercise self-determination. In the absence of support from others, many individuals with disabilities may never develop the capacities necessary to take personal control over their lives. In the case of individuals with severe disabili- ties, some support from others may always be necessary if self-determination is to be effectively exercised.

Professionals, family members, and people with disabilities themselves must take responsibility for ensuring that the supports necessary for self- determination are available to all people with disabilities. This is likely to be an arduous task. Intervention at the macrosystem level, however, has the potential to ensure that the supports necessary for self-determination are available. Over the long run, it will also produce the changes in attitudes and values necessary to enhance the personal control exercised by people with disabilities.

Self-Advocacy The most obvious way for an individual to stimulate the societal change necessary to enhance self-determination is through taking part in coordinated advocacy efforts for people with disabilities at local, state, and national levels. A second form of intervention likely to prove useful in enhancing self-determination entails the support of existing self-advocacy organizations that have the potential to bring about needed social change. Gaining its initial momentum in 1974 with the establishment of an initial People First organization, the self-advocacy movement has experienced phenomenal growth over the past 15 years (Browning, Rhoades, & Thorin, 1986; Browning, Thorin, & Rhoades, 1984; Shoultz, 1991). Although the impact of the self-advocacy movement on the delivery of services to people with disabilities has not been well documented in the research literature, the impact of these efforts appear to be substantial (Hayden & Shoultz, 1991; Williams, 1989). One study suggested that one of the most powerful predictors of a state's financial commitment to services for people with developmental disabilities is the strength and activity level of consumer advocacy groups (Braddock & Bachelder, 1990). Documentation of systems change associated with the efforts of self-advocacy groups is also readily available (People First of Washington, 1991; Rupp, 1991; Shoultz, 1991).

Self-advocacy organizations can be supported in a variety of ways, including providing consumers with information about local self-advocacy groups, encouraging people to attend group meetings, organizing necessary transportation, or serving as an advisor to a group. Actions of this nature have the potential to strengthen the self-advocacy movement thereby increasing the likelihood that these organizations, in a manner and in areas decided upon by people with disabilities themselves, can effectively influence those in power to provide the supports necessary for enhanced self-determination.

Increasing Public Knowledge A third avenue through which to intervene at a societal level focuses on a task that almost all individuals can undertake—increasing the public's knowledge about disabilities. As long as myths and misconceptions about people with disabilities exist, exercising the right to self-determination will be difficult. Using available resources such as the schools and the media, extensive public education should focus on the gifts and capacities of individuals with disabilities, their contributions to society, and the potential they possess to lead productive lives. Many barriers to self-determination are based upon a cultural value system that, at best, permits, and at worst, encourages individuals with disabilities to be perceived as a drain on society and of little value. As Mercer (1973) suggested, these misconceptions make it easy for society to deny people with disabilities many of their basic rights, including the right to self-determination.

CONCLUSIONS

At the start of this chapter, a conceptualization of self-determination was offered to the reader. This notion focused on the importance of acknowledging the synergistic interplay of personal characteristics and the environment when considering the construct. The remainder of the chapter highlighted the impact of environmental factors on the development of the self-determined individual. This approach was taken, not to minimize the importance of personal competencies, but rather to focus attention on the ecology of self-determination that is currently poorly understood. These ecological influences, considered by themselves, are quite numerous. When the individual is added into the equation, the complexity increases further. This reflects the complexity of human behavior, the uniqueness of each person, and the fact that all people live and develop within a vast array of environments that both shape the individual and are themselves likely to be changed by the individual. Considered in this light, we believe that most people will conclude that self-determination is in fact a complex, multifaceted process.

The complexity of self-determination and the need to consider it a result of a dynamic interaction between the individual and the environment should not be viewed as a drawback. In fact, this perspective has several distinct advantages. If it is only *internal processes* that are important to self-determination, one might conclude that many individuals are not capable of exercising any real degree of personal control over their lives. Some of the internal processes that have been hypothesized to be necessary for self-determination are not available to children until they reach middle to late childhood. People with severe disabilities may never develop a number of these competencies despite efforts to do so. Does this mean such individuals are not capable of self-determination? Parents of young children as well as people with severe disabilities will attest to the fact that many of these individuals exercise some degree of control over their environment. In most cases they cannot accomplish this alone. In the presence of a responsive, supportive environment, however, even very rudimentary behavior (e.g., a cry or vocalization) can result in desired changes being made and individuals beginning to realize that they can exert personal control.

If environmental accommodations and support can be used to enhance self-determination, even for those with severe disabilities or who are very young, a myriad of intervention possibilities open up that have yet to be considered. No longer will interventions need to solely be conceptualized as efforts to change the person. Rather, they can focus on providing individuals with the environmental accommodations they need to take greater control over their lives. Rid of the assumption that the job of educational and human services professionals is to make people with disabilities, as much as possible, "like the rest of us," concentrated efforts can begin to develop educational, residential, employment, and other community environments in a manner such that they nurture, support, and reinforce the efforts of individuals to exercise personal control. These endeavors might include working with caregivers to enhance their skills at providing appropriate opportunities for goal setting and choice making, raising their responsiveness to subtle indications of personal preference, or increasing the extent to which they reinforce attempts to exercise personal control. Interventions could also focus on changing relevant features of the service environment such as modifying existing residential and employment regulations and rules, changing staff attitudes, increasing the options from which consumers can choose, or restructuring staff roles and responsibilities. Given research evidence that suggests that environmental factors play as important, if not more important, a role in self-determination than the personal characteristics of the consumer, such an approach promises to be both more successful and cost-effective than efforts that rely solely upon skills training.

REFERENCES

Abery, B.H. (1994). A conceptual framework for enhancing self-determination. In M.F. Hayden & B.H. Abery (Eds.), *Challenges for a service system in transition: Ensuring quality community experiences for persons with developmental disabilities* (pp. 345–380). Baltimore: Paul H. Brookes Publishing Co.

Abery, B.H., & Eggebeen, A. (1993, June). *A descriptive study of the self-determination skills and opportunities of youth with mental retardation.* Paper presented at the Annual Conference of the American Association on Mental Retardation, Washington, DC.

Abery, B.H., Eggebeen, A., Rudrud, L., Arndt, K., Tetu., L., Barosko, J., Hinga, A., McBride, M., Greger, P., & Peterson, K. (1994) *Self-determination for youth with disabilities: A family education curriculum.* Minneapolis: University of Minnesota, Institute on Community Integration.

Abery, B.H., Eggebeen, A., Rudrud, L., & Sharpe, M. (1991). *The self-determination of youth with disabilities: Stakeholder perspectives.* Minneapolis: University of Minnesota, Institute on Community Integration.

Abery, B.H., McGrew, K., & Smith, J. (1995). *The contributions of individual characteristics and environmental factors to the self-determination of children and youth with disabilities.* Manuscript in preparation.

Abery, B.H., Rudrud, L., Arndt, K., Schauben, L., & Eggebeen, A. (1995). Evaluating a multicomponent program for enhancing self-determination of youth with disabilities. *Intervention in School and Clinic, 30,* 170–179.

Ainsworth, M.D.S. (1979). Attachment as related to mother-infant interaction. In J.S. Rosenblatt, R.A. Hinde, C. Beer, & M. Bushnel (Eds.), *Advances in the study of behavior* (Vol. 9). Orlando, FL: Academic Press

Americans with Disabilities Act of 1990 (ADA), PL 101-336. (July 26, 1990). Title 42, U.S.C. 12101 et seq: *U.S. Statutes at Large, 104,* 327–378.

Anderson, B.L. (1993). The stages of systematic change. *Educational Leadership, 51,* 14–17.

Baker, B.L., Seltzer, G.B., & Seltzer, M.M. (1974). *As close as possible: Community residences for retarded adults.* Boston: Little, Brown.

Baker, B.L., Seltzer, G.B., & Seltzer, M.M. (1977). *As close as possible: Community residences for retarded adults* (2nd ed.). Boston: Little, Brown.

Bandura, A. (1977). Self-efficacy: Toward a unified theory of behavioral change. *Psychological Review, 84*, 191–215.

Barlow, J., & Kirby, N. (1991). Residential satisfaction of people with an intellectual disability living in an institution or in the community. *Australia and New Zealand Journal of Developmental Disabilities, 17*, 7–23.

Bartnik, E., & Winkler, R.C. (1981). Discrepant judgements of community adjustment of mentally retarded adults: The contribution of personal responsibility. *American Journal on Mental Deficiency, 86*, 260–266.

Baumrind, D. (1967). Child care practices anteceding three patterns of preschool behavior. *Genetic Psychology Monographs, 75*, 43–88.

Baumrind, D. (1977, March). *Socialization determinants of personal agency.* Paper presented at the biennial meeting of the Society for Research in Child Development, New Orleans.

Beare, P.L., Severson, S.J., Lynch, E.C., & Schneider, D. (1992). Small agency conversion to community-based employment: Overcoming the barriers. *Journal of The Association for Persons with Severe Handicaps, 17, 170*–178.

Becher, R.M. (1984). *Parent involvement: A review of research and principles of effective practice.* Urbana, IL: ERIC Clearinghouse on Elementary and Early Childhood Education.

Bennett, M., Shaddock, A., & Guggenheimer, S. (1992, July). *The complexities of providing choice in a community group home for people with severe intellectual disabilities.* Paper presented at the Ninth World Congress of the International Association for the Scientific Study of Mental Deficiency, Broadbeach, Queensland, Australia.

Braddock, D., & Bachelder, L. (1990). *Comparative analysis of public support for mental retardation and mental health services in the United States* (Public Policy Monograph Series No. 48). Chicago: University Affiliated Program in Developmental Disabilities, University of Illinois at Chicago.

Bronfenbrenner, U. (1977). Toward an experimental ecology of human development. *American Psychologist, 32*, 513–531.

Bronfenbrenner, U. (1979). *The ecology of human development: Experiments by nature and design.* Cambridge, MA: Harvard University Press.

Bronfenbrenner, U. (1989). Ecological systems theory. *Annals of Child Development, 6*, 187–249.

Brown, R.I., Bayer, M.B., & Brown, P.M. (1992). *Empowerment and developmental handicaps: Choices and quality of life.* North York, Ontario, Canada: Captus University Publication/Chapman & Hall.

Browning, P., Rhoades, C., & Thorin, E. (1986). *The impact of nationwide training programs to promote self-advocacy for people with developmental disabilities.* Eugene: University of Oregon, Rehabilitation, Research and Training Center in Mental Retardation.

Browning, P., Thorin, E., & Rhoades, C. (1984). A national profile of self-help/self-advocacy groups of people with mental retardation. *Mental Retardation, 22*, 226–230.

Burchard, S.N., Hasazi, J.E., Gordon, L.R., & Yoe, J. (1991). An examination of lifestyle and adjustment in three community residential alternatives. *Research in Developmental Disabilities, 12*, 127–142.

Cattermole, M., Jahoda, A., & Markova, I. (1988). Leaving home: The experience of people with mental handicap. *Journal of Mental Deficiency Research, 32*, 47–57.

Christenson, S.L., Rounds, T., & Franklin, M.J. (1992). Home–school collaboration: Effects, issues, and opportunities. In S.L. Christenson & J.C. Conoley (Eds.), *Home–school collaboration: Enhancing children's academic and social competence* (pp. 19–48). Silver Spring, MD: National Association of School Psychologists.

Christenson, S.L., Rounds, T., & Gorney, D. (1992). Family processes and student achievement: Applying what we know for student success. *School Psychology Quarterly, 7*(3), 178–200.

Colorado Division for Developmental Disabilities. (1992). *Director's Report, 2*(2).

Dattilo, J., & Mirenda, P. (1987). An application of a leisure preference assessment protocol for people with severe handicaps. *Journal of The Association for Persons with Severe Handicaps, 12*, 306–311.

Davies, D. (1987). Looking for an ecological solution for improving the education of disadvantaged children. *Equity and Choice, 4*(1), 3–7.

Dornbusch, S. (1986). *Helping your kids make the grade.* Reston, VA: National Association of Secondary School Principles (NASSP). (ERIC Document Reproduction Service No. ED 275 406)

Education for All Handicapped Children Act of 1975, PL 94-142. (August 23, 1975). Title 20, U.S.C. 1401 et seq: *U.S. Statutes at Large, 89,* 773–796.

Egeland, B., & Farber, E.A. (1984). Mother-infant attachment: Factors related to its development and changes over time. *Child Development, 55,* 753–771.

Epstein, J.L. (1986). Parents' reactions to teacher practices of parent involvement. *The Elementary School Journal, 86,* 277–294.

Epstein, J.L. (1987). Toward a theory of family-school connections: Teacher practices and family involvement. In K. Hurrelmann, F. Kaufmann, & F. Losel (Eds.), *Social intervention: Potential and constraint* (pp. 121–136). New York: deGruyter.

Epstein, J.L. (1988). Effects on student achievement of teachers' practices of parent involvement. In S. Silver (Ed.), *Literacy through family, community, and school interaction.* Greenwich, CT: JAI Press.

Field, S., & Hoffman, A. (1994). Development of a model for self-determination. *Career Development for Exceptional Individuals, 17,* 159–169

Flower, C.D. (1994). Legal guardianship: The implications of law, procedure, and policy for the lives of people with developmental disabilities. In M.F. Hayden & B.H. Abery (Eds.), *Challenges for a service system in transition: Ensuring quality community experiences for persons with developmental disabilities* (pp. 427–447). Baltimore: Paul H. Brookes Publishing Co.

Forest, M., & Lusthaus, E. (1987). The kaleidoscope: Challenge to the cascade. In M. Forest (Ed.), *More education/integration* (pp. 1–16). Downsview, Ontario, Canada: G. Allan Roeher Institute.

Foxx, R.M., Faw, G.D., Taylor, S., Davis, P.K., & Fulia, R. (1993). "Would I be able to . . .?" Teaching clients to assess the availability of their community living life style preferences. *American Journal on Mental Retardation, 98,* 235–248.

Fullan, M. (1991). *The new meaning of educational change.* New York: Teachers College Press.

Fullan, M. (1993). Innovation, reform, and restructuring strategies. In G. Cawelti (Ed.), *Challenges and achievements of American education (1993 Yearbook of the Association for Supervision and Curriculum Development)* (pp. 116–133). Alexandria, VA: Association for Supervision and Curriculum Development.

Garbarino, J. (1982). *Children and families in the social environment.* New York: Aldine Press.

Goldstein, S., Strickland, B., & Turnbull, A.P. (1980). An observational analysis of the IEP conference. *Exceptional Children, 46,* 278–286.

Gollay, E., Freedman, R., Wyngaarden, M., & Kurtz, N.R. (1978). *Coming back: The community experiences of deinstitutionalized mentally retarded people.* Cambridge, MA: ABT Books.

Green, C.W., Reid, D.H., White, L.K. Halford, R.C., Brittain, D.P., & Gardner, S.M. (1988). Identifying reinforcers for people with profound handicaps: Staff opinion versus systematic assessment of preferences. *Journal of Applied Behavior Analysis, 21,* 31–43.

Guess, D., Benson, H.A., & Siegel-Causey, E. (1985). Concepts and issues related to choice-making and autonomy among people with severe handicaps. *Journal of The Association for Persons with Severe Handicaps, 10,* 79–86.

Guess, D., & Siegel-Causey, E. (1985). Behavioral control and education of severely handicapped students: Who's doing what to whom? And why? In D. Bricker & J. Filler (Eds.), *Severe mental retardation: From theory to practice* (pp. 230–244). Reston, VA: Council for Exceptional Children.

Halpern, A.S., Close, D.W., & Nelson, D.J. (1986). *On my own: The impact of semi-independent living programs for adults with mental retardation.* Baltimore: Paul H. Brookes Publishing Co.

Harner, C.J., & Heal, L.W. (1993). The multifaceted lifestyle evaluation scale (MLSS): Psychometric properties of an interview schedule for assessing personal satisfaction of adults with limited intelligence. *Research in Developmental Disabilities, 14,* 221–236.

Hayden, M.F., & Shoultz, B. (Eds.). (1991). *IMPACT: The Newsletter of the Institute on Community Integration* (Feature Issue on Self-Advocacy), *3*(4).

Heller, T. (1978). Group decision-making by mentally retarded adults. *American Journal of Mental Deficiency, 82,* 480–486.

Henderson, A. (1988). Parents are a school's best friend. *Phi Delta Kappan, 70,* 149–153.

Hill, B.K., Lakin, K.C., & Bruininks, R.H. (1988). Characteristics of residential facilities. In L.W. Heal, J.I. Haney, & A.R. Novak Amado (Eds.), *Integration of developmentally disabled individuals into the community* (2nd ed., pp. 89–123). Baltimore: Paul H. Brookes Publishing Co.

Hoffman, A., & Field, S. (1995). Promoting self-determination through effective curriculum development. *Intervention in School and Clinic, 30,* 134–141.

Houghton, J., Bronicki, J.B., & Guess, D. (1987). Opportunities to express preferences and make choices among students with severe disabilities in classroom settings. *Journal of The Association for Persons with Severe Handicaps, 12,* 18–27.

Hunt, P. (1995). *Exemplary transition programs in Minnesota.* Minneapolis: University of Minnesota, Institute on Community Integration.

Individuals with Disabilities Education Act of 1990 (IDEA), PL 101-476. (October 30, 1990). Title 20, U.S.C. 1400 et seq: *U.S. Statutes at Large, 104,* 1103–1151.

Jenkinson, J., Copeland, C., Drivas, V., Scoon, H., & Yap, M.L. (1992). Decision making by community residents with an intellectual disability. *Australia and New Zealand Journal of Developmental Disabilities, 18,* 1–8.

Jiranek, D., & Kirby, N. (1990). The job satisfaction and/or psychological well being of young adults with an intellectual disability and nondisabled young adults in either sheltered employment, competitive employment or unemployment. *Australia and New Zealand Journal of Developmental Disabilities, 16,* 133–148.

Johnson, D.R., Wallace, T., & Krawetz, N. (1994). *Exemplary programs for people with disabilities in transition, supported employment, and parent-professional collaboration.* Minneapolis: University of Minnesota, Institute on Community Integration

Kagan, S.L. (1984). *Parent involvement research: A field in search of itself (Report #8).* Boston: Institute for Responsive Education.

Kishi, G., Teelucksingh, B., Zollers, N., Park-Lee, S., & Meyer, L. (1988). Daily decision-making in community residences: A social comparison of adults with and without mental retardation. *American Journal on Mental Retardation, 92,* 430–435.

Kozleski, E.B., & Sands, D.J. (1992). The yardstick of social validity: Evaluating quality of life as perceived by adults without disabilities. *Education and Training in Mental Retardation, 27*, 119–131.

Levine, H.G., & Langness, L.L. (1985). Everyday cognition among mildly mentally retarded adults: An ethnographic approach. *American Journal of Mental Deficiency, 90*, 18–26.

Lindsey, P. (1994). Assessing the ability of adults with mental retardation to give direct consent for residential placement: A follow-up study for the Consent Screening Interview. *Education and Training in Mental Retardation and Developmental Disabilities, 29*, 155–164

Ludi, D.C., & Martin, L. (1995). The road to personal freedom: Self-determination. *Intervention in School and Clinic, 30*, 164–169.

Malette, P., Mirenda, P., Kandborg, T., Jones, P., Bunz, T., & Rogow, S. (1992). Application of a lifestyle development process for people with severe intellectual disabilities: A case study report.*Journal of The Association for Persons with Severe Handicaps, 17*, 179–191.

Martin, J.E., & Marshall, L.H. (1995). ChoiceMaker: A comprehensive self-determination transition program. *Intervention in School and Clinic, 30*, 147–156.

Mercer, J.R. (1973). *Labeling the mentally retarded.* Berkeley: University of California Press.

Mischel, W. (1968). *Personality and assessment.* New York: John Wiley & Sons.

Mithaug, D.E. (1991). *Self-determined kids.* Lexington, MA: Lexington Books.

Mithaug, D.E., & Mar, D.K. (1980). The relationship between choosing and working prevocational tasks in two severely retarded young adults. *Journal of Applied Behavior Analysis, 13*, 177–182.

Mount, B. (1987). *Personal futures planning: Finding directions for change.* Ann Arbor, MI: UMI Dissertation Information Service.

Mount, B., & Zwernik, K. (1988). *It's never too early, it's never too late.* St. Paul, MN: Metropolitan Council.

Newton, J.S., Horner, R.H., & Lund, L. (1991). Honoring activity preferences in individualized plan development: A descriptive analysis. *Journal of The Association for Persons with Severe Handicaps, 16*, 207–212.

O'Brien, J. (1987). A guide to lifestyle planning: Using the activity catalogue to integrate services and natural support systems. In B. Wilcox & G.T. Bellamy (Eds.), *A comprehensive guide to the activities catalog: An alternative curriculum for youth and adults with severe disabilities* (pp. 175–189). Baltimore: Paul H. Brookes Publishing Co.

Olson, D.H. (1993). Circumplex model of marital and family systems assessing family functioning. In F. Walsh (Ed.), *Normal family processes* (pp. 104–137). New York: Guilford Press.

O'Neil, J. (1993). Turning the system on its head. *Educational Leadership, 51*(1), 8–11.

Orlansky, M.D. (1979). Sam's day: A simulated observation of a severely handicapped child's education program. *AAESPH Review, 4*, 251–258.

Pace, G.M., Ivancic, M.T., Edwards, G.L., Iwata, B.A., & Page, T.J. (1985). Assessment of stimulus preference and reinforcer value with profoundly retarded individuals. *Journal of Applied Behavior Analysis, 18*, 249–255.

Packer, J., & Wright, J. (1983). *I like where I live.* Canberra, Australia: Department of Social Security.

Parent, W. (1993). Quality of life and consumer choice. In P. Wehman (Ed.), *The ADA mandate for social change* (pp. 19–41). Baltimore: Paul H. Brookes Publishing Co.

Parmenter, T.R., Briggs, L., & Sullivan, R. (1991). Quality of life: Intellectual disabilities and community living. *Evaluation Journal of Australia, 3*, 12–25.

Parsons, M.B., McCarn, J.E., & Reid, D.H. (1993). Evaluating and increasing meal-related choices throughout a service setting for people with severe disabilities. *Journal of The Association for Persons with Severe Handicaps, 18*, 253–260.

Parsons, M.B., & Reid, D.H. (1990). Assessing food preferences among people with profound mental retardation: Providing opportunities to make choices. *Journal of Applied Behavior Analysis, 23*, 183–195.

Parsons, M.B., Reid, D.H., Reynolds, J., & Bumgarner, M. (1990). Effects of chosen versus assigned jobs on the work performance of people with severe handicaps. *Journal of Applied Behavior Analysis, 23*, 253–258.

Pearpoint, J., O'Brien, J., & Forest, M. (1993). *PATH. Planning alternative tomorrows with hope: A workbook for planning better futures.* Toronto: Center for Integrated Education and Communities.

Peck, C.A. (1985). Increasing opportunities for social control by children with autism and severe handicaps: Effects on student behavior and perceived classroom climate. *Journal of The Association for Persons with Severe Handicaps, 10*(4), 183–193.

Peck, C.A., & Schuler, A.L. (1983). Classroom based intervention for children with autism: Theoretical and practical considerations for the speech and language specialist. *Seminars in Speech and Language, 4*, 93–103.

People First of Washington (1991). People first members teach transit. In M.F. Hayden & B. Shoultz (Eds.), *IMPACT: The Newsletter of the Institute on Community Integration* (Special issue on self-advocacy), *3*(4), 9.

Perry, J.C. (1980). Neonate and adult head movement: No and yes revisited. *Developmental Psychology, 16*, 245–250.

Racino, J.A., & Taylor, S.J. (1993). "People first": Approaches to housing and support. In J.A. Racino, P. Walker, S. O'Connor, & S.J. Taylor (Eds.), *Housing, support, and community: Choices and strategies for adults with disabilities* (pp. 33–56). Baltimore: Paul H. Brookes Publishing Co.

Racino, J.A., Walker, P., O'Connor, S., & Taylor, S.J. (Eds.). (1993). *Housing, support, and community: Choices and strategies for adults with disabilities.* Baltimore: Paul H. Brookes Publishing Co.

Raynes, N.V., Johnson, M., Sumpton, R.C., & Thorp, D. (1987). Comparison of the daily lives of four young adults who are mentally retarded. *Journal of Mental Deficiency Research, 31*, 303–310.

Realon, R.E., Favell, J.E., & Lowerre, A. (1990). The effects of making choices on engagement levels with people who are profoundly multiply handicapped. *Education and Training in Mental Retardation, 25*, 299–305.

Reese, R.M. (1986). *Teaching individual and group problem solving to adults with mental retardation.* Unpublished doctoral dissertation, University of Kansas, Lawrence.

Rietveld, C.M. (1983). The training of choice behaviors in Down's syndrome and nonretarded preschool children. *Australia and New Zealand Journal of Developmental Disabilities, 9*, 75–83.

Rupp, W. (1991). Self-advocates and the legislature: Making voices heard at the Capitol. In M.F. Hayden & B. Shoultz (Eds.), *IMPACT: The Newsletter of the Institute on Community Integration* (Special issue on self-advocacy), *3*(4), 6.

Sands, D.J., & Kozleski, E.B. (1994). Quality of life differences between adults with and without disabilities. *Education and Training in Mental Retardation and Developmental Disabilities, 29*, 90–101.

Schalock, R.L. (1994). The concept of quality of life and its current applications in the field of mental retardation/developmental disabilities. In D. Goode (Ed.), *Quality of life for people with disabilities: International perspectives and issues* (pp. 266–284). Cambridge, MA: Brookline Books.

Schalock, R.L., Keith, K.D., & Hoffman, K. (1990). *1990 Quality of life questionnaire: Standardization manual.* Hastings, NE: Mid-Nebraska Mental Retardation Services.

Seltzer, G.B., & Seltzer, M.M. (1978). *Context for competence: A study of retarded adults living and working in the community.* Cambridge, MA: Educational Projects.

Serna, L.A., & Lau-Smith, J. (1995). Learning with a purpose. Self-determination skills for students who are at risk for school and community failure. *Intervention in School and Clinic, 30,* 142–146.

Shaddock, A.J. (1993, July). *Choice making by people with intellectual disabilities: Issues and strategies for the future.* Keynote address to the Australian Association of Special Education, Inc. (Tasmanian Chapter), Conference on Transition from School to Adult Life, Hobart.

Shaddock, A.J., & Bramston, P. (1991). Individual service plans: The policy-practice gap. *Australia and New Zealand Journal of Developmental Disabilities, 17,* 73–80.

Shoultz, B. (1991). A short history of American self-advocacy. In M.F. Hayden & B. Shoultz (Eds.), *IMPACT: The Newsletter of the Institute on Community Integration* (Special issue on self-advocacy), *3*(4), 2.

Shoultz, B. (1993). Regenerating a community: The story of Residential, Inc. In J.A. Racino, P. Walker, S. O'Connor, & S. Taylor (Eds.), *Housing, support, and community: Choices and strategies for adults with disabilities* (pp. 281–298). Baltimore: Paul H. Brookes Publishing Co.

Skinner, B.F. (1953). *Science and human behavior.* New York: MacMillan.

Sroufe, L.A., Fox, N.E., & Pancake, V.R. (1983). Attachment and dependency in developmental perspective. *Child Development, 54,* 1615–1627.

Stancliffe, R.J. (1991). Choice making by adults in supported community accommodation: Hobson's choice? *Interaction, 5,* 23–33.

Stancliffe, R.J. (1994a, October). *Guardianship, behavior management and people with intellectual disability: Policy and practice in Australia.* Paper presented at the National Guardianship Association Conference, Fort Worth, TX.

Stancliffe, R.J. (1994b, December). *Choice making and community living: An Australian perspective.* Paper presented at the 1994 TASH Conference, Atlanta.

Stancliffe, R.J. (1995). Assessing opportunities for choice making: A comparison of self- and staff reports. *American Journal on Mental Retardation, 99,* 418–429.

Stancliffe, R.J., & Wehmeyer, M.L. (1995). Variability in the availability of choice to adults with mental retardation. *Journal of Vocational Rehabilitation, 5,* 319–328.

Tymchuk, A.J. (1985). *Effective decision making for the developmentally disabled.* Portland, OR: EDNICK Communications.

Tymchuk, A.J., Andron, L., & Rahbar, B. (1988). Effective decision-making/problem-solving training with mothers who have mental retardation. *American Journal on Mental Retardation, 92,* 510–516.

Vandercook, T., York, J., & Forest, M. (1989). MAPS: A strategy for building the vision. *Journal of The Association for Persons with Severe Handicaps, 14,* 205–215.

Vaughn, S., Bos, C.S., Harrell, J.E., & Laskey, G. (1988). Parent participation in the initial placement/IEP conference ten years after mandated involvement. *Journal of Learning Disabilities, 21,* 82–87.

Wagner, T. (1993). Systemic change: Rethinking the purpose of school. *Educational Leadership, 51*(1), 24–28.

Ward, M.J. (1994). Self-determination: A means to an end. In B. Abery, L.A. Dahl, & G. Chelberg (Eds.), *IMPACT, 6,* 8.

Watson, J.B. (1925). *Behaviorism.* New York: Norton.

Wehmeyer, M.L. (1992). Self-determination and the education of students with mental retardation. *Education and Training in Mental Retardation, 27,* 302–314.

Wehmeyer, M.L. (1994). Perceptions of self-determination and psychological empowerment of adolescents with mental retardation. *Education and Training in Mental Retardation and Developmental Disability, 29*, 9–21.

Wehmeyer, M.L. (1995). A career education approach: Self-determination for youth with
mild cognitive disabilities. *Intervention in School and Clinic, 30*, 157–163.

Wehmeyer, M.L., & Metzler, C.A. (1995). How self-determined are people with mental
retardation? The national consumer survey. *Mental Retardation, 33*, 111–119.

Williams, R.R. (1989, January). *Creating a new world of opportunity: Expanding choice
and self-determination in the lives of Americans with severe disability by 1992 and beyond.* Keynote address presented at the National Conference on Self-Determination,
Arlington, VA.

Ysseldyke, J., Christenson, S., & Thurlow, M.T. (1993). *Project SLICK final report to the
U.S. Department of Education.* Minneapolis: University of Minnesota.

Zetlin, A.G., Turner, J., & Winik, L. (1987). Socialization effects on the community adap-
tion of adults who have mild mental retardation. In S. Landesman & P. Vietze (Eds.),
Living environments and mental retardation (pp. 293–313). Washington, DC: American
Association on Mental Retardation.

Chapter 8

THE OPTIMAL PROSPECTS PRINCIPLE

A Theoretical Basis for Rethinking Instructional Practices for Self-Determination

Dennis E. Mithaug

ALTHOUGH VIRTUALLY ALL students self-determine to some extent, not all do so with equal success. Some know what they need and want and then regulate their thoughts and actions from moment to moment and day to day by anticipating the consequences of alternative plans and actions and then selecting the best course to get them where they want to go. Consider Doris, for example, a bright blonde sixth-grade student who has learned to regulate her behavior to get what she wants over the long haul. She is an experienced achiever. She is determined to do well in school because she knows that good grades will help her get what she wants after she graduates. Doris also knows what she can do and how to compensate for what gives her difficulty. She sets goals that are consistent with her needs and interests, strives to achieve them, and then experiences great satisfaction when she makes progress. Most important, Doris expects to achieve goals that are *just beyond* what she achieved in the past, which often requires more work and better methods of producing gain than what she has done previously. No one tells her *what* goals she should set or *how* she should meet them, although she often seeks advice when she gets confused and does not know where to begin. Doris has the habit of performing at or near her capacity in most of what she does. After meeting one goal she sets a slightly more ambitious goal the next time. This increases her capacity and improves her opportunity to act in self-determined ways.

Parts of this chapter are adapted from Mithaug, D.E. (in press). *Equal opportunity theory.* Newbury Park, CA: Sage Publications.

Now consider Carey, a sociable sixth grader who lacks determination in all that she does. She is a poor student, dislikes school, avoids homework, and spends much of her time watching television and hanging out with friends. She dreams about what she might be when she grows up but lacks confidence that she will ever become what she wants to be. Moreover, she has no idea what steps are necessary to pursue her dreams. When asked what grades she expects to earn each semester, she gives inconsistent answers. Sometimes she says she will get all A's, and other times she says she expects to fail all her courses. This is typical of how she looks at the future. Her goals are either so high she cannot achieve them or so low she is certain of achieving them. Either way, she has no intention of changing what she does or how she thinks. This is because when she sets expectations that are too high, no amount of planning and working will make any difference, and when she sets expectations that are too low, any amount of planning and working will be effective. Consequently, there is never any connection between what Carey expects and what she does. Frequently, this causes her to feel depressed and helpless because she depends so much on external events or people for direction and stimulation. She doesn't know what to improve about herself or how to improve herself, and she doesn't know how to enhance her opportunities. She is a poor self-regulator, too. Carey lacks self-determination.

Self-determined students fulfill their potential by setting expectations *slightly higher* than they think they are capable of achieving and then choosing behaviors and strategies that produce results that match those expectations. After each adjustment episode, they compare actual outcomes with expectations for gain and then adjust strategies, expectations, or both. They repeat this cycle until they match what they expect with what they can produce in order to maximize gain toward reaching their goals. Self-determined students are self-regulated problem solvers. Students who are not self-determined, by contrast, fail to fulfill their potential because 1) they set expectations that are too high or too low, 2) they fail to find a strategy that will meet those expectations, and 3) they fail to adjust their expectations or their choice of strategies. By setting expectations too high, they have little chance of meeting those expectations no matter what strategy they choose; likewise, by setting expectations too low, they also cannot meet their expectations regardless of a chosen strategy. In both cases, the selection and use of a strategy are irrelevant to goal attainment. Consequently, it is reasonable for them to believe luck or some other external, uncontrollable force decides their success or failure.

Students who do not act in self-determined ways do not know how to conduct *means–ends* problem solving to get what they want at school or in other areas of their lives. Their deficits in *ends* management show up when 1) they fail to set goals; 2) they have set goals, but have failed to select standards for judging when they have met those goals; or 3) they fail to specify their expectations for producing incremental gain toward goal attainment. Their deficits in *means* management show up when they fail to 1) consider different options and then choose the most profitable one for producing incremental gain, 2) produce results that move them toward their goals, or 3) compare results of their choices with their expectations for incremental gain and then adjust subsequent choices and performances accordingly. Lacking both sets of skills and experiences, they have little chance of connecting a given end with an available mean successfully. As a consequence, they depend upon others to not only set goals for them but to tell them what strategies to use to reach those goals as well.

Many students in special education exhibit these deficits. Consequently, their teachers spend a good deal of time identifying their needs, designing programs to reduce those needs, and then administering programs to maximize their progress. An unfortunate consequence of this well-meaning process is that it bypasses student involvement in their own problem solving to reach goals. This may not be a serious problem for students with skill-based rather than regulation-based needs because students who are good means–ends problem solvers can use their self-regulation skills to work independently at home, in the resource room, and in inclusive classrooms. They can even develop their own strategies for minimizing the effects of their disabling condition. But what about students whose primary obstacle to getting along in life is their failure to self-regulate effectively and efficiently? Do they benefit from instructional practices that provide little opportunity to learn and to practice self-regulated problem solving to meet goals? Will they be prepared to be self-determined once they leave school?

LACK OF SELF-DETERMINATION

Some have argued that lack of self-determination is the major problem for special education graduates. Students who leave special education after graduating from school do not know what they like, what they want, or what they can do. Consequently they lack self-initiative; they don't know how to self-direct or self-correct (Mithaug, Martin, & Agran, 1987; Mithaug, Martin, Agran, & Rusch, 1988). The claim is that in special education there are too many students like Carey and too few students like Doris. In fact, assessments of students' levels of self-determination confirm this claim. Levels of self-determination for students with disabilities are lower than for students without disabilities (Wolman, Campeau, DuBois, Mithaug, & Stolarski, 1994). These findings validate the reasoning behind the OSERS (Office of Special Education and Rehabilitative Services) initiative to teach the behaviors and skills necessary for self-determination among children and youth with disabilities (see Ward, Chapter 1). Also underscored is the importance of teaching students to be more self-determining during their early years so they will be more effective in getting what they need and want in their adult years (see Doll, Sands, Wehmeyer, & Palmer, Chapter 5).

Unfortunately, the federal initiative responsible for encouraging the teaching of self-determination skills to students with disabilities is coming to a close at a time when expectations for improving student outcomes are increasing. This places substantial pressure on teachers to adopt instructional practices that will encourage more independence and self-determination in their students, even though there remain substantial obstacles to widespread adoption and application of instructional methods that can accomplish these ends. First, there is the obstacle of getting teachers to respond to student needs and interests in fundamentally different ways than many are accustomed to doing. The assumption that student deficits should drive all instructional activity often prevents teachers from focusing on what students want to pursue and, as a consequence, promotes learned helplessness as students learn to depend on teachers to solve their problems. The focus on self-determination requires teachers to identify student needs and interests and then to assist students as they develop their own plans to pursue those ends. This orientation to student learning is diametrically opposed to much of what goes on in special education. So getting teachers to adopt a student-directed orientation is unlikely to occur on its own.

Second, there is the equally difficult problem of getting students to accept greater responsibility for their education and for their actions with respect to that education. Shifting responsibility can be perceived as threatening when students have grown accustomed to teachers' identifying what the problem is, deciding how to solve it, and then instructing them on what to do to follow through. This happens every day and has the effect of decreasing students' risk of failure while increasing their chance of success. But this, too, incurs a cost—in the form of increased boredom and passivity and decreased initiative and risk taking. The greatest cost, however, is the fact that it produces many students like Carey, who never seek out opportunity or optimize circumstance, and too few students like Doris, who continually reach for a slightly greater challenge to expand their capacity and change their available opportunity. If special education teachers were to provide their students with the experience of self-directed learning and achieving, they would be increasing their students' experiences of self-determination by allowing them to regulate their own problem solving to meet their own goals. Teachers would also be working with students who were intrinsically motivated because students would be working for their own benefit and enjoyment.

The third and perhaps most difficult obstacle has to do with what must be taught in order for students to become self-determined. The difficulty here is that the perceptions, knowledge, and abilities comprising the process of self-determination are not easily deconstructed or task analyzed, taught separately, and then reconstructed into the functional process of self-determination—problem solving to meet personal goals. In fact, the very processes of deconstruction, of building skills one at a time, and then of reconstructing the learned components to solve real-life problems can take so long that the learner loses sight of the purpose and value of what she or he is learning. Add to this the fact that teachers and students are already wedded to a pattern of interaction that prohibits student-directed problem solving to meet personal goals, and one has to conclude that students are unlikely to improve their levels of self-determination any time soon.

WHEN DO PEOPLE SELF-DETERMINE?

These daunting obstacles suggest that perhaps educators should step back for a moment and ask a more basic question before they rush to teach students another set of "essential" skills or train them to perform another repertoire of "appropriate" behaviors. Perhaps we should ask ourselves, "When are *we* most likely to self-determine?", because to answer this question is to know something about the conditions that are *optimally conducive* to our own self-determined thought and action. In fact, to know about these conditions is to understand that all people, not just people with disabilities, respond to the same conditions that promote self-determination. And knowing when these conditions are present to encourage self-determination is to know about how *just-right* circumstances motivate all people to pursue the opportunity to expand their capacity to get the things they desire and to become the persons they want to be.

The problem with instructional approaches for students with disabilities is that they often fail to take into account the process of self-regulation that everyone experiences within a context of engaging specific circumstances in life to get what they need and want. So when teachers examine only the student, and when that student has a disability, they overlook the fundamental process of self-regulation that is *ongoing* for that student as well as the *social context* within which that student's regulatory process is functioning to secure a favorable adjustment. Consequently educators are oblivious of the form and substance of those interactions between student and environment that make one pattern of self-regulation an instance of *self*-determination and another pattern of self-regulation an instance of *other*-determination. What is missing in instructional approaches is an understanding of the difference between the pattern of self-regulation by which some individuals *adjust* to changing circumstance in order to *maintain* what they have in life and the pattern of self-regulation by which other individuals adjust in order to *expand* what they have in life.

The Experience of Self-Determination

Self-regulation theory helps us understand how this process works for all individuals—for those who are self-determined as well as for those who are not. The theory describes these different patterns of self-regulation by explaining how individuals vary in their *capacity* and *opportunity* to self-determine. It accounts for the fact that some individuals have substantial capacity and frequent opportunity, others have ample capacity but few opportunities, others lack capacity but have frequent opportunities, and still others lack both capacity and opportunity. The theory also helps us understand that these different capacity–opportunity patterns vary according to the resource being sought and the end in life being pursued. Consequently, the experience of control comes and goes according to the means and the end defining the pursuit. What an individual wants in life affects her experience of self-determination because her capacity and available opportunity determine success or failure in getting what she wants. If an individual wants substantially more than her capacity or opportunity allows, she may become frustrated and feel impotent because her goals are unrealistic. In these circumstances, she experiences what many others have experienced from time to time. So she is likely to do what they have done, too. She will adjust her expectations to eliminate the source of frustration and disappointment. She will set her expectations to match her capacity.

This is the first step in self-regulation. It involves adjusting to life's circumstances by determining what ends are achievable and what ends are not. By ignoring those outcomes that are unattainable, we eliminate the discrepancy condition that prompts us to commence problem solving to meet a goal. With the disappearance of the discrepancy goes any interest in pursuing opportunities to change what we are, who we want to become, or what we need to achieve a new status in life. We become "realistic" because we have adjusted expectations to what we perceive to be our current capacity and present opportunity.

So the first step in self-regulation is *deciding whether or not to seek out and engage new opportunity for gain*. And, as often than not, we decide to abort; we decide to adjust expectations *downward* so that they match our existing capacity and circumstance. We avoid risking failure and its anticipated cost to our existing capacity. Of course, for people who are least advantaged in life, this risk is especially onerous because they must adjust to life's circumstances with limited capacity and constrained opportunity. The cost of failure is proportionately greater because these individuals lack the surplus resources needed to carry on satisfactorily if they fail. Loss of access to the resources they already have to *maintain* what they have in life would be too costly to endure.

The experience of self-determination depends upon decisions to search for opportunities to secure access to resources currently lacking in one's life. Decisions that avoid new opportunities constrain the individual's access to valued resources, and this, in turn, reduces her or his capacity for satisfying unmet needs in life. It creates a cycle of declining prospects for self-determination: Lowered expectations decrease motivation to search, lack of motivation to search decreases the frequency of engagement in new opportunity, lack of engagement of new opportunity decreases the chances of enhancing capacity, and limitations in capacity for satisfying unmet needs creates feelings of powerlessness over life's circumstances. This lack of control over life translates into an experience of *other*-determination. The external world, not the individual, is controlling the individual's life. This condition explains Carey's approach to solving problems.

The opposite occurs when expectations increase to create discrepancies between actual and needed capacity that causes the individual to seek out and engage new opportunity, use results to enhance capacity, and then use this enhanced capacity to fulfill what is missing in the individual's life. Now the operable cycle is change and expansion rather than stasis and contraction. Enhanced capacity gives rise to higher expectations that motivate new searches, new engagements, more success, and additional capacity. This enhancement of capacity allows a person to improve her or his ability to search for new opportunity, to engage it successfully, and then to enhance her or his capacity in order to optimize ever more challenging opportunity. It allows an individual to become successively more powerful in all of her or his pursuits. This condition explains Doris's approach to life's circumstances.

People like Doris, who enjoy the experience of self-determination, have three conditions favoring their adjustment to life's circumstances:

1. They know how to regulate the use of existing resources to secure control over the additional means necessary to satisfy unmet needs and interests in life.
2. They are free from constraints created by a lack of personal, social, economic, or technical resources necessary to engage new opportunity for gain.
3. They are free to pursue new opportunity because there are sufficient options from which to select one that matches their capacity to optimize circumstance.

These people *become* self-determined because they gain sufficient capacity and opportunity to change their environments to get what they want out of life.

The Just-Right Condition

These operations on the environment are most likely when individuals find just-right matches between their capacity and their opportunity. Under these conditions of *optimal prospects*, individuals are, according to MacCallum's definition of freedom, autonomous persons free from Y to pursue Z (Gray, 1991). They are free to regulate their resources *on their own* by choosing the means of getting what they need and want from a set of reasonably favorable opportunities or options that empower them to satisfy unmet needs. Optimal prospects are just-right matches between capacity and opportunity when they encourage individuals to think and act independently of others to decide what is important in life, to set goals that specify what they want to pursue in order to satisfy unmet needs, and then to regulate problem solving toward those ends. Self-regulated problem solving to meet a goal involves

1. Finding the match between capacity and opportunity that is necessary to commence goal pursuit
2. Developing a strategy for optimizing opportunity for gain
3. Acting on that strategy to change environmental circumstance to produce expected gain
4. Adjusting to results by repeating the cycle until the goal has been either attained or abandoned

Individuals vary in capacity to self-regulate to the extent that they can solve these types of problems. First, they vary in the extent to which they are able to *search environments for opportunity* to produce the gain needed to reduce the discrepancy between actual and expected capacity. Success in this effort depends upon an individual's assessment of her or his needs and interests, what is best for her or him over the long term, and what resources she or he has available to pursue opportunities that will satisfy unmet needs. It also depends on the individual's *beliefs* about the causal factors operating in the environment and how to use this understanding to identify new opportunity for gain. A person must be able to estimate the resources she will expend to operate on these causal factors in order to optimize her circumstance. Can she afford the possibility of failing to produce the expected gain? Finally, her success depends on finding that opportunity or option that promises to produce the greatest gain at the lowest cost. In the best of all searches, the individual will find a just-right match between her capacity and an opportunity that has a risk-benefit ratio she believes to be a good prospect for gaining what she needs to meet one of her goals in life.

A second way individuals vary in capacity to self-regulate is in their ability to *convert opportunities into a net resource gain* for themselves, that is, the extent to which they know how to optimize circumstances for gain production. In this second set of problem-solving activities, the individual must decide what strategies to employ, what resources to allocate, and when and how to deploy these resources. Here the individual develops a plan he believes will optimize circumstances for the greatest gain at the lowest cost. He constructs an optimizing strategy that is consistent with his estimate of the opportunity's cost-benefit ratio and probability of success. In other words, the individual estimates the optimality of that opportunity. He infers this optimality from his assessment of his prospects of converting the circumstances of a given situation into a net resource gain for himself.

The third way individuals vary in capacity to self-regulate is in their ability to *act on their plans to optimize opportunity*. As the individual strives to overcome obstacles to the conversion of an existing circumstance to a more favorable condition, she gathers information on results of her actions to identify what to change in order to improve her circumstances with new action. The individual's capacity to overcome obstacles that threaten to increase costs, reduce gains, and decrease prospects for success depend upon accurate information about what she is doing, what gain she is producing, and how results compare with expectations for gain. By gathering feedback and adjusting subsequent problem solving repeatedly over time and over many self-regulation episodes, the individual increases her capacity incrementally. And this, in turn, optimizes subsequent opportunity for net gain.

In sum, the self-regulated problem solver is *motivated* and *focused*. She or he is motivated when experiencing a discrepancy between her or his actual capacity to produce what she or he needs and wants in life and the capacity necessary to attain those ends. The self-regulated problem solver exhibits this motivation by engaging in three types of problem solving: 1) *finding opportunities to be optimized* through use of expendable resources; 2) *producing a strategy for using existing resources* to optimize opportunity at the lowest cost and at the highest probability of success; and 3) *acting on that strategy* to produce gain, evaluate results, and adjust subsequent episodes of self-regulated problem solving. Individuals with capacities to solve problems effectively and efficiently optimize their adjustments and maximize their gain. They reduce discrepancies between what they have and what they need in order to satisfy their ends in life within the limits defined by their circumstances. In other words, *they do the best they can with what they have available to them.*

Optimal Adjustment

Self-regulation theory explains how people take advantage of the opportunities available to them—that is, how they optimize adjustments to maximize gain. Its four propositions describe conditions that affect how they set expectations for gain, how they select opportunities for producing gain, how they act on those choices or opportunities, and how the gain they produce affects the optimalities of subsequent expectations, choices, and actions. These four propositions were described by Mithaug (1993) as follows:

1. *The Expectation Proposition*: The closer to optimal the past gain toward goal attainment and the smaller the discrepancy between the actual state and goal state, the closer to optimal the expectation for gain
2. *The Choice Proposition*: The closer to optimal the past gain toward goal attainment and the more salient the differences between options, the closer to optimal the choice
3. *The Response Proposition*: The closer to optimal the past gain, expectations, and choices, then the closer to optimal the distribution of responses between task completion to meet the goal and feedback about goal state-actual state discrepancies, options, task performance, and gain
4. *The Gain Proposition*: The closer to optimal the past gain, expectations, choices, and responses, then the closer to maximum the gain toward goal attainment. (p. 59)

The expectation proposition states that two factors—experience in producing gain and the size of the discrepancy between current and expected capacity—affect one's ability to set optimal expectations for gain (the highest expectations possible from a given opportunity).

Experience in producing gain toward goal attainment increases the individual's capacity to judge what is possible under the circumstances (options). The size of the discrepancy affects the individual's judgments, too. For example, the smaller the discrepancy, the more likely the person will find a gain (solution) that will either eliminate the difference or maximize its reduction. Conversely, as discrepancies between goal states and actual states increase, the probability of finding completely effective solutions decreases. Large discrepancy reductions frequently require multiple solutions with varying reduction effects. This makes it difficult to identify the option that produces the greatest incremental gain toward goal attainment. (Mithaug, 1993, p. 58)

The choice proposition states that optimal choice making depends upon previous choice making, which is no surprise. It also identifies salience between opportunities or options as being important for choosing optimally. When one opportunity is clearly superior to others, chances are good that the chooser will notice the difference and pursue that opportunity (if it is the most favorable one). The proposition also alerts us to the effects of ambiguity, which is an impediment to good choice making.

> The choice proposition specifies conditions under which the individual chooses the operation that produces the greatest gain at the lowest cost. Again, there are two factors that influence optimal choosing. The first is experience or past gain toward the goal: the closer to optimal the past gain, the more likely the person will select the best operation to produce expected gain. The second factor is the difficulty of identifying important differences between options. The proposition states that the more salient the difference between options, then the more likely the individual will choose optimally. During less than ideal choice circumstances where differences are subtle and options are many, discriminations are difficult and time consuming (costly). They reduce the likelihood of choosing optimally. (Mithaug, 1993, pp. 58–59)

The response proposition specifies conditions that determine the effectiveness and efficiency of an individual's actions to produce gain. Again, past gain, expectations for gain, and choices are influential. When one has little experience with a pending pursuit, when one's expectations for gain are unrealistic, and when one chooses opportunities that demand more skill and greater resources than one has at her or his disposal, then the individual must expend so much time and energy gathering information and learning what to do that the cost of the pursuit increases as the gain it promises decreases. This changes when the individual is competent in the area of pursuit in which she or he is seeking gain. Then, the person knows how to identify the option that is most likely to produce the expected gain, and he or she also knows how to perform the tasks required to optimize the circumstances of the situation. Consequently, the individual spends less time and effort learning what to do and more time completing tasks that will get the individual to where she or he wants to go. In other words, the more competent we are, the fewer errors we make, and the less time we take, the greater the gain we produce. We respond effectively and efficiently to the opportunities we pursue.

> The response proposition specifies the conditions under which the individual maximizes responses to produce gain and minimizes responses that seek feedback. . . . Improvements in any of these conditions [of past gain optimalities, expectation optimalities, or choice optimalities] indicate the regulator's greater experience and understanding of what causes what. This leads to more effective and efficient distribution of responses. The person spends less time and effort monitoring performance accuracy, goal state-actual state discrepancies, options, and results and more time and effort performing the operations necessary to produce gain toward goal attainment. (Mithaug, 1993, pp. 59–60)

Finally, the gain proposition explains what happens when expectations, choices, and responses are optimal: Gain toward goal attainment maximizes. Under these conditions, gain equals expectations, expectations are as high as possible under the circumstances, choices are the best of the options available, and actions are as efficient and effective as possible. Error responses minimize and effective responses maximize. The result is optimal adjustment and maximum gain.

> The gain proposition describes the effects of adjustment optimalities on gain toward the goal. The proposition states that as past gains, expectations, choices, and responses approach maximum optimalities, gain toward reducing the discrepancy between the actual state and goal state maximizes, too. The upper limit—maximum gain—occurs when (1) past gain equals expected gain, (2) expectations for gain equal the maximum possible from the options available, (3) choices produce the greatest gain at the lowest cost, and (4) resource allocations maximize responding to produce gain and minimize feedback seeking on goal states, choices, performances, and gains. . . .
>
> In summary, self-regulation theory states that we maximize progress toward goals when (1) past gains match expectations, (2) present expectations are the maximum possible, (3) choices are the best possible, and (4) follow-through on choice is as effective and efficient as possible. Under these conditions, regulation is optimal and return from the environment is maximal. (Mithaug, 1993, pp. 60–61)

Cycles of Optimal and Suboptimal Adjustment

One implication of self-regulation theory is its prediction of *cumulative* effects created by interaction among the four optimality factors: past gain, expectations for gain, choices, and actions. Change in one optimality factor produces change in the others, and the emergent effect of these interactions is reflected in an accumulation of positive or negative experiences of self-determination. For example, cycles of optimal adjustment yield feelings of optimism, empowerment, and confidence and cycles of suboptimal adjustment create feelings of hopelessness, impotence, and despair. Suboptimal cycles begin when an adjustment produces less gain than expected, thereby 1) affecting the next self-regulation episode by producing a suboptimal expectation for producing gain, 2) reducing motivation to search for an optimal opportunity, 3) yielding a suboptimal choice, and 4) generating less gain than would be possible with a better selection. From there, the spiral will continue downward when the actions on the suboptimal opportunity are also suboptimal, which reduces gain production to negatively affect the next self-regulation episode by further reducing expectations. The result is decreased motivation, infrequent search for new opportunity, reduced engagement of new opportunity, declining gain in resource production, and constrained capacity to self-determine. Left to itself, the negative cycle of self-regulation creates a sense of helplessness and despair that characterizes people whose prospects for self-determination have reached an all-time low.

These cycles of suboptimal adjustment occur when self-regulated problem solving is repeatedly unsuccessful over time—that is, when interaction among the four optimality factors work together to accelerate the creation of increasingly suboptimal adjustments. If it continues, the negative cycle will leave the regulator with little motivation, capacity, or opportunity to direct problem solving toward the capacity building necessary to secure resources that will satisfy important needs in life. It will leave the regulator bereft of the *experience* of self-determination that is necessary to exercise the *right* to self-determination. Consequently, the only problems the individual will be likely to solve will be those she or he is forced to solve in order to maintain subsistence-level adjustment to life's circumstances. This is Carey's experience of "other-determination."

Self-regulation cycles can also lead to opposite, end-state patterns of adjustment when people like Doris, for example, generate experiences of self-determination and empowerment that build self-esteem and self-respect. During these cycles, the four optimality factors interact in ways that create their own momentum because everything seems to go as expected. The person sets expectations that are just right, she or he chooses the best option from those available, acts on that option with her or his best performance, and produces results she or he expects. Moreover, the positive experience of one self-regulation episode affects the next, which enables and encourages the individual to repeat the cycle and the previous success by setting slightly higher expectations that provide the just-right challenge that motivates the individual to enhance her or his capacity further. The person feels empowered because she or he is *optimally challenged* by the match between capacity and opportunity. Mihaly Csikszentmihalyi calls this the optimal experience or "flow":

> The optimal state of inner experience is one in which there is *order in consciousness*. This happens when psychic energy—or attention—is invested in realistic goals, and when skills match the opportunities for action. The pursuit of a goal brings order in awareness because a person must concentrate attention on the task at hand and momentarily forget everything else. These periods of struggling to overcome challenges are what people find to be the most enjoyable times of their lives. . . . A person who has achieved control over psychic energy and has invested it in consciously chosen goals cannot help but grow into a more complex being. By stretching skills, by reaching toward higher challenges, such a person becomes an increasingly extraordinary individual. (Csikszentmihalyi, 1990, p. 6)

Central to flow is the sense of power that comes with ordering one's consciousness toward expectations, choices, and performances that produce exactly what one expects and wants from the optimal challenge. It is the same experience Gilbert Brim describes as a search for "just manageable difficulties":

> When we win, the response is to increase the degree of difficulty. We set a shorter timetable for the next endeavor, raising expectations of how much we can achieve, even broadening out and adding new goals. We will try to get there earlier or faster, and to get more or better. . . .

Winning raises our hopes; losing lowers them [italics added]. As Tocqueville wrote about democracy in the United States when it was a new nation, social movements are not caused by failure and frustration but spring from rising strength. . . .

There are broad implications here for what happens to people when they are successful at work. Once you get good at a particular job, it no longer takes most of your ability to do it well. *So you set your sights higher and push on to more demanding work* [italics added].

But here's the hitch. People can become psychologically trapped by their own success as they race to keep up with the rising expectations bred by each new achievement. With each success, they raise their level of difficulty, climbing up a ladder of subgoals, moving faster, raising aspirations, and at some point reaching the limit of their capacity. (Brim, 1992, pp. 31–32)

The experience generated during self-regulation is a function of *repeated interaction* between capacity and opportunity over time. Consequently, as capacity waxes and wanes, optimalities of opportunity wax and wane, and as optimalities of opportunity increase and decrease, capacities to regulate effectively and efficiently change to create different experiences. Some of these experiences are empowering, some are discouraging, and some experiences are neutral. However, when capacity and opportunity interact to produce repeated patterns of optimal adjustment and maximum gain, individuals cease searching for new opportunity for gain because their routines are sufficient to produce those ends in life they expect to achieve. The same occurs when capacity and opportunity interact to produce repeated patterns of suboptimal adjustment and minimum gain. These people also cease searching for new opportunity because their routines are sufficient to produce those ends in life they expect to reach. In both situations, capacity–opportunity interactions stabilize to maintain an accepted and expected exchange with the environment.

This constitutes what people who are most and least advantaged in society have in common. *They are equally motivated to keep what they have.* Those who are most advantaged have maximized the acquisition of new resources so that they regulate their problem solving to maintain their access to resources already under their control, while those least advantaged in society have reached the limits of the resources they can afford to lose so that they regulate their problem solving to maintain access to resources they need simply to survive. Psychologically, the motivation of the two groups is similar, although the basis of that motivation is different. People who are advantaged have surplus capacity to prevent the experience of marginal adjustment, while people who are disadvantaged have no surplus so they must experience marginal adjustment and the erosion of self-confidence and self-respect it stimulates.

THE OPTIMAL PROSPECTS SOLUTION

Understanding the underlying process affecting prospects for self-determination for all people should enable educators to help people like Carey who are trapped in a declining spiral of capacity–opportunity interaction that diminishes their prospects for self-determination. The fact that these individuals may have a disability *is a side issue* to the moral problem created by diminished prospects for self-determination. It is a side issue because the moral claim for the right to freedom trumps all other claims for social or education redress when that right is abrogated. For too long, violations of this fundamental right have been in the background when considering what ought to be the priority in determining educational opportunity for students with disabilities. Now this is changing as educators rethink the principle of individualized instruction that guides intervention paradigms in special education.

The Right to Self-Determine

The *National Agenda for Achieving Better Results for Children and Youth with Disabilities* (U.S. Department of Education, 1994) has articulated a vision in the year 2000 that "begins with images of children and youth with disabilities having access to supports and services that lead to self-actualization, self-determination, and independence" (p. 4–5). This is but a reaffirmation of what most people have long believed to be a condition of life in every democratic society—that *all people* have a right to self-determination. Indeed, Article 1 of the *International Covenant on Civil and Political Rights* adopted by the General Assembly of the United Nations states that "All peoples have the right to self-determination. By virtue of that right they freely determine their political status and freely pursue their economic, social and cultural development" (Humana, 1992, p. 385).

Equal opportunity theory addresses the moral problem created by the discrepancy between the right and the experience of self-determination—a condition that is often felt by people with disabilities. It locates the cause of this discrepancy in lack of capacity and opportunity among individuals whose personal, social, and economic circumstances are beyond their control. By claiming that every member of society deserves an optimal chance of securing the good in life, the theory explains society's collective responsibility for assuring fair prospects for all. The theory shows that when prospects for self-determination are distributed fairly, they are equally optimal for all. Although one person's pursuits will be different from another person's, prospects are nonetheless comparable because all individuals have roughly the same chance of pursuing or not pursuing, of fulfilling or not fulfilling, their own ends over the long term.

Thus the problem of inequality is a problem of unequal prospects for engaging and succeeding in self-determined pursuits. When prospects for pursuing the individually defined good in life are not distributed equally among members of a society, the ideal of liberty for all is jeopardized. And in all countries of the world, including the United States, this is the case. Substantial numbers of individuals fail to engage and succeed in their own pursuits and, as a consequence, lose control over life's circumstances. The persistent pattern of failure they experience leads to a loss of hope and a growing sense of helplessness and despair that destroys the very basis of their self-respect. They become victims in a cycle of personal, social, and economic decline that debilitates and erodes their capacity for improving their own prospects for life. These individuals need and deserve help to experience the self-determined life. Children and youth with disabilities are among those who need and deserve this assistance.

The optimal prospects solution seeks to embody equal opportunity theory by justifying social redress on behalf of people who are least well situated in society by claiming the following (Mithaug, 1995):

1. All persons have the right to self-determination.
2. Psychological and social conditions of freedom cause some individuals and groups to experience unfair advantages in determining their future.
3. Declines in prospects for self-determination among the less fortunate are due to social forces beyond their control.
4. As a consequence of these declines, there is a collective obligation to improve prospects for self-determination among least well-situated groups.

The collective action proposed by equal opportunity theory is to *optimize prospects* for self-determination among the less fortunate by improving their capacity for autonomous thought and action, by improving the opportunities available to them for effective choice and action, and by optimizing the match between individual capacity and social opportunity.

Optimal Prospects: Principles and Application

The assumptions undergirding the optimal prospects principle, which operationalizes the equal opportunity value, are that 1) every person is an individual with a special set of talents, interests, and needs; 2) every person deserves a fair chance to express those unique attributes in pursuit of self-defined ends in life; and 3) as a consequence, there can be no overarching social mechanism for sorting individuals into categories of deserving and undeserving when it comes to distributing access to the fair chance. Every person deserves an equal chance—a fair prospect—for pursuing a self-determined life.

The redress recommended by the optimal prospects principle for those denied a fair prospect is to focus on the *means* for creating the experience of self-determination, that is, the individual's capacity and opportunity to choose and enact choice in pursuit of self-defined life goals. The principle is based upon the understanding that when either capacity or opportunity to self-determine is diminished or constrained, the *probability* of self-determination diminishes, and when one's chances of engaging in self-determined pursuits decline, then fairness in liberty for all is threatened. The optimal prospects principle is based upon an understanding of how individuals interact with opportunity to improve their chances of getting what they need and want in life. When opportunities are just-right challenges—when they offer the right amount of risk for the gain expected—then those opportunities will be pursued. All people, regardless of who they are, where they come from, or whether or not they have a disability or a disadvantaged background, will think and act on just-right opportunities *repeatedly* to learn what they need to learn and to adjust what they need to adjust in order to reach the goals they most desire. In other words, all people have the ability to regulate their thoughts, feelings, and actions in pursuit of goals that enable them to be self-determined people who identify themselves as being free.

Application of the optimal prospects principle on behalf of individuals in need of social redress results in just-right matches between opportunity and capacity. These just-right matches, in turn, engage the thoughts and actions of those receiving that redress by empowering them to enhance their own capacity and to improve their own opportunities for living a self-determined life. It matters little if the individuals empowered are with or without disabilities, impoverished, or enriched because the goal is the same for all—*increased engagement in challenging opportunity to pursue desirable life goals.* Indeed, in past decades, this has been the direction, if not the content, of compensatory policies emanating from equal opportunity programs designed to improve prospects for individuals with disabilities and/or disadvantaged backgrounds. Court decisions and legislative mandates in the 1960s and 1970s focused upon building capacity for learning through programs such as Head Start for disadvantaged youth and through individualized education planning and instruction for students with disabilities. They also attempted to restructure social opportunity by requiring capacity building to take place in desegregated schools for African American students and in least restrictive environments for students with disabilities. The intention was for these early experiences to improve prospects for pursuing adult opportunity after school. Schooling was to provide comprehensive social reparation through capacity building and opportunity enhancement.

THE SPECIAL EDUCATION OPPORTUNITY

This perspective provides coherence in our understanding of the evolution of social policy from the judicial precedent set by *Brown v. Board of Education* in 1954 to the legislative precedents established by the Education for All Handicapped Children Act of 1975 (PL 94-142), the Individuals with Disabilities Education Act of 1990 (IDEA) (PL 101-476), and the Americans with Disabilities Act of 1990 (PL 101-336). Such precedents reveal the right to self-determination to be the underlying moral ideal driving social policy and specify a redress principle implied by the moral and legal obligation to promote the realization of that right.

Equal opportunity theory explains this moral claim for fairness in liberty for all by showing how the discrepancy between the right and the experience of self-determination depends upon an individual's capacity and opportunity to choose and enact choice in pursuit of self-determined needs and interests. When either capacity or opportunity to self-determine is diminished or constrained, the experience of self-determination diminishes; when this diminished experience persists, the right to self-determination is abrogated (Mithaug, 1995). The solution to this problem is to improve prospects for self-determination by providing opportunities that constitute just-right challenges for engagement in the self-directed life. The implication of this solution is that all people, regardless of who they are, where they come from, or whether or not they have a disability, will think and act on just-right opportunity because by learning what they need to learn and adjusting what they need to adjust, they will reach the goals in life that are most valuable to them. In other words, all persons will regulate their thoughts, feelings, and actions in pursuit of goals that define themselves as self-determining persons.

Special education opportunity has the capacity to provide just-right challenges for all children and youth with disabilities. In fact, it has a moral obligation to do just that—to engage students' thoughts and actions in learning that leads to enhanced capacity and improved adult opportunity for a self-determined life after school. Moreover, this appears to be the direction of federal school-to-work policies that seek to increase correspondence between learning in school and working in the community so students can adjust more successfully to adult life. Again, the underlying assumption is that matching student capacity with community opportunity is necessary for students to have a fair chance at determining their own future as adults.

Unfortunately, the debate about the direction of special education reform tends to separate student capacity from social opportunity by claiming one or the other of these conditions should be the sole criterion for determining what is an appropriate education. One position emphasizes the improvement of students' capacities through instruction that meets individual needs and the other emphasizes enhancement of students' social opportunities through various inclusive educational placements. The problem with both positions is that neither attaches an ultimate purpose to the particular version of the special education opportunity it advocates. This problem is solved when the purpose attached to all special education opportunity is to increase students' prospects for self-determination. With this reattachment of means to ultimate ends, the relationship between capacity and opportunity becomes coherent, and the purpose and challenge for educators becomes clear: to identify those optimally challenging connections between student capacity and social opportunity that maximize students' prospects for self-determination in adult life.

CONCLUSIONS

This chapter began with a description of two special education students: Doris, who learned to regulate her behavior to get what she wanted over the long haul, and Carey, who lacked any self-defined direction in what she did. While Doris strived continuously and succeeded frequently, Carey rarely strived and when she did she usually failed. According to self-regulation theory, Carey was experiencing a suboptimal match between her capacity and her opportunities. Or, stated in terms that Carey might understand, she lacked the ability to find those just-right challenges that would engage her mind and encourage her pursuit. Consequently, she spent her time dreaming and avoiding challenging opportunity. For Doris, by contrast, there was an optimal match between her capacity and her opportunity, and as a result she spent her time pursuing those ends in life she most desired.

Self-regulation theory helps us understand these differences in how Doris and Carey regulate themselves to get what they need and want in life. Although both students regulate their behaviors to produce desirable outcomes, they do so in very different ways. Doris regulates herself to control her circumstances by *choosing* those opportunities that she has a reasonable chance of engaging successfully, while Carey avoids making such choices by waiting for something to happen to her. And, more often than not, nothing very positive does happen.

This chapter described the optimal prospect principle for guiding our interventions on behalf of students like Carey. According to this principle, we should focus on the match between a student's capacity and her opportunity by striving to find that just-right challenge that engages her in the opportunity. Self-induced engagement is what we need to promote first; specific learning outcomes are a natural consequence of this engagement. The reasoning behind this new focus for individualized instruction is that engagement is always prior to learning, and self-induced engagement is always prior to the application and generalization of that learning to meaningful problems and circumstances in life. Moreover, when we observe this engagement in self-selected challenges, we call it self-determination.

REFERENCES

Americans with Disabilities Act of 1990 (ADA), PL 101-336. (July 26, 1990). Title 42, U.S.C. 12101 et seq: *U.S. Statutes at Large, 104,* 327–378.
Brim, G. (1992). *Ambition: How we manage success and failure throughout our lives.* New York: Basic Books.
Brown v. Board of Education. (1954). 347 U.S. 483, 493–495.
Csikszentmihalyi, M. (1990). *Flow: The psychology of optimal experience.* New York: Harper & Row.
Education for All Handicapped Children Act of 1975, PL 94-142. (August 23, 1977). Title 20, U.S.C. 1401 et seq: *U.S. Statutes at Large, 89,* 773–796.
Gray, T. (1991). *Freedom.* Atlantic Highlands, NJ: Humanities Press International.
Humana, C. (1992). *World human rights guide* (3rd ed.). New York: Oxford University Press.
Individuals with Disabilities Education Act of 1990 (IDEA), PL 101-476. (October 30, 1990). Title 20, U.S.C. 1400 et seq: *U.S. Statutes at Large, 104,* 1103–1151.
Mithaug, D.E. (in press). *Equal opportunity theory.* Newbury Park, CA: Sage Publications.
Mithaug, D.E. (1993). *Self-regulation theory: How optimal adjustment maximizes gain.* Westport, CT: Praeger.
Mithaug, D.E., Martin, J.E., & Agran, M. (1987). Adaptability instruction: The goal of transitional programming. *Exceptional Children, 53,* 500–505.

Mithaug, D.E., Martin, J.E., Agran, M., & Rusch, F.R. (1988). *Why special education graduates fail: How to teach them to succeed.* Colorado Springs, CO: Ascent Publications.

U.S. Department of Education. (1994). *The national agenda for achieving better results for children and youth with disabilities.* Washington, DC: Author.

Wolman, M., Campeau, P.L., DuBois, P.A., Mithaug, D.E., & Stolarski, V.S. (1994). *AIR self-determination scale and user guide.* Palo Alto, CA: American Institutes for Research.

Section II

PROMOTING SELF-DETERMINATION ACROSS THE LIFE SPAN

Chapter 9

SELF-DETERMINATION AS A GOAL OF EARLY CHILDHOOD AND ELEMENTARY EDUCATION

Brian Abery and Robert Zajac

IN SPITE OF the potential importance of self-determination to the quality of life experienced by children and adults alike, there is much that is still not known about this construct. Based upon available research, however, it appears that the emergence of self-determination entails a developmental process involving not only the acquisition of skills, but also the integration of these competencies with each other and with the knowledge the individual has accumulated through experience (see also Doll, Sands, Wehmeyer, & Palmer, Chapter 5). This process is not a short-term endeavor that can be completed within a few years. Rather, it is an undertaking initiated shortly after birth that continues over the entire course of one's life (Abery, 1994a; Cohen & Brown, 1993).

In an effort to encourage the consideration of self-determination as a critical outcome of early childhood and elementary special education, this chapter 1) provides a rationale for addressing self-determination at the early childhood and elementary levels and 2) describes applications for early childhood and elementary educators with a focus on the specific roles that the school and family can play in this developmental process.

Preparation of this chapter was supported by a research project funded through the U.S. Department of Education, Office of Special Education Programs, Grant No. H023J2001, and by a cooperative agreement between the National Institute on Disability and Rehabilitation Research (NIDRR) and the Research and Training Center on Residential Services and Community Living at the University of Minnesota, College of Education and Human Development, located within the Institute on Community Integration. The opinions expressed herein are those of the authors.

FACILITATING SELF-DETERMINATION DURING THE EARLY YEARS: A RATIONALE

If one accepts the assumption that self-determination is a developmental process (e.g., see Doll et al., Chapter 5), it makes little sense to wait until a child has matured into an adult before providing instruction to enhance this outcome. Conceptualizing self-determination as a developmental process has a number of advantages, especially for children with disabilities. First, as children with disabilities often take longer to master complex skills, starting instruction in this area at an early age allows sufficient time for the development of the competencies necessary for the exercise of personal control. Second, taking this approach encourages significant adults to provide opportunities for age-appropriate decision making at a time when they can easily supervise and support children. Third, the provision of early instruction allows children to practice and refine their self-determination capacities by making relatively simple choices. Fourth, early efforts to enhance self-determination have the potential to prevent children with disabilities from developing long histories of overdependence, a low sense of self-efficacy, and an external locus of control. Fifth, because many of the skills, attitudes, and knowledge required for the assumption of personal control have their roots in child development, it is relatively easy to infuse learning opportunities naturalistically into early childhood and elementary education programs.

Unfortunately, when parents and professionals speak about self-determination, it is typically young adults to whom they are referring. The educational and home environments of many young children with disabilities are not designed to maximize opportunities for control or the acquisition of the competencies necessary for self-determination (Cook, Brotherson, Weigel-Garrey, & Mize, Chapter 6). Special education programs at both the early childhood and elementary levels continue to stress classroom routines that feature strong adult control over student behavior and compliance with teacher directives (Guess & Siegel-Causey, 1985; Houghton, Bronicki, & Guess, 1987; Orlansky,1979; Peck, 1985).

If professionals and parents want to facilitate the autonomous functioning of children with disabilities when they reach adulthood, they need to provide multiple opportunities for the acquisition, practice, and refinement of the necessary competencies for self-determination at as early an age as possible (Abery, 1994b). Skill training, opportunities for control, and environmental supports will need to be made available on a regular basis, infused into the ongoing curriculum and daily activities. This will require a major change in the manner in which early childhood and elementary special education services are conceptualized and delivered so that children with disabilities are challenged, encouraged to take reasonable risks, and allowed to make mistakes as well as experience their consequences.

SELF-DETERMINATION AND SOCIAL RELATIONSHIPS

Cohen and Brown (1993) suggested that many of the foundations for adult behavior, including self-determination, can be traced to childhood. Between infancy and the later elementary school years, children develop the ability to effectively communicate their needs and desires, move about in and manipulate the physical environment, regulate their own behavior, set personal goals, make choices based upon individual preferences, and advocate for themselves. In addition, it is during this period of development that an awareness of self and a sense of self-efficacy emerge (Doll et al., Chapter 5).

The majority of these competencies develop as a result of interactions between the individual and the environment (Abery, 1994a, 1994b). Often, the most salient features of those environments are the individuals who populate them. Initially, the context for child development is relatively small and centers around relationships with primary caregivers. As a child matures, interactions with friends and acquaintances leave their own mark on development. Entry into preschool or elementary school presents children with extended opportunities for interactions with peers and with the chance to establish relationships with unrelated adults. As children mature, they do not give up one context for another. Rather, the potential for an interplay between the family, school, and community emerges.

Interactions, in turn, are grounded in the relationships that have been established between children and their parents, family members, educators, and friends. A discussion of self-determination as it relates to early childhood and elementary school children would be incomplete without consideration of these influences. Although there are a myriad of relationships that are likely to have an impact on self-determination, the following section focuses on a limited number of these, including the attachment relationship, parenting and family interaction style, and the nature of instructional environments.

Caregiver–Infant Interaction and Self-Determination

The development of a secure attachment relationship with a caregiver is an issue that has generated considerable interest among developmental psychologists since the early 1970s. The core concept of attachment is that of a two-way control system learned as a result of interactions between the infant and caregiver (Ainsworth, Blehar, Waters, & Wall, 1978). This relationship is designed to increase the safety and security of the infant by ensuring that a caregiver will be available when needed (Bowlby, 1969, 1973, 1980). The quality of the attachment relationship is also likely to have a direct impact on the emergence of a number of capacities related to the development of self-determination.

Ainsworth and her associates (Ainsworth, Blehar, Waters, & Walls, 1978) postulated that attachment relationships typically fall into one of two basic categories: secure or insecure. Since the mid-1970s, the results of a number of research studies have indicated that there are long-term correlates to such attachments. Children categorized as securely attached as infants have, at later dates, been found to be more curious, self-reliant, eager to solve problems independently, likely to serve in leadership roles, and less dependent upon adults than their insecurely attached counterparts (Arend, Gove, & Sroufe, 1979; Barrett & Trevitt, 1991; Speltz, Greenberg, & Deklyen, 1990; Sroufe, 1983; Sroufe & Fleeson, 1988; Waters, Wippman, & Sroufe, 1979). As Belsky and his colleagues have noted, it is not that securely attached children are more intellectually advanced than their insecurely attached peers, but that they appear more willing to apply their competencies and take on new challenges (Belsky, Garduque, & Hrncir, 1984).

The behavioral characteristics associated with secure attachment are among the most important precursors of self-determination. Confidence, curiosity, self-reliance, and independent problem solving are all basic capacities necessary for individuals to exercise control over their lives. The attachment relationship also provides infants with a secure base from which to explore (Sroufe & Fleeson, 1988). Understanding that a primary caregiver is available to provide support, securely attached children effectively explore their environments because they trust that, if difficulties are encountered, support will be forthcoming. Through this relationship they learn at an early age that if they can effectively communicate their needs, they can create a desired effect within their environment.

The degree to which there are similarities and differences in the attachment relationships of infants with and without disabilities is still open to debate. Studies of children with disabilities have reported relatively normal distributions of infants among attachment categories (i.e., severe and insecure) (Hadadian, 1995; Lederberg & Mobley, 1990; Rogers, Ozonoff, & Maslin-Cole, 1991). Most of these studies, however, have not included infants with severe disabilities. In addition, recent research has found significant relationships between cognitive, linquistic, and gross motor development levels (Rogers et al., 1991) and parental attitudes towards disability (Hadadian, 1995), suggesting the possibility of poorer attachment quality for children with severe and multiple disabilities. Regardless of this research, it must be remembered that a relatively large number of all children (30%–40%) are typically found to be insecurely attached (Ainsworth, 1979; Lederberg & Mobley, 1990).

At the current time, little information is available as to the developmental outcomes of insecurely attached infants with disabilities. What research has demonstrated to date are significant differences in the manner in which infants with and without disabilities respond to their parents and how their parents interact with them. Numerous studies have found that infants with disabilities 1) are less active and responsive (Crnic, Ragozin, Greenberg, Robinson, & Basham, 1983), 2) engage in lower frequencies of mutual eye-gaze (Crnic et al., 1983; Malatesta, Grigoryev, Lamb, Albin, & Culver, 1986), 3) provide less readily readable cues (Rogers, 1988), and 4) smile less than typically developing infants (Brooks-Gunn & Lewis, 1982). Although the evidence is less than unequivocal, caregivers appear to respond to these differences by 1) showing less positive affect in the relationship (Rogers, 1988), 2) decreasing their responsiveness to the infant over time (Brooks-Gunn & Lewis, 1982; Kogan, Tyler, & Turner, 1974; Wasserman & Allen, 1985), and 3) being more directive and controlling within the context of interactions (Barrera & Vella, 1987; Lambrenos, Cox, Weindling, & Calam, 1991; Tannock, 1988). Given data that clearly indicate the relation between these aspects of caregiver–infant interaction, attachment, and later developmental outcomes, infants with disabilities would appear to be at risk for less than optimal self-determination during their later years (Barrett & Trevitt, 1991; Goldberg, Lojkasek, Gartner, & Corter, 1989; Speltz et al., 1990).

Family Interaction, Parenting Style, and Self-Determination

Due to the characteristics inherent in many disabling conditions and the assumptions that members of society frequently make about such individuals, children with disabilities often do not experience opportunities for personal control outside of the family setting. This magnifies the importance of the home environment in fostering self-determination (Cook et al., Chapter 6). If family members become highly skilled at recognizing and responding to unspoken preferences, provide few opportunities for control, or fail to allow the child to experience the consequences of personal choices, the end result may be a child who rarely expresses preferences, has a difficult time making decisions, and cannot effectively problem-solve. Family life, however, also has the potential to facilitate the development of self-determination.

Research has clearly established a relationship between family interaction and developmental outcomes for children with and without disabilities. Baumrind (1967) and her colleagues delineated three modes of family interaction/parenting style that have been found to be closely associated with a variety of aspects of child competence directly related to self-determination. An *authoritarian* style of parenting is characterized by high levels of demanding and low levels of responsivity on the part of parents. In these families, parents attempt to direct, control, and evaluate the behavior and attitudes of their children in accordance with a strict set of standards. A second pattern identified is termed *permissive*. These types of parents make few, if any, demands; are tolerant of their children's impulses; and rarely mete out discipline. The third style of parenting distinguished by Baumrind is referred to as *authoritative*. This pattern of parent–child interaction is characterized by parental warmth, clear standard setting, firm rule enforcement, encouragement of the child's independence and individuality, and recognition of the rights of both children and parents.

During the preschool years, children of authoritative parents have been found to be self-reliant, self-controlled, and socially responsible. Children raised in families in which an authoritarian style of parenting is employed have been characterized as detached and controlling, with low levels of independence and social responsibility. Immaturity, a lack of impulse control, and the lowest levels of independence and social responsibility describe preschool children of permissive parents (Baumrind, 1991; Baumrind & Black, 1967).

Baumrind continued her studies of these families when child participants were 8–9 years old and again at 15 years of age. At both of these ages, children of authoritative parents remained the most competent of all three groups. Compared to their peers, children from authoritative/democratic families were individuated, mature, resilient, self-regulated, and socially responsible, with high self-esteem and an internal locus of control. Children in families in which parenting remained authoritarian in style were found to be lacking in individuation, autonomy, and social consciousness and had an external locus of control. Relatively low levels of social responsibility, self-regulation, and achievement orientation characterized children of permissive/nondirective parents (Baumrind, 1971, 1973, 1991).

In the years since Baumrind first initiated her studies, a number of other researchers have investigated the correlates of parenting style from preschool to adolescence. The results of these investigations clearly indicate that parental warmth and responsiveness, firm rule setting and enforcement, and encouragement toward independence and individuality are associated with positive developmental outcomes. This includes high levels of academic achievement (Dornbusch, Ritter, Leiderman, Roberts, & Fralleigh, 1987; Hess & McDevitt, 1984; Steinberg, Elman, & Mounts, 1989; Switzer, 1990), self-esteem (Parish & McCluskey, 1994), self-assertion (Crockenberg & Litman, 1990), effective behavior management skills (Spivack & Cianci, 1987), and problem-solving capabilities (Schaefer, 1985).

The most systematic attempt to assess the impact of family functioning on children with disabilities has been a series of studies undertaken by Nihira and her colleagues (Mink & Nihira, 1987; Mink, Nihira, & Meyers, 1983; Nihira, Meyers, & Mink, 1983; Nihira, Mink, & Meyers, 1981, 1985). Using a variety of measures of family interaction, this research team found that the social competence of children with disabilities (i.e., their ability to socially interact with peers and adults in a positive manner) was closely related to the harmony and quality of the parental relationship, educational and cognitive stimulation provided in the home, and the degree of emotional support and approval children with disabilities received from family members. Social adjustment (the ability of the child to function within established behavioral guidelines and rules), however, was found to be significantly related to cohesion and harmony within the family environment as a whole. In a research effort of a similar vein, the social, behavioral, and academic competence of children with Down syndrome was found to be closely associated with moderate levels of family cohesion and family flexibility (Abery, 1990).

Much of the current evidence connecting family interaction/parenting style to self-determination is indirect in nature, consisting of links that have been established between the quality of these relationships and capacities hypothesized as necessary for the exercise of personal control. What has directly been demonstrated is that children with disabilities raised in families that provide opportunities for self-determination that are appropriate with respect to both age and ability do, in fact, assume greater control over their lives than their counterparts who do not have these opportunities available. These results appear valid for children with mild as well as moderate–severe disabilities ranging in age from 5 to 21 years (Abery, McGrew, & Smith, 1995).

Self-Determination and School Experiences

In 1987, the National Association for the Education of Young Children took the position that the growth of young children is best served by providing them with opportunities within the context of the classroom to initiate their own activities and become self-directed learners (Bredekamp, 1987). The rationale for this approach is based upon a substantial body of knowledge suggesting the differential impact of teacher-centered versus student-centered learning. Approaches to early and elementary education supportive of student autonomy and choice have been associated with high intrinsic motivation and self-esteem (Deci & Ryan, 1982, 1985, 1987), increased attention span and greater persistence (Hauser-Cramm, Bronson, & Upshur, 1993; Hutt, Tyler, Hutt, & Christopherson, 1989), higher levels of positive social interaction (Hauser-Cramm et al., 1993; Robson,1991), and increased ability to self-regulate behavior (Robson, 1991), as well as assisting young children in becoming independent, self-directed learners (Jowett & Sylva, 1986). Incongruence between students' desire to have input into classroom decision making and their perceptions of the availability of such opportunities has been associated with declines in their motivation, increased misbehavior, and lowered ratings of interest in and perceptions of the usefulness of school (Mac Iver, Klingel, & Reuman, 1986; Mac Iver & Reuman, 1988).

Given this research, one might expect to find that the majority of early childhood and elementary special education classrooms provide ongoing opportunities for choice and support student self-determination. Unfortunately, this does not appear to be the case. A number of observers (e.g., Deci, Hodges, Pierson, & Tomassone, 1992; Hanline & Fox, 1993; Mahoney, O'Sullivan, & Fors, 1989; Mahoney, Robinson, & Powell, 1992; Odom & McEvoy, 1990) have noted that early childhood special education programs, despite employing many recommended practices, are typically teacher-directed, highly structured in nature, and narrowly focused on skill development. The emphasis on performing specific behaviors in order to obtain extrinsic reinforcement focuses teachers away from self-directed learning and child preferences and toward the encouragement of conformity and compliance with directives.

Contemporary early childhood education is grounded in developmental theory (Bredekamp, 1991), with its primary program goal entailing the mastery of basic developmental tasks. Programs implementing early childhood education recommended practice procedures are based on child-initiated, child-directed, teacher-supported play (Hanline & Fox, 1993; Mahoney et al., 1992). These programs maximize childrens' opportunities to make choices, initiate and engage in activities based upon their own preferences, and learn in a self-directed manner. This does not mean that teachers in such classrooms are mere observers, as they use a variety of strategies to maximize the learning that occurs based upon the unique competencies of each child (Johnson & Johnson, 1992; Kostelnik, 1992). A considerable body of research supports the efficacy of these child-centered approaches (see Guralnick, 1993; Johnson & Johnson, 1992; Mahoney et al., 1992).

Although available data suggest that the classroom environments of many preschool children with disabilities are not maximally conducive to self-determination, one might hope that as these children matured, they would be encouraged to assume greater control within the classroom. Most of these students, however, regardless of age, appear to have few opportunities for control within the context of the school day (Abery & Eggebeen, 1993; Abery, McGrew, et al., 1995; Guess & Siegel-Causey, 1985; Guess, Benson, & Siegel-Causey, 1985; Houghton et al., 1987; Peck, 1985). In addition, as Cohen and Brown (1993) discovered in their study of the IEP goals and objectives of children with disabilities, little attention is typically given to incorporating instruction that will specifically enhance students' capacities for self-determination. The outcome of this state of affairs is that our educational system is socializing students with disabilities to remain dependent upon others to set goals, make choices, problem-solve, and advocate for them. Nevertheless, once they reach adulthood, these students are expected to take charge of their own lives.

ENHANCING SELF-DETERMINATION: THE NEED FOR A COLLABORATIVE EFFORT

Over the past 5 years, a number of researchers and policy makers have argued that self-determination should be one of the primary educational goals for students with disabilities (Abery, 1994a, 1994b; Ward, 1994; Wehmeyer, 1992, 1994). Beginning in 1990, the Transition Programs Division of the Office of Special Education and Rehabilitative Services provided funding directed at developing programs aimed at achieving this goal (Ward, Chapter 1). These efforts, however, have had a negligible effect upon the developing self-determination of preschool and elementary school children with disabilities. Although it makes little sense to view self-determination solely as an issue of early adulthood, educators still appear to be taking this approach despite indications that many, if not most, of the fundamental roots of personal control lie within developmental processes initiated during early childhood and the elementary school years (see Doll et al., Chapter 5).

Significant changes will need to take place in the manner in which young children with disabilities are educated if the enhancement of their self-determination is to be achieved. This approach will require exposure to a curriculum into which opportunities for the acquisition of the skills, knowledge, and attitudes/beliefs necessary for self-determination are infused on a daily basis and at as early an age as possible. Robson (1992) has presented a model that can serve as a framework for discussing many of the issues relevant to developing early childhood and elementary classroom environments that will facilitate self-determination. This model focuses on structures that can be created within schools that are advantageous to a child's developing self-determination including 1) the structure of classroom organization, 2) structures related to children's tasks and activities, and 3) the structure of relationships. Although this model was clearly developed with the school in mind, it can also be used to examine some of the more salient family and parenting issues related to self-determination described on the following pages.

Classroom and Family Structure

All classroom and home environments have some form of structure (Cook et al., Chapter 6; Robson, 1992). Some classrooms and families have a *child-directed* orientation (Deci & Ryan, 1982; Nihira et al., 1985). This type of organizational structure allows children to solve their own problems, assess their own competence, and provides a considerable degree of freedom within adult-set limits with respect to what children do, when they do it, and the manner in which it is accomplished. Focusing on the ideas of Hutt et al. (1989) and Rowland (1987), Robson (1992) argued that, in order to foster autonomy and self-determination, emphasis must be placed on developing structures that do not result in children giving authority and responsibility back to adults, but rather encourage them to develop powers of choice and judgment based upon the idea of shared control. This notion is not new, for a number of research findings indicate that at some points in development, parents and children typically share controlling functions (Dornbusch et al., 1987). Maccoby (1984) refers to this period, which occurs during late childhood and early adolescence, as being characterized by the process of *co-regulation.* During this phase of development, parents continue to exercise general supervisory control—monitoring, guiding, and supporting from a distance and helping children to develop the skills that will allow them to effectively control their own behavior—while children wield moment-to-moment control. Within the context of this model, the role of teachers and parents is one of facilitator and supporter.

Teaching and parenting on the basis of a child-directed approach requires structuring (or restructuring) the environment to encourage children's attention in self-initiated and self-directed learning (Hanline & Fox, 1993). Available research indicates that the physical arrangement of the environment can do much to stimulate this type of engagement on the part of the child (Bailey & Wolery, 1992; Spodek, Saracho, & Davis, 1991; Wolfgang & Wolfgang, 1992). One way to ensure that the environment supports self-determination is to give children as much say as possible with respect to the organization of their surroundings. Whether the area in question is a bedroom, playroom, or classroom, providing children with an opportunity to decide which of the available pieces of furniture they will use, where these will be placed, and the specific functions they will serve is a first step in assisting them to gain some control over their environment. Flexibility in the manner in which space is used is a second critical aspect of the classroom or home environment that can serve to either facilitate or hinder self-determination. Although materials need to be placed in a manner that facilitates choice and accessibility, it is important that adults do not view the use of various areas in an inflexible, manner. A third structural aspect of all systems likely to have an impact on self-determination is the manner in which time is viewed. Hartley (1987) observed that classroom environments that treat time in a regimented fashion, allocate it in exactly the same manner for all children, and fail to provide choices to students with respect to the use of time are unlikely to promote feelings of personal control.

Structure and Nature of Children's Tasks and Activities

The specific activities that will foster a developing sense of self-determination must obviously be selected on the basis of the unique capacities and support needs of each child. As Gothelf and Brown (1996) have discussed, however, there are a general set of guidelines that can be used to ensure that the program developed for any specific child facilitates enhanced personal control. First, the program must employ flexible curricula that allow students to make choices on a daily basis. These choices must be respected and attempts to exercise personal control reinforced through respectful, nonjudgmental responses to children. Second, learning opportunities should be provided that enhance students' understanding of the potential they have to exercise control over their environment. Third, the program must facilitate students acquiring, practicing, and refining the capacities for self-determination.

Allowing Student Choice   Earlier in this chapter, a comparison was made between traditional approaches to early childhood and elementary special education and the strategies now recommended for early childhood education programs. While the former focuses on children engaging in a preselected set of skill-building activities, the latter emphasizes educators promoting, supporting, and building upon child-initiated activities and respecting the preferences and current interests of the student. A number of educators (e.g., Hanline & Fox, 1993; Mahoney et al., 1992; Robson, 1992) have suggested that this latter approach is just as, if not more, effective in facilitating skill development as traditional methods employed by special educators.

A child-directed approach to education benefits children by providing them with ongoing opportunities to make choices within a wide variety of areas and to experience the consequences of their decisions in a supportive environment. This can be accomplished by deemphasizing the work aspects of learning and accentuating those aspects that focus on play and encourage children to initiate active learning, including exploration, manipulation, and problem solving. Although most children associate learning with work, the impact of play upon the acquisition of skills, knowledge, and beliefs has been known for some time (e.g., see Piaget, 1950, 1954). Play provides a flexible practice ground for the development of many of the skills necessary for self-determination. When engaged in self-initiated activities, children learn how to 1) set goals for themselves, 2) make decisions, 3) effectively problem-solve, 4) communicate with others, and 5) take responsibility for their behavior. To date, approaches of this nature have primarily been used within early childhood education programs. Their application to the education of elementary school children with disabilities, however, appears quite promising.

Emphasizing the playful aspects of learning does not mean that teaching does not occur. Within the context of a child-directed program, children are offered a variety of activities from which they can choose that are motivating and support the acquisition of developmental skills targeted for instruction. The application of this approach does not mean that adults stand idle observing children. Teachers and parents must structure the environment to foster children's learning through exploration. In addition, they serve as a resource to the child providing the necessary scaffolding for learning (Meadows & Cashdan, 1988). This might include support and encouragement, focusing attention, redirecting student behavior, and modeling new ideas.

Enhancing Student Understanding of Self-Determination Outcomes A second programmatic characteristic that has the potential to facilitate self-determination is the ongoing provision of opportunities for children to better understand the potential they have to exercise control over their environment and the possible outcomes of this control. All too often, family members and the professionals who serve children with disabilities have become so adept at accurately "reading" the preferences of these children that they inadvertently short-circuit the self-determination process. Over time, the frequent selection of activities on the part of adults is likely to lead to the child decreasing his or her attempts to exercise control. In addition, children need to be allowed to experience the negative as well as the positive consequences of their decisions. If this does not occur, and adults intervene every time a poor choice is made, it is likely that little time and effort will be expended on the part of the child in carefully thinking through each alternative prior to making a choice.

Consider the example of a young child with a disability who has few of the skills needed for independently finding his or her way around the community. One strategy to increase the child's knowledge and understanding of the environment, as well as enhance his or her feeling of personal competence, might be to encourage the child to assist teachers when they need small items picked up or delivered to other sites within the school. Although such a student might take some wrong turns when initially serving in this capacity, those mistakes provide an excellent opportunity for learning to find one's way in the environment. Through first providing a physical orientation to the environment, teaching the child how to ask for directions from others, and routinely notifying colleagues prior to sending the student to deliver or pick up materials, a teacher can minimize the child's vulnerability while at the same time challenging him or her to learn a new set of behaviors, the effects of which would contribute to their enhanced self-determination. Although efforts within this area obviously must take safety into consideration, eliminating children's opportunities to make challenging choices and experience their mistakes also suspends the possibility of learning within the context of these situations.

Most young children, especially children with disabilities, have a tendency to make choices with little consideration of the impact these decisions have upon others (see Doll et al., Chapter 5). The enhancement of children's understanding of the potential outcomes of self-determination can serve an important function of increasing their appreciation of the responsibility that accompanies the exercise of personal control. Incorporating a time for reflection upon choice making provides an important opportunity for children to carefully examine the impact of their choices on both others and themselves. Deciding to continue a popular activity that can accommodate only a limited number of children near the conclusion of the day, for example, not only will limit the opportunities of other children to engage in the task but will also curtail the occasion for the child in question to take part in alternative valued activities. Acknowledgment of such dilemmas is likely to build a sense of responsibility to the larger group and will also encourage children to make choices based upon knowledge of their personal preference hierarchies at any given time.

Facilitating the Acquisition of Self-Determination Competencies   If early childhood and elementary education programs are to effectively enhance those capacities that serve as the foundations of self-determination, efforts to infuse daily opportunities for the acquisition and refinement of these skills will need to be undertaken in both the classroom and at home. In addition, it will be necessary to ensure that all students have the resources and supports to accommodate them when their disabilities delay or preclude the development of such capacities. Although it is not possible to prescribe specific interventions that will enhance the self-determination of children with disabilities without a particular child in mind, there are number of guidelines that can be used to increase the probability that such programming will have a positive effect on development within this area.

Motor and Mobility Skills   One aspect of childhood development that has an impact on self-determination and is particularly relevent to early childhood educators is the development of motor skills. During the first months of life, infants have little mobility and relatively poorly developed motor skills. Gradually children begin to control selective movements voluntarily and rely less on reflexive reactions to environmental stimulation (Eckert, 1987). By 6–8 months of age, most infants have developed mobility in the prone position, are able to roll over in both directions, and sit independently (Eckert, 1987).

When children acquire the capacity for self-produced locomotion (i.e., crawling and walking) and enhanced prehensile skills (i.e., the palmar grasp), they quickly expand their capacity to explore and manipulate their environment (Eckert, 1987). The greater part of motor development, however, is not complete until children are at least 5–6 years of age and have the opportunity to practice and refine their abilities within this area (Eckert, 1987). As these abilities develop, children reduce the dependence on caregivers that had so dominated earlier relationships.

Gross and fine motor skills and increased mobility are acquired much more slowly, if at all, by many infants and toddlers with disabilities. If children are not mobile, are unable to lift their heads, or have yet to develop the skills necessary to physically manipulate objects, then exploration of the environment is curtailed. There are a relatively large number of disabilities of differing etiology that have the potential to restrict movement to such a degree as to serve as a barrier to self-determination. A description of the specific interventions necessary to improve functioning within these areas is beyond the scope of this chapter. The general goal of intervention as it relates to self-determination, however, is to help the child move as normally as possible, use movement to initiate interactions with and exercise control over the environment, and provide opportunities for increased independence. Keeping these goals in mind, it is essential that parents and professionals work collaboratively to develop strategies that assist the child in minimizing abnormal and involuntary movement patterns and maximizing functional motor skills. Employment of alternative handling methods as well as specialized equipment (e.g., prone boards) can make the child's environment more user-friendly and aid in gross and fine motor skills development.

Keeping in mind the importance of a child-directed approach to intervention, opportunities for the exercise and refinement of specific gross and fine motor skills can be integrated into daily activities from which the child is asked to choose rather than presented solely as isolated, teacher-directed exercises. The use of a prone board placed within activity areas selected by the child, for example, can help transform activities in which it would be difficult for the child to engage into opportunities for learning. Providing access to and instruction in the use of powered mobility equipment (e.g., electric wheelchairs) at as early an age as possible is critical if the child with limited physical mobility is to acquire knowledge necessary to exercise control over the environment. Both of these strategies aim to afford children greater access to a variety of activities and enable them to more adequately explore and manipulate their home and school environments in a manner that will facilitate the self-determination process.

Communication Skills   One of the most basic skills necessary for children to exercise control over their environment is the ability to clearly communicate preferences. Historically, attempts to teach children with disabilities new communication skills were confined to highly structured programs. Unfortunately, interventions of this nature often did not lead to the development and use of functional communication (Dattilo & Camarata, 1991). Within the past several years, a variety of approaches to instruction within this area have been developed that not only promise to enhance basic communication skills more effectively, but also are likely to lead to increased self-determination.

More than any other characteristic, approaches to communication intervention that are supportive of a child's developing self-determination are *functional* in nature. As Rowland and Schweigert (1993) suggested, such approaches stress communication that occurs within natural settings, results in real consequences, and is used spontaneously. The philosophy of providing instruction within natural settings takes advantage of the many communication opportunities available to children both inside and outside of school. As they play, dress, and take part in other activities, natural opportunities for instruction occur that are likely to be considerably more meaningful than 1-hour therapy sessions in a professional's office. This increases the likelihood that acquired skills will generalize to other environments and that a student will be motivated to use available abilities (Halle, 1988).

Many of the communicative attempts of young students with disabilities, especially children experiencing speech and language difficulties, are not responded to by others (Houghton et al., 1987; Peck, 1989). As with any behavior, a lack of responsiveness to communication initiations over an extended period of time may result in the extinction of communication attempts. The interaction styles and responsiveness of adults can do much to minimize the occurrence of such an undesirable outcome.

Over the past 20 years, research results have consistently indicated that facilitative rather than directive styles of social interaction enhance children's communicative performance and that high levels of listener responsiveness are a critical component of communication interactions (Dunst & Lowe, 1986; McDade & Varnedoe, 1987; Peck, 1989). In addition, teachers and parents can use a variety of strategies when interacting with students to encourage the development of their communication skills including expanding children's utterances (Chapman, 1988; Cross, 1984), prompting for higher levels of response that require progressively more advanced communication skills (Warren, McQuarter, & Rogers-Warren, 1984), and promoting peer interaction (Goldstein & Strain, 1988; Romski, Sevcik, & Wilkinson, 1994).

Many students with disabilities, while having learned specific sets of communication skills, fail to use them in a spontaneous fashion (Reichle & Sigafoos, 1991). Ensuring that communication is elicited through natural cues (e.g., a verbal or nonverbal initiation on the part of a peer) within the environment is essential if those skills are to be used to enhance self-determination. Teaching communication within the context of natural settings as well as linking its use to

personal control are likely to be at least partially effective in facilitating spontaneous usage (Dyer, 1989). The additional use of a variety of response prompting
and fading techniques designed to transfer stimulus control including time delay,
verbal prompt-free techniques, and interrupted behavior chain strategies may
also be indicated (Gee, Graham, Goetz, Oshima, & Yoshioka, 1991; Locke &
Mirenda, 1988).

Self-Determination Skills   The specific skills necessary for self-
determination include goal setting, choice making, problem solving, self-
regulation, and personal advocacy competencies. Similar to skill development
within other areas, these capacities that serve as the primary basis for self-
determination are best taught in the natural environment through procedures that
draw upon the daily needs and desires of children. Opportunities to acquire,
practice, and refine these behaviors are abundant throughout the course of the day
both within school and at home. Child-directed early and elementary education
programs, such as those described by Robson (1992), Hanline and Fox (1993),
and Mahoney and his colleagues (1992), provide natural opportunities for
students to practice the exercise of personal control.

Brown and her colleagues (Brown, Belz, Corsi, & Wenig, 1993), for example, have identified several types of choices that can be made within the context
of a child's typical day. These include choosing *within* the context of an activity,
selecting *between two or more activities*, deciding *when* to complete a task, selecting *persons* along with whom to undertake activities, choosing *where* to complete a task, *refusing* to participate in an activity, and choosing to *terminate* a
task. As children develop their problem-solving and self-regulation skills, a more
complex form of personal control can be added to this list which entails children
choosing *how* they will complete an activity (Abery, Rudrud, Arndt, Schauben, &
Eggebeen, 1995). Gothelf and her associates (e.g., Gothelf & Brown, 1996;
Gothelf, Crimmins, Mercer, & Finocchiaro, 1993, 1994) have presented a con-
cise step-by-step process for choice-making instruction within the school environment. Although focused specifically on choice making and developed for children who are deaf-blind, this approach is easily adaptable to enhance other
self-determination capacities and for use with younger children and those with
other types of disabilities.

Working with Lisa   The first author of this chapter used similar procedures to teach a 6-year-old with moderate mental retardation, cerebral palsy, and
few communication skills to take greater control over her school day. Work with
Lisa first began by assisting her to establish a cue she could give to others to
signal that she desired to engage in or terminate a specific classroom activity (a
simple on–off microswitch communication system). Upon entering the class each
day, Lisa was wheeled from one activity area to the next until she cued the
educational aide with whom she worked that she desired to remain at the activity.
When she wished to communicate a desire to change activities, a similar
procedure was followed. Once this process was well established, miniatures (e.g.,

a small block to signify the block building activity area) were introduced to serve as symbolic representations of available classroom activities. At this point, choice of activity was made through a simple pointing response. Photographs and eventually line drawings that could be incorporated into a communication board were, over time, substituted for the miniatures with the result that Lisa could more easily symbolically indicate to others those activities in which she desired to engage. Over the course of several months, proficiency at using this system developed to the extent that Lisa was able to choose those activities in which she desired to engage as well as terminate such tasks when she desired.

The procedures used with Lisa initially focused on providing instruction that would facilitate her choice-making capacities. Over the course of the school year, however, it became clear that with appropriate instructional support, she could do far more than engage in moment-to-moment choice making. An instructional process based upon work in the area of self-regulation (see Bambera & Ager, 1992; Sawyer, Graham, & Harris, 1992) was therefore implemented to enhance Lisa's ability to plan her educational experiences over an extended period of time. Instruction in weekly self-scheduling involved teaching Lisa to use a self-instructional routine that included goal setting, planning, and self-monitoring.

Weekly self-scheduling involved Lisa working with an educational aide each Friday afternoon during which time she selected cards containing line drawings representing the many activities in which she could engage. After selection, each card was placed in a slot representing the specific days the following week in which she desired to take part in the activity. This weekly scheduling was taught through modeling and prompting when necessary. When she arrived at school each morning, Lisa followed a similar procedure to select the sequence of activities she desired to undertake over the course of the day. At this time she was allowed to add any additional activities or remove tasks in which she no longer desired to engage. At the end of each day, Lisa's educational aide reviewed her daily activities with her and, through use of her communication board, she indicated whether she would have desired to have spent more or less time on those activities in which she took part over the course of the day. Using these procedures, Lisa was able to dramatically increase her self-determination within the classroom. In addition, she acquired skills that would eventually allow her to assume greater control in her family life.

As children mature and gain experience in making simple choices, it is important to gradually introduce more complex situations in which decisions need to be made. Although most individuals do not always make their choices in a logical, step-by-step manner, instruction in the processes underlying complex decision making has been shown to be an effective strategy to enhance the quality of decisions made by students with disabilities of various ages. The first step in this process involves conducting an assessment of the existing choice-making skills of the student in question. Following the identification of those processes in which the student has demonstrated a need for improvement, instruction focusing on these aspects of the choice-making process can be incorporated into naturally occurring decision-making situations throughout the school day. The modeling of decision-making sequences along with prompts, when necessary, has been effective in teaching students to 1) learn to independently identify choice-making opportunities, 2) delay choice making until they have considered all available alternatives, 3) evaluate the potential positive and negative consequences of alternatives, 4) choose from among these alternatives, and 5) evaluate personal satisfaction with the choice(s) made (Abery, Rudrud, et al., 1995; Rietveld, 1983).

Structure of Relationships

The family and school are obviously social communities. The nature of the relationships that develop between parents and children, teachers and students, and friends all have an impact on the learning that takes place within these contexts as well as its behavioral manifestations. These relationships have the potential to either support the developing self-determination of the child or hinder its emergence.

Self-Determination and Family Relationships Family relationships, especially those that exist between parents and children, have both a direct and an indirect impact upon the developing child's self-determination. Professionals working with parents of infants and young children with disabilities need to be aware of these influences and provide the necessary support to ensure that the home is a context within which the self-determination of the child is valued and respected, encouraged and reinforced (see Cook et al., Chapter 6). Because parents fulfill their roles in as diverse a manner as educators, it is necessary for educational staff to cultivate an understanding of the family system. This entails an awareness of the extent to which family members understand the construct of self-determination, its importance, and the capacity of people with disabilities to take charge of their own lives. In addition, it involves recognition of the degree to which the family comprehends the necessity of encouraging the development of those capacities necessary for self-determination in their child and the degree to which the home supports this endeavor. An understanding of the family's cultural and religious beliefs as they relate to self-determination, disability, and parent–child relationships is also critical for the educator to possess.

Much of this information can be discerned by talking to family members within their home. Discussion of family members' expectations, desires, and aspirations; the fears they have regarding the child's developing self-determination; and the strategies they currently use to support the acquisition of capacities within this area can easily be obtained in this manner. At the same time, staff can observe parents' interactions with their children as well as the extent to which the home physically supports self-determination. Once an understanding of the family system has been developed, educators can begin to support, where necessary, parents and other family members as they create an environment within which self-determination can thrive. One of the most critical aspects of this environment is the parent–child relationship.

Parents of children with disabilities may need education and support if their interactions with their children are to facilitate self-determination. Reviews of the parent–infant research literature clearly indicate that many infants with disabilities provide less readily readable cues, demonstrate less or more muted affect, and may have difficulties synchronizing turn-taking. Parents tend to react to this by becoming more directive and active at first. Over time, however, their responsiveness to the infant may significantly decrease (Rogers, 1988). Behaviors on the part of both parent and infant have the potential to lead to insecure attachment, decrements in the quantity and quality of the stimulation received by the infant, and difficulties for the child in establishing cause–effect relationships. During this period, early childhood professionals can assist parents to more accurately read their child's cues and work with them to identify the manner in which their child communicates pleasure or displeasure, a need for attention, and the desire to temporarily withdraw to reduce overstimulation (Eggebeen & Leigh, 1994). As children mature and develop the desire to explore their environment and communicate with others more extensively, educators can collaborate with families to facilitate these interactions. Work with parents might include educating them about how to properly position their infant so that the child can reach and grasp objects or supporting them in acquiring and teaching their child to use adaptive switches with toys.

During the preschool and elementary years, children naturally develop the desire to be more in control of their lives. Many parents, however, are unsure as to the specific choices to offer to their children or how to present them. Educational staff can use their knowledge of disabilities and child development to ensure that choice-making opportunities are available to the child that are both developmentally appropriate and occur on a frequent enough basis as to stimulate the development of self-determination. In addition, parents can be taught how to effectively involve their child with a disability in family decision making. Abery and his colleagues (Abery et al., 1994) have developed a family education program designed to enhance family members' abilities to support the developing self-determination of children with disabilities. This program is composed of 15 modules covering a variety of topics related to supporting self-determination. Although initially developed for young adults, this program is easily adaptable for use with older elementary school children.

Self-Determination and Relationships within the School   The school is a significant context for introducing children to interactions with unrelated adults and other children. Unfortunately, most adult–child relationships in this setting take place within the context of a very clear power hierarchy. Many students with disabilities also spend the majority of their school day in segregated classes, hindering their ability to establish relationships with a diverse group of peers. Given that the school relationships of many children with disabilities do little to facilitate self-determination, what needs to change?

Teacher–Student Relationships Children's relationships with their teachers are an often ignored aspect of the school experience, even though most parents will state that it is precisely this relationship that makes a school year a success or failure. Most teacher–student relationships are hierarchical in nature and tend to foster conformity. This type of relationship does little to facilitate the development of self-determination. Relationships based upon shared control or co-regulation, however, create an environment in which all involved experience a degree of control (Robson, 1992). It is this type of environment in which the collaboration, cooperation, and freedom necessary for the development of self-determination is most likely to occur. Within the classroom, teachers make their purposes and reasons for action known. Students feel free to inquire as to "why" they are being asked to undertake a task, ask for the reasons behind a teacher's behavior, and negotiate boundaries and activities with the adults by whom they are served (Robson, 1991). Educational staff and children who have developed relationships based upon shared control discuss the specific activities each child should undertake, when they need to be completed, and the manner in which a finished product will be produced. Some tasks may be developed for specific children based upon their educational needs, others selected on the basis of the child's intrinsic interests (Meadows & Cashdan, 1988).

Teacher–student relationships based upon shared control are likely to promote self-determination because affiliations of this type give students ongoing opportunities to exercise control over meaningful events in their lives. This type of relationship, however, does not mean that educators give up control of the classroom. Decision making is conceptualized as a shared endeavor with both teachers *and* students accepting responsibility for outcomes. The degree of control exercised by each party is likely to vary considerably based upon the competencies of individual students. Optimal levels of adult control within the context of teacher–student relationships vary as children mature and develop new capacities. Viewed from the perspective of person–environment fit theory (Hunt, 1975), it is the degree of congruence between a child's need and capacity for personal control and the opportunities available for self-determination that are critical for achieving optimal developmental outcomes within this area.

Peer Group Relationships A second set of relationships within schools that have the potential to facilitate self-determination are those developed among peers. Piaget (1932) articulated the important role that interaction within the peer group plays in child development in general. Children's interaction with friends and acquaintances, especially those that occur when adults are not present, also provide fertile ground for the development of those capacities necessary for self-determination. When adults are absent, children make decisions, negotiate, problem-solve, regulate their own behavior, and resolve conflicts on their own. Regardless of the quality of the choices made, they typically experience the consequences. Peers are models for behavior, have powerful reinforcement value, and may even serve a direct teaching function (Piaget, 1932; Robson, 1992). Unfortunately, many young children with disabilities remain socially isolated both inside and outside of the school (Guralnick & Groom, 1987; McConnell & Odom, 1986; Odom, McConnell, & McEvoy, 1992).

Facilitating the development of social relationships between children with disabilities and their typically developing peers has drawn considerable attention over the past decade. Although the results of this research are far from unequivocal, it does appear that, within inclusive educational settings, relationships between children with and without disabilities do develop (Hall, 1994; Haring, 1991; Meyer & Putnam, 1988; Odom & McEvoy, 1990) and that in at least some cases there are considerable gains in social competence on the part of children with disabilities (Cole & Meyer, 1991). The development of social relationships between children with and without disabilities within inclusive educational settings will by no means guarantee enhanced self-determination. The increased availability of peers, along with the greater opportunities for control experienced by children educated within such settings, however, all suggest that this is a possible avenue through which to support the developing self-determination of students with disabilities at all ages (Hauser-Cramm et al., 1993).

CONCLUSIONS

At the beginning of this chapter, the point was made that the basic foundations for self-determination are laid in early childhood and the elementary school years and that the growth of capacities within this area should be considered one of the primary goals of early childhood and elementary education. The remainder of the chapter explored some of the basic developmental processes underlying the acquisition of self-determination capacities and offered some preliminary ideas as to the manner in which functioning within these areas might be enhanced. In concluding this chapter, one question that remains to be answered is whether our society is currently doing all that is possible during the early childhood and elementary school years to foster the self-determination of young children with disabilities. Based upon the available evidence, this would not appear to be the case. Within many schools and families, self-determination is at best ignored and at worst actively discouraged.

In talking with parents and educators, it has become clear that, before one can expect children with disabilities to routinely be provided with experiences facilitative of self-determination, the exercise of personal control on the part of these children needs to be valued and respected at a societal level. Societal attitudes towards persons with disabilities, however, although having changed in a positive direction, remain focused on disability rather than capability, dependence as opposed to independence, and conformity rather than autonomy. One needs only to examine the individualized education programs of a sample of students with disabilities to find support for this postulation. For the most part, these programs are barren of goals and objectives related to the development of self-determination (Cohen & Brown, 1993). In the case of many students, goals and objectives are written in such a manner as to foster dependence rather than enhanced personal control. The situation within most families is not much better. A relatively large proportion of children grow up in homes in which compliance with parental directives rather than self-determined thought and behavior are reinforced.

Blame for the lack of self-determination exhibited by many children with disabilities should not be placed solely upon the shoulders of teachers and parents. In today's classroom, teachers are faced with providing services to ever-increasing numbers of students. The preservice training they have received is likely to have stressed the importance of structure rather than flexibility, compliance with teacher directives as opposed to initiative. One also needs to inquire as to whether recent moves to standardize curricula and behavioral control procedures will hinder the development of self-determination. Such procedures have the potential to cause both children and teachers to feel less in control of what happens to them (Robson, 1992). Within the home, a similar situation exists. In the early 1990s, parents were being asked to spend longer hours at work, leaving them less time to spend with their children. As a result, many children have had few opportunities to make basic choices related to their daily lives. In our efforts to standardize education and run efficient households, we must ask ourselves whether we have forgotten the intrinsic nature of all persons to desire some degree of control over their lives.

Today's schools are serving many children with and without disabilities who see little purpose to education and being in the classroom other than as a place to socialize with friends. This may be one of the primary factors leading to the high drop-out rates of students with disabilities when they reach early adulthood (Wagner, D'Amico, Marder, Newman, & Blackorby, 1992). We must begin to question whether this outcome is, at least partially, due to our failure to make education a self-determining experience. The child's experiences in school and at home during the preschool and elementary school years set the tone, not only for what will be learned in junior and senior high school, but for developmental outcomes that will last a lifetime. If the goal of parents and educators is to facilitate children with disabilities developing into adults who are capable of responsibly controlling their own lives, early childhood and elementary school educators, as well as the family, will need to more successfully foster the development of self-determination.

REFERENCES

Abery, B.H. (1990, May). *Family interaction and the school-based competence of children with Down syndrome.* Paper presented at the Annual Conference of the American Association on Mental Retardation, Washington, DC.

Abery, B.H. (1994a). A conceptual framework for enhancing self-determination. In M.F. Hayden & B.H. Abery (Eds.), *Challenges for a service system in transition: Ensuring quality community experiences for persons with developmental disabilities* (pp. 345–380). Baltimore: Paul H. Brookes Publishing Co.

Abery, B.H. (1994b). Self-determination: It's not just for adults. *IMPACT, 6*(4), 2–3.

Abery, B.H., & Eggebeen, A. (June, 1993). *The self-determination of youth with disabilities: A descriptive study* (Technical Report No. 2). Minneapolis: University of Minnesota, Institute on Community Integration.

Abery, B.H., Eggebeen, A., Rudrud, L., Arndt, K., Tetu, L., Barosko, J., Hinga, A., McBride, M., Greger, P., & Peterson, K. (1994). *Self-determination for youth with disabilities: A family education curriculum.* Minneapolis: University of Minnesota, Institute on Community Integration.

Abery, B.H., McGrew, K., & Smith, J. (1995). *The contributions of individual characteristics and environmental factors to the self-determination of children and youth with disabilities.* Minneapolis: University of Minnesota, Institute on Community Integration.

Abery, B., Rudrud, L., Arndt, K., Schauben, L., & Eggebeen, A. (1995). Evaluating a multicomponent program for enhancing self-determination of youth with disabilities. *Intervention in School and Clinic, 30*, 170–179.

Ainsworth, M.D.S. (1979). Attachment as related to mother–infant interaction. In J.S. Rosenblatt, R.A. Hinde, C. Beer, & M. Busnell (Eds.), *Advances in the study of behavior* (Vol. 9). Orlando, FL: Academic Press.

Ainsworth, M.D.S. (1982). Attachment: Retrospect and prospect. In C.M. Parkes & J. Stevenson (Eds.), *The place of attachment in human behavior* (pp. 3–30). London: Tavistock.

Ainsworth, M.D.S., Blehar, M.C., Waters, E., & Wall, S. (1978). *Patterns of attachment: A psychological study of the strange situation.* Hillsdale, NJ: Lawrence Erlbaum Associates.

Arend, R., Gove, F.L., & Sroufe, L.A. (1979). Continuity of individual adaptation from infancy to kindergarten: A predictive study of ego-resiliency and curiosity in preschoolers. *Child Development, 50*, 950–959.

Bailey, D.B., & Wolery, M. (1992). *Teaching infants and preschoolers with disabilities.* Columbus, OH: Charles E. Merrill.

Bambera, L.M., & Ager, C. (1992). Using self-scheduling to promote self-directed leisure activity in home and community settings. *Journal of The Association for Persons with Severe Handicaps, 17*, 67–77.

Barrera, M.E., & Vella, D.M. (1987). Disabled and un-disabled infants' interactions with their mothers. *American Journal of Occupational Therapy, 41*, 168–172.

Barrett, M., & Trevitt, J. (1991). *Attachment behaviour and the schoolchild.* London: Tavistock/Routledge.

Baumrind, D. (1967). Child care practices anteceding three patterns of preschool behavior. *Genetic Psychology Monographs, 75*, 43–88.

Baumrind, D. (1971). Current patterns of parental authority. *Developmental Psychology Monographs, 4*(1), 1–103.

Baumrind, D. (1973). The development of instrumental competence through socialization. In A. Pick (Ed.), *Minnesota symposia on child psychology* (Vol. 7, pp. 3–46). Minneapolis: University of Minnesota Press.

Baumrind, D. (1991). The influence of parenting style on adolescent competence and substance use. *Journal of Early Adolescence, 11*(1), 56–95.

Baumrind, D., & Black, A.E. (1967). Socialization practices associated with dimensions of competence in preschool boys and girls. *Child Development, 38*, 291–327.

Belsky, J., Garduque, L., & Hrncir, E. (1984). Assessing performance, competence, and executive capacity in infant play: Relations to home environment and security of attachment. *Developmental Psychology, 20*, 406–417.

Bowlby, J. (1969). *Attachment and loss: Vol. I. Attachment.* New York: Basic Books.

Bowlby, J. (1973). *Attachment and loss: Vol. II. Separation.* New York: Basic Books.

Bowlby, J. (1980). *Attachment and loss: Vol. III. Sadness and depression.* New York: Basic Books.

Bredekamp, S. (1987). *Developmentally appropriate practice in early childhood programs serving children from birth through age 8.* Washington, DC: National Association for the Education of Young Children.

Bredekamp, S. (Ed.). (1991). *Developmentally appropriate practice in early childhood programs serving children from birth through age 8* (exp. ed.). Washington, DC: National Association for the Education of Young Children.

Brooks-Gunn, J., & Lewis, M. (1982). Affective exchanges between normal and handicapped infants and their mothers. In T. Field & A. Fogel (Eds.), *Emotion and interaction: Normal and high-risk infants* (pp. 432–456). Hillsdale, NJ: Lawrence Erlbaum Associates.

Brown, F., Belz, P., Corsi, L., & Wenig, B. (1993). Choice diversity for people with severe disabilities. *Education and Training in Mental Retardation, 28*, 318–326.

Chapman, R.S. (1988). Language acquisition in the child. In N.J. Lass, L.V. McReynolds, J.L. Northern, & D.E. Yoder (Eds.), *Handbook of speech language pathology and audiology* (pp. 309–353). Toronto, Canada: B.C. Decker.

Cohen, S., & Brown, F. (1993). *Self-determination and young children.* Manuscript submitted for publication.

Cole, D.A., & Meyer, L.H. (1991). Social integration and severe disabilities: A longitudinal analysis of child outcomes. *Journal of Special Education, 25*, 340–351.

Crnic, K.A., Ragozin, A.S., Greenberg, M.T., Robinson, N.M., & Basham, R.B. (1983). Social interaction and developmental competence of pre-term and full-term infants during the first year of life. *Child Development, 54*, 1199–1210.

Crockenberg, S., & Litman, C. (1990). Autonomy as competence in 2-year-olds: Maternal correlates of child defiance, compliance and self-assertion. *Developmental Psychology, 26*(6), 961–971.

Cross, T.G. (1984). Habilitating the language impaired child: Ideas from studies of parent–child interaction. *Topics in Language Disorders, 4*, 1–14.

Dattilo, J., & Camarata, S. (1991). Facilitating conversation through self-initiated augmentative communication treatment. *Journal of Applied Behavior Analysis, 24*, 369–378.

Deci, E.L., Hodges, R., Pierson, L., & Tomassone, J. (1992). Autonomy and competence as motivational factors in students with learning disabilities and emotional handicaps. *Journal of Learning Disabilities, 25*, 457–471.

Deci, E.L., & Ryan, R.M. (1982). *Curiosity and self-directed learning: The role of motivation in education* (Vol. 4). New Jersey: Ablex.

Deci, E.L., & Ryan, R.M. (1985). *Intrinsic motivation and self determination in human behavior.* New York: Plenum.

Deci, E.L., & Ryan, R.M. (1987). The support of autonomy and control of behavior. *Journal of Personality and Social Psychology, 53*, 1024–1037.

Dornbusch, S.M., Ritter, P.H., Leiderman, P.H., Roberts, D.F., & Fraleigh, M.J. (1987). The relation of parenting style to adolescent performance. *Child Development, 58*, 1244–1257.

Dunst, C.J., & Lowe, L.W. (1986). From reflex to symbol: Describing, explaining, and fostering communicative competence. *Augmentative and Alternative Communication*, 2, 11–18.

Dyer, K. (1989). The effects of preference on spontaneous verbal requests in individuals with autism. *Journal of The Association for Persons with Severe Handicaps*, 14(3), 184–189.

Eckert, H.M. (1987). *Motor development*. Indianapolis, IN: Benchmark Press.

Eggebeen, A., & Leigh, A. (1994). Facilitating self-determination through early intervention. *IMPACT*, 6, 4.

Gee, K., Graham, N., Goetz, L., Oshima, G., & Yoshioka, K. (1991). Teaching students to request the continuation of routine activities by using time delay and decreasing physical assistance in the context of chain interruption. *Journal of The Association for Persons with Severe Handicaps*, 16(3), 154–167.

Goldberg, S., Lojkasek, M., Gartner, G., & Corter, C. (1989). Maternal responsiveness and social development in preterm infants. In M.H. Bornstein (Ed.), *New directions for child development maternal responsiveness: Characteristics and consequences* (pp. 75–87). San Francisco: Jossey-Bass.

Goldstein, H., & Strain, P.S. (1988). Peers as communication intervention agents: Some new strategies and research findings. *Topics in Language Disorders*, 9(1), 44–57.

Gothelf, C.R., & Brown, F. (1996). Instructional support for self determination in individuals who are deaf-blind with profound disabilities. In D.H. Lehr & F. Brown (Eds.), *People with disabilities who challenge the system* (pp. 355–377). Baltimore: Paul H. Brookes Publishing Co.

Gothelf, C.R., Crimmins, D.B., Mercer, C.A., & Finocchiaro, P.A. (1993). Teaching students who are deaf-blind and cognitively disabled to effectively communicate choices during mealtimes. *Deaf-Blind Perspectives*, 1, 6–8.

Gothelf, C.R., Crimmins, D.B., Mercer, C.A., & Finocchiaro, P.A. (1994). Teaching choice-making skills to students who are deaf-blind. *Teaching Exceptional Children*, 26, 13–15.

Guess, D., Benson, H., & Siegel-Causey, E. (1985). Concepts and issues related to choice making and autonomy among persons with severe disabilities. *Journal of The Association for Persons with Severe Handicaps*, 10, 29–37.

Guess, D., & Siegel-Causey, E. (1985). Behavioral control and education of severely handicapped students: Who's doing what to whom? And why? In D. Bricker & J. Filler (Eds.), *Education of learners with severe handicaps: Exemplary service strategies* (pp. 230–244). Lancaster, PA: The Division on Mental Retardation of the Council for Exceptional Children, Lancaster Press.

Guralnick, M.J. (1993). Developmentally appropriate practice in the assessment and intervention of children's peer relations. *Topics in Early Childhood Special Education*, 13, 344–371.

Guralnick, M.J., & Groom, J.M. (1987). The peer relations of mildly delayed and non-handicapped preschool children in mainstreamed playgroups. *Child Development*, 58, 1556–1572.

Hadadian, A. (1995). Attitudes toward deafness and security of attachment relationships among young deaf children and their parents. *Early Education and Development*, 6(2), 181–191.

Hall, L. (1994). A descriptive assessment of social relationships in integrated classrooms. *Journal of The Association for Persons with Severe Handicaps*, 19(4), 302–313.

Halle, J.W. (1988). Adopting the natural environment as the context of training. In S.N. Calculator & J.L. Bedrosian (Eds.), *Communication assessment and intervention for adults with mental retardation* (pp. 155–185). Boston: College-Hill Press.

Hanline, M.F., & Fox, L. (1993). Learning within the context of play: Providing typical early childhood experiences for children with severe disabilities. *Journal of The Association for Persons with Severe Handicaps, 18*(2), 121–129.

Haring, T. (1991). Social relationships. In L.H. Meyer, C.H. Peck, & L. Brown (Eds.), *Critical issues in the lives of people with severe disabilities* (pp. 195–217). Baltimore: Paul H. Brookes Publishing Co.

Hartley, D. (1987). The time of their lives: Bureaucracy and the nursery school. In A. Pollard (Ed.), *Children and their primary schools* (pp. 161–179). London: Falmer.

Hauser-Cramm, P., Bronson, M.B., & Upshur, C.C. (1993). The effects of classroom environment on the social and mastery behavior of preschool children with disabilities. *Early Childhood Research Quarterly, 8*, 479–497.

Hess, R.D., & McDevitt, T.M. (1984). Some cognitive consequences of maternal intervention techniques: A longitudinal study. *Child Development, 55*, 2017–2030.

Houghton, J., Bronicki, G.J.B., & Guess, D. (1987). Opportunities to express preferences and make choices among students with severe disabilities in classroom settings. *Journal of The Association for Persons with Severe Handicaps, 12*, 18–27.

Hunt, D.E. (1975). Person–environment interaction: A challenge found wanting before it was tried. *Review of Educational Research, 45*, 209–230.

Hutt, S.J., Tyler, S., Hutt, C., & Christopherson, H. (1989). *Play, exploration, and learning: A natural history of the pre-school.* London: Routledge Education.

Johnson, J.E., & Johnson, K.M. (1992). Clarifying the developmental perspective in response to Carta, Schwartz, Atwater, and McConnell. *Topics in Early Childhood Special Education, 12*(4), 439–457.

Jowett, S., & Sylva, K. (1986). Does kind of pre-school matter? *Educational Research, 28*, 1.

Kogan, K.L., Tyler, N., & Turner, P. (1974). The process of interpersonal adaptation between mothers and their cerebral palsied children. *Developmental Medicine and Child Neurology, 16*, 518–527.

Kostelnik, M.J. (1992). Myths associated with developmentally appropriate programs. *Young Children, 47*, 17–23.

Lambrenos, K., Cox, A., Weindling, M., & Calam, R. (1991, October). *The impact of psycho-therapy intervention on the mother–child relationship of children predicted to develop cerebral palsy.* Paper presented at the annual meeting of the Cerebral Palsy Research Association, Liverpool, England.

Lederberg, A.R., & Mobley, C.E. (1990). The effects of hearing impairment on the quality of attachment and mother–toddler interaction. *Child Development, 61*, 1590–1604.

Locke, P.A., & Mirenda, P. (1988). A computer-supported communication approach for a child with severe communication, visual and cognitive impairments: A case study. *Augmentative and Alternative Communication, 4*, 15–22.

Mac Iver, D., Klingel, D.M., & Reuman, D.A. (1986, April). *Students' decision-making congruence in mathematics classrooms: A person-environment fit analysis.* Paper presented at the annual meeting of the American Educational Research Association, San Francisco.

Mac Iver, D., & Reuman, D.A. (1988, April). *Decision-making in the classroom and early adolescents' valuing of mathematics.* Paper presented at the meeting of the American Educational Research Association, San Francisco.

Maccoby, E.E. (1984). Middle childhood in the context of the family. In W.A. Collins (Ed.), *Development during the middle childhood: The years from six to twelve* (pp. 184–239). Washington, DC: National Academy of Sciences Press.

Mahoney, G., O'Sullivan, G., & G. Fors, S. (1989). Special education practices with young handicapped children. *Journal of Early Intervention, 13*, 261–269.

Mahoney, G., Robinson, C., & Powell, A. (1992). Focusing on parent–child interaction: The bridge to developmentally appropriate practices. *Topics in Early Childhood Special Education, 12,* 105–120.

Malatesta, C.Z., Grigoryev, P., Lamb, C., Albin, M., & Culver, C. (1986). Emotion, socialization and expressive development in the pre-term and full-term infant. *Child Development, 57,* 316–330.

McConnell, S.R., & Odom, S.L. (1986). Sociometrics: Peer-referenced measures and the assessment of social competence. In P.S. Strain, M.J. Guralnick, & H.M. Walker (Eds.), *Children's social behavior* (pp. 215–284). New York: Academic Press.

McDade, H.L., & Varnedoe, D.R. (1987). Training parents to be language facilitators. *Topics in Language Disorders, 7,* 19–30.

Meadows, S., & Cashdan, A. (1988). *Helping children learn: Contributions to a cognitive curriculum.* London: David Fulton.

Meyer, L.H., & Putnam, J. (1988). Social integration. In V.B. Van Hasselt, P.S. Strain, & M. Hersen (Eds.), *Handbook of developmental and physical disabilities* (pp. 107–133). New York: Pergamon.

Mink, I., & Nihira, K. (1987). Direction of effects: Family life-styles and the behavior of TMR children. *American Journal of Mental Deficiency, 92,* 57–64.

Mink, I.T., Nihira, K., & Meyers, C.E. (1983). Taxonomy of family life styles: I. Homes with TMR children. *American Journal of Mental Deficiency, 87,* 484–497.

Nihira, K., Meyers, C.E., & Mink, I.T. (1983). Reciprocal relationship between home environment and development of TMR adolescents. *American Journal of Mental Deficiency, 88,* 139–149.

Nihira, K., Mink, I.T., & Meyers, C.E. (1981). Relationship between home environment and school adjustment of TMR children. *American Journal of Mental Deficiency, 86,* 8–15.

Nihira, K., Mink, I.T., & Meyers, C.E. (1985). Home environment and development of slow-learning adolescents: Reciprocal relationships. *Developmental Psychology, 21,* 784–794.

Odom, S.L., McConnell, S.R., & McEvoy, M.A. (1992). Peer-related social competence and its significance for young children with disabilities. In S.L. Odom, S.R. McConnell, & M.A. McEvoy (Eds.), *Social competence of young children with disabilities* (pp. 3–35). Baltimore: Paul H. Brookes Publishing Co.

Odom, S.L., & McEvoy, M.A. (1990). Mainstreaming at the preschool level: Potential barriers and tasks for the field. *Topics in Early Childhood Special Education, 10,* 48–61.

Orlansky, M.D. (1979). Sam's day: A simulated observation of a severely handicapped child's education program. *AAESPH Review, 4,* 251–258.

Parish, T.S., & McCluskey, J.J. (1994). The relationship between parenting styles and young adults' self-concepts and evaluations of parents. *Family Therapy, 21*(3), 223–226.

Peck, C.A. (1985). Increasing opportunities for social control by children with autism and severe handicaps: Effects on student behavior and perceived classroom climate. *Journal of The Association for Persons with Severe Handicaps, 10,* 183–193.

Peck, C.A. (1989). Assessment of social communicative competence: Evaluating environments. *Seminars in Speech and Language, 10*(1), 1–15.

Piaget, J. (1932). *The moral judgement of the child.* London: Routledge Kegan Paul.

Piaget, J. (1950). *The psychology of intelligence.* San Diego: Harcourt Brace Jovanovich.

Piaget, J. (1954). *The construction of reality in the child.* New York: Basic Books.

Reichle, J., & Sigafoos, J. (1991). Establishing spontaneity and generalization. In J. Reichle, J. York, & J. Sigafoos, *Implementing augmentative and alternative communication: Strategies for learners with severe disabilities* (pp. 157–171). Baltimore: Paul H. Brookes Publishing Co.

Rietveld, C.M. (1983). The training of choice behaviours in Down's syndrome and nonretarded preschool children. *Australia and New Zealand Journal of Developmental Disabilities*, 9(2), 75–83.

Robson, S. (1991). Developing autonomous children in the first school. *Early Child Development and Care*, 77, 17–35.

Robson, S. (1992). How can autonomy be achieved in school? *Early Child Development and Care*, 79, 73–88.

Rogers, S.J. (1988). Characteristics of social interactions between mothers and their disabled infants: A review. *Child Care, Health and Development*, 14, 301–317.

Rogers, S.J., Ozonoff, S., & Maslin-Cole, C. (1991). A comparative study of attachment behavior in young children with autism or other psychiatric disorders. *Journal of the American Academy of Child and Adolescent Psychiatry*, 30(3), 483–488.

Romski, M.A., Sevcik, R.A., & Wilkinson, K.M. (1994). Peer-directed communicative interactions of augmented language learners with mental retardation. *American Journal on Mental Retardation*, 98(4), 527–538.

Rowland, S. (1987). Child in control: Towards an interpretive model of teaching and learning. In A. Pollard (Ed.), *Children and their primary schools* (pp. 237–263). London: Falmer.

Rowland, C., & Schweigert, P. (1993). Analyzing the communication environment to increase functional communication. *Journal of The Association for Persons with Severe Handicaps*, 18(3), 161–176.

Sawyer, R.J., Graham, S., & Harris, K.R. (1992). Direct teaching, strategy instruction, and strategy instruction with explicit self-regulation: Effects on the composition skills and self-efficacy of students with learning disabilities. *Journal of Education Psychology*, 84, 340–353.

Schaefer, E. (1985). Parent and child correlates of parental modernity. In I. Sigel (Ed.), *Parental belief systems: The psychological consequences for children* (pp. 287–318). Hillsdale, NJ: Lawrence Erlbaum Associates.

Speltz, M., Greenberg, M.T., & Deklyen, M. (1990). Attachment in pre-schoolers with disruptive behaviour: A comparison of clinic-referred and non-problem children. *Child Development and Psychopathology*, 2, 31–46.

Spivack, G., & Cianci, N. (1987). High-risk early behavior patterns and later delinquency. In J. Burchard & S. Burchard (Eds.), *Prevention of delinquent behavior* (pp. 44–74). Newbury Park, CA: Sage Publications.

Spodek, B., Saracho, O.N., & Davis, M.D. (1991). *Foundations of early childhood education* (2nd ed.). Englewood Cliffs, NJ: Prentice Hall.

Sroufe, L.A. (1983). Infant–caregiver attachment and patterns of adaptation in preschool: The roots of maladaptation and incompetence. In M. Perlmuter (Ed.), *Minnesota symposium in child development* (Vol. 16, 41–83). Hillsdale, NJ: Lawrence Erlbaum Associates.

Sroufe, L.A., & Fleeson, J. (1988). The coherence of family relationships. In R. Hinde & J. Stevenson-Hinde (Eds.), *Relationships with families: Mutual influences* (pp. 27–47). Oxford: Oxford University Press.

Steinberg, L., Elman, J.D., & Mounts, N.S. (1989). Authoritative parenting, psychosocial maturity, and academic success among adolescents. *Child Development*, 60, 1424–1436.

Switzer, L.S. (1990). Family factors associated with academic progress in children with learning disabilities. *Elementary School Guidance and Counseling*, 24, 200–206.

Tannock, R. (1988). Mothers' directiveness in their interactions with their children with and without Down syndrome. *American Journal on Mental Retardation*, 93(2), 154–165.

196 ■ ABERY AND ZAJAC

Wagner, M., D'Amico, R., Marder, C., Newman, L., & Blackorby, J. (1992, December). *What happens next? Trends in post-school outcomes of youth with disabilities. The second comprehensive report from the National Longitudinal Transition Study of Special Education Students.* Washington, DC: U.S. Department of Education, Office of Special Education Programs (SRI International).

Ward, M.J. (1994). Self-determination: A means to an end. *IMPACT, 6*(4), 8.

Warren, S., McQuarter, R., & Rogers-Warren, A. (1984). The effects of mands and models on the speech of unresponsive language-delayed preschool children. *Journal of Speech and Hearing Disorders, 49,* 43–52.

Wasserman, G.A., & Allen, R. (1985). Maternal withdrawal from handicapped toddlers. *Journal of Child Psychology and Psychology, 26,* 381–387.

Waters, E., Wippman, J., & Sroufe, L.A. (1979). Attachment, positive affect, and competence in the peer group: Two studies in construct validation. *Child Development, 50,* 821–829.

Wehmeyer, M.L. (1992). Self-determination and the education of students with mental retardation. *Education and Training in Mental Retardation, 27,* 302–314.

Wehmeyer, M. (1994). Self-determination as an educational outcome. *IMPACT, 6*(4), 6–7.

Wolfgang, C.H., & Wolfgang, M.E. (1992). *School for young children: Developmentally appropriate practice.* Needham, MA: Allyn & Bacon.

Chapter 10

PROMOTING SELF-DETERMINATION IN SCHOOL REFORM, INDIVIDUALIZED PLANNING, AND CURRICULUM EFFORTS

Sharon Field and Alan Hoffman

THERE IS A growing emphasis in the disability community on self-determination. As described by Ward (Chapter 1), the independent living movement, organized around a self-help and mutual support strategy by adults with physical disabilities, has played a major role in highlighting the civil rights of people with disabilities, including the right to make decisions that affect their lives. There is often a myriad of service providers and a bureaucratic web of agencies involved in the lives of people with disabilities (Will, 1984). As a result, many advocates, parents, educators, and service providers have found a need to ensure that disability-related services are provided in a student-centered or client-centered manner, where the focus of control resides with the person who is receiving services (Wehman, 1992). This growing awareness of the rights of people with disabilities to assume control of decisions affecting their lives is evident in both popular and academic publications. It also has become a part of legislation affecting both education and rehabilitative services for people with disabilities.

As documented by Wehmeyer (Chapter 2), much of the focus on self-determination has been generated from a human rights perspective. Research findings on instructional effectiveness lend additional support to the need for self-determination in schools. Wehmeyer (1992) cited numerous research studies that found that instructional programs are more effective when students are involved in setting goals and developing their own educational programs.

Funding to support the development of this chapter was partially provided by Grant nos. H158K00036 and H023J20004 from the U.S. Department of Education, Office of Special Education and Rehabilitative Services (OSERS), awarded to Wayne State University. Opinions expressed herein do not necessarily reflect those of OSERS.

The emerging focus on self-determination for people with disabilities has been paralleled by a similar emphasis on greater control and participation in decision making by employees in the workplace. Participative management practices are no longer considered novel in either the private or the public sector. For example, a recent survey of human resources professionals reported that employee involvement was ranked as one of the top three issues in human resources (Mathes, 1993). Furthermore, total quality management (TQM) is increasingly being accepted as a philosophy of management and a mainstay of company life (Omachonu & Ross, 1994). According to Omachonu and Ross (1994), "TQM is the integration of all functions and processes within an organization in order to achieve continuous improvement in the quality of goods and services" (p. 3). Omachonu and Ross state that one important component of TQM is employee involvement.

Likewise, school management practices that emphasize site-based management and involvement by stakeholders in decision making are an emerging trend (Myers & Myers, 1995). According to Myers and Myers (1995), site-based management delegates as much decision-making authority as possible to people who are directly involved with students at individual school buildings. These authors stated that the concept of site-based management is drawn from similar management efforts in business and is tied to research on effective schools.

The common denominator in each of the school and workplace management styles noted above is an emphasis on activities that, through participative practices, 1) take into account the perceptions, needs, and concerns of individuals within those settings and 2) provide for a large degree of control by those who will be most affected by the decisions that are made. This common denominator recognizes the importance of considering the perspectives of, and creating ownership by, individuals in the school or workplace for key policy and management decisions to ensure the success of the organization. These concepts are highly consistent with the concept of self-determination. Essentially, these management practices, evident in workplaces and schools, provide for the self-determination of the organization as a whole.

Self-determination is a concept that can provide a foundation for school improvement, individualized education programming, and curriculum development for students with and without disabilities. It is a concept that is pertinent to success in both general and special education, both at the organizational and the individual levels.

This chapter presents two models: 1) a model for self-determination and 2) a model for school improvement and individualized planning for students with and without disabilities, based on the model for self-determination. A curriculum is described that promotes student knowledge, beliefs, and skills leading to self-determination. Finally, student, parent, and teacher reactions to the curriculum are presented, including their suggestions for its successful implementation.

A MODEL FOR SELF-DETERMINATION

A brief overview of the model for self-determination that forms the basis for the intervention efforts described in this chapter is provided subsequently. This description is based on a more detailed discussion about the model and the process used to develop it by Field and Hoffman (1994a).

Our model of self-determination was developed over a 3-year research effort. This research included 1) interviews regarding the nature of self-determination conducted with adults with and without disabilities as well as students with disabilities, 2) observations of students in school environments, and 3) findings from the self-determination literature and input from three state advisory panels and one national advisory panel of experts representing consumerism/self-advocacy, parent involvement, education, and adult services. We based our model on the following definition of self-determination: "the ability to identify and achieve goals based on a foundation of knowing and valuing oneself" (Field & Hoffman, 1994a, p. 161). According to the model, self-determination is affected by skills, knowledge, and beliefs of the individual and factors that are environmental in nature (e.g., attitudes of others, opportunities for choice). The model delineating the individual knowledge, beliefs, and skills that contribute to self-determination is depicted in Figure 1.

As illustrated, the model has five primary components: 1) *Know Yourself*, 2) *Value Yourself*, 3) *Plan*, 4) *Act*, and 5) *Experience Outcomes and Learn*. Specific subcomponents are delineated for each of the five components of the model. The first two components, Know Yourself and Value Yourself, provide the foundation and the content for becoming self-determined. The last three components, Plan, Act, and Experience Outcomes and Learn, describe the skills that enable the individual to attain what he or she desires.

A MODEL FOR SELF-DETERMINED SCHOOL IMPROVEMENT AND INDIVIDUALIZED PLANNING

While the word *self-determination* is seldom used, the concept of self-determination is evident throughout the school improvement literature. Components of our self-determination model, described previously, have many correlates in school improvement recommended practices. For example, in a discussion on school reform, Fullan and Miles (1992) described change as a learning, evolutionary process. Their description of change is similar to our self-determination model component—Experience Outcomes and Learn—where actual outcomes are compared with anticipated outcomes, actual performance is compared with anticipated performance, and the goal of learning is increased positive performance and outcomes in the future. Lipsky (1992) focused on the concept of respect in the school improvement process. This focus on respect could be directly linked to aspects of the Value Yourself component of the self-

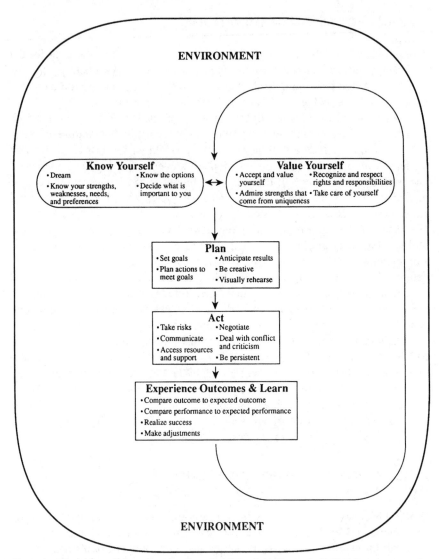

Figure 1. Model for self-determination. (From Field, S., & Hoffman, A. [1994]. Development of a model for self-determination. *Career Development for Exceptional Individuals, 17*, 159–169; reprinted by permission.)

determination model. There is a high degree of consistency between commonly accepted school improvement practices and the notion of self-determination. Recommended practices in school improvement/school reform provide support for the use of a collaborative school improvement process incorporating principles of self-determination.

In addition, there is a growing emphasis on self-determination in the special education individualized education program process. According to the Individuals with Disabilities Education Act of 1990 (IDEA), students must be included as participants in their transition planning meetings and their preferences and interests must be taken into account when developing their transition plans. Self-determination in educational planning goes hand-in-hand with self-determination in the school improvement process. As practices and materials are developed through the school improvement process, increased resources are available to serve individual students; as student needs'and solutions to meet those needs are developed through the individualized planning process, additional information and resources can be provided to the school improvement process. A model for self-determined school improvement, which incorporates an individualized planning process is depicted in Figure 2.

School Improvement

The school reform/school improvement literature documents numerous ways to effectively involve participants in a collaborative process to create change in school settings (e.g., Fullan & Miles, 1992; Harkavy & Puckett, 1991; Hopfenberg, Levin, Meister, & Rogers, 1990). A premise of site-based management and recommended practices in school reform and school improvement is that those who have responsibility for change need to be involved in the school improvement planning and implementation process. The purpose of this involvement is twofold: 1) to create changes that are sensitive to the needs of individuals and local communities and 2) to develop ownership on the part of individuals who have responsibility for program implementation.

The model for self-determined school improvement provided in Figure 2 suggests a structure and a process for collaborative school improvement teams to develop recruitment strategies, curriculum, instructional strategies, individual planning procedures, and support designed to meet the needs of youth with special needs in their local community. In this model, a collaborative school improvement team is responsible for developing curriculum, instruction, and support in five major areas: 1) self-determination, 2) on-the-job training, 3) functional life skills, 4) functional literacy, and 5) community-based instruction. These five areas were selected because they represent major themes in the literature on recommended practices for meeting the needs of youth with disabilities and/or youth who are at risk (Field & Hoffman, 1994b). The collaborative school improvement team is also responsible for designing a process, based on self-determination, for individualized education and transition planning.

The collaborative school improvement team comprises all key stakeholders who have an interest in the success of the school. The team includes youth, parents, educators, human services agency representatives, adult services providers,

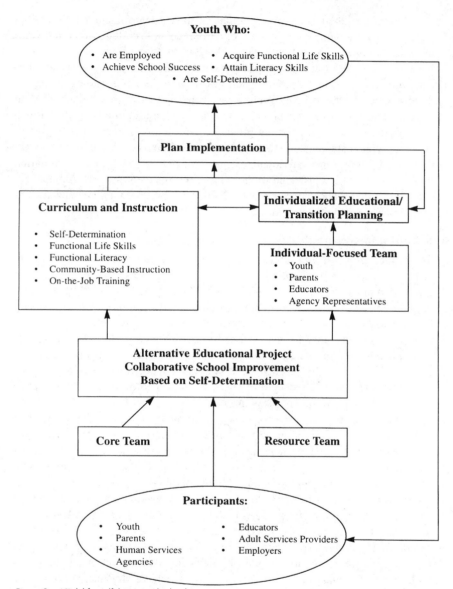

Figure 2. Model for self-determined school improvement.

and employers. The collaborative school improvement team has two components: 1) the core team and 2) the resource team. The smaller core team (8–10 people) is responsible for overall coordination of all planning and implementation efforts. Resource team members are responsible for assisting the core team with components of program development and implementation related to their specific areas of expertise.

Individualized Planning

The instructional and support opportunities designed by the collaborative school improvement team in the five major areas delineated above provide resources that can be used by individual-focused teams in student-centered planning efforts. According to the model, the school improvement and the individualized planning processes are interactive. Resources developed through the school improvement process are available to individualized teams and issues and solutions addressed in individualized planning inform and provide resources for the school improvement process. In this model, the collaborative school improvement team develops or selects an individualized planning process that is consistent with and builds on the five components of the self-determination model (i.e., Know Yourself, Value Yourself, Plan, Act, Experience Outcomes and Learn).

Two educational planning processes consistent with self-determination are the *Self-Directed IEP* (individualized education program) (Martin & Marshall, 1993) and IPLAN (VanReusen & Bos, 1990). The purpose of the *Self-Directed IEP* is to help students learn how to assume a leadership role in their educational program. The *Self-Directed IEP* includes a curriculum matrix, assessment instruments, and videos and lesson plans teachers can use to help students develop skills that will help them assert themselves in the educational planning process. The *Self-Directed IEP* is described in detail in this volume (Chapter 11).

The IPLAN strategy is intended to help students learn how to play a more participative, central role in the education planning process (VanReusen & Bos, 1990). IPLAN uses a five-step strategy to help students learn and remember key components of being effectively involved in the IEP meeting. The steps are as follows:

1. I   Inventory your strengths, weaknesses you need to improve, goals and interests, and choices for learning.
2. P   Provide your inventory information.
3. L   Listen and respond.
4. A   Ask questions.
5. N   Name your goals.

The five steps form the acronym IPLAN, which is used to help students remember the steps of the strategy.

In the self-determined school improvement model, new curriculum and instruction options are created as the individualized plans are developed to meet unique student needs. As these plans are implemented and evaluated, feedback is provided to the collaborative school improvement team. This feedback helps the team to improve instruction, services, and supports available through the program and to refine the individualized planning process. Curriculum and instructional strategies designed to meet specific individual needs through the planning process add to what is available through the program.

According to Kennedy (1984), most decisions resulting in educational change are based on *working knowledge* and the way in which new knowledge is incorporated into working knowledge. Williams and Bank (1984) discussed working knowledge as follows: "One does not have to seek such information— one is immersed in it" (p. 267). In this model for school improvement and individual planning, participants' working knowledge is used to make decisions that are relevant and appropriate to the needs of individual students and their local communities. In addition, the self-determined school improvement process provides the opportunity for new knowledge to become part of participants' working knowledge repertoire.

The process used in this school improvement model assures that the perspectives of those whom the program is intended to serve—the students and those who are most closely involved with them—are addressed in the planning process, at both the schoolwide and the individual levels. The model adds assurance that local needs are met and that there is ownership in the plan by those who implement it. The structure dictates that key elements needed to help youth be successful are addressed.

SELF-DETERMINATION IN CURRICULUM DEVELOPMENT

One of the five components targeted for curriculum and instruction in the self-determined school improvement model is self-determination. The model of self-determination described previously provides the foundation for the development of a curriculum that promotes knowledge, beliefs, and skills that lead to self-determination in youth with and without disabilities. We developed, piloted, and field tested this curriculum with students with and without disabilities. The curriculum was piloted with students who attended an urban, midwestern high school. In addition to the students, two special education teachers, one general education teacher, and one school psychologist participated in the piloting of the curriculum. As authors of the curriculum, we also participated in each of the pilot sessions with the students and teachers. At the end of each session, students and teachers shared their impressions about the effectiveness of the session's activities as well as their recommendations for improvement. The curriculum was then revised based on the comments of the students and teachers and the observations of the sessions by the authors. The revised curriculum was field-tested in two midwestern high schools the following year. The field-test group included students from both urban and suburban environments and from a range of socioeconomic backgrounds. Students who participated in the curriculum field-test represented diverse ethnic groups and disability types.

Curriculum Organization and Content

The *Steps to Self-Determination* curriculum (Field & Hoffman, in press) is a 17-session curriculum that provides instruction related to each of the elements in our self-determination model. It was designed to be used in secondary school programs, with students with and without disabilities, using a variety of scheduling arrangements (e.g., infused into an existing class, as an extracurricular activity, as part of a weekly group). The curriculum includes lesson plans, transparency masters, and handout masters for a 55-minute orientation session, a 6-hour workshop session, and sixteen 55-minute sessions that individually focus on one of the components of the self-determination model. Students' parents or another significant adult in their lives participate with the students in the workshop session and provide support for the students' weekly homework assignments. The curriculum is experientially based, and students identify and work toward their personal goals as part of the curriculum.

A topical focus for each session of the curriculum is provided in Table 1. While each of the sessions has a topical focus for instructional purposes, self-determination components are woven together at several points throughout the

Table 1. Topical focus for each session of the *Steps to Self-Determination* curriculum

Orientation Session:	Overview of Curriculum/Planning for the Workshop
Workshop:	Getting to Know Each Other
	Overview of Self-Determination
	Self-Awareness
	Self-Acceptance
	Rights and Responsibilities
	Accessing Support from Families and Friends
	Supporting the Self-Determination of Others
Session 1:	Dreaming to Open Possibilities
Session 2:	What Is Important to Me?
Session 3:	Creating Options for Long-Term Goals
Session 4:	Setting Goals
Session 5:	Steps to Short-Term Goals
Session 6:	Planning Steps to Reach Short-Term Goals
Session 7:	Planning Activities to Reach Short-Term Goals
Session 8:	Taking the First Step (Risk Taking)
Session 9:	Creative Barrier Breaking
Session 10:	A Little Help from My Friends (The Power of the Group in Solving Problems)
Session 11:	Journey to Self-Determination (Role Models: Disability and Self-Determination)
Session 12:	Assertive Communication I
Session 13:	Assertive Communication II
Session 14:	Negotiation
Session 15:	Conflict Resolution
Session 16:	Where Do We Go from Here?

Reprinted with minor revisions from Hoffman, A., & Field, S. (1995). Promoting self-determination through effective curriculum development. *Intervention in School and Clinic, 30,* 134–141; reprinted by permission.

curriculum to help students apply and experience self-determination knowledge and skills in their lives.

There are 10 cornerstones that provide the foundation for the curriculum (Hoffman & Field, 1995). These cornerstones are infused throughout the curriculum materials and include 1) establishing a co-learner role for teachers, 2) emphasizing modeling as an instructional strategy, 3) using cooperative learning to help students acquire knowledge and skills, 4) promoting experiential learning, 5) using integrated or inclusive environments, 6) obtaining support from family and friends, 7) emphasizing the importance of listening, 8) incorporating interdisciplinary team teaching, 9) using humor appropriately, and 10) capitalizing on teachable moments.

A Sample Lesson

A sample lesson, "Session 8: Taking the First Step," is discussed here as an example of how the concepts described above are put into practice in the curriculum. The intent of this session is to 1) review the overall model for self-determination and 2) help students prepare to take action to achieve their identified goals. A copy of the outline for this session is provided in Table 2. A narrative detailing the content for each of the topics in the outline is provided in the curriculum itself.

Students begin the session by reviewing their homework from the last session. In the previous session, students were asked to share their short-term goals

Table 2. Sample lesson outline (Session 8: Taking the First Step) from the *Steps to Self-Determination* curriculum

I. Introduction (5 min.)
  A. Review homework
  B. Review agenda *(Overhead [OH]: Taking the First Step, Agenda)*
II. Review model, *Self-Determination* (10 min.)
  A. Review "Know Yourself," "Value Yourself," and "Plan" *(OH: Self-Determination)*
  B. Introduce "Act" and "Learn"
III. Taking Action
  A. Introduction *(OH: Preparing Ourselves to Act)* (5 min.)
  B. Anticipating the results of our actions (20 min.)
    1) Introduction
    2) Activity and worksheet: *Tyrone's Dilemma*
    3) Select activity for the week
    4) Activity and worksheet: *Anticipating Results*
  C. Rehearse (10 min.)
IV. Summary (5 min.)
  A. Review
  B. Homework
  C. Looking forward

From Field, S., & Hoffman, A. (in press). *Steps to self-determination*. Austin, TX: PRO-ED; reprinted by permission.

with a parent or friend and to obtain feedback from these individuals. The teachers, who are also working to increase their self-determination and are completing the same activities as the students, share their experiences in the same activity with the group. This emphasis on teachers as co-learners helps create a classroom environment that is conducive to promoting student self-esteem as well as providing students with appropriate role models. A discussion is conducted that asks students to consider what they learned about finding support from others for self-determination. Then, to provide an advance organizer, the students have the opportunity to review the agenda for the remainder of the class session with the teacher.

Next, the students spend approximately 10 minutes reviewing the overall model for self-determination by sharing what they have learned about themselves related to each of the first three components of the model (i.e., Know Yourself, Value Yourself, and Plan). This discussion builds the foundation for the next component of the model, (Act), which is being introduced in session eight.

There are two major points of the Act component that are stressed in this session: 1) anticipating results and 2) visually rehearsing. The first point addressed is anticipating results. The students' discussion examines why it is important to try to predict possible results of their planned action. The teacher's role during the discussion is to clarify and summarize students' responses and emphasize that it is important to predict results of our actions so we can decide whether we want to 1) go ahead with a planned action; 2) modify the planned action to avoid, or deal with, any possible negative consequences; or 3) discard the plan.

Students then complete the worksheet "Tyrone's Dilemma" (see Figure 3). This worksheet gives students the opportunity to identify alternative actions and possible results in a hypothetical situation. It is a situation that, in piloting and field-testing, students found entertaining and humorous. Students complete the activity in small groups and then discuss key issues in the large group.

Students and teachers then have the opportunity to apply the strategy of anticipating results in their own lives. Each of the group participants decides what action he or she would like to take this week toward the first step of his or her short-term goal and states that intention to the small group. (Note: Participants have already established their short-term goals in an earlier session.) The facilitator for the group assures that each participant chooses a specific action. Small groups are used frequently throughout the curriculum. It is recommended that a facilitator be provided for each small group. The small group facilitator role may be filled by teachers, support services staff (e.g., psychologists, counselors), administrators, students who have completed the curriculum, or community volunteers. In small groups, students complete the Anticipating Results worksheet (Figure 4) for the action they would like to take this week. Teachers have already completed this worksheet for themselves before the session and they share it with students in their small groups as a model. This worksheet helps participants think through possible consequences and alternatives before taking action. In the small

---

TYRONE'S DILEMMA

Tyrone has a test in English tomorrow. It is a big exam and his grade currently is right between a B and a C. He has had some difficulty understanding the material that will be covered in the exam, and he feels he needs more time to study if he is going to perform well on the test. Just as he sits down to study, the phone rings. It is Cathy, a girl he has liked for some time. He has talked with her several times at school, but she has never called him at home before. Cathy wants to see if he is going to the basketball game tonight. She says she is planning to go, and she hopes she will see him there. Tyrone has been waiting to go out with Cathy for a long time, and now that she has finally called, he can't imagine saying no.

Write down three possible actions Tyrone could take and what you think possible consequences of those actions would be.

Action One:

    Possible Consequences:

Action Two:

    Possible Consequences:

Action Three:

    Possible Consequences:

Figure 3. Tyrone's dilemma worksheet. (From Field, S., & Hoffman, A. [in press]. *Steps to self-determination.* Austin, TX: PRO-ED; reprinted [with minor revisions] by permission.)

groups, teachers structure their questions to students, encouraging them to give detailed, specific feedback to one another. Students then return to the large group and discuss what they learned in the small groups. The action that each session member (students and teachers) plans to take that week is recorded on poster paper. The next session begins with a discussion of each of the participants' outcomes.

After the planning activity, approximately 10 minutes is taken to address the concept of rehearsing. Students are asked if they have ever rehearsed for anything (e.g., dance, music, sports) and, if so, how that helped prepare them for the event. Students take a few minutes to rehearse their planned actions by imagining

---

ANTICIPATING RESULTS

Planned action:

Possible results:

After thinking about the possible results, which of the following do you want to do?

_____ Modify the plan

What would you change?

_____ Discard the plan

_____ Go for it, without any changes

Figure 4. Anticipating results worksheet. (From Field, S., & Hoffman, A. [in press]. *Steps to self-determination*. Austin, TX: PRO-ED; reprinted by permission.)

themselves completing the actions successfully. The lesson is completed by briefly reviewing 1) the steps in the self-determination model, 2) the planned actions for the coming week, and 3) how the next session will start with their reporting on the actions they took toward reaching their goals during the previous week.

CURRICULUM EFFECTIVENESS

As mentioned previously, the curriculum was field-tested in two high schools in the midwest United States with students with and without disabilities (Hoffman & Field, 1995). The field-test consisted of an intervention group, who received the *Steps to Self-Determination* curriculum, and a control group, who did not receive the curriculum. A test of the intervention and the control group indicated a significant increase ($p = .002$) in the correct responses on a Self-Determination Knowledge Scale (SDKS) for the intervention group (Hoffman, Field, & Sawilowsky, in press). In addition, the effect of a pretest–posttest intervention versus control group of the effectiveness of the curriculum showed a significant increase ($p = .000$) for the intervention group in students' behaviors that are considered correlates of self-determination. The Self-Determination Observational Checklist (SDOC), a component of the Self-Determination Assessment Battery (Hoffman, Field, & Sawilowsky, 1995) was used to measure change in students' behaviors.

Student, Parent, and Teacher Responses

Field-test teachers were asked to keep logs as they taught the *Steps to Self-Determination* curriculum indicating what worked, what didn't, and any suggestions they had to enhance the curriculum. In addition, students and parents were asked to give the same feedback when the curriculum was completed. Themes emerged from the reactions, suggestions, and ideas provided by students, parents, and teachers. For example, when asked what they learned, the primary responses of students were that they learned 1) more about themselves and 2) how to set goals. Parents also reported that learning how to set goals was a primary outcome of curriculum participation. In addition, parents commented that students learned to speak more assertively. One teacher responded that the curriculum provided a "step-by-step guide to responsibility and taking charge of one's life." The areas about which students, teachers, and parents most frequently commented can be grouped into three major topics: 1) the workshop, 2) reactions to other activities within the curriculum, and 3) suggestions for scheduling and need for follow-up.

Workshop Implementation and Effectiveness The 6-hour workshop, which included students' parents or another significant adult, was consistently seen as the most rewarding activity by students, parents, and teachers. It was also generally viewed as the most challenging activity by teachers, primarily in the areas of scheduling and ensuring participation by parents. One teacher commented, "The response to the workshop was great—much better than anticipated. It was really touching watching students, their parents, and/or friends interact."

Two of the teachers who participated in the field-test took their co-learner roles very seriously by bringing their own parents to the workshop with them. The students were intrigued by the opportunity to get to know their teachers' parents. The teachers' involvement of their parents in the workshop seemed to ease some students' anxiety about bringing their own parents to school. An interesting spin-off benefit reported was that one of the teachers' parents voted for a school funding measure for the first time in his life after spending time with the students.

Students who did not have a parent support person to participate in the workshop were assisted in finding another adult who could support them in this activity. Some students elected to be paired with school personnel. In one school, building level and central office administrators were paired with students who did not bring parents to the workshop activity. The administrators who participated stated that the workshop provided them with an opportunity to spend time with students in a positive, informal setting. They commented that the involvement was valuable to them as they were able to listen to and learn from the students and gave them an opportunity to build positive relationships with students on a proactive basis.

Responses to Specific Curriculum Activities

Students There is one activity in the curriculum where a story is read to the students. Although it was initially thought that this might seem too childish to the high school students, they consistently commented that they enjoyed this activity. Students also commented frequently about the climate in the self-determination classes. Students made the following comments related to class climate:

- "I like that we all worked together. Nobody was by themselves."
- "[I liked] the cooperative effect it had on people."
- "It didn't feel like a class. It felt like somewhat of a family."

Some students in a school where the curriculum was taught as part of a general education sophomore English class commented that they thought some of the activities were redundant. Comments included

- "It seemed redundant, common-sense type thinking."
- "[I didn't like how] the worksheets were so repetitive and the way that work-sheets asked about goals in 100 different ways."

These comments suggest that teachers may need to adapt the level of sophistication related to concepts addressed in the curriculum.

Teachers Teachers found that students appreciated both the individual attention given to their goals and being listened to by the teachers and other students. This observation of teachers was supported by the student responses described above regarding the feeling or climate of the group. Teachers found that students sometimes felt uneasy revealing thoughts that seemed personal. They found it important to allow students to keep their thoughts and notebooks private when they wanted and to only share information voluntarily. They also found it necessary to sometimes redirect students if they had difficulty being serious in response to a personal question, such as "What is important to you?"

Teachers also commented on the strength of interactive, experiential activities for the students. They consistently stated that the activities that were strongest were those where students were most highly involved, either through activity or verbal interaction. Furthermore, they commented that student–teacher interaction was one of the strengths of the curriculum.

Parents and Friends Parents and friends who participated in the curriculum with the students and responded to the follow-up evaluation rated the homework activities as highly supportive of their relationship with the student. In response to the question, "Please rate the value of your participation in the student's self-determination homework regarding building and/or maintaining a good relationship between you and the student", the mean response for the parents and friends was 4.75 (1 = poor; 5 = great). However, these same parents rated the importance of their involvement in the homework with regard to students becoming self-determined somewhat less favorably, 3.88 on the same 5-point scale.

Suggestions for Scheduling and Follow-Up   All of the comments regarding scheduling were made by teachers or students. Teachers found *Steps to Self-Determination* easier to infuse into existing coursework when they had greater control over the curriculum. For example, in a special education/general education, co-taught Career English class, teachers cited no difficulty infusing the self-determination curriculum into the class. However, in the general education/special education, co-taught sophomore English class, which had more districtwide curriculum requirements, teachers reported difficulty completing all of the self-determination classes in one semester and finishing the course requirements. In the same school, the special education teacher used the *Steps to Self-Determination* curriculum with her resource room class with no difficulty. Teachers suggested that it may be more feasible to schedule the self-determination curriculum over the entire school year, rather than one semester, when it is used in classes where there are more academic requirements to be met. Furthermore, teachers suggested that the curriculum would be strengthened by applying concepts learned in the self-determination curriculum in the general curriculum. While the curriculum suggests that teachers capitalize on "teachable moments" to help students apply concepts from the curriculum in real-life situations throughout the day, there is not currently a formal mechanism with which to structure this application.

Some students commented that they thought the class should be longer, some stated that it should be taught more than once each week, and some suggested that it should be offered over two semesters. A student who participated in the curriculum as part of a special group that was established specifically to receive the curriculum (as opposed to it being infused into an ongoing class) stated that, although she liked the curriculum, she did not like missing her regularly scheduled class each week.

SUMMARY

Self-determination can serve as an important organizing tool and philosophical underpinning for school improvement, educational planning, and curriculum efforts. It is a meaningful concept to be stressed for students with and without disabilities. Results of research suggest that increased student involvement is linked to more effective learning acquisition (Wehmeyer, 1992). By using self-determination as a central concept in school reform, individualized planning, and curriculum design, school staff can help ensure that educational programs meet individual student needs in a meaningful way. Research has found use of a self-determination curriculum to be effective in increasing student knowledge, skills, and behaviors associated with self-determination in students with and without disabilities (Hoffman & Field, 1995). Because self-determination is important to *all* students, the concept can be used in integrated or inclusive settings, thus helping to bridge the gap between general and special education programming. This comment supports a concern commonly associated with pull-out programs and suggests that scheduling arrangements must be sensitive to the overall needs of the students.

REFERENCES

Field, S., & Hoffman, A. (1994a). Development of a model for self-determination. *Career Development for Exceptional Individuals, 17,* 159–169.

Field, S., & Hoffman, A. (1994b). *Promoting successful outcomes through self-determination: Demonstration of a model for youth with disabilities who have dropped out of school or are at risk of dropping out of school.* Detroit, MI: Wayne State University.

Field, S., & Hoffman, A. (in press). *Steps to self-determination.* Austin, TX: PRO-ED.

Fullan, M.F., & Miles, M.B. (1992). Getting reform right: What works and what doesn't. *Phi Delta Kappan, 73*(10), 745–752.

Harkavy, I., & Puckett, J.L. (1991). Toward effective university public school partnerships: An analysis of a contemporary model. *Teachers College Record, 92,* 557–580.

Hoffman, A., & Field, S. (1995). Promoting self-determination through effective curriculum development. *Intervention in School and Clinic, 30,* 134–141.

Hoffman, A., Field, S., & Sawilowsky, S. (1995). *Self-determination assessment battery.* Detroit, MI: Wayne State University.

Hoffman, A., Field, S., & Sawilowsky, S. (in press). *Self-Determination Knowledge Scale.* Austin, TX: PRO-ED.

Hopfenberg, W.S., Levin, H.M., Meister, G., & Rogers, J. (1990). *Accelerated schools.* Stanford, CA: Accelerated Schools Project, Stanford University.

Individuals with Disabilities Education Act of 1990 (IDEA), PL 101-476. (October 30, 1990). Title 20, U.S.C. 1400 et seq: *U.S. Statutes at Large, 104,* 1103–1151.

Kennedy, M.M. (1984). How evidence alters understanding and decisions. *Education Evaluation and Policy Analysis, 6,* 207–226.

Lipsky, D.K. (1992). We need a third wave of education reform. *Social Policy, 22*(3), 43–45.

Martin, J., & Marshall, L. (1993). *The self-directed IEP.* Colorado Springs: University of Colorado.

Mathes, K. (1993, January). A look ahead for 93. *HR Focus, 1,* 4.

Myers, C.B., & Myers, L.K. (1995). *The professional educator.* Belmont, CA: Wadsworth.

Omachonu, V.K., & Ross, J.E. (1994). *Principles of total quality.* Delray Beach, FL: St. Lucie Press.

VanReusen, A.K., & Bos, C.S. (1990). IPLAN: Helping students communicate in planning conferences. *Teaching Exceptional Children, 22,* 30–32.

Wehman, P. (1992). *Life beyond the classroom: Transition strategies for young people with disabilities.* Baltimore: Paul H. Brookes Publishing Co.

Wehmeyer, M.L. (1992). Self-determination and the education of students with mental retardation. *Education and Training in Mental Retardation, 27,* 302–314.

Will, M. (1984). *OSERS programming for the transition of youth with disabilities: Bridges from school to working life.* Washington, DC: U.S. Department of Education, Office of Special Education and Rehabilitative Services.

Williams, R.C., & Bank, A. (1984). Assessing instructional information systems in two districts: The search for impact. *Educational Evaluation and Policy Analysis, 6*(3), 267–282.

Chapter 11

CHOICEMAKER

Infusing Self-Determination Instruction into the IEP and Transition Process

James E. Martin and Laura Huber Marshall

SPECIAL EDUCATION IS a system for delivering services to students with special needs. But mostly, special education is about teaching. In particular it is instruction specially designed to meet students' *unique* needs (Bateman, 1992). The heart, soul, and consciousness of this enterprise is the individualized education program (IEP) (Strickland & Turnbull, 1990). In addition to being a legally binding document, the IEP is a technical and process tool with which to develop and implement specialized instruction to obtain specified outcomes. The IEP process is used to determine where students are now; predict where they are going; and state how they will get there, how long it will take, and how all involved will know when they arrive (Bierly, 1978). The IEP is a unique educational practice.

This chapter does three things. First, it discusses student involvement in the IEP process, shows why this important, and explains the benefits. Second, it introduces the ChoiceMaker self-determination materials as a method to facilitate student leadership of their own IEP process. Third, it examines the IEP itself, reviews the IEP's most basic concepts, and shows how to infuse self-determination constructs into the IEP document.

This chapter would not have been possible without the feedback and advice from several educators in the Colorado Springs area. We wish to express our appreciation to Laurie Maxson, Vocational Director, Academy School District; Patty Jerman, Coronado High School in the Colorado Springs School District; and Debbie Thompson, Transition Specialist for the Colorado Springs School District. We would also like to thank Terry Miller, John Oliphint, and Paul Sale from the Special Education Program at the University of Colorado at Colorado Springs for their assistance. Support for this chapter was provided in part by a self-determination outreach grant from the U.S. Department of Education #H158Q40027.

STUDENT PARTICIPATION IN THE IEP PROCESS

Benefits of Active Student Participation

Since its inception, the premise behind the Education for All Handicapped Children Act of 1975 (PL 94-142) has been active student participation and decision making in the IEP process (Strickland & Turnbull, 1990). Because the student is the focal point of the IEP and "will play an important part in its accomplishment, his involvement is vital" (Strickland & Turnbull, 1990, p. 196). This concept is so important that training materials from the Colorado Department of Education (Palmer, Longo, Brewer, Bechard, & Amon, 1995), for instance, state that the "parent, the child, and school personnel are all equal participants in the sharing of information and decision making" (sec. 5, p. 7). Strickland and Turnbull (1990) listed the following potential benefits derived from active student participation in the IEP:

1. Students can contribute firsthand information regarding areas that present the greatest and least amount of difficulty. They can also evaluate methods of intervention in terms of their effectiveness in providing helpful strategies for learning.
2. Student presence at the IEP meeting can personalize the meeting for committee members, who may not know the student. Committee members can ask the student directly about his interests, skills, and so on, rather than relying solely on reports of others.
3. Including the student in the IEP conference indicates to the student that parents and teachers are receptive to the student's input and consider what students say as important.
4. Participation in the IEP development and/or in the IEP conference promotes the notion that the student is expected to behave maturely and responsibly.
5. Student participation in the IEP process may foster self-advocacy by providing an opportunity for the student to speak for himself regarding interests, academics, and the educational program. (p. 196)

But do students really participate to the best of their ability in the special education decision-making process? Unfortunately, this dream is far from a reality (Gillespie & Turnbull, 1983; VanReusen & Bos, 1990, 1994).

Student Participation in the IEP: "Whenever Appropriate" Means Never

The writers of the original PL 94-142 special education legislation included an almost forgotten phrase that called for student participation in IEP meetings "whenever appropriate" (Gillespie & Turnbull, 1983). For most students receiving special education services, "whenever appropriate" simply means never.

Goldstein, Strickland, Turnbull, and Curry (1980) studied IEP meetings. They found the special education teacher to be the most dominant speaker, who directed most of her conversation toward the parents. Gillespie (1981) reported that over 75% of students and 90% of parents did not know that students could attend their own IEP meetings. When asked about their attitude toward student participation, over 90% of the parents and 75% of the students strongly agreed with the concept of student participation. Gillespie and Turnbull (1983) characterized student participation in the IEP process as follows:

> Although a great deal of progress has been made by education agencies in implementing parent participation in education planning, very little has been done to include students with special needs in planning their own program. The potential of this involvement for furthering students' growth, maturity, and the exercise of appropriate power over their own lives is tremendous. While most persons are aware that school officials and parents are involved in IEP planning, many are not aware that the student may be included in helping to develop the IEP. (p. 27)

The situation changed little a decade later:

> Student involvement . . ., even at the secondary level, is for the most part either nonexistent or passive. If special educators plan and carry out instructional activities without involving or considering the adolescent's perceptions and priorities, they may be minimizing the student's *self-determination* [italics added]. (Van Reusen & Bos, 1990)

Nor has student participation in the IEP improved today: "Most students enrolled in special education programs are not being given the opportunity to participate in the development of their IEPs" (VanReusen & Bos, 1994, p. 466).

Teacher-Directed IEPs

The teacher-directed IEP process is under attack. Smith (1990) found that traditional teacher-directed IEPs do not foster specially designed instruction, teachers do not use the IEP in their daily educational activities, they lack a positive response from general education, and most parents are passive at teacher-directed conferences. Smith concluded his review with a scathing epithet: "We should acknowledge the IEP as nonviable and impractical and pursue other methods" (p. 12). Perhaps because student input is not considered and student involvement is minimal at best, the traditional teacher-directed IEP has failed to find meaning in a *student's* educational experience (Martin, Huber Marshall, & Maxson, 1993).

Repeating the Same Mistakes in Transition Planning The Individuals with Disabilities Education Act (IDEA) (PL 101-476) transition legislation encourages students, educators, and parents to plan for students' post–high school life, but if changes are not made, there is a danger of making the same mistakes with transition planning as are being made with individualized education programming (Stowitschek & Kelso, 1989). That is, transition planning will become just like teacher-directed IEPs—an administrative paperwork hassle that has little impact on actual instructional practices (Smith, 1990).

Lack of Student Empowerment Unfortunately, special education practices implemented in the past did little to empower youth with learning and behavior problems to control their own lives. As a result, many students did not learn the self-regulation skills needed to manage their lives (Mithaug, 1993). These students remain dependent upon others to make decisions, provide support, and make needed changes (Mithaug, Martin, & Agran, 1987). Their educational system exerted little effort to teach students how to gain control of their lives and to adapt to changes in their environments (Martin & Huber Marshall, 1995a). Perhaps the biggest culprit in this process is the IEP as it is now being implemented. Ironically, it may have the potential to provide the best tool with which to teach students to become self-determined.

THE IEP PROCESS AND BEHAVIORS FOR SUCCESS

Successful people know what they want and they persistently go after it (Hill, 1960; Hill & Stone, 1987). These individuals decide upon major goals, set a timeline, develop specific plans to attain their goals, determine the benefits that reaching the goals will bring, close off discouraging influences and thought, and build coalitions with others who share similar goals and who will engage with them in mutual encouragements.

Garfield (1986) found that successful people in any field excel at making decisions, self-managing their behavior, and adapting to changing circumstances. When these individuals made decisions, they 1) chose a mission leading to action; 2) communicated a clear mission; and 3) developed an action plan consisting of specific goals and benchmarks to evaluate the timing, quality, and quantity of the results. Successful people, according to Garfield (1986),

- Learn as they go, taking educated risks and building confidence in their skills along the way. "It is not fear of failure that drives them along, but a strong desire for achievement" (p. 138).
- See themselves "as the originator of actions in . . . life . . . [viewing] events in life as opportunities for taking action and [seeing] themselves as the agents who must precipitate action" (p. 141).
- Adapt by making course corrections and managing change through lifelong learning, expecting to succeed, mapping alternative futures, and updating their mission.

Garfield (1986) reached two conclusions: First, regardless of age, education, or profession, the most successful people share the same basic set of skills. Second, and perhaps most important, individuals can *learn* these skills.

INDIVIDUALS WITH DISABILITIES AND SUCCESS

These same success behaviors apply to people with disabilities. In a unique study, Gerber, Ginsberg, and Reiff (1992) interviewed a group of adults with learning disabilities to determine why some were successful and others were not. They found that successful individuals with learning disabilities

- Take control of their lives and surroundings
- Have a desire to succeed
- Have well-thought-out goals
- Are persistent
- Adapt to their environment
- Build a social support network that facilitates their success

After conducting the interviews, Gerber et al. (1992) realized that successful individuals decided, long before they became successful, that they would be successful. The authors concluded that successful adults with severe learning disabilities wanted to succeed, set achievable goals, and confronted their learning disability so that appropriate measures could be taken to increase the likelihood of success. One highly successful young man explained it like this: "Successful people have a plan. You have to have a plan, goals, strategy, otherwise you are flying through the clouds and then you hit the mountain" (Gerber et al., 1992, p. 480).

It is our belief that the IEP process offers the opportunity to teach these success behaviors. Recent changes in the IDEA transition regulations make this possible on a nationwide scale.

IDEA Transition Requirements
Operationalize IEP Instruction in Self-Determination

The IDEA operationalizes IEP instruction in self-determination by mandating student participation and decision making in the IEP process. Students 16 years of age and older must now be invited to their own IEP meeting unless a reason exists for them not to do so (although we would be hard pressed to envision such a reason). The spirit of these new rules requires that students of transition age determine, when able and with input and support from the IEP team, their own goals, objectives, and activities based upon *self-perceived* needs, preferences, and interests—not simply those expressed by parents and educators in the student's best interest.

Federal law mandates that a statement of needed transition services be included in the IEPs of transition-age students. IDEA defines transition services as a coordinated set of activities to promote movement from school to postschool activities. For the first time, educational activities must be based on sudents' expressed preferences and interests. These activities include instruction; community experiences; employment and other adult living objectives; and, when appropriate, functional vocational evaluation.

CHOICEMAKER CURRICULUM

The IEP is a self-determination metaphor (McAlonan & Longo, 1995). As a metaphor of the IEP process, self-determination instructional methodology and materials teach students how to predict where they are going, and determine how they will get there, how long it will take, and how all will know when they arrive. From learning to be aware of high school, post–high school, employment, personal, and housing and daily living needs, students learn to choose goals based upon their interests, skills, and limits. They learn how to express their needs and goals and how to obtain support for them. Students learn how to take action on their goals by planning, using self-management strategies, acting on that plan, self-evaluating their progress, and making adjustments as needed (Martin & Huber Marshall, 1995a).

The *ChoiceMaker Self-Determination Transition Curriculum* (Martin & Huber Marshall, 1995b) is one of a growing number of lesson packages designed to teach these crucial skills through student self-management of the IEP and transition process (Martin et al., 1996). This curriculum teaches students to self-manage their IEP and transition process. It consists of three sections: 1) choosing goals, 2) expressing goals, and 3) taking action (see Table 1). Each section contains from two to four teaching goals and several teaching objectives addressing six transition domains. These transition domains are 1) high school, 2) employment, 3) post–high school, 4) personal, 5) housing and daily living, and 6) community participation. Figure 1 shows the flow between transition domains and the ChoiceMaker IEP process. As students learn to manage their own IEP, they do so by making decisions and taking action on specific transition domains across the three major IEP process stages: 1) choosing goals, 2) expressing goals, and 3) taking action.

Martin and Huber Marshall (1995, 1996) socially validated the *Choice-Maker Self-Determination Transition Curriculum* through a four-step process. First, an extensive literature review and interview process produced a comprehensive list of 37 self-determination concepts grouped into seven areas (see Table 2). These areas are

1. Self-awareness
2. Self-advocacy
3. Self-efficacy
4. Decision making
5. Independent performance
6. Self-evaluation
7. Adjustment

Second, each concept was defined and then placed into a curriculum matrix format. Third, teachers, adults with disabilities, parents, and university-based transition experts from across the country validated the self-determination concepts and the curriculum matrix. Fourth, focus groups, practicing educators who co-authored the materials, and extensive field tests fine-tuned the curriculum and instructional materials.

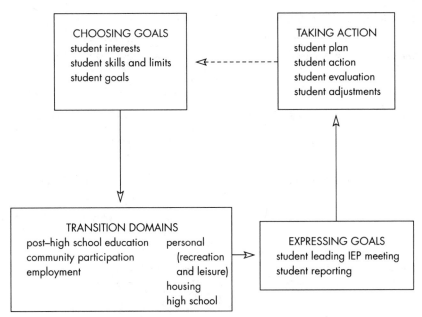

Figure 1. The flow between transition domains and the ChoiceMaker IEP process.

ChoiceMaker Assessment

The *ChoiceMaker Self-Determination Transition Assessment* (Martin & Huber Marshall, 1996) is a curriculum-based tool keyed to the *ChoiceMaker Self-Determination Transition Curriculum* (Martin & Huber Marshall, 1995). Each assessment item matches a curriculum objective. To complete the assessment, the teacher rates "Student Skills" and determines the "Opportunity at School" to perform that skill in the student's present environment on a 0–4 scale. The teacher completes each item based upon what he or she has seen students or the school actually do, not upon what he or she thinks students or the school could do. (See Figure 2 for an example.) A graphic summary profile is then prepared comparing student skills to their opportunity at school across the three curriculum sections. The *ChoiceMaker Self-Determination Transition Assessment* is useful to document student and program change across time, and it may help an IEP team determine need and present level of performance statements for the IEP meeting and document.

ChoiceMaker Lesson Packages

The ChoiceMaker lesson packages describe the methodology and provide the material to teach the objectives of the ChoiceMaker curriculum (see Table 3). Each lesson package is designed to be infused into existing school coursework

Table 1. The ChoiceMaker Self-Determination Transition Curriculum

Sections	Teaching goals	Teaching objectives		
1: Choosing Goals (through school & community experience)	A. Student Interests	A1. Express **high school** interests	A2. Express **employment** interests	A3. Express **post–high school education** interests
	B. Student Skills and Limits	B1. Express **high school** skills & limits	B2. Express **employment** skills & limits	B3. Express **post–high school education** skills & limits
	C. Student Goals	C1. Indicate options & choose **high school** goals	C2. Indicate options & choose **employment** goals	C3. Indicate options & choose **post–high school education** goals
2: Expressing Goals	D. Student Leading Meeting	D1. Begin meeting by stating purpose	D2. Introduce participants	D3. Review past goals and performance
	E. Student Reporting	E1. Express interests (from A1–7)	E2. Express skills & limits (from B1–6)	E3. Express options & goals (from C1–6)
3: Taking Action	F. Student Plan	F1. Break general goals into specific goals that can be done now	F2. Establish **standard** for specific goals	F3. Determine how to get **feedback** from environment
	G. Student Action	G1. Record or report performance	G2. Perform specific goals to **standard**	G3. Obtain **feedback** on performance
	H. Student Evaluation	H1. Determine if goals are achieved	H2. Compare performance to task **standards**	H3. Evaluate **feedback**
	I. Student Adjustment	I1. Adjust goals if necessary	I2. Adjust goal **standards**	I3. Adjust or repeat method for **feedback**

From Martin, J.E., & Huber Marshall, L. (1995). ChoiceMaker: A comprehensive self-determination transition program. *Intervention in School and Clinic, 30*(3), 147–156; reprinted by permission.

(continued)

Table 1. *(continued)*

A4. Express **personal** interests	A5. Express **housing & daily living** interests	A6. Express **community participation** interests	A7. Express what is most important	
B4. Express **personal** skills & limits	B5. Express **housing & daily living** skills & limits	B6. Express **community participation** skills & limits		
C4. Indicate options & choose **personal** goals	C5. Indicate options & choose **housing & daily living** goals	C6. Indicate options & choose **community participation** goals		
D4. Ask for feedback from group members	D5. Ask questions if student doesn't understand	D6. Deal with differences of opinion	D7. State needed support	D8. Close meeting by summarizing decisions

F4. Indicate **motivation** to complete specific goals	F5. Indicate **strategies** for completing specific goals	F6. Determine **support** needed to complete specific goals	F7. Prioritize & **schedule** to complete specific goals	F8. Express **belief** that goals can be obtained
G4. **Motivate** self to complete specific goals	G5. Use **strategies** to perform specific goals	G6. Obtain **support** needed	G7. Follow **schedule**	
H4. Evaluate **motivation**	H5. Evaluate effectiveness of **strategies**	H6. Evaluate **support** used	H7. Evaluate **schedule**	H8. Evaluate **belief**
I4. Adjust **motivation**	I5. Adjust or repeat **strategies**	I6. Adjust or repeat **support**	I7. Adjust or repeat **schedule**	I8. Adjust **belief** that goals can be obtained

Table 2. Self-determination constructs grouped into seven categories

Self-Awareness
  Identify needs
  Identify interests
  Identify and understand strengths
  Identify and understand limitations
  Identify own values

Self-Advocacy
  Assertively state wants
  Assertively state rights
  Determine support needs
  Pursue needed support
  Obtain and evaluate needed support
  Conduct own affairs

Self-Efficacy
  Expects to obtain goals

Decision Making
  Assess situational demands
  Set goals
  Set standards
  Identify information needed to make decisions
  Consider past solutions for new situations
  Generate new, creative solutions
  Consider options
  Choose best option
  Develop plan

Independent Performance
  Initiate tasks on time
  Complete tasks on time
  Use self-management strategies
  Perform tasks to standard
  Follow-through on own plan

Self-Evaluation
  Monitor task performance
  Compare performance to standard
  Evaluate effectiveness of self-management strategies
  Determine if plan is completed and goal met

Adjustment
  Change goals
  Change standards
  Change plan
  Change strategies
  Change support
  Persistently adjust
  Use environmental feedback to aid adjustment

Part I: ChoiceMaker Self-Determination Transition Assessment

SECTION 1: CHOOSING GOALS

	Student Skills (Does the student do this?)	Opportunity at School (Does school provide structured time?)

B. _Student Interests_ - Does the student:

	Student Skills	Opportunity at School
B1. Express **school** interests (e.g., classes, sports, clubs)?	0 1 2 3 4	0 1 2 3 4
B2. Express **employment** interests (e.g., jobs, careers)?	0 1 2 3 4	0 1 2 3 4
B3. Express **post-high school education** interests (e.g., colleges, trade schools)?	0 1 2 3 4	0 1 2 3 4
B4. Express **personal matters** interests (e.g., social, leisure, health, financial, legal)?	0 1 2 3 4	0 1 2 3 4
B5. Express **housing and daily living** interests?	0 1 2 3 4	0 1 2 3 4
B6. Express **community participation** interests (e.g., transportation, adult services)?	0 1 2 3 4	0 1 2 3 4
	Subtotal	_Subtotal_

C. _Student Skills and Limits_- Does the student:

	Student Skills	Opportunity at School
C1. Express **school** skills and limits?	0 1 2 3 4	0 1 2 3 4
C2. Express **employment** skills and limits?	0 1 2 3 4	0 1 2 3 4
C3. Express **post-high school education** skills and limits?	0 1 2 3 4	0 1 2 3 4
C4. Express **personal matters** skills and limits?	0 1 2 3 4	0 1 2 3 4
C5. Express **housing and daily living** skills and limits?	0 1 2 3 4	0 1 2 3 4
C6. Express **community participation** skills and limits?	0 1 2 3 4	0 1 2 3 4
	Subtotal	_Subtotal_

Figure 2. Sample section from the _ChoiceMaker Self-Determination Transition Assessment_ tool. (From Martin, J.E., & Huber Marshall, L.H. [1996]. _ChoiceMaker Self-Determination Transition Assessment._ Longmont, CO: Sopris West; reprinted by permission.)

225

Table 3. ChoiceMaker Self-Determination Transition curriculum sections, goals, and lessons

Section	Goals	Lessons
1. Choosing Goals	A. Student Interests B. Student Skills and Limits C. Student Goals	• Choosing Employment Goals (completed) • Choosing Personal Goals (completed) • Choosing Post–High School Education Goals (to be completed) • Choosing Secondary School Goals (to be completed) • Choosing Housing and Daily Living Goals (to be completed) • Choosing Community Participation Goals (to be completed)
2. Expressing Goals	D. Student Leading Meeting E. Student Reporting	• Self-Directed IEP (completed)
3. Taking Action	F. Student Plan G. Student Action H. Student Evaluation I. Student Adjustment	• Take Action (completed)

and programs. Because the Choosing Goals and Taking Action materials (curriculum sections 1 and 3) are compatible with many middle and high school content areas, they can be used with general education as well as special education students in either general education classrooms or in specialized teaching environments. The *Self-Directed IEP* (the Expressing Goals section of the curriculum; Martin, Huber Marshall, Maxson, & Jerman, 1996), as well as the accompanying *ChoiceMaker Self-Determination Transition Assessment*, are designed for use with students receiving special education services. These lesson packages are described in greater detail in the following sections.

Choosing Goals Lesson Modules   The Choosing Goals lesson modules teach students the necessary skills and personal information needed to articulate their interests, skills, limits, and goals across the five transition areas. A videotape introduces the concept of choosing goals by showing actual high school students learning and using the choosing goals process. Students from Colorado Springs area high schools made the videotape highlighting their concerns from the different transition domains.

The lessons take students through a series of systematic school- and community-based experiences across five different transition areas. Worksheets keyed to students' experiences assist them to match their skills, limits, and preferences to various in-school and community opportunities. Because the lesson sequence is flexible, each lesson may be mixed and matched to correspond with the content and opportunities presented by existing school curriculum and schedules.

Choosing Employment Goals (Huber Marshall, Martin, Maxson, & Jerman, 1996) is one of the Choosing Goals lesson modules. It provides a structured set of materials and methodology for students to experientially examine their employment interests, skills, and limits in order to set vocational goals. An example from this module is the "Job Characteristics I Like" lesson (see Figure 3). In this lesson, students compare the job characteristics they would like to what exists at their current job sites. Students graph their preferred characteristics to create over time a visual picture of their preferred and nonpreferred job characteristics. Students combine this information with many other factors to help determine their own unique employment goals.

Expressing Goals The Expressing Goals section of the ChoiceMaker curriculum is taught using the *Self-Directed IEP* (Martin, Huber Marshall, Maxson, et al., 1996). It is the only part of the ChoiceMaker curriculum itself designed specifically for students receiving special education services. Rather than being passive participants at their IEP meetings, the *Self-Directed IEP* teaches students to direct their meetings to the greatest extent of their ability and eagerness. While completing the lessons, students watch a videotape showing "Zeke" leading his own IEP meeting. Students complete workbook assignments lesson-by-lesson and apply each new lesson to their own IEP.

The lessons teach students 11 steps for leading their own IEP meetings. Sample steps include Step 1, Begin meeting by stating purpose; Step 2, Introduce everyone; working on interpersonal and social skills such as in Step 6, Ask questions if you don't understand; and Step 7, Deal with differences in opinion. The lessons are generally taught two to three times a week over a 3-week period and then reviewed prior to when the student's IEP meeting is scheduled.

Through the use of the *Self-Directed IEP* procedures and practice in their actual meetings, students learn the leadership skills necessary to manage their IEP meetings and to publicly disclose their interests, skills, limits, and goals gleaned from the Choosing Goals lessons.

Taking Action The *Taking Action* module (Huber Marshall, Martin, McGill, Maxson, & Jerman, 1996) teaches students to break their long-range goals into specific short-term objectives. As with the other curriculum sections, this module is introduced with a student-oriented videotape demonstrating the Taking Action concepts. As presented in Figure 4, Taking Action lessons teach students to plan how they will attain their goals by establishing 1) a standard for goal performance, 2) a means to get performance feedback, 3) what motivates them to accomplish this goal, 4) the strategies they will use, 5) needed supports, and 6) schedule for action. This leads to student action, evaluation, and adjustment. Rather than teachers, parents, or support staff telling students what to do, when to do it, and how they did, students assume these responsibilities themselves. Of course, this requires a learning process that fades teacher

---

JOB CHARACTERISTICS I LIKE WORKSHEET

NAME: _____ JOB SITE: _____ DATE: _____

Directions:

WHAT I LIKE column: Circle the job characteristics that you like best in each box.
WHAT IS HERE column: Circle the job characteristic that best describes what is at this job.
MATCHES column: Circle YES if the first two columns are the same. Circle NO if they are not.

	WHAT I LIKE	WHAT IS HERE	MATCHES
1.	work alone lots of people around	work alone lots of people around	YES NO
2.	quiet workplace noisy workplace	quiet workplace noisy workplace	YES NO
3.	work close to home distance to job doesn't matter	work close to home distance to job doesn't matter	YES NO
4.	weekends only weekends too	weekends only weekends too	YES NO
5.	easy job challenging job	easy job challenging job	YES NO

Figure 3. Sample lesson from the Choosing Goals Lesson modules. (From Huber Marshall, L., Martin, J.E., McGill, T., Maxson, L.L., & Jerman, P. [1996]. *Taking action*. Colorado Springs: University of Colorado, School of Education; reprinted by permission.)

instruction as students learn the crucial skills. These lessons can be applied to any goal or project and thus are excellent for use as part of regular, ongoing classes.

INFUSING SELF-DETERMINATION INTO THE IEP PROCESS

Youths who receive special education services possess far fewer self-determination skills than do secondary general education students (Wolman, Campeau, DuBois, Mithaug, & Stolarski, 1994). As self-determination skills are seldom directly taught, most students in general education acquired these skills through the daily interactions in their lives. Students with learning and behavior problems for whatever reasons acquire very few self-determination skills in their daily lives.

The importance of self-determination skills to postschool success is without question (Deci & Chandler, 1986; Field & Hoffman, 1994; Mithaug, 1991; Wehmeyer, 1992). Fortunately, as Garfield (1986) realized, self-determined success behavior can and must be taught. We firmly believe that for students to learn and use self-determination behaviors in their everyday life, self-determination constructs must become a part of students' daily instructional routine. To make this happen for students who have not acquired or who do not use these success behaviors, IEP teams need to strongly consider students' self-determination needs.

Directions

General and Specific Goals Write your general goal and specific goal on the lines below.

Specific goals are smaller goals that lead to your general goal. Specific goals are things you can work on during the next week.

1. *Student Plan* Write a plan to accomplish your specific goal. Complete the six parts of the plan by answering the questions in each box.

2. *Action* Next week, review your action. Answer the questions in each box.

3. *Evaluate Plan* After you complete 2. Action, evaluate whether each part of your plan worked. Write the reasons they did or didn't work in each box.

4. *Main Reason for Results* Look at your reasons in 3. Evaluate Plan. Decide which of those is the main reason you got the results you did. Write it on the lines under the question.

5. *Adjust Plan* Decide if you want to adjust the parts of your plan that didn't work. Write the changes in the boxes. Remember which parts of your plan did work so you can use them again

General Goal   GET OUT OF DEBT

Specific Goal   PAY OFF VISA CARD

1. Student Plan

STANDARD What will I be satisfied with?	FEEDBACK How will I get information on my performance?	MOTIVATION Why do I want to do this?	STRATEGY What methods should I use?	SUPPORT What help do I need?	SCHEDULE When will I do it?
ZERO BALANCE ON VISA CARD	GETTING THE VISA STATEMENT	HAVE GOOD CREDIT	WORK AND PAY VISA BALANCE EACH MONTH	KEEP JOB AND WORK STEADY HOURS	PAY BALANCE EVERY MONTH

Figure 4.   Sample Taking Action Student plan. [From Huber Marshall, L., Martin, J.E., McGill, T., Maxson, L.L., & Jerman, P. [1996]. *Taking action.* Colorado Springs: University of Colorado, School of Education; reprinted by permission.]

229

To help accomplish this goal, this section describes the IEP process and shows how to infuse self-determination constructs into each IEP component. If educators are serious about teaching students self-determination skills, then self-determination instruction must occur. Making self-determination a part of the IEP document is the first step to take.

Individualized Instruction

The IEP process addresses students' needs and determines the instruction, services, modifications, and accommodations needed to meet those needs. The IEP concerns itself only with that part of the student's education that must be individualized.

To facilitate individualized instruction, the IEP process serves several functions, these include its use as a

1. Communication tool for parents, school personnel, and students to decide student needs, services to meet those needs, and expected outcomes
2. Means for parents, school staff, and students to resolve differences in opinion about student needs
3. Management tool to ensure that each student is provided appropriate special education and related services
4. Monitoring tool to determine the extent of student progress toward meeting the expected outcomes
5. Legal tool to ensure accountability in program planning and service delivery through the production of a tangible document detailing each student's educational program (Strickland & Turnbull, 1990)

Each of these functions assist in establishing self-determination as a transition priority.

Questions IEP Team Must Ask

The IEP team asks three basic questions (Bateman, 1992): What are the student's unique educational needs as defined through the present level of performance? What will the school do or provide to meet these needs? What goals and objectives will the student and educational system attempt to accomplish?

Until self-determination needs are routinely considered by each IEP team, the key to infusing self-determination constructs into the IEP document is to rephrase Bateman's (1992) three questions. Answers to these questions will go a long way to infuse self-determination into the IEP and everyday life of each student who receives special education services. Looking at self-determination as an essential consideration of the IEP, the IEP team must ask:

1. What are the student's unique self-determination needs as defined through the present level of performance?
2. What will the school do or provide to meet these self-determination needs?
3. What self-determination goals and objectives will the student and educational system attempt to accomplish?

Steps to Writing the IEP

Bateman's (1992) method to write the IEP document consists of four active steps. First, identify the student's unique characteristics and needs. Second, describe the student's present level of performance. Third, note the areas of needed service. Fourth, write down goals and objectives. Adaptations to this format exist all across the country, but these basic concepts are in every IEP.

Identify Unique Characteristics and Needs The first step in completing an IEP is the identification of unique student needs. These describe the effect of the disability on the student's performance in any affected educational area. To increase the likelihood of secondary school and transition success, the IEP team needs to consider self-determination as a unique, if not one of the most important, need areas. This list of needs should not only look at today, but also describe the student's future needs as well based upon perceived long-term outcomes. Long-term outcomes provide a direction and route to follow based upon the student's interests, preferences, and strengths. They incorporate students' and parents' dreams for the future and may focus upon the next transition point in a student's life, such as high school graduation. The statement of needs should be self-explanatory and clear to all participants in the IEP meeting. Bateman (1992) provides several examples of academic and non-academic needs:

- The student's handwriting is nearly illegible due to size and spacing of letters and words.
- The student works very slowly and becomes upset when a mistake is made or corrected.
- The student does not comprehend material read independently.
- The student does not know how to approach teachers to seek assistance.
- The student has difficulty in following oral instructions from supervisor at work.
- The student talks inappropriately about monsters, blood, and death.

Following Bateman's lead, below are several sample self-determination needs:

- The student does not establish goals and a sequence of time-related tasks needed to complete long-term assignments.
- The student is very disorganized and does not keep track of due dates and assignments.
- The student wants a job that matches his interests, skills, and limits.
- The student does not self-evaluate and compare completed work to the expected grading criteria before turning in class products.
- The student needs to identify and tell teachers what educational support is needed to prepare for academic life at the local community college.

Although not required by federal mandates, some IEP teams review and profile student strengths before the needs are specified. This addition starts the meeting in a positive framework and provides the opportunity for objectives developed later in the meeting to build on student strengths. If strengths are discussed, the IEP team may want to describe the student's self-determination strengths, as well.

Describe Present Level of Performance The present level of performance (PLOP) profiles the student today. PLOPs describe the needs that the remainder of the IEP addresses (Bateman, 1992). Like the statement of needs, PLOPs must be clear, understandable to all team members (including the parent and student), and precise so that measurement can occur. The PLOP is an elaboration of the identified needs. For instance, if the need is illegible handwriting due to size and spacing of letters and words, the PLOP could be "writes six words per minute, with four to five words illegible." Formal or informal evaluation results are often a good source to help develop PLOP statements. Like the needs list, the PLOP is unique to each student. The IEP team determines the PLOP statements and uses them as the starting point for the development of goals and objectives. Three sample self-determination need and PLOP statements might be as follows:

1. *Need*: To establish goals and a sequence of time-related tasks needed to complete long-term assignments
   PLOP: Turns in 90% of nightly assignments but does not turn in any long-term assignments from any class
2. *Need*: To learn what available jobs match his interests, skills, and limits
   PLOP: Over the past semester stated five different job choices, three of which are not available in the community he plans to live in after leaving school and two for which he clearly does not meet the entry-level requirements
3. *Need*: To self-evaluate own work or compare it to the expected grading criteria or instruction before turning in class products
   PLOP: Almost 60% of turned-in assignments and tests show missing segments or sections completed incorrectly

Note Areas of Needed Services In response to the student's needs, the IEP team develops a listing of services. Bateman (1992) suggests that the IEP team develop the services by discussing "special education, related services, regular class modifications, and other creative, flexible, innovative, and often inexpensive need-meters" (p. 60). As services are identified, the team must think of special education not as a place but rather a system of supports brought to the student. A listing of services that put the student in a place is inadequate (Bateman, 1992). Interestingly, intervention methodology to meet the needs do not have to be identified. Except in very rare instances, school staff select the methodology, not the IEP team. Examples of special education and related services include

- Extending time for completion of essays and content area assignments
- Providing a tape recorder and headphone for use in classes
- Providing instruction in an IEP self-management program that enables the student to manage meeting her own goals and objectives through building supports and managing interventions
- Providing instruction in a self-managed homework system that includes a calendar and due date, strategy, and progress checklist system
- Assigning a study-buddy
- Building into each class a continuous and cumulative material review
- Providing situational community-based vocational assessment
- Providing a learning strategies and study skills class
- Team teaching content area class, with the special education teacher teaching learning strategies, self-management skills, and goal analysis while the general education teacher instructs on the existing content and assignments

Write Down Goals and Objectives   IEP goals and objectives evaluate the services being provided (Bateman, 1992). They tell the IEP team how far the student will progress toward the annual goal and by when it will most likely happen. IEP goals answer the question, "If the service we're providing is effective, what will we see in Todd's behavior that tells us so?" (Bateman, 1992, p. 60). They are written only for the special services provided, not for all the components of the student's educational program. A direct relationship exists between the PLOP statements and the annual goals:

1. *Need*:   To establish goals and a sequence of time-related tasks needed to complete long-term assignments
    PLOP: Turns in 90% of daily homework assignments but does not turn in any long-term assignments from any class
    Service to Be Provided: Goal setting, assignment analysis, and task breakdown instruction in a learning/study skills strategy class; and team teaching with special education teacher providing similar strategy support in the content area
    Annual Goal: Will turn in at least 80% of long-term assignments (due at least 2 class days from when assigned) from each class
2. *Need*:   To learn what available jobs match his interests, skills, and limits
    PLOP: Over the past semester stated five different job choices, three of which are not available in the community he plans to live in after leaving school, and two for which he clearly does not meet the entry-level requirements
    Services to Be Provided: Situational community-based vocational assessment and in-class support
    Annual Goal: Will consistently identify at least three available community jobs that match his interest, skills, and limits

3. *Need*: To self-evaluate own work or compare it to the expected grading criteria or instruction before turning in class products

   PLOP: Almost 60% of turned-in assignments and tests show missing segments

   Services to Be Provided: Goal setting assignment analysis, and task breakdown instruction in a learning/study skills strategy class; team teaching with special education teacher providing similar strategy support in the content area

   Annual Goal: 80% or more of the assignments and tests turned in will not have missing segments or sections completed incorrectly because of obvious disregard for stated grading criteria or instruction

The importance of self-determination for postschool success, and the lack of self-determination skills in so many youth who receive special education services, make it imperative that self-determination skills be taught. The Choice-Maker curriculum, and other self-determination instructional packages, facilitate this process. But, we believe in order to make a true difference, self-determination needs must be discussed at the IEP meeting. This is the only way that self-determination needs, services, and goals will emerge from IEP team discussions and assessments. When students interact directly with the IEP process and faculty facilitate this process, the likelihood of students learning these crucial skills is increased.

Notes from One District

Academy School District in Colorado Springs is taking a lead in the effort to infuse self-determination into the IEP process. A school and community committee wrote their transition policy, which the school board then approved. This policy takes advantage of the opportunity provided by the IEP process to teach and provide students repeated opportunities to practice self-determination behaviors. Student leadership of the IEP process is the foundation of this policy statement (Martin et al., 1993a). The policy outlines a developmental IEP sequence. Students in elementary schools attend their own IEP meeting. By middle school, students start to actively participate, and by high school, students learn to direct their own IEP process to their greatest ability.

SUMMARY

Transition programming attempts to facilitate successful adjustment to life after public school. To assist in this effort, self-determination instruction is quickly becoming a means by which to increase the likelihood of post-school success and quality life. Self-determination instruction pulls together success behaviors, self-advocacy, goal-setting, problem solving, self-management, and self-efficacy research and thoughts into a consistent intervention package.

This chapter presented the ChoiceMaker lessons and materials and described how they operationalize self-determination to teach these crucial skills through the IEP process. If we expect students to be successful and self-determined once they leave school, then we need to teach them how to control their own lives while they are still in school. Key to this process is infusing self-determination concepts into the IEP and transition process. Thanks to federal support, a variety of methodologies for teaching self-determination skills are being developed. Infusing these into existing school programs, especially into the IEP process, is our challenge.

REFERENCES

Bateman, B.D. (1992). *Better IEPs.* Creswell, OR: Otter Ink.

Bierly, K. (1978). Public Law 94-142: Answers to the questions your're asking. *Instructor, 87*(9), 63–67.

Deci, E.L., & Chandler, C.L. (1986). The importance of motivation for the future of the LD field. *Journal of Learning Disabilities, 19*, 587–594.

Education for All Handicapped Children Act of 1975, PL 94-142. (August 23, 1977). Title 20, U.S.C. 1400 et seq: *U.S. Statutes at Large, 89*, 773–796.

Field, S., & Hoffman, A. (1994). Development of a model for self-determination. *Career Development for Exceptional Individuals, 17*, 159–169.

Garfield, G. (1986). *Peak performers: The new heroes of American business.* New York: Avon.

Gerber, P.J., Ginsberg, R., & Reiff, H.B. (1992). Identifying alterable patterns in employment success for highly successful adults with learning disabilities. *Journal of Learning Disabilities, 25*, 475–487.

Gillespie, E.B. (1981). *Student participation in the development of individualized education programs: Perspectives of parents and students.* Unpublished doctoral dissertation, University of North Carolina at Chapel Hill.

Gillespie, E.B., & Turnbull, A.P. (1983). It's my IEP! Involving students in the planning process. *Teaching Exceptional Children, 16*, 27–29.

Goldstein, S., Strickland, B., Turnbull, A.P., & Curry, L. (1980). An observational analysis of the IEP conference. *Exceptional Children, 46*(4), 278–286.

Hill, N.H. (1960). *Think and grow rich.* New York: Ballantine Books.

Hill, N.H., & Stone, W.C. (1987). *Success through a positive mental attitude.* New York: Prentice Hall.

Huber Marshall, L., Martin, J.E., Maxson, L.L., & Jerman, P. (1996). *Choosing employment goals.* Longmont, CO: Sopris West.

Huber Marshall, L., Martin, J.E., McGill, T., Maxson, L.L., & Jerman, P. (1996). *Taking action.* Longmont, CO: Sopris West.

Individuals with Disabilities Education Act of 1990 (IDEA), PL 101-476. (October 30, 1990). Title 20, U.S.C. 1400 et seq: *U.S. Statutes at Large, 104*, 1103–1151.

Martin, J.E., & Huber Marshall, L.H. (1995). ChoiceMaker: A comprehensive self-determination transition program. *Intervention in School and Clinic, 30*, 147–156.

Martin, J.E., & Huber Marshall, L.H. (1996). *ChoiceMaker Self-Determination Transition Assessment.* Longmont, CO: Sopris West.

Martin, J.E., Huber Marshall, L., Miller, T.L., Kregar, G., & Hughes, W. (1996). [Analysis of various transition related self-determination curriculum]. Unpublished raw data.

Martin, J.E., Huber Marshall, L., & Maxson, L.L. (1993). Transition policy: Infusing self-determination and self-advocacy into transition programs. *Career Development for Exceptional Individuals, 16,* 53–61.

Martin, J.E., Huber Marshall, L., Maxson, L.L., & Jerman, P. (1996). *Self-directed IEP.* Longmont, CO: Sopris West.

McAlonan, S.J., & Longo, P.A. (1995, March). *KEDS: Kids empowerment drives the system.* Paper presented at the Seventh Collaborative Conference for Special Education, Colorado Springs, CO.

Mithaug, D.E. (1991). *Self-determined kids: Rasising satisfied and successful children.* Lexington, MA: D.C. Health.

Mithaug, D.E. (1993). *Self-regulation theory: How optimal adjustment maximizes gain.* Westport, CT: Praeger.

Mithaug, D.E., Martin, J.E., & Agran, M. (1987). Adaptability instruction: The goal of transitional programs. *Exceptional Children, 53,* 500–505.

Palmer, B., Longo, P., Brewer, R., Bechard, S., & Amon, C. (1995). *Planning and preparing quality individualized education programs.* Denver: Colorado Department of Education.

Smith, S.W. (1990). Individualized education programs (IEPs) in special education: From intent to acquiescence. *Exceptional Children, 57,* 6–14.

Stowitschek, J.J., & Kelso, C.A. (1989). Are we in danger of making the same mistakes with ITPs as were made with IEPs? *Career Development for Exceptional Individuals, 12,* 139–151.

Strickland, B.B., & Turnbull, A.P. (1990). *Developing and implementing individualized education programs.* Columbus, OH: Charles E. Merrill.

VanReusen, A.K., & Bos, C.S. (1990). IPLAN: Helping students communicate in planning conferences. *Teaching Exceptional Children, 22,* 30–32.

VanReusen, A.K., & Bos, C.S. (1994). Facilitating student participation in individualized education programs through motivation strategy instruction. *Exceptional Children, 60,* 466–475.

Wehmeyer, M.L. (1992). Self-determination: Critical skills for outcome-oriented transition services. *The Journal for Vocational Special Needs Education, 15,* 3–9.

Wolman, M., Campeau, P.L., DuBois, P.A., Mithaug, D.E., & Stolarski, V.S. (1994). *AIR self-determination scale and userguide.* Palo Alto, CA: American Institute for Research.

Chapter 12

ENHANCING SELF-DETERMINATION THROUGH GROUP ACTION PLANNING

A Holistic Emphasis

Ann P. Turnbull, Martha J. Blue-Banning,
Emma Longan Anderson, H. Rutherford Turnbull,
Kimberly A. Seaton, and Patricia A. Dinas

THE FIELD OF special education has been characterized as taking a "fix-it" approach to disability (Gliedman & Roth, 1980; Heshusius, 1982; Turnbull & Turnbull, 1985; Zola, 1982). The "fix-it" approach emphasizes that the goal of special education is remediation of deficits that exist within the individual. It assumes that once those deficits are remediated, individuals with a disability will be able to participate in society in an independent (i.e., unassisted) manner. The "fix-it" approach is reflected in the area of self-determination by approaches that exclusively enumerate a list of important skills that individuals with disabilities must master in order to be considered self-determining. Typically, once the list is developed, efforts are directed at systematically teaching these skills to achieve self-determination. This conceptualization of self-determination assumes that individual skills alone are enough for an individual to achieve autonomy in meeting environmental challenges and expectations.

As an alternative to this unidimensional emphasis on individual skills, we have suggested that self-determination has three key components: 1) motivation, 2) individual skills, and 3) a responsive context. Consistent with the identification of these three components, we have defined self-determination as follows: "Self-determination means choosing how to live one's life consistent with per-

A portion of this research was funded by the Office of Special Education Programs, U.S. Department of Education, Grant #H158K20035, Self-Determination Through Group Action Planning Project, to Full Citizenship, Inc., Lawrence, Kansas; no official endorsement should be implied.

sonal values and preferences. A self-determining individual can choose to make decisions singularly and/or choose whose support to invite in his or her decision-making process" (Turnbull & Turnbull, 1985).

Becoming self-determined involves an interplay of motivation, skills, and a responsive context. This interaction develops dynamically and fluidly over time. Motivation and skills relate to aspects of the individual, whereas the component of a responsive context relates to environmental support and opportunity. Motivation refers to intrinsic desire, energy, and positive anticipation of the future that result in an openness to learn, undertake challenges, and solve problems. Skills involve a broad range of domains including knowledge and acceptance of self, problem solving, communicating, learning from successes and failures, accessing individual and agency support, and being reciprocal in relationships. A responsive context consists of environments in which opportunities are available for enjoyable and reciprocal relationships, nonjudgmental and informative feedback, a reasonable degree of successive challenges, negotiation of reasonable and constructive limits, open and honest communication, facilitating but not controlling support, and celebratory affirmations of progress.

The focus in this chapter is primarily on the creation of a responsive context. Although this particular component is highlighted, we emphasize that the three components are highly interdependent. Thus, when a context is appropriately responsive, one should expect that it will influence the individual in terms of enhancing both motivation and skill development.

This chapter describes a particular model, one that we have developed and call Group Action Planning, which has a wide range of applications, including the enhancement of self-determination. Group Action Planning is a form of person-centered planning that shares many features of other person-centered approaches such as Making Action Plans (Forest & Pearpoint, 1992) (formerly the McGill Action Planning System), Personal Futures Planning (Mount & Zwernik, 1988), and Essential Lifestyles Planning (Smull & Harrison, 1992). Table 1 compares and contrasts traditional planning methods (e.g., individualized education program [IEP] conferences) and a person-centered approach (e.g., Group Action Planning). Group Action Planning is a flexible process that can be used at any point in a person's life. Although this chapter focuses primarily on Group Action Planning as a strategy for supporting students with disabilities who are moving from high school to adulthood, the process is just as applicable for infants as it is for adolescents or people who are elderly.

GROUP ACTION PLANNING

Group Action Planning is a process of creating a reliable alliance among an individual with a disability, family members, professionals, and friends. The purpose of the process is to support the individual with a disability to create a vision of how he or she wants to live life and then to make a long-term commitment to the individual to transform that vision into reality.

Table 1. Comparison of traditional and person-centered planning approaches

IEP conferences— traditional planning	Group action planning— person-centered planning
Professionally directed, unequal ratio of professionals to family members and friends	Approximately equal proportion of participants from the groups of friends, community citizens, family members, and professionals
Structured, formal process	Reflective, creative process that focuses on divergent problem solving
Regulated by mandated paperwork for monitoring compliance	Not mandated or regulated; facilitated by an individual skilled in collaborative communication
Held in professional setting (e.g., conference room)	Held in an informal setting, most often the home of family or friends
Serious atmosphere in which the focus of attention is on the student's developmental needs	Relational, fun, affirming atmosphere in which the strengths, capabilities, contributions, and dreams are the focus of attention
Meets once or twice a year	Meets regularly (usually monthly) to accomplish next steps
Developmental assessment and outcomes guide the process	Visions and relationships guide the process
Professionals and agencies are primarily responsible for implementing programs to accomplish developmental outcomes	Group members form a reliable alliance with every member assuming responsibility for transforming visions to reality

From Turnbull, A.P., Turnbull, H.R., & Blue-Banning, M. (1994). Enhancing inclusion of infants and toddlers with disabilities and their families: A theoretical and programmatic analysis. *Infants and Young Children, 7*(2), p. 8; copyright © 1994 Aspen Publishers, Inc.; reprinted by permission.
IEP, Individualized education program.

The fundamental characteristics of Action Groups are that they

1. Actively invite people who can be helpful to participate in a reciprocal and interdependent manner
2. Create a context of social connectedness and caring among all participants
3. Foster dynamic and creative problem solving fueled by great expectations
4. Continuously affirm and celebrate the progress that is being made

When these characteristics of Action Groups occur at an optimal level, the outcome is synergy. Synergy has been defined as "the capacity of an individual or group to increase the satisfaction of all participants by intentionally generating increased energy and creativity, all of which is used to co-create a more rewarding present and future" (Craig & Craig, 1974, p. 62). This synergy, in turn, empowers both an adolescent individually and his or her network of key supporters, with the result being that "the whole is truly greater than the sum of the parts." This is a radically different concept than the "fix-it" approach that primarily emphasizes the development of an individual repertoire of skills.

The information presented here is based in part on a 3-year model demonstration project funded by the Office of Special Education Programs within the U.S. Department of Education. This project, entitled "Self-Determination

Through Group Action Planning," is currently in its final year of implementation. It consists of 1) a high school course on self-determination and 2) the development and implementation of Action Groups for each student in the course.

The self-determination course, facilitated by project staff and high school personnel, used process-oriented teaching strategies. The students were involved in the development of the course, outlining the curriculum in the first week of class and generating ground rules for their individual and collective work. The course facilitators concentrated on enhancing individual motivation and skills. The course was supplemented by participation in Group Action Planning, which, in a sense, served as a practicum component for the course.

The Action Groups provided an environment in which the students could express, practice, and benefit from their newly developing skills. It became clear that the "fix-it" approach of teaching skills associated with self-determination is necessary but is not sufficient for the full utilization of these skills in making crucial transitional decisions. Instead, those skills have to be activated (through motivation), developed, and used by the student in a supportive context. Thus, Group Action Planning is a way to approach self-determination holistically because it focuses on the motivation and skills of the individual and the responsiveness of the context. The essence of this approach is to create a network of people who nurture, support, and encourage the student to make choices about his or her present and future life.

The following sections explain the "who," "where," and "when" of Group Action Planning by emphasizing general guidelines and following the implementation of Ryan and Katie's Action Groups (see the following case studies). The emphasis is on general guidelines and suggestions, as the key to successful Group Action Planning is flexibility and absolute focus on each individual student's needs in his or her community, culture, and family contexts.

Ryan is a 17-year-old high school student with cognitive disabilities who likes Nintendo, sports, music, and pizza. Ryan has been in a segregated special education setting for most of his life. His mother and father have been very involved in initiating change in his life. When his Action Group started, he was identified as having "behavior problems." He acted out in class, was not motivated to go to school, was lonely, and generally appeared to be unhappy. He was unaccustomed to expressing his preferences, and his attention span was short. His ability to comprehend the complexity of decision making or to contribute his own input was thought to be "severely limited."

Katie is a bright, competent 19-year-old high school student with cerebral palsy who is preparing to graduate. Although Katie was placed in a special education classroom for students with cognitive disabilities at an early age, she has no cognitive disabilities.

Katie was raised by her maternal grandmother. After her grandmother died when Katie was 15 years old, Katie moved to a group home for adults with severe and profound mental retardation. Katie is a very patient person who enjoys people and wants to work with children after graduation. She is interested in looking into postsecondary education. When Katie entered the self-determination class, she was interested in leaving the group home to live independently, thinking about graduation, and experiencing difficulties being assertive with friends and service providers.

Who Participates in Group Action Planning?

The focus member of the group is, first and foremost, the individual with a disability. The evolving self-determination of adolescents can most comprehensively be supported through a family systems orientation (Turnbull & Turnbull, in press-b); therefore, groups also typically include family members (not limited to mothers only, as too often happens in home–school partnerships). Other people are invited to join the group, and the invitation depends primarily on 1) the transition issues facing the person and group, 2) the lifestyle preferences of the person and group, and 3) the ability and preferences of those invitees to participate in the group and to be part of the reliable transition alliance. Table 2 specifies issues in six domains of transition planning and suggests people who might be invited to participate in Action Groups based on their ability to systematically address these issues.

Action Group participation can be arranged on both a permanent and temporary basis. The permanent members are the core people most committed to the student who will likely be available over a long period of time. These are the people who not only support the student to express his or her visions for the future, but also provide support for the daily challenges of implementing those visions. Other participants, however, can be temporary in the sense that they can be invited to participate in one or more meetings that address specific issues. For example, in Table 2 a number of different people are specified related to living situations—Section 8/HUD housing personnel, social services personnel, and landlords. It may be that these individuals would not be appropriate to include as permanent members of a student's Action Group but would be appropriate as invitees to specific meetings where the issues to be addressed have to do with finding desirable housing.

A key group member is the facilitator, whose role is vital to the Action Group's success. We will discuss the facilitator's role later in the chapter.

Ryan's core Action Group members have included Ryan, a facilitator, his parents, his sister, his teacher, two classmates from school, two peers from his church, a couple of university faculty members, and several family friends. Some of the temporary members have

Table 2. Identifying key issues and people to invite

EMPLOYMENT
Issues
Is the student currently working? Is it a paid position or an unpaid position? What kind of work experience does the student have? What are his or her vocational interests? Has there been an employment evaluation? If the student is not currently working, is he or she interested in finding a job? What are future employment goals?

People to invite to Group Action Planning meeting

Co-workers, supervisor	Vocational rehabilitation personnel
Family	Independent living center personnel
Student connections	Generic employment agency personnel
School personnel	
Vocational coordinator	
Teachers	
Job coach	

LIVING
Issues
Where is the student currently living? Where does he or she want to live 5 years from now? With whom does he or she want to live? What can we do now to make the vision a reality? How is it going with his or her current living situation? Any problems, issues to deal with now?

People to invite to the Group Action Planning meeting

Friends	Section 8/HUD housing personnel
Roommates, landlord	Independent living center personnel
Attendants, paid staff	

TRANSPORTATION
Issues
How does the student usually get around? Is transportation an issue? Does he or she know how to access public transportation? Is he or she interested in obtaining a driver's license? Taking driver's education classes?

People to invite to the Group Action Planning meeting

Friends	Paratransit systems
Cab company personnel	People who may be open to carpooling
Bus company personnel	Driver's license examiner

FINANCIAL
Issues
Does the student currently have a bank account? Does she or he know about banking procedures? Does he or she have a budget? Is there something for which the student needs to be saving—something he or she wants to do or buy? Does the student know how to purchase something from a store? Are there issues in regard to guardianship or conservatorship?

People to invite to the Group Action Planning meeting

Service providers, service coordinators	Supplemental Security Income (SSI) personnel
Conservator, guardian	Social services personnel (food stamps, financial aid)
Advocacy and protective services personnel	

(continued)

Table 2. (continued)

SOCIAL

Issues

What does he or she do now for fun? What are preferred hobbies or sports? What about friendships and dating? What are possible community resources related to social interests?

People to invite to the Group Action Planning meeting

Friends, classmates	Athletic club participants
Church members	Recreational services staff
Neighbors	Community members with similar hobbies

SCHOOL

Issues

How are things going at school? Is the educational program appropriate? What is the status of the transitional planning process? Are sufficient related services being provided? How is the communication between the school and family? Is school appropriately preparing the student for adult life?

People to invite to the Group Action Planning meeting

Friends, classmates	Related services providers
Inclusion specialist	Job coaches
Transition specialist	Counselors
Teachers	School administrators
Paraprofessionals	Advocacy organization representatives

been music students from the local university, several members of a fraternity at the local university, a speech and language therapist, and teachers and transition specialists from his school.

Katie's core Action Group members have included Katie, a facilitator, her special education teacher, her vocational rehabilitation counselor, her job coach, a speech and occupational therapist, a services coordinator from the state Medicaid waiver program, her friends, and a transition specialist from the high school. Temporary members have included a representative from a literacy project, an independent living specialist, a representative from Advocacy and Protective Services, and her home care attendants.

Where Do Action Groups Convene?

Action Groups meet in a comfortable, nonthreatening environment. The environment can significantly impede the outcome of the meeting for the student and his or her family if it is intimidating. Thus, groups should meet anywhere that is comfortable and where professional control is not the norm. Meeting places can include group members' homes, a library or community building, restaurant, or church. Whereas traditional team meetings, such as IEP conferences, typically meet around tables with everyone having a set of papers in front of them, Action Groups are best convened more informally.

> Ryan's group usually meets at his home. Group members sit around the living room and munch on snacks. Over the last couple of years, the group has also met at a friend's house, Ryan's church fellowship hall, and a park.

> Katie's group meets in a local bakery close to her apartment, restaurants, her apartment, the high school, and a neutral office setting. Katie's meetings are always very large, but people always manage to pull together into a circle.

When Do Action Groups Meet?

Groups may meet when convenient and as often as necessary. Monthly meetings are the general rule, with more frequent meetings during times of crises or upcoming deadlines. It is essential to remember that the bottom line of Action Groups is *action*—the perception and reality of which are critical to enhancing the student's motivation and skill related to self-determination. Thus, groups need to meet regularly and fairly often, with group members working on tasks between meetings.

> Ryan's group meets approximately once a month. The group has met more frequently during times when Ryan has experienced more intense behavior challenges or when greater changes are needed in his school schedule, such as when he became the first student with a cognitive disability at the local high school to be fully included in the general education program.

> Katie's group also meets on a monthly basis. The group met more frequently when Katie was preparing to move into her own apartment. When other critical issues arise, members gather in smaller groups to have more intensive brainstorming sessions with Katie.

Group Members' Roles

Although all Action Group members contribute by offering support, providing resources, and developing action plans, there are some specific roles that members typically assume. The roles of the student, family, facilitator, and other group members are described on the following pages.

Student Roles Student involvement may range from being present to setting the agenda, leading the discussion, and creating the action plan. It is critical that the student be involved and remain the center or focus of the group, as the purpose of the Action Group is to be a responsive context in which the student chooses how to live his or her life and to provide the necessary support to actualize those preferences. Even if the student's current motivation and skills are such that his or her involvement in the Action Group is limited, supportive participation with coaching can be the catalyst for developing self-determination skills. Group members run the risk of making students dependent on the group if they assume control of decision making, rather than supporting them to make the choices they prefer.

Family Roles   The roles of the family or primary caregiver should complement the student's ability to be involved. Families of students with more advanced skills can assume more of a support role in the group, encouraging their family member with a disability to express preferences and participate actively in decision making. Family members of students with more significant disabilities are often most attuned to their family member's specific preferences and can communicate his or her visions and preferred options for taking action.

Parents, siblings, and extended family can all make valuable contributions. In a recent study of student perspectives of family involvement in transition planning, students frequently cited brothers and sisters, aunts, uncles, cousins, parents, and grandparents as people on whom they would prefer to rely for long-term support in securing employment and housing (Morningstar, Turnbull, & Turnbull, 1995). Some students, such as Katie, do not have family to call upon, and it is especially important in those instances to call on long-term support from friends.

> *In Ryan's Action Group, his family was very involved from the beginning as the primary catalyst for visions and priorities. In addition to his parents and sister, his friends from school and church helped all group members "stand in Ryan's shoes" and see things from the perspective of a 17-year-old. In fact, Ryan's motivation to participate greatly increased because of participation in his Action Group meeting by his friends. He especially looks forward to the times when these friends come to his house for meetings, and he always wants to sit by them. Since the first meeting, Ryan has greatly extended his skills in expressing his opinions and preferences in an assertive manner. All group members have responded by asking for his opinions and making sure that any options discussed meet with his approval from the outset. His family has been able to encourage the same level of active participation in decision making throughout his daily and weekly routine.*

> *Katie has led her Action Group from the start. She has worked with the facilitator to prepare for the meetings—setting agendas, inviting people to attend, establishing meeting times and places, and developing action plans. In many ways, the members of Katie's Action Group have created a network of support much like an extended family.*

Facilitator Roles As stated previously, Group Action Planning can be characterized primarily as a process that promotes self-determination through 1) inviting support, 2) creating connections, 3) solving problems with fuel created by great expectations, and 4) affirming and celebrating progress. Action Groups work best when a facilitator is specifically designated to promote these four vital functions. Table 3 lists tips for effective facilitation.

The facilitator's role in inviting support is to enable the student to identify the people on whom he or she would most like to rely for support when creating and actualizing a vision for adult life. This task involves identifying key issues and people who can help with those issues, brainstorming about the best way to issue an invitation to join the Action Group, supporting the student (and family) in issuing invitations, and explaining their potential roles to the people being invited to the Action Group.

The facilitator's role related to social connectedness is to make sure that people feel comfortable with one another, ensure that each person experiences a

Table 3.   Tips for effective facilitation

- Listen to the student with a disability and ensure that his or her message is heard by all group members.
- If the student is not able to communicate assertively, watch for body language that indicates a desire to communicate or participate in decision making. Create a safe and supportive context for participation to be manifested.
- Anticipate what the priority issues will be and identify key resources that can be helpful in addressing them.
- Create a positive, upbeat, and socially alive atmosphere within the meetings.
- Make sure that every participant is welcomed and perceives a sense of connection to the student, family, and to other group members.
- Inject humor, laughter, and warmth into discussions.
- Remember that the goal of the meeting is action, and keep the discussion focused on moving through the steps of the problem-solving process. Do this in a way that is comfortable and refrain from putting pressure on or creating stress for other group members.
- Encourage creative visions filled with great expectations of the future.
- When inviting people to join the group, issue the invitation in a way that promotes the dignity of the student and family.
- Make sure that the action plan is specific in terms of tasks to be accomplished, who is to assume responsibility, and the preferred timeline. Reach closure on issues and summarize to make sure that people understand.
- In brainstorming, create an environment where creativity and divergent thinking can be expressed. Refrain from evaluating options as they are suggested.
- Always emphasize the human side of communication and refrain from distancing oneself or taking a clinical orientation.
- Create a comfortable pace for the meetings that is consistent with the family's cultural style and tempo.
- Affirm the progress that the student is making in demonstrating self-determination skills. Reinforce those skills and encourage others in the group to do the same.
- Enjoy yourself. The more there is a genuine "joy quotient," the more the Action Group will be creating an atmosphere in which to best foster self-determination.

sense of belonging and contribution, maintain an upbeat and energized atmosphere during the meetings, and see that participants experience a sense of connection with the student. Essentially, the facilitator's role is to ensure a vital and reciprocal social support atmosphere within the Action Group.

The third major role is to encourage the group to follow a creative and systematic problem-solving process. The steps we recommend for problem solving are outlined in Table 4. Although most traditional team meetings are constituted to make vital decisions affecting the lives of individuals with disabilities, too often these meetings are devoid of a creative and systematic problem-solving process (Turbiville, Turnbull, Garland, & Lee, in press). Given this history of typical team meetings, it becomes obvious that creative and systematic problem solving cannot be expected to happen automatically. Many professionals and families do not have a mastery of the problem-solving skills necessary for self-determination, and many students with disabilities do not know how to be problem solvers. Thus, in Action Groups students benefit from having a facilitator who generally guides the problem-solving process, empowering students to demonstrate the problem-solving skills that they are learning in their self-determination coursework. As students develop these skills, they naturally move into the role of leader. As students are increasingly able to lead their group, which involves identifying key issues, goals, and action plans, the facilitator's role becomes more of a support person to the leader, coordinating communication and action. In the initial and middle stages of development, the facilitator should model the skills necessary for problem solving and decision making.

Finally, facilitators have a key role in ensuring that Action Groups are characterized by the celebration of success. Both students and families have characterized a process of planning for the future as being highly stressful (Morningstar et al., 1995; Turnbull, Turnbull, Bronicki, Summers, & Roeder-Gordon, 1989). Thus, a key aspect of Action Groups becoming a responsive context for self-determination is the creation of opportunities for students to practice and refine self-determination skills while simultaneously minimizing the discomfort and

Table 4. Steps of the problem-solving process

1. Identify a problem/issue and specify a desirable outcome. Assess the level of risk.
2. Brainstorm options. Set a specific amount of time, and list as many ideas as possible. Do not explain or judge the ideas. Be silly, be outrageous—you never know what ideas will work or what they will inspire in others. Write down all of the ideas for later discussion.
3. Evaluate options and weigh alternatives. Look at the advantages and disadvantages of each option. Identify potential obstacles and consequences. Remember that every decision has both positive and negative consequences.
4. Assert preferences.
5. Make and implement an action plan. Outline tasks, person(s) who will assume responsibility, and a timeline.
6. Evaluate the outcome (and revise plan as necessary).

maximizing the enjoyment associated with the process. Indeed, the more fun, the more group members will stay involved as part of the reliable alliance. Thus, the facilitator can take the lead to initiate celebratory activities. The role of celebration is discussed in greater detail later in the chapter.

> *The facilitator of Ryan's Action Group, from the outset, enabled Ryan and his family to identify people to invite as group members. As the group progressed through its first two years, Ryan's participation became stronger. He became the host for the evening, enhancing the social connectedness among participants and sharing his dreams, preferences, and concerns about his school program and job possibilities. One of the particular roles of the facilitator was to highlight the success that Ryan was experiencing and to help all group members recognize the important contributions they were making to his evolving self-determination.*
>
> *In Katie's group, the facilitator primarily supported Katie in her role as group leader—sharing her concerns and brainstorming alternatives for those concerns. Sometimes the facilitator served as a mediator between group members who had differing opinions, and at other times the facilitator primarily encouraged the participation of all members. As Katie was increasingly able to do these tasks herself, the facilitator was primarily present in a supportive role.*

Group Members' Roles   Every group member has the role of being a creative problem solver, namely, 1) supporting the student's self-determination by enhancing his or her motivation and skills and 2) participating in the hard work of creating desirable transition supports and services. This is accomplished on a month-by-month basis by implementing the "next steps" that are generated at each meeting. Whereas traditional team meetings set annual goals and objectives that typically are not expected to be implemented on an immediate basis, Action Groups determine "next steps" that are to be accomplished prior to the next meeting. The more specific, concrete, and doable each person's action and the sooner it must be taken and accounted for to the group, the better.

A specific responsibility related to problem solving is to record the major decisions that the Action Group makes and the specific "next steps" that each member agrees to carry out. The facilitator or a designee should take notes and prepare a simple "to-do list" to be sent to group members after each meeting, with a reminder of the time and place of the following meeting. The tasks on the "to-do list" are critical because the essence of Action Groups is *accomplishing tasks* that translate the student's visions into preferred and responsive supports and services.

Another specific responsibility that often needs to be designated to a particular group member is to serve as an advocate for the student's self-determination.

One of the dangers of group meetings is that there are a number of adults who may be accustomed to a fast-paced agenda, rapidly moving through the steps of problem solving. As a result, the student may be left out of the critical decision-making process. The advocate's role is to ensure that the student has every possible opportunity to participate and clearly understands the contributions that others are making. This can involve providing explanations to the student or cautions to group members to slow down. Advocates can monitor the extent to which group members are keeping the student's interest as the focus of the discussion. This responsibility needs to be assumed by a person who is especially familiar with the student and has both the capacity and desire to communicate the student's preferences and interests.

Other creative roles that group members can assume include a "yaysayer" and a "naysayer." Especially when conflicts or controversial issues are being discussed, it may be important to have people who can specifically advocate a "why not" approach, as well as people who can bring up the "yes, but" issues. If these roles are implemented, it is helpful to rotate them so that certain individuals do not always fall into the routine of taking an extreme pro or con position.

Ryan's friends in the group were wonderful "yaysayers." When discussing school inclusion and options available, such as Ryan participating in the high school marching band or on the wrestling team, his friends consistently offered rationales for why Ryan should get to do what everyone else in the school had opportunities to do. They had a special knack for cutting through bureaucratic barriers and seeing possibilities, whereas some of the adults might just see the barriers. One friend commented that the Action Group could accomplish almost anything because Ryan had adult support coupled with his peers' creativity, inventiveness, and grassroots knowledge about how students make things happen for each other.

Due to Katie's difficulty in verbal communication, she was at risk of being left out or "spoken for" when the group began excitedly brainstorming and discussing ideas. In response to this risk, a special relationship developed between Katie and an independent living specialist named Diane. Diane worked with Katie on how to best present her ideas and opinions. In this way, Diane acted as Katie's advocate, always ensuring that other group members heard what Katie had to say.

CONDUCTING GROUP ACTION PLANNING

Because Group Action Planning is a process, implementation varies according to whether the Action Group is in a preliminary stage or if it has been ongoing for a significant period of time. This variance is addressed by focusing on implementation issues associated with 1) initial planning, 2) the first meeting, 3) the life of the Action Group, and 4) celebrating success at each step of the way. These issues are discussed below.

Initial Planning

The catalyst for Group Action Planning, in Katie's situation, came from the demonstration project's paid staff who were interested in implementing this approach. Ryan's group was initiated by the two senior authors, who served in the role of facilitator and parent, respectively. They were not part of the demonstration project. Action groups can also be initiated by individuals with disabilities, family members, friends of the individual or family, or professionals who support them (Turnbull & Turnbull, 1996; Turnbull, Turnbull, & Blue-Banning, 1994). Regardless of who the catalyst is, one of the most critical first steps in getting started is to identify a facilitator.

The facilitator can meet with the student and others who are committed to starting an Action Group. Initial conversations need to focus generally on the student's visions for the future and the specific priorities that he or she would most like to address. Facilitators can be helpful in asking specific questions about employment, housing, postsecondary education, or other domains of future consideration (see Table 2). They can also brainstorm a broad array of options for students and family members who may not be aware of the full range of future possibilities.

As visions and preferences begin to be identified, the facilitator, student, and family can select people who would be most appropriate to invite to the first Action Group meeting (again, see Table 2). After these individuals are designated, another important decision would be to determine who will issue the invitation and how this will be done. The student may have both the motivation and skills necessary to invite support, or he or she may need various levels of assistance to carry out this initial task. Regardless of how inviting participants is done, students should have the opportunity to enhance their motivation and skill in reaching out to others, explaining the rationale for this process, and inviting participation in it.

Obviously, logistics for the first meeting need to be arranged, including location, time, and refreshments. Major consideration needs to be given to comfort and connection so that the Action Group can, from the outset, develop the social ambience that differs from traditional team meetings.

First Meeting

The first meeting is critical for setting the tone for the entire Group Action Planning process. Again, major emphasis needs to be given to social connectedness, an upbeat atmosphere, and energy for envisioning a preferred lifestyle and learning how to implement it. Rather than the meeting being a serious and somber process, the students, family, and facilitator can work together to create a welcoming, energized, and active atmosphere. During this first meeting, envisioning the future is the priority focus. The student, if possible, can share his or her dreams in terms of preferred lifestyle options.

At the first meeting, Katie and her group members generated many ideas and action plans to help Katie realize her goals. Katie and her group also began to deal with critical issues at hand. One topic of immediate concern was guardianship, because one of Katie's service providers was vying to become Katie's guardian.

Some people have never had the opportunity to articulate a vision and may not be able to do so from the outset. Also, many cultural traditions focus on a strong present rather than future orientation. But most group members generally have an idea of the student's present preferences. Our experience suggests that visions grow in ever-increasing circles as the student's motivation and skills for self-determination are enhanced. Thus, it is possible for Action Groups to get started on one specific task (e.g., getting a part-time job, arranging for Supplemental Security Income [SSI] benefits, learning to use public transportation) while other, larger visions are incubating.

Whether Action Groups start with a student's specific preference or with a fully developed future vision, the first meeting needs to delineate one or two priority issues for the group's focus. Action Groups focus on manageable tasks— one after another in successive approximation. Rather than trying to work on all preferences and needs simultaneously, a key for Group Action Planning is to explicate the specific next step that would act on the student's preferences and then to develop and implement an action plan to accomplish that next step. Once that task is completed, the Action Group proceeds to the next priority. The focus at the first meeting should be on the development of a blueprint for the Action Group with particular focus on gaining an understanding of how the student wants to live his or her life. From this vision, the first task of importance is identified. If there is time at the meeting (most meetings last 1–2 hours), the group can begin to formulate an action plan using creative problem solving to address the first task.

By the end of the meeting, the Action Group should have the issue of first consideration identified. As members consider that issue, they may want to recommend other people who might be invited to join the group. For example, if the first goal relates to participating more actively in community recreation and the student particularly enjoys sports, other people in the community who particularly enjoy sports might be asked to join the Action Group as well as someone from the City Parks and Recreation program. Membership should be flexible so that people with particular interest in and expertise on issues under consideration are invited to share their suggestions and resources.

Ryan's visions at the first meeting included participating more in the extracurricular activities at his school and having friends with whom he could hang out. That was one of the reasons why it was especially important to have friends as members of the Action Group. At the first meeting, members generated school activities that might be of particular interest to Ryan. It became obvious that the school's pep club was a natural as Ryan so much enjoys sports and also likes to be in an energized, rowdy atmosphere. Ryan and his family were clearly excited about these new possibilities.

From the outset, Katie was very clear about her future goals. She wanted to graduate from high school, live in her own apartment, have a job after high school, and be her own guardian. At the first meeting, Katie and her group members generated many ideas and action plans to help Katie realize her goals. Katie and her group also began to deal with critical issues at hand. One topic of immediate concern was guardianship because one of Katie's service providers was vying to become Katie's guardian.

Life of Group Action Planning

After the first meeting, the Action Group participants proceed through future meetings with successive action plan development and implementation. It is critical to realize that the actual Action Group meeting is the designated time for planning, but the designated time for implementation is the period *between* meetings. Thus, the goal of each meeting is to create an action plan with a "to-do list" of tasks that various group members will implement prior to the following meeting. If each member takes on one or two tasks, then a whole host of tasks can be accomplished within a relatively short period of time. Each meeting needs to begin with a review of the "to-do list" from the previous meeting, with each participant reporting on what he or she has accomplished. This kind of immediate accountability at each meeting supports the motivation of group members to accomplish their tasks and helps provide an individual and collective sense of group momentum. As the student perceives significant progress toward realizing visions, his or her motivation and skills related to self-determination are affirmed.

Generally, Action Groups move from one significant task to another. Translating visions into reality, particularly at the time of transition from high school to adult life, is a complex and time-consuming process. Some Action Groups that have created radical lifestyle change have taken 5 or 6 years for all necessary changes to occur (Turnbull & Turnbull, 1996).

One of the goals of Action Groups is to develop social connectedness and personal commitment so that members choose to stay together over long periods of time. In some sense, the Action Group can become almost an extended family, not only for the student but for all group members.

Celebrating Success Along the Way

In almost every family, work and celebration go hand in hand. Indeed, one of the key ingredients of Action Groups that is missing in many of the other efforts to support people with disabilities is even a modicum of celebration. Typically, students, families, and professionals address issues of future planning and self-determination in a somber and serious way always focusing on the tasks still not successfully achieved. In asking families and teachers to reflect on IEP conferences, a frequent reaction is a big sense of relief once the meeting is over (Turnbull & Turnbull, 1990). Drudgery is probably not too harsh of a term to apply to the general demeanor of approaching transitional planning.

As an alternative, Group Action Planning is designed to generate significant action in accomplishing visions and then celebrating progress that is associated with that action. Emphasis is placed on enlivening the hard work of planning and implementation by adding as much celebration and spirit as possible. Thus, achieving and celebrating successes are the lifeblood of the Group Action Planning process.

At the end of 1 year, Ryan and his Action Planning Group had accomplished many things. After working on extracurricular involvement in the pep club at his junior high, the Action Group went on to address Ryan's greatest vision, which was to be a member of the school's wrestling team. That vision was accomplished and one of the highlights of Ryan's school career has been participating in a wrestling match. As time progressed and visions grew, Ryan then decided that he wanted to be fully included in the local high school. Although students in his community with his degree of disability had not experienced this extent of inclusion previously, the Action Group went to work over many months to help put these supports in place. Currently, Ryan is finishing his first semester in full inclusion. Biology is his favorite academic class, but the real highlight of the semester has been participating in the percussion section of the high school marching band. Ryan's family and teachers marvel at the improvement in his behavior as he has increasingly learned to express and act on his own preferences.

At the end of 1 year, Katie's life has changed tremendously. She graduated from high school with a standard diploma. She currently lives on her own with support from home care providers that she has hired. She is working to become her own guardian—a struggle in the courts for over 1 year now. She is also exploring employment options and working independently to build her communication and literacy skills through programs offered at the university. Katie is surrounded by many friends, including a boyfriend. She has become

*more assertive and is therefore able to communicate her needs and
wishes to the various service providers in her life.*

Considering Cultural Diversity in Group Action Planning

MacGugen (1991) emphasized the importance of reexamining how culture
frames both the definition of self-determination and the process by which one
strives to become self-determined. The typical definition of self-determination in
the literature that primarily emphasizes personal autonomy is in many ways a
"white, western, linear, and product oriented" (MacGugen, 1991, p. 6) concept
that consequently needs to be culturally reframed to better fit minority students
with disabilities and their families.

The following guidelines have been helpful to us in reframing the concept
of self-determination and relating it to the Group Action Planning. First, it is
important to consider the individual and family's cultural context, including level
of acculturation, family composition, and community supports. Are the self-
determination skills the student is learning congruent with his or her cultural values?
Will these skills be appreciated as self-determination when expressed in a culturally relevant manner?

Second, the problem-solving focus of Group Action Planning may appear
more linear than intended. Honoring how the family has successfully initiated
positive change in the past is the best predictor of future success. What has
worked? Who have been the key players? This process of discovering the unique
problem-solving process of a given family may not be easy. It is important to reflect on the family's context and respond in a manner congruent with the family's
values.

Finally, the self-determination skills acquired via this culturally relevant
process must be considered in light of utility within the dominant culture. We
concur with MacGugen that "minority students with disabilities . . . , like their
parents and families, stand with one foot in their family-culture and another foot
in the dominant culture" (MacGugen, 1991, p. 3). How can the individual and
family successfully utilize these newly acquired skills in the larger social context
while still acknowledging the validity of their familial–cultural context? While
keeping one foot in two different contexts is necessary, we contend that negating
the family–culture is not only detrimental for the student and family, but also significantly diminishes the learning that can occur for people from both dominant
and minority contexts.

SUMMARY

We have found Group Action Planning to be an effective means of fostering self-
determination and creating a responsive context, a network of ongoing support
for the individual, family, and service providers. A summary of Group Action

Planning is encapsulated by an Action Group member of another student, Steve, who participated in the demonstration project.

If I understand it right, . . . the whole intention behind the Action Group process . . . is that people aren't doing this out of an obligation, or that this is their community service for the month, or anything. They go there [to the Action Group meetings] because it's fun, it's fun to sit down and talk about how to make things better for this person. You know, you're having something to eat, it's a casual situation, it's not a meeting where everybody's uptight. . . . It's more a discussion about the great things that Steve has achieved, and how they can work together to help each other in the following weeks. And they may not always have common interests with each other—that's one way to have a group come together—but they can disagree adamantly about philosophy or religion or really any of those heavy issues. But as long as they have a strong interest in Steve, and he cares about them, that seems to be what allows the group to continually reinvent itself. And the family and Steve are always consistent, and usually a few other long-term, key people, but other people come in and out as . . . friendships change over time. And, so then, the group never fades.

REFERENCES

Craig, J.H., & Craig, M. (1974). *Synergic power: Beyond domination and permissiveness.* Berkeley, CA: Proactive Press.

Forest, M., & Pearpoint, J.C. (1992, October). Putting kids on the MAP. *Educational Leadership, 50,* 26–31.

Gliedman, J., & Roth, W. (1980). *The unexpected minority: Handicapped children in America.* New York: Harcourt Brace Jovanovich.

Heshusius, L. (1982). At the heart of the advocacy dilemma: A mechanistic world view. *Exceptional Children, 49,* 6–13.

MacGugen, M.K. (1991). *Self-determination and cultural relevance.* Albuquerque, NM: Protection and Advocacy System.

Morningstar, M.E., Turnbull, A.P., & Turnbull, H.R. (1995). What do students with disabilities tell us about the importance of family involvement in transition from school to adult life? *Exceptional Children, 62,* 249–260.

Mount, B., & Zwernik, K. (1988). *It's never too early, it's never too late: A booklet about personal planning for persons with developmental disabilities, their families and friends, case managers, service providers, and advocates.* St. Paul, MN: Metropolitan Council.

Smull, M., & Harrison, S.B. (1992). *Supporting people with severe reputations in the community.* Alexandria, VA: National Association of State Mental Retardation Program Directors.

Turbiville, V., Turnbull, A.P., Garland, C.W., & Lee, I.M. (in press). Development and implementation of IFSPs and IEPs: Opportunities for empowerment. In S. Odom & M. McLean (Eds.), *Recommended practices in early intervention.* Austin, TX: PRO-ED.

Turnbull, A.P., & Turnbull, H.R. (1985). Developing independence. *Journal of Adolescent Health Care, 6,* 108–119.

Turnbull, A.P., & Turnbull, H.R. (1990). *Families, professionals, and exceptionality: A special partnership* (2nd ed.). Columbus, OH: Charles E. Merrill.

Turnbull, A.P., & Turnbull, H.R. (1996). Group Action Planning as a strategy for providing comprehensive family support. In R.L. Koegel, L.K. Koegel, & G. Dunlap (Eds.), *Positive behavioral support: Including people with difficult behavior in the community* (pp. 99–114). Baltimore: Paul H. Brookes Publishing Co.

Turnbull, A.P., & Turnbull, H.R. (1996). An analysis of self-determination within a culturally responsive family systems perspective: Balancing the family mobile. In L. Powers, G. Singer, & J. Sowers (Eds.), *On the road to autonomy: Promoting self-competence in children and youth with disabilities* (pp. 195–220). Baltimore: Paul H. Brookes Publishing Co.

Turnbull, A.P., Turnbull, H.R., & Blue-Banning, M.J. (1994). Enhancing inclusion of infants and toddlers with disabilities and their families: A theoretical and programmatic analysis. *Infants & Young Children, 7*, 1–14.

Turnbull, H.R., III, Turnbull, A.P., Bronicki, G.J., Summers, J.A., & Roeder-Gordon, C. (1989). *Disability and the family: A guide to decisions for adulthood.* Baltimore: Paul H. Brookes Publishing Co.

Zola, I.K. (1982). Disincentives to independent living. *Research and Training Center on Independent Living Monographs, 1.* Lawrence: University of Kansas.

Chapter 13

FACILITATING ADOLESCENT SELF-DETERMINATION

What Does It Take?

Laurie E. Powers, Roxanne Wilson, Jeanne Matuszewski,
Amy Phillips, Claudia Rein, Dona Schumacher, and Janet Gensert

ADOLESCENCE IS TYPICALLY a period of dramatic physical, intellectual, and socioemotional development. Expansions in self-awareness, participation in extrafamilial social relationships, and personal autonomy are associated with increasing desires for independence, assertion of personal identity, and assumption of new responsibilities (Burchard, 1996). For youth with challenges, such as disability, typical progression through this developmental period is often complicated by additional personal and societal barriers. These obstacles include limitations directly imposed by disability or health instability, restricted access to age-appropriate experiences and social interaction, and attitudinal and architectural barriers (Garrison & McQuiston, 1989).

Much progress has been realized in efforts to enhance the functional competence of youth who experience disabilities. An impressive array of educational technologies have been developed for teaching a wide range of skills within instructional, vocational, and independent living domains (e.g., Bellamy, Horner, & Inman, 1979; Graham & Harris, 1989; Horner, Meyer, & Fredericks, 1986; Sowers & Powers, 1989; Wehman, 1981). Many supports and services have been established to support youth with challenges, and, clearly, there are increasing opportunities available to facilitate their community integration.

This chapter was funded, in part, by grants H158K20006 and H08642006 awarded by the U.S. Department of Education, Office of Special Education and Rehabilitative Services (OSERS). The opinions expressed herein are exclusively those of the authors, and no official endorsement by OSERS should be inferred.

However, despite these advances, it is clear that adolescents and young adults with disabilities continue to experience significant barriers in their evolution toward a successful adult life. Adolescents with disabilities drop out of high school at a higher rate than adolescents without disabilities (Valdes, Williamson, & Wagner, 1990). Unemployment rates of young adult males with disabilities are approximately 3 times those of their peers without disabilities, while unemployment rates for females with disabilities are approximately 4.5 times the unemployment rates for young women without disabilities. Additionally, youth with disabilities attend postsecondary education or training institutions at much lower rates than do young adults without disabilities (U.S. Department of Health and Human Services, Maternal and Child Health Bureau, 1992). Approximately 70% of young adults with disabilities continue to live with their parents 2 years following their graduation from high school, and a large proportion of young adults with functional challenges depend on family members for personal care and home management (Valdes, Williamson, & Wagner, 1990). Youth and their families are also often required to negotiate complex systems of regulations and services that inadvertently reinforce youthful dependency by emphasizing assistance and direction provided by others.

Since the mid-1980s, significant attention has focused on the benefits of empowering consumers to shape educational and adult services and supports. In particular, parents have gained increasing power and respect in influencing regulations and services designed to assist their children. Parent empowerment has been particularly visible in initiatives in early education, educational planning, family-centered care, and family support (Dunst & Trivette, 1989; Santelli, Turnbull, Lerner, & Marquis, 1993; Shelton, Jeppeson, & Johnson, 1989). Most agree that consumer involvement will facilitate both empowerment and the provision of supports that more appropriately address the needs of consumers. We have also come to value the importance of parent–professional collaboration in the design and implementation of effective services.

Traditionally, education, and special education in particular, has not emphasized youth empowerment or partnership. Instead, most efforts have focused on exposing youth to curricula and programs considered essential by professionals and families. Youth have generally been involved as passive participants in this process. Although most would agree that one of the overarching goals of education is to promote self-sufficiency and competence among youth, many or most of our own efforts to assist youth have been fairly directive, aimed at providing youth with informational and experiential building blocks upon which they might somehow spontaneously launch their lives after leaving school.

Encouraging youth still in school to assume major roles in decision making and collaborating with youth in the design of educational services is a fairly recent trend. Educators have been called to task to identify ways to promote youth self-direction and to strengthen their capacities to support youth success. Much of this work has been accomplished through federally funded initiatives to identify and demonstrate strategies to promote the self-determination of youn disabilities (Brown, 1992; Ward & Kohler, 1996; Ward, Chapter 1). Self-determination refers to personal attitudes and abilities that facilitate an individual's identification and pursuit of goals (Powers, Sowers, Turner, et al., 1996). The expression of self-determination is reflected in personal attitudes of empowerment, active participation in decision making, and self-directed action to achieve personally valued goals. Self-determined youth identify goals and accomplish the functional requisites to achieve those goals. Professionals and families who promote the self-determination of youth assist them to learn and successfully apply approaches for goal identification and achievement. Self-determination is expressed by youth who experience various levels of ability. Selecting courses, actively participating in career planning, helping to implement school reform programs, or indicating basic preferences by pointing or activating a communication switch are all potential examples of self-determined behavior.

There is growing agreement regarding the importance of youth learning to take charge of their lives and to develop partnerships with others to further their success. Life following high school is uncertain and overwhelming for many young people, and supports are typically hard to find. To have a chance at success, it is critical that youth be as prepared as possible to manage the challenges they will face. It is clear that self-determination is not a unique need, right, or desire for people with disabilities. It is an essential requirement for the future success and personal fulfillment of *all* youth.

The purpose of this chapter is to discuss key conditions necessary to promote the self-determination of adolescents with and without identified challenges, including facilitative factors for youth, required shifts in attitudes and practices, and supports necessary to promote the empowerment capacities of professionals and parents. The concepts and practices espoused are based on a review of current literature in self-determination and findings resulting from our implementation of *TAKE CHARGE*, a supported self-help model to promote the self-determination of adolescents (a detailed description of *TAKE CHARGE* is found in Powers, Sowers, Turner, et al., 1996).

CONCEPTUAL FOUNDATIONS OF SELF-DETERMINATION

Self-determination can be understood as antithetical to learned helplessness and as a logical outcome of promoting mastery motivation and self-efficacy expectations. This section explains these three issues and their implications for either the discouragement or promotion of self-determination in youth.

Learned Helplessness

Learned helplessness is an *acquired* behavioral disposition characterized by passivity, self-denigration, and internalization of devalued social status (Seligman, 1975). It is induced through repeated failed attempts to impact the environment, and it is perpetuated through permanent, pervasive, internalized negative self-attributions (Seligman, 1990). Learned helplessness is associated with impaired autonomy, lack of perseverance when faced with a challenge, and poor problem-solving skills (Luchow, Crowl, & Kahn, 1985; Margalit & Shulman, 1986; Peterson & Stunkard, 1989; Zeaman & House, 1960).

Learned helplessness is reinforced by environmental factors that encourage passivity by 1) providing little opportunity for an individual to actively make choices and generate successful responses, 2) communicating expectations of noninvolvement or failure, or 3) reinforcing failure or not reinforcing striving (Houghton, Bronicki, & Guess, 1987; Hoy, 1986). Factors that promote learned helplessness include overprotection and economic, academic, or social deprivation. As a result of these influences, youth are at risk for orientations of hopelessness, dependency, and passivity. Such passivity, in association with restricted access to opportunities to learn and practice mastery skills, substantially reduces the ability of adolescents with disabilities to exercise the self-determination required to access, use, and benefit from adult independent living, interpersonal, and vocational opportunities (Clark, Mack, & Pennington, 1988; Thomas et al., 1985).

Mastery Motivation

In contrast to learned helplessness, a model of mastery motivation proposed by Harter (1981) provides a framework for understanding how youth acquire a generalized positive disposition toward achievement and striving. Mastery motivation is characterized by perceived competence, self-esteem, maintenance of an internal locus of control, and internalization of goals and rewards. It is achieved through repeated attempts paired with reinforcement for successes. Youth who possess mastery motivation exhibit a demonstrated willingness to expend effort in domains in which, historically, they have experienced success. Such children try hard to achieve goals and often succeed more often than do children who lack such motivation (Clark, 1980). Parents and professionals who encourage mastery motivation set goals that are slightly beyond the present capabilities of a child; they do not require too little of the child and thereby reinforce passivity, nor do they demand too much and thereby set the stage for failure (Lindemann, 1981). As children mature, they are encouraged by their parents to set their own goals, to take acceptable risks, and to self-advocate (Powers, Singer, & Todis, 1996).

Self-Efficacy Expectations

Self-efficacy theory provides a detailed framework for understanding specific influences on the development of self-determination (Bandura, 1977, 1986). Self-efficacy consists of outcome expectations and efficacy expectations. Efficacy expectations are personal beliefs regarding one's capability to realize a desired behavior in a specific context. Efficacy expectations do not refer to a person's skills, but rather to one's judgment of what one can do with whatever skills one possesses. Outcome expectations are personal beliefs about whether a particular behavior will lead to a particular consequence. Youth who exhibit high levels of self-efficacy believe that they have the necessary capabilities to accomplish their goals and that they will achieve these goals if they exercise those capabilities.

Youth with high levels of self-efficacy will be more likely to make choices, attempt new behaviors, and persevere through difficult tasks than will youth with low self-efficacy (Bandura, 1986). Self-efficacy beliefs are an important predictor of academic success (Graham & Harris, 1989), motivation (Schunk, 1989), and functional well-being (Dolce, 1987) for people with disabilities. Adolescents with high self-efficacy are also less likely to experience depression (Ehrenberg, Cox, & Koopman, 1991).

Self-efficacy appraisals are affected by four specific sources: enactive attainment, vicarious experience, social persuasion, and physiological information.

Enactive Attainment The most important source of self-efficacy information, enactive attainment, is derived from repeated performance accomplishments (Bandura, 1986). Performance accomplishments are fostered through specific opportunities in which youth can experience success through achievement and effective coping with challenge. Such opportunities must maximize youths' self-attribution of success. It is not sufficient to orchestrate enjoyable activities for youth or to ensure their success by performing key activity elements for them. Rather, opportunities must be created for youth to exercise their own capabilities and to achieve outcomes that they value. Ideally, opportunities should facilitate youth self-help, provide those supports necessary to give them a reasonable chance for success, and highlight their accomplishments (Arborelius & Bremberg, 1991; Hughes, Korinek, & Gorman, 1991).

Vicarious Experience A second source for the promotion of self-efficacy expectations is vicarious experience, particularly in novel contexts with ambiguous task demands (Bandura, 1986). Self-efficacy appraisals are bolstered by observing similar others' success and their effective management of challenges. This type of learning typically occurs in the course of contact with peers and other members of the individual's informal social network (Fewell & Vadasy, 1986). Role models are another source of vicarious learning. Through exposure to successful role models, students with challenges have an opportunity to learn and practice disability-related strategies for overcoming obstacles and developing personal identity and pride (Powers, Sowers, & Stevens, 1995; Rousso, 1988).

Social Persuasion A third source for self-efficacy appraisals is social persuasion, which can take the form of encouragement, evaluative feedback, reinforcement, or challenge. Evidence indicates that youth who are reinforced for their attempts demonstrate motivation and success in learning (Brophy & Good, 1974; Lindemann, 1981). Social persuasion is particularly effective when it leads people to expend increased effort required to successfully accomplish activities (Bandura, 1986). Children who are persuaded that they are capable of mastering tasks and challenges are likely to mobilize greater effort and thus more likely to achieve success (Schunk, 1982). They are most likely to be influenced when they believe that the person persuading them is credible by virtue of personal knowledge and skill and experience in judging the requirements for performing the activity (Crundall & Foddy, 1981). Persuasion is believable and effective when focused on inspiring a person to achieve slightly beyond his or her current levels (Bandura, 1986). By providing encouragement in conjunction with information about realistic activity requirements, parents, educators, and mentors may assist youth to identify and successfully strive toward short-term goals.

Physiological Information   A fourth source for self-efficacy appraisals is physiological information. Heightened arousal is associated with expectancy for failure and, consequently, lowered self-efficacy (Bandura, 1986). Those who perceive themselves to be ineffective are especially prone to misjudge arousal as a sign of coping deficiency. Experiences that reduce fear and arousal or stimulate change in self-appraisal of the reason for arousal are likely to increase self-efficacy (Bandura, 1986). Skills such as relaxation (Sowers & Powers, 1991) and positive self-talk can be used to both increase motor performance and reduce negative self-attributions that can affect a student's self-efficacy expectations.

FACILITATIVE CONDITIONS FOR SELF-DETERMINATION

The preceding conceptual discussion highlighted three key conditions required for promoting self-determination for adolescents with disabilities and health impairments. As depicted in Figure 1, self-determining youth must have access to 1) opportunities for mastery experiences, through both performance accomplishments and successful management of obstacles to success; 2) information and skills that will facilitate their success; and 3) support from others in the form of encouragement, persuasion, praise, or challenge. These conditions are likely to promote self-determination to the extent that they foster positive self-attributions of personal capabilities.

Opportunities for Mastery Experiences

Access to opportunities for mastery experiences is the primary requisite for bolstering self-determination; examples include opportunities to make decisions, communicate ideas, attempt new activities, assume responsibilities, negotiate privileges, and gain experience managing obstacles to success. Opportunities are maximized by supporting youth to make decisions and engage in activities that they deem important and that they can most likely perform or participate in performing successfully. It is critical that adults listen to what youth say is important to them. During a presentation by an adolescent with learning and health concerns, a professional from the audience asked what she could do to help youth achieve their goals. The youth responded by saying, "Just listen to us, listen before you decide what's best for us."

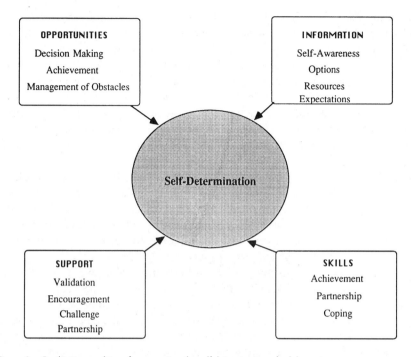

OPPORTUNITIES	INFORMATION
Decision Making	Self-Awareness
Achievement	Options
Management of Obstacles	Resources
	Expectations

Self-Determination

SUPPORT	SKILLS
Validation	Achievement
Encouragement	Partnership
Challenge	Coping
Partnership	

Figure 1. Facilitative conditions for promoting the self-determination of adolescents.

Decision Making   In addition to listening, it is important to permit youth to make choices and decisions—choices such as what clothes to wear, what music to listen to, whether to wear make-up and decisions about courses to take, about the ways in which their schools should be organized to promote their learning, about their future goals. Few experiences are more empowering than communicating respect and trust for someone's decision-making skills. Much of the time, we are afraid to let youth make decisions because we are concerned that they may not select the best options.

When well-informed and respected, our experience suggests that youth generally make thoughtful and responsible decisions. For example, when given free reign to select any goals they wanted in areas from dating to academics, 8 out of 10 youth in one of our *TAKE CHARGE* self-determination classes independently selected *academic* goals—goals such as doing homework, raising a grade, or studying for SATs. Even more impressive was that each of these students achieved the goal he or she set. These students had had many adults telling them to do these activities for years, but it wasn't until they were given opportunity to assume control—to own their goals—that they attained success.

It is clear that some decisions have a higher response cost than others, and there are situations in which it may be prudent to limit the decision-making power of an adolescent. In situations in which an adolescent's decision is likely to result in adverse outcomes, it may become the responsibility of more knowledgeable adults to intervene. Ideally, intervention should come early, prior to giving control for the decision over to the adolescent. In this case, the teenager's viewpoint should still be sought, and adults should be prepared to provide the adolescent with their rationale for alternative decisions that are made. It is essential that adults are thoughtful in their deliberations about which decisions truly carry a response cost high enough to warrant adult intervention and which decisions could be made by an adolescent. After all, it is typically through experiencing the consequences of personal decisions that adolescents learn to become wise decision makers.

Many adolescents can benefit from assistance in defining options that have potential for success and from support to help them bridge the gaps between their current capabilities and requirements for the successful performance of activities. This may be particularly true for adolescents who have limited life experience and therefore little basis upon which to either identify goals with potential for achievement or implement strategies to successfully achieve goals.

One approach to assisting adolescents to identify viable goals is to define for them a range of potential activities that are likely to be achievable and to encourage them to select goals from the options provided. This strategy is commonly used by parents and professionals; however, particularly for adolescents, it can be overly constrictive, appearing like a well-orchestrated attempt to provide opportunities for youth to work toward goals selected by others. This strategy also fails to provide youth with secondary opportunities to learn *how* to identify goal options that have potential for success. As a result, youth are likely to remain dependent on others to define and offer goal options rather than learn how they might generate their own options.

A second, and perhaps preferable, approach involves first assisting youth to articulate their criteria for desirable goals, then assisting them to identify decision options. This strategy involves assisting youth to identify 1) what is most important to them and 2) possible goals to work toward. For example, youth may decide that they want their goals to be important to some aspect of their current life (e.g., being a better student, making friends) or to be important for their future success (e.g., getting ready to live more independently, working toward getting a job, preparing to get into college).

Most adolescents will also agree that it makes sense to select short-term goals that are currently doable *and* will help them move forward toward achieving their larger, more remote goals. For example, many socially isolated youth want to make friends. An adolescent may at first think that the best way to make friends is to have a big party; however, upon realizing that he or she has nobody to invite to a party, the youth will typically agree that more modest goals such as saying "hi" to a peer or calling another adolescent on the telephone are probably good first steps that will help to build a base of acquaintances to invite to a future party. Although a bit more controversial, many adolescents will also agree that the best goals are those that important adults in their lives will not block. Our experience suggests that just as most youth recognize they need to progress in small steps, most will also acknowledge that it generally works best to select goals that provide opportunities for adults to grant them autonomy in small steps rather than forcing major confrontations that adults are likely to win.

The majority of adolescents, including youth with cognitive disabilities, are able to articulate some of the criteria for goals that are important to them. Additional criteria can also be proposed and youth can be assisted to identify their standards for personally valued goals. This process will help adolescents both learn an important approach for identifying future goals and help to maximize their positive self-attributions associated with subsequent goal attainment ("I succeeded at something that was important to me").

Achievement Self-determination is promoted by motivation and self-efficacy derived through successive mastery experiences. As such, it is critical that youth experience some success as they strive to achieve goals. Success can come in the form of goal attainment, achievement of substeps toward goal attainment, or through self-perceived efforts to try one's best. Although encouraging youth to value their efforts independent of their objective accomplishments is critical for self-acceptance and coping efficacy, youth must also have opportunities to experience achievement success. Achievement success can be bolstered by providing youth with the support necessary to maintain their progress toward goals while also providing them with opportunities to experience the benefits of their own hard work. Adolescents are likely to lose momentum in goal pursuit if every substep is arduous. Likewise, they are unlikely to perceive that they accomplished something valuable if every step is accomplished for them. In contrast to spontaneously providing help, youth typically benefit from coaching to help them to identify difficult steps in goal attainment and to address their assistance needs. As with goal identification, this type of coaching both helps youth achieve their goals and provides them with opportunities to learn metacognitive strategies for identifying and soliciting assistance. This approach also enables youth who might require a lot of help to accomplish goals to attribute their achievement to their self-management of that help. As adolescents demonstrate increasing capacities to accomplish goal steps more independently, support should be faded and youth should be encouraged and challenged to attempt more steps on their own.

Management of Obstacles Critical to facilitating self-determination experiences for adolescents is assisting them to identify and apply strategies to cope with obstacles that impede their progress: personal obstacles such as communication challenges, academic difficulties, limitations in mobility, or difficulties in emotional regulation and contextual barriers such as discrimination, lack or complexity of services, and disincentives to independence and self-direction. Once again, coaching youth to identify strategies to manage obstacles in conjunction with offering needed support is typically preferable to managing problems for them. It is through this approach that youth have opportunities to identify methods they might use to manage similar challenges in the future, to build confidence in their abilities to overcome barriers, and to maximize their self-attributions of coping efficacy.

The best kinds of self-determination opportunities are those that maximize the probability of success, either in achieving goals or managing barriers. Yet self-determination is also bolstered by taking risks, and youth can not be insulated from occasional failure. If, despite their efforts and adult supports, adolescents fail to achieve goals or their decisions prove unwise, it becomes adults' responsibility to assist them to become wiser as a result of their experiences. Self-determination will be threatened in situations in which youth attribute failure as permanent, pervasive, and internal (Seligman, 1990) ("I failed because I am a failure; everything I do is wrong and I will always be this way"). In failure situations, it is important to coach adolescents to consider what worked and what did not (limited vs. pervasive attributions), to attribute failure to their strategies rather than to themselves (external vs. internal attributions), and to focus on options for identifying new strategies that may be more successful in the future (temporary vs. permanent attributions). This approach does not imply that youth are not responsible for their failures as well as their successes. Rather, it encourages youth to assume responsibility for responding appropriately and productively.

Access to Information

Promoting the self-determination of youth necessitates that they have access to information that they can gain from self-exploration and use to make informed decisions.

Self-Exploration Self-awareness is important if adolescents are to optimally identify their interests and desires and to select self-determination options that are relevant to their goals. However, it is important to realize that the development of self-awareness is a lifelong process achieved at various levels as a function of personal introspectiveness, metacognitive capabilities, and contextual encouragement. Adolescence is an intense period of introspection for some youth; however, other youth are more likely to gain self-awareness through participating in, and reflecting on, the outcomes of multiple life experiences. Likewise, many adolescents who have difficulty thinking abstractly or engaging in personal reflection are still capable of making decisions, setting specific goals, and demonstrating high levels of self-determination as they strive toward goals. As such, it is important to realize that self-awareness is bolstered through different approaches, and efforts to assist youth to enhance their self-awareness must be tailored to their individual learning styles. Furthermore, although encouraging self-exploration is often helpful, requiring youth to demonstrate specific levels of self-awareness is not a necessary prerequisite for permitting them to move forward in making new decisions and attempting new behaviors.

Self-exploration can be promoted by many methods that assist youth to obtain and interpret information about themselves, to identify and strive toward goals that are consistent with their preferences, and to interpret the personal meanings of information they gain through new experiences. Methods useful for assisting adolescents to obtain information about themselves include the following:

1. Helping youth explore their future dreams through mapping strategies (see, e.g., Bolles, 1995; Powers et al., 1996)
2. Encouraging youth to explore their interests through activities such as taking standardized interest inventories or job shadowing
3. Helping youth to identify their personal capabilities through analysis of academic and interpersonal strengths

As highlighted in the preceding discussion, methods such as coaching youth to identify criteria for personally relevant goals and assisting them to generate and choose from goal options can be effective ways to facilitate youth self-awareness. Finally, coaching adolescents to sort out their responses to experiences and the implications of those responses for future preferences and plans are valuable methods to assist youth to identify and interpret incoming information about themselves.

Informed Decision Making To make informed decisions, adolescents need to know what their options are for courses, support services, after-school activities, educational planning goals, and postsecondary education and employment experiences. Professionals and parents hold much of this information and it is essential that they make such information accessible to youth. Too often professionals avoid providing information to adolescents because of its complexity. Withholding information isn't the answer; we have to discover ways to provide information in consumer-friendly formats and to encourage and trust adolescents to tell us what they need and how they want it presented. Youth will learn to become more informed consumers of information about life options and resources if such information is infused into inclusive curriculum and made a part of standard learning in school.

When providing information to adolescents about options and resources, it is essential that professionals be careful not to restrict the dreams of youth to specific programs currently offered. Although it is common for schools and community organizations to develop specific packaged programs to address the needs of large constituencies (e.g., a work experience program for all special education juniors), adolescents often develop more individualized goals (e.g., "Get an after-school job at the mall when I'm 15"); we need to be flexible in responding to those individual needs. This requires creativity in identifying possible strategies for mixing and matching current program elements, collaboration with other organizations to maximize options and resources, and administrative support to promote the identification of flexible resources. Accomplishing this systems redesign is perhaps our greatest challenge. However, if we are to truly support adolescents to identify and strive toward their personal dreams, we must be willing to both listen to youth and do our best to address their needs. This requires us to be honest about our capacities and to work toward enhancing the options available to support youth.

Self-Determination Skills

The third prerequisite for promoting the self-determination of adolescents involves facilitating their acquisition and successful application of self-determination skills. Self-determination is not something mysterious or something only accessible to a few who are born with high levels of intelligence or outgoing personalities. Self-determination is a skill—a skill that is developed through instruction, practice, and achievement. That self-determination is a skill is a clear advantage in that it can be learned and it can be nurtured—not by autocratic teaching but by collaborative strategies such as cooperative learning, coaching, and facilitation. Typically, adolescents do not develop self-determination skills through osmosis; they require systematic coaching through specific self-determination curricula that *integrates* knowledge development and practicum experience. Self-determination curricula and practicum can be integrated within instruction in standard subjects such as health education and social studies. It is critical that parents and professionals advocate for the inclusion of self-determination skill development within standard educational practices.

There are specific skills parents and professionals can impart to youth to promote their capacities for self-determined behavior. Examples of such skills include the application of academic knowledge, using a communication device, or taking the bus. Other skills are generic in that they provide students with lifelong strategies to achieve success in their lives. Generic self-determination skills include goal setting, problem solving, assertiveness, coping with challenges, self-regulation, and management of helping partnerships (Powers et al., 1996; Ward & Kohler, 1996; Wehmeyer, 1992). Our experience suggests that youth self-determination is bolstered through the acquisition and application of specific achievement, partnership, and coping skills, as discussed in the following subsections. (Powers et al., 1996). Each of these skills can be broken down into discrete generic steps that adolescents can apply to achieve current and future self-determination goals.

Achievement Skills   Achievement skills focus on the identification and attainment of personal goals. Such skills include the following:

• Identifying future dreams
• Setting goals
• Problem solving to achieve goals
• Preparing to successfully undertake activities
• Performing activities necessary for goal achievement

Identifying Future Dreams   The importance of identifying future dreams for enhancing both personal motivation and future planning is well recognized (e.g., Bolles 1995; Pearpoint, O'Brien, & Forest, 1992; Turnbull et al., Chapter 12). Articulating one's future dreams is a skill that requires creativity, knowledge of life options, and strategies for organizing and integrating the many facets of future life. Some adolescents, particularly those exposed to economic and cultural deprivation, have difficulty acknowledging or exploring their dreams. It is essential that these youth have their challenges validated *and* be encouraged to risk developing dreams for a more hopeful future. It is also common for youth to develop far-reaching dreams that their parents or teachers may believe are inappropriate or unrealistic. However, the specific nature of a youth's dream is less important than the enthusiasm dreaming generates for goal achievement. Our experience also suggests that future dreams become more realistic as adolescents mature, learn about future life options, and have opportunities to work toward specific goals.

Goal Setting   Goal setting may be the most important self-determination skill (Brotherson, Backus, Summers, & Turnbull, 1986; Gardner, 1986; Mitchell, 1988). Individuals typically choose goals that they value and are empowered through creating opportunities to achieve desired outcomes. They tend to infer high self-efficacy from success achieved through effort on tasks that are perceived to be difficult. In contrast, they infer low self-efficacy if they have to work hard to master easy tasks (de Vries, Dijkstra, & Kuhlman, 1988). As such, youth should be encouraged to select moderately challenging goals that have a reasonable probability of success.

Goal setting can be learned as a series of generic steps that include 1) identifying one's goal options, 2) selecting short-term goals that will facilitate progress toward future dreams, and 3) narrowing goals to a series of specific activities that can be feasibly performed and monitored for successful completion. Adolescents often experience difficulty setting goals and require structure, encouragement, and assistance. Youth may benefit from coaching to help them identify options for narrowing their goals. For example, "getting a job" can be narrowed to "applying for specific jobs," "making a resume," or "participating in an informational interview." Ultimately, the specific activities selected are less important for building self-determination than is valuing and achieving whatever activity goals are picked.

Problem Solving   Evidence indicates that youth with significant disabilities can effectively apply problem-solving strategies if they are provided with systematic, in situ training (Hughes & Rusch, 1989). Generic problem solving can be learned as a straightforward three-step approach. The first step is to identify the parts or subactivities that have to be accomplished by anyone to perform the activity. In effect, adolescents learn how to perform rudimentary task analyses. The second step of problem solving involves youth identifying exactly what will be hard for them in performing each step. Identifying these hard parts can be accomplished through abstract reasoning, by asking the opinions of others aware of the requirements of the activity and the youth's capabilities, or by actually trying each step. The final step involves youth using brainstorming to identify all sorts of possible ways to make each hard part easier and selecting the best strategy to try. Generally, the best strategy is the method that is both feasible for a youth and maximizes his or her independence.

Problem solving is initially difficult for many adolescents, at least partially because they often have a history of limited access to life experiences and information about the requirements of activities and solution options (McCarthy, 1986). Many youth with challenges also have a history of being provided with well-meaning assistance from others that inadvertently deprives them of opportunities to learn problem-solving skills. As a result, youth often need coaching to identify activity requirements and potential solutions. As youth become more familiar with the process, coaching can be faded and expectations for successful performance can be increased.

Those youth who have ongoing difficulty performing problem-solving can still learn to become responsible for directing the problem-solving assistance that they receive from others. For example, youth can learn to communicate their activity goals and then solicit help from others to identify the parts they will have to complete and potential strategies to make the hard parts easier to do. Youth can also solicit recommendations regarding preferred strategies and then make their own decisions regarding which preferred strategy to try.

Preparation   The successful performance of most activities requires thorough preparation. After adolescents problem-solve exactly how they will perform activities, they must learn how to identify and carry out arrangements that are required to execute their strategies. It is fairly common for adolescents to have difficulty following through in their execution of preparation activities. It is critical that they are provided with 1) adequate assistance to identify strategies for completing preparation activities that are within the scope of their current capabilities and 2) support to accomplish preparation activities that they aren't able to perform independently. Otherwise, they are likely to experience preparation as a punishing experience that isn't worth their efforts and to give up working toward their goals.

Achievement of Activity Goals   It is through successful, self-attributed achievement of activity goals that adolescents ultimately promote their self-determination. It is critical that youth gain experience in repeatedly achieving their goals and that facilitators provide coaching necessary to ensure youth have reasonable probabilities of success. Once adolescents experience their personal success, they often demonstrate increasing enthusiasm for working toward additional goals and become more resilient when faced with challenges (Seligman, 1990).

Partnership Skills   Independence can be expressed either through independent action or by actively soliciting and managing the assistance provided by others. Neither of these strategies is less valuable for independence than the other, however independent action is considered the strategy of choice when feasible for the individual. To promote their preparation for adult life, their abilities to advocate for needed services, and their personal empowerment, it is critical that youth learn to assume control for mobilizing and directing partnerships with others. Schmoozing, assertiveness, negotiation, and management of assistance are four generic partnership skills essential for the expression of self-determination.

Schmoozing To schmooze is to "be friendly," "chat," or otherwise engage in positive conversation with others (*The American Heritage Dictionary*, 1985). Schmoozing helps to create an environment of positive interaction in which more directive communication is conducted. Schmoozing is often utilized by skilled communicators. Most adolescents have difficulty schmoozing, particularly with adults with whom they wish to express their viewpoints and assert their independence. Youth must be encouraged to integrate a positive presentation of their desires and plans with expressions of appreciation for others' support and interest in others' lives and opinions.

Assertiveness Assertiveness refers to the ability to express needs directly and to act with self-confidence (Des Jardins, 1986). Component skills such as establishing positive body language, communicating clearly, using stop action communication techniques, and managing others' resistance are important components of assertiveness (Jakubowski & Lange, 1978). Many adolescents are motivated to behave assertively; however, they typically have a propensity for passive or aggressive responses that fail to provide opportunities for them to demonstrate their competence or build positive rapport. Youth can learn to apply a three-step assertiveness strategy: 1) look others in the eye; 2) speak calmly and firmly; and 3) if they disagree, repeat what you want and explain your reasoning. Following thorough preparation, most youth are able to positively and clearly communicate their goals and solicit support.

Negotiation Possessing negotiation skill is essential if one is to navigate the many systemic and interpersonal obstacles to goal achievement. Engagement in skillful win–win negotiation can be a fairly complex and demanding process (Fisher & Ury, 1981). Yet even a skill as sophisticated as negotiation can be learned at a rudimentary level as a series of steps: 1) listen to what others want, 2) decide what you can live with, and 3) compromise (find a solution both parties can accept). Our experience suggests that adolescents of diverse cognitive abilities can learn to enhance their negotiation skills. Critical for this success is the opportunity for youth to consider acceptable alternatives in advance and to rehearse negotiation interactions.

Management of Assistance Youth who are able to direct their support through active participation and management are likely both to feel a sense of added control over their lives and to experience a higher quality of life (DeJong, 1979; Sailor, Gee, Goetz, & Graham, 1988; Ulicny & Jones, 1987). Learning generic strategies for getting information, requesting a favor from another, and managing ongoing help is essential if adolescents are to achieve optimal levels of independence and self-determination. Youth should also be encouraged to identify ways that they may be able to assist others, promoting reciprocity and mutual support in their relationships.

Coping Skills   It is clear from the preceding discussion that effective coping with personal challenges is critical for the development of self-esteem, self-confidence, and self-determination. Specific coping skills integral to the promotion of self-determination include thinking positively, noticing personal accomplishments, managing frustration, and self-monitoring and reinforcing personal success.

Thinking Positively   There is a growing body of literature indicating that feedback such as positive self-talk can effectively assist people to shape their own behavior (Dush, Hirt, & Schroeder, 1989). Positive self-talk, although an extremely valuable skill, is difficult for many adolescents to understand and to learn how to modify. Adolescents are typically unaware that they engage in internal dialogues that influence how they respond to difficult situations. To promote their acquisition of positive self-talk, youth may be coached to generate positive self-statements and then encouraged to analyze specific self-statements in association with events such as preparing for communication encounters with parents. Adolescents can be encouraged to "immunize" themselves with positive affirmations and to refute pervasive negative self-statements.

Through self-monitoring of their accomplishments, people have opportunities to observe their competence and, as a result, begin to view themselves as more competent (Dowrick, 1983). In turn, they actually begin to demonstrate higher levels of skill (Gonzales & Dowrick, 1983). Adolescents, like the rest of us, seldom attend to their accomplishments or positive experiences. On a regular basis, adolescents should be invited to note accomplishments of which they are proud and be encouraged to boast about their successes with peers and adults. Our experience has been that although many youth initially regard noting their accomplishments as a "dumb" exercise, they gradually express growing pride in their efforts and capabilities.

Managing Frustration   Frustration is a normal response to situations in which goals are not achieved quickly or effectively. Learning to productively manage frustration is important if adolescents are to avoid demoralization and maintain their momentum for goal attainment. Youth skilled in the use of problem-focused and emotion-focused coping strategies are optimally prepared to effectively respond to obstacles (Compas, 1987). Problem-focused techniques, such as problem solving, are appropriate coping strategies in situations in which an obstacle can be overcome, whereas emotion-focused strategies are helpful in instances in which an outcome cannot be controlled (Folkman & Lazarus, 1980). Generally, coping responses that emphasize situational, depersonalized, and temporary interpretations of negative events are associated with heightened perseverance in the face of failure and frustration (Seligman, 1990). Youth should be encouraged to use positive self-talk to reframe their failure as a temporary, situational event. They should also be encouraged to depersonalize their failures by attributing the problem to a flawed game plan rather than to personal failings. To the extent that adolescents learn to attribute failure to a flawed plan, they are able to respond by problem-solving new strategies that will bolster their probability for future success.

Tracking and Reinforcing One's Progress Tracking and rewarding one's progress toward goal attainment is a form of self-regulation. Self-regulation is associated with enhancement of personal empowerment, autonomy, and internal locus of control (Brigham, 1989; Williams & Long, 1979). These skills are critical for adolescents who are transitioning from controlled school environments into an adult world in which rules are often ambiguous and external reinforcement unavailable. Self-regulation is also an important skill for promoting autonomy in situations where others seek to exert influence or control. Accurate self-monitoring, self-feedback, and contingent self-delivery of valued rewards by youth appears to provide an effective method to enhance self-determination.

Youth should be provided repeated opportunities to monitor and reinforce their efforts and progress toward goal attainment. They can be encouraged to identify and deliver personal rewards in association with acknowledgment of their accomplishments and efforts toward achieving their goals. Rewards can range from calling a special friend to buying a compact disc to sleeping in late on Saturday.

Support from Others

The final major element necessary to promote the self-determination of youth is support. Support can be provided as encouragement, challenge, praise, and partnership. Letting youth know they are doing a good job, challenging them to take risks, using humor to validate their dilemmas, providing honest feedback, and being available to provide needed assistance are all important support strategies.

Although youth often benefit from some traditional instruction, self-determination is most effectively promoted with broader coaching methodologies. Coaches can provide opportunities for adolescents to learn and apply generic strategies to achieve their personal goals, model the application of strategies, cheer their progress, occasionally challenge them to take action, make themselves available to help youth rehearse their use of particular strategies (e.g., role-play negotiating a goal with a teacher), or assist youth to perform particular activities necessary for goal achievement (e.g., call an agency on the student's behalf to obtain information). Coaches may be teachers, guidance counselors, staff from community agencies, or community volunteers. The essence of coaching involves establishing relationships with youth that validate their perceptions of their strengths and challenges while also empowering them to make their lives different, to take control, and to risk attempting new ways of thinking and behaving.

Parents who encourage self-determination set goals that are slightly beyond the present capabilities of their child (Lindemann, 1981). As children move through adolescence and young adulthood, such parents encourage them to make decisions, to set their own goals, to act assertively, to manage their own challenges, to take acceptable risks, and to self-advocate (Powers, Singer, & Todis, 1996). Suggestions for promoting the support capacities of educators, parents, and peers are discussed in the following subsections.

Promoting Support Capacities of Educators   Most educators agree that self-determination is important for adolescents. However, like the youth they serve, they lack opportunities, information, skills, and support needed to impact the self-determination of youth. Promoting self-determination is seldom a focus of preservice and in-service training for educators. Most educators are also required to function within educational structures that emphasize uniformity and compliance ahead of individualized programming, youth or educator self-direction, and partnership. Finally, as clearly articulated by Field and Hoffman (1996), it is imperative that educators attain personal levels of self-determination sufficient to positively affect the self-determination of youth whom they serve.

If educators are to facilitate the self-determination of youth effectively, they must have access to information about specific methodologies and curricula, opportunities to apply those methodologies within individual and classroom settings, and support from their colleagues and administrators. As discussed earlier, access to support is particularly critical when an educator's effective facilitation of the self-determination of a youth stimulates a need for system flexibility. Finally, educators will be successful in promoting the self-determination of youth to the extent to which they themselves are self-determined. Educational systems and training approaches that focus on assisting educators to acquire and apply personal self-determination skills will ultimately facilitate their capacities to provide quality coaching and support for youth.

Promoting Support Capacities of Parents   Our experience suggests that parents generally try their best to facilitate their children's development of self-determination and are keenly aware of barriers to their efforts. Parents of adolescents often encounter five major obstacles as they attempt to promote their children's self-determination. First, many parents are unclear about how much self-determination they should expect from their children. They may lack reference points about typical levels of self-determination expressed by adolescents at varying ages. If this information is available, parents may have difficulty translating it into appropriate expectations for their own children. Second, parents may be uncertain of strategies they could effectively use to prompt their children's self-determination. Their uncertainty may be based upon inadequate information regarding potential strategies or concerns about selecting strategies that are likely to promote their children's success yet guard against threats to child safety if such strategies are unsuccessful. In this instance, parents generally want to be reasonably sure that serious harm will not result from permitting their children to take certain risks. Third, some families may have different cultural meanings and expectations for their children's expression of self-determination. These families may find that their deviation from common Anglo American expectations may pose their greatest obstacle, as their viewpoints and child-rearing practices may not be well understood or integrated into educational efforts to assist their children. A fourth obstacle for some families is the presence of multiple stressors that prevent parents from supporting the self-determination of their children. Such stressors may include poverty, unemployment, health problems, marital discord, or problems affecting other children in the family. Finally, a fifth obstacle many parents of adolescents also experience is stress and fatigue associated with years of struggling to advocate for their children with little support available to bolster their efforts.

It is essential that those wishing to promote the self-determination of youth acknowledge, respect, and respond to parent perspectives regarding their desires, capabilities, and barriers to promoting the self-determination of their children. Methods that might be used to support parents' encouragement of self-determination include the following:

- Acknowledgment of the many ways in which parents already successfully support their children (Summers, Behr, & Turnbull, 1989)
- Respect for family norms guiding child expression of self-determination (Turnbull & Turnbull, 1996)
- Technical assistance to help parents identify potential strategies they would like to use to promote the self-determination of their children
- Providing parents with information about the typical emergence of self-determination during adolescence and resources available to support their children's optimal expression of self-determination (Sowers, 1989)
- Introducing parents to self-determined adults who experience challenges similar to their children's (Powers, Sowers, & Stevens, 1995)
- Supporting parents as they attempt to balance encouraging self-determination with providing a safety net for the autonomous activities of their children (Espinosa & Shearer, 1986)
- Assisting parents as they manage family stressors that impede their capacities to support the well-being of family members (Singer & Irvin, 1989)

Promoting Support Capacities of Peers and Adults with Similar Challenges   Although support from professionals and parents is critical for the facilitation of self-determination, others can also be instrumental. Most notable is support provided by role models or mentors and support provided by peers who experience similar challenges. Mentoring is a popular approach for promoting living skills; a positive view of disability, and knowledge, self-confidence, and motivation in youth with disabilities (Fredericks, 1988; Jones & Ulicny, 1986; Rhodes, 1994). Evidence suggests that interaction with adult role models who experience disabilities enhances the disability-related knowledge and self-confidence of adolescents with disabilities and parent perceptions of the knowledge and capabilities of their children with disabilities (Powers, Sowers, & Stevens, 1995).

Many youth with disabilities and their families don't get the chance to meet successful adults with similar challenges. When these opportunities occur, youth and families often respond with excitement and enthusiasm. Riding in an adapted van one's mentor is driving, seeing an adult with one's same disability supervising others at work, and learning tips about dating or using community resources are just a few of the experiences that youth can have with mentors.

Since the 1980s, much emphasis has been focused on the importance of promoting interaction between youth with disabilities and youth without disabilities. It is clear that the development of relationships between youth of diverse capabilities generally promotes the well-being of all participants (Bricker, 1978; Gaylord-Ross, Haring, Breen, & Pitts-Conway, 1984). However, it is important to remember that an inadvertent impact of inclusion is that youth with disabilities may lose access to learning and sharing about disability-related issues with peers who have similar challenges. Although interaction with peers without disabilites is very important, the importance of providing youth with options for also developing relationships with students who experience similar challenges should not be negated.

Peer support among people with disabilities can be a powerful method to enhance self-determination, self-acceptance, and leadership (Jones & Ulicny, 1986; Williams & Shoultz, 1984). Intervention by a peer counselor with a disability can also significantly accelerate the transition to independent living for an individual with a disability (Saxton, 1983). Through interaction with their peers with disabilities, youth have opportunities to learn and practice self-determination and leadership skills, to share strategies for managing disability-related barriers, and to receive support for self-acceptance.

Strategies to promote peer support and mentoring may include 1) integrating challenge-related peer support into existing peer counseling programs in schools; 2) developing databases of current students, young adults exiting school, and adults who are interested in supporting others; 3) establishing relationships with independent living centers, college disabled services programs, and self-advocacy groups to network youth and adults; and 4) hiring people with disabilities to work in school buildings. Although it is important to employ people with disabilities at state and federal levels, it is only by promoting hiring in schools that the lives of students with disabilities will be touched directly.

SHIFTS IN ATTITUDES AND APPROACHES

The centerpiece of promoting self-determination among youth is access to relevant opportunities, information, skills, and supports. However, the accomplishment of these objectives necessitates a significant shift in current attitudes and approaches.

Viewing Youth as Change Agents

Professionals must shift from attitudes of control to attitudes of empowerment and trust. In doing this, they will become better listeners and enter into shared decision making with youth. Approaches to promote the self-determination of youth must respect youth as effective change agents in their own lives, capable of exercising personal control and decision making. Interventions must provide for primary implementation of strategies by youth, with other participants acting as facilitators and support providers. Educators and community resource personnel must convey confidence in adolescents' abilities to make effective judgments while also providing these youth with appropriate limits and supports to maximize their capacities for success.

Redefining Professional Roles

Professionals are traditionally trained to perceive themselves as experts whose primary role is to impart content knowledge to youth. Although this role is important, professionals must also realize that achieving success in life also demands self-confidence, striving, coping, and perseverance. Professional roles must be expanded to include bolstering these capacities as well—combining the transfer of expertise *to* youth with the validation and support of expertise *within* youth, even when such expertise may be hard to identify. Even the most challenged, disheartened, angry, and self-destructive youth have strengths and focusing on their strengths is often the most effective entrée into helping them address their challenges. Professionals must believe in youth and partner with them to collaboratively identify skills, information, and practice opportunities needed to foster their self-determination development. To accomplish this role shift, professionals must be provided with opportunities to learn and apply facilitative strategies for establishing cooperative relationships with youth and parents (Goetz, Anderson, & Laten, 1989; Slater, Martinez, & Habersang, 1989; Walker, 1989).

Adopting a Whole-Person Focus

Youth spend the majority of their lives outside of school, and their future success will be gauged based upon their achievements across life domains. Although many youth value academic goals, many others view their greatest needs in areas such as independent living, friendship, employment, or recreation. If educational professionals are limited to intervening with youth in solely academically related domains, their capacities to further both the general development and the academic skills of youth will be compromised. Professionals must be encouraged to adopt a whole-person focus with youth and supported to intervene in areas beyond academics and the school building. Professional assistance provided to identify and implement strategies to productively use free time, to establish supportive relationships with peers and role models, or to manage threats to personal safety will, in the long run, enhance the academic focus and capacities of many youth.

Committing to Short-Term
Investment to Achieve Long-Term Success

Promoting self-determination can be a time-consuming and resource-demanding process: Youth may require regular coaching over a period of years, their parents may require intensive assistance to manage family barriers that impede their capacities to support their children, and professionals may need additional time to reach out to youth in their communities. Yet if we do not attend to this aspect of youths' lives, they are at risk of becoming stuck in patterns of indecisiveness, underachievement, or destructiveness to themselves and others, at a high long-term cost to society. It is essential that organizations and professionals commit to making intensive short-term investments that will bolster youth in their efforts to prevent and manage long-term life challenges. Approaches to promote youth self-determination provide generic methodologies for enhancing the current and future success of youth and for ultimately conserving resources.

Embracing Organizational Collaboration

Our world has grown to a point where no one individual or person in a specific role can influence the kinds of changes necessary to ensure quality supports for youth. Regardless of whether underlying problems lie in youth being exposed to too many options, family discord, poverty, or disability, it is up to youth, professionals, and families to work together to confront challenges and to promote the current and future capacities of youth. We must shift from believing we can use isolated approaches to embracing and seeking opportunities for collaboration. We must learn to identify and build partnerships with and between youth, successful adults, parents, schools, and community organizations.

Asking How to Make Self-Determination Possible

Finally, and most importantly, we must shift from thinking about competence in yes or no terms to focusing on what it will take to promote the highest levels of competence possible for each youth. In the early 1980s, professionals met and debated whether people with disabilities could work in their communities. Some said yes, while others said it couldn't be done. However, it was only when we began to ask another question—not can people work, but what will it take to make it possible—that we moved forward to identify numerous strategies to effectively promote community-based, naturally supported employment. Promoting youth success in other areas is no different. We must stop asking if it's possible and reframe the question to ask, "What will it take?"

JAKE: A STORY OF SELF-DETERMINATION

We end this chapter by describing the experiences of a 14-year-old youth who participated in our *TAKE CHARGE* self-determination intervention (Powers et al., 1996). "Jake" has muscular dystrophy, uses a wheelchair, and has cognitive challenges requiring lower levels of assistance. He became involved in the self-determination program because he was very passive, had no friends, and had no opportunity to go into his community except with his family. After identifying some preliminary dreams for his future (youth with life-limiting challenges also have dreams), Jake set a goal of learning to ride the bus to a mall where many of his peers hang out. He had no experiences with buses—he didn't know buses had drivers, and he was excited and amazed to hear that they did!

With help from his coach at school, Jake problem-solved exactly how he would use the bus. His mentor from the independent living center went on a few practice runs with him, and Jake was able to ride the bus independently after a few practice sessions. His mom, who was anxious about permitting Jake to take the bus, was offered encouragement by a parent staff person from a Parent to Parent organization, and she was introduced to other parents who also provided support.

As Jake mastered the bus, he became interested in asking a peer at school, Stephen, to go to the mall with him. He then asked his coach to assist him to problem-solve how to ask Stephen to go along. Stephen said yes and he and Jake now regularly go to the mall and other places in town to participate in activities and hang with other youth. Jake also takes the bus independently, and his mom now jokes about her difficulty in keeping track of Jake.

While working on these goals, Jake's individualized education program (IEP) was scheduled. He had never participated in his IEP, but this time he indicated he wanted to attend and advocate for a computer to do his school work. He asked his coach to help him figure out what to say. He was anxious in the meeting, but he managed to express what he wanted and why it was important to him. The staff appeared shocked, as was his mom. The director of special education was so impressed that he left the meeting temporarily, checked his discretionary budget, and returned to immediately authorize funds to help purchase the computer. The IEP team then brainstormed with Jake on ways to obtain additional funds. Jake decided that he would write a letter to a local fraternal organization to request their support. Jake left his IEP meeting feeling proud of his efforts and expressing interest in working toward specific academic goals. Jake's coach assisted him to prepare the letter and, within a brief period of time, the organization responded by donating a computer to Jake as well as five additional computers to his school.

Jake now looks people in the eye, has power struggles with his parents like most teenagers, and has identified and is working toward several additional goals. He has become more independent in problem solving and directing the assistance he needs. His mother is now increasingly defining her expectations for Jake based upon what other teenagers his age would be expected to do.

Jake experienced the spark of his own self-determination and he created new momentum for himself that could only have come through developing his personal sense of control and achievement. Jake's success was made possible through the numerous partnerships that he developed with people and organizations who were willing to listen and try their best to help. There are many youth like Jake. They may experience different types of challenges, however they all have the potential to move forward toward self-determined lives. It is up to us to work with them to transform their dreams into realities.

REFERENCES

Arborelius, E., & Bremberg, S. (1991). How do teenagers respond to a consistently student-centered program of health education at school? *International Journal of Adolescent Medicine and Health, 5*(2), 95–112.

Bandura, A. (1977). Self-efficacy: Toward a unifying theory of behavior change. *Psychological Review, 84*, 191–215.

Bandura, A. (1986). *Social foundation of thought and action: A social cognitive theory.* New York: Prentice Hall.

Bellamy, G.T., Horner, R.H., & Inman, D.P. (1979). *Vocational habilitation of severely retarded adults.* Baltimore: University Park Press.

Bolles, R.N. (1995). *The 1995 what color is your parachute? A practical manual for job-hunters and career-changers.* Berkeley, CA: Ten Speed Press.

Bricker, D.D. (1978). A rationale for the integration of handicapped preschool children. In M.J. Guralnick (Ed.), *Early intervention and the integrating of handicapped and non-handicapped children* (pp. 3–26). Baltimore: University Park Press.

Brigham, T.A. (1989). *Self-management for adolescents: A skills training program.* New York: Guilford Press.

Brophy, J., & Good, T. (1974). *Teacher–student relationships: Causes and consequences.* New York: Holt, Rinehart & Winston.

Brotherson, M.J., Backus, L.H., Summers, J.A., & Turnbull, A.P. (1986). Transition to adulthood. In J.A. Summers (Ed.), *The right to grow up: An introduction to adults with developmental disabilities* (pp. 17–44). Baltimore: Paul H. Brookes Publishing Co.

Brown, D.S. (1992, Fall). Empowerment through peer counseling. *OSERS: News in Print, 5*, 27–29.

Burchard, S.M. (1996). Mastering the developmental challenges of childhood and adolescence. In L.E. Powers, G.H.S. Singer, & J. Sowers (Eds.), *On the road to autonomy: Promoting self-competence for children and youth with disabilities* (pp. 29–52). Baltimore: Paul H. Brookes Publishing Co.

Clark, F.A., Mack, W., & Pennington, V. (1988). Transition needs assessment of severely disabled high school students and their parents and teachers. *The Occupational Therapy Journal of Research, 8*, 323–344.

Clark, R.M. (1980). *Family life and school achievement: Why poor black children succeed or fail.* Chicago: University of Chicago Press.

Compas, B.E. (1987). Coping with stress during childhood and adolescence. *Psychological Bulletin, 101*, 393–403.

Crundall, I., & Foddy, M. (1981). Vicarious exposure to a task as a basis of evaluative competence. *Social Psychology Quarterly, 44*, 331–338.

de Vries, H., Dijkstra, M., & Kuhlman, P. (1988). Self-efficacy: The third factor besides attitude and subjective norm as a predictor of behavioral intentions. *Health Education Research, 3*, 273–282.

DeJong, G. (1979). *The movement for independent living: Origins, ideology, and implications for disability research.* Ann Arbor, MI: University Centers for International Rehabilitation.

Des Jardins, C. (1986). Assertiveness is/is not. In F. Weiner (Ed.), *No apologies: A guide to living with a disability, written by the real authorities—People with disabilities, their families and friends* (pp. 122–123). New York: St. Martin's Press.

Dolce, J.J. (1987). Self-efficacy and disability beliefs in behavioral treatment of pain. Special Issue: Chronic pain. *Behavior Research & Therapy, 25,* 289–299.

Dowrick, P.W. (1983). Self-modeling. In P.W. Dowrick & S.J. Biggs (Eds.), *Using video: Psychological and social applications* (pp. 105–124). London: John Wiley & Sons.

Dunst, C.J., & Trivette, C.M. (1989). An enablement and empowerment perspective of case management. *Topics in Early Childhood Education, 8,* 87–102.

Dush, D.M., Hirt, M.L., & Schroeder, H.E. (1989). Self-statement modification in the treatment of child behavior disorders: A meta-analysis. *Psychological Bulletin, 106*(1), 97–106.

Ehrenberg, M.F., Cox, D.N., & Koopman, R.F. (1991, Summer). The relationship between self-efficacy and depression in adolescents. *Adolescence, 26*(102), 361–374.

Espinosa, L., & Shearer, M. (1986). Family support in public school programs. In R.R. Fewell & P.F. Vadasy (Eds.), *Families of handicapped children: Needs and supports across the life span* (pp. 253–277). Austin, TX: PRO-ED.

Fewell, R.R., & Vadasy, P.F. (Eds.). (1986). *Families of handicapped children: Needs and support across the life span.* Austin, TX: PRO-ED.

Field, S., & Hoffman, A. (1996). Increasing the ability of educators to support youth self-determination. In L.E. Powers, G.H.S. Singer, & J. Sowers (Eds.), *On the road to autonomy: Promoting self-competence for children and youth with disabilities* (pp. 171–187). Baltimore: Paul H. Brookes Publishing Co.

Fisher, R., & Ury, W. (1981). *Getting to yes: Negotiation agreement without giving in.* New York: Penguin Books.

Folkman, S., & Lazarus, R.S. (1980). An analysis of coping in a middle-aged community sample. *Journal of Health and Social Behavior, 21,* 219–239.

Fredericks, B. (1988). Tim becomes an Eagle Scout. *Transition Summary, 5,* 8–9.

Gardner, N.S. (1986). Sexuality. In J.A. Summers (Ed.), *The right to grow up: An introduction to adults with developmental disabilities* (pp. 45–66). Baltimore: Paul H. Brookes Publishing Co.

Garrison, W.T., & McQuiston, S. (1989). *Developmental Clinical Psychology and Psychiatry: Vol. 19. Chronic illness during childhood and adolescence: Psychological aspects.* Newbury Park, CA: Sage Publications.

Gaylord-Ross, R.J., Haring, T.G., Breen, C., & Pitts-Conway, V. (1984). The training and generalization of social interaction skills with autistic youth. *Journal of Applied Behavior Analysis, 17,* 229–247.

Goetz, L., Anderson, J., & Laten, S. (1989). Facilitation of family support through public school programs. In G.H.S. Singer & L.K. Irvin (Eds.), *Support for caregiving families: Enabling positive adaptation to disability* (pp. 239–252). Baltimore: Paul H. Brookes Publishing Co.

Gonzales, F.P., & Dowrick, P.W. (1983, October). *Effects of video self-modeling in "feedforward" training hand/eye coordination.* Unpublished manuscript, University of Alaska, Anchorage.

Graham, S., & Harris, K.R. (1989). Components analysis of cognitive strategy instruction: Effects on learning disabled students' compositions and self-efficacy. *Journal of Educational Psychology, 81,* 353–361.

Harter, S. (1981). A model of mastery motivation in children: Individual differences and developmental change. In S. Collins (Ed.), *Minnesota symposium on child psychology* (Vol. 14, pp. 215–255). Hillsdale, NJ: Lawrence Erlbaum Associates.

Horner, R.H., Meyer, L.H., & Fredericks, H.D.B. (Eds.). (1986). *Education of learners with severe handicaps: Exemplary service strategies.* Baltimore: Paul H. Brookes Publishing Co.

Houghton, J., Bronicki, G.J., & Guess, D. (1987). Opportunities to express preferences and make choices among students with severe disabilities in classroom settings. *Journal of The Association for Persons with Severe Handicaps, 12*(1), 18–27.

Hoy, C. (1986). Preventing learned helplessness. *Academic Therapy, 22,* 11–18.

Hughes, C., & Rusch, F.R. (1989). Teaching supported employees with severe mental retardation to solve problems. *Journal of Applied Behavior Analysis, 22,* 365–372.

Hughes, C.A., Korinek, L., & Gorman, J. (1991). Self-management for students with mental retardation in public school settings: A research review. *Education and Training in Mental Retardation, 26,* 271–291.

Jakubowski, P., & Lange, A.J. (1978). *The assertive option: Your rights & responsibilities.* Champaign, IL: Research Press.

Jones, M.L., & Ulicny, G.R. (1986). The independent living perspective: Applications to services for adults with developmental disabilities. In J.A. Summers (Ed.), *The right to grow up: An introduction to adults with developmental disabilities* (pp. 227–244). Baltimore: Paul H. Brookes Publishing Co.

Lindemann, J.E. (1981). Cerebral palsy. In J.E. Lindemann (Ed.), *Psychological and behavioral aspects of physical disability* (pp. 117–145). New York: Plenum.

Luchow, J.P., Crowl, T.K., & Kahn, J.P. (1985). Learned helplessness: Perceived effect of ability and effort on academic performance among EH and LD/EH children. *Journal of Learning Disabilities, 18,* 470–474.

Margalit, M., & Shulman, S. (1986). Autonomy perceptions and anxiety expressions of learning disabled adolescents. *Journal of Learning Disabilities, 19,* 291–293.

McCarthy, H. (1986). Making it in able-bodied America: Career development in young adults with physical disabilities. *Journal of Applied Rehabilitation Counseling, 17,* 30–38.

Mitchell, B. (1988). Who chooses? *Transition Summary, 5,* 4–5.

Pearpoint, J., O'Brien, J., & Forest, M. (1992). *PATH: A workbook for planning better futures,* Version 1.1. Toronto: Inclusion Press.

Peterson, C., & Stunkard, A.J. (1989). Personal control and health promotion. *Social Science Medicine, 28,* 819–828.

Powers, L.E., Singer, G.H.S., & Todis, B. (1996). Reflections on competence: Perspectives of successful adults. In L.E. Powers, G.H.S. Singer, & J. Sowers (Eds.), *On the road to autonomy: Promoting self-competence for children and youth with disabilities* (pp. 69–92). Baltimore: Paul H. Brookes Publishing Co.

Powers, L.E., Sowers, J., & Stevens, T. (1995). An exploratory, randomized study of the impact of mentoring on the self-efficacy of adolescents with physical health challenges. *Journal of Rehabilitation, 61*(1), 33–41.

Powers, L.E., Sowers, J., Turner, A., Nesbitt, M., Knowles, A., & Ellison, R. (1996). *TAKE CHARGE*: A model for promoting self-determination among adolescents with challenges. In L.E. Powers, G.H.S. Singer, & J. Sowers (Eds.), *On the road to autonomy: Promoting self-competence for children and youth with disabilities* (pp. 291–322). Baltimore: Paul H. Brookes Publishing Co.

Rhodes, J.E. (1994, Spring). Older and wiser: Mentoring relationships in childhood and adolescence. *Journal of Primary Prevention, 14,* 187–196.

Rousso, H. (1988). *Mentoring empowers! How to start a networking project for disabled women and girls in your community.* New York: The Networking Project for Disabled Women and Girls, YWCA of the City of New York.

Sailor, W., Gee, K., Goetz, L., & Graham, N. (1988). Progress in educating students with the most severe disabilities: Is there any? *Journal of The Association for Persons with Severe Handicaps, 13*, 87–99.

Santelli, B., Turnbull, A.P, Lerner, E., & Marquis, J. (1993). Parent to parent programs: A unique form of mutual support for families of persons with disabilities. In G.H.S. Singer & L.E. Powers (Eds.), *Families, disability, and empowerment: Active coping skills and strategies for family interventions* (pp. 27–57). Baltimore: Paul H. Brookes Publishing Co.

Saxton, M. (1983). Peer counseling. In N.M. Crewe & K.Z. Irving (Eds.), *Independent living for physically disabled people* (pp. 171–186). San Francisco: Jossey-Bass.

Schunk, D.H. (1982). Effects of effort attributional feedback on children's perceived self-efficacy and achievement. *Journal of Educational Psychology, 74*, 548–556.

Schunk, D.H. (1989). Self-efficacy and cognitive achievement: Implications for students with learning problems. *Journal of Learning Disabilities, 22*, 14–22.

Seligman, M.E.P. (1975). *Helplessness: On depression, development, and death.* San Francisco: W.H. Freeman.

Seligman, M.E.P. (1990). *Learned optimism.* New York: Pocket Books.

Shelton, T.L., Jeppeson, E.S., & Johnson, B.H. (1989, June). *Family-centered care for children with special health care needs* (2nd ed.). Washington, DC: Association for the Care of Children's Health.

Singer, G.H.S., & Irvin, L.K. (1989). Family caregiving, stress, and support. In G.H.S. Singer & L.K. Irvin (Eds.), *Support for caregiving families: Enabling positive adaptation to disability* (pp. 3–25) Baltimore: Paul H. Brookes Publishing Co.

Slater, M.A., Martinez, M., & Habersang, R. (1989). Normalized family resources: A model for professionals serving families with a chronically ill or handicapped child. In G.H.S. Singer & L.K. Irvin (Eds.), *Support for caregiving families: Enabling positive adaptation to disability* (pp. 161–173). Baltimore: Paul H. Brookes Publishing Co.

Sowers, J. (1989). Supported employment: Critical parent roles. In G.H.S. Singer & L.K. Irvin (Eds.), *Support for caregiving families: Enabling positive adaptation to disability* (pp. 269–282). Baltimore: Paul H. Brookes Publishing Co.

Sowers, J., & Powers, L. (1989). Preparing students with cerebral palsy and mental retardation for the transition from school to community-based employment. *Career Development for Exceptional Individuals, 12*, 25–35.

Sowers, J. & Powers, L. (1991). *Vocational preparation and employment of students with physical and multiple disabilities.* Baltimore: Paul H. Brookes Publishing Co.

Summers, J.A., Behr, S.K., & Turnbull, A.P. (1989). Positive adaptation and coping strengths of families who have children with disabilities. In G.H.S. Singer & L.K. Irvin (Eds.), *Support for caregiving families: Enabling positive adaptation to disability* (pp. 27–40). Baltimore: Paul H. Brookes Publishing Co.

The American Heritage Dictionary (2nd College Ed.). (1985). Boston: Houghton Mifflin.

Thomas, A., Bax, M., Coombes, K., Goldson, E., Smyth, D., & Whitmore, K. (1985). The health and social needs of physically handicapped young adults: Are they being met by the statutory services? *Developmental Medicine & Child Neurology, 27*(Suppl. 50), 1–20.

Turnbull, A.P., & Turnbull, H.R. (1996). An analysis of self-determination within a culturally responsive family systems perspective: Balancing the family mobile. In L.E. Powers, G.H.S. Singer, & J. Sowers (Eds.), *On the road to autonomy: Promoting self-competence for children and youth with disabilities* (pp. 195–220). Baltimore: Paul H. Brookes Publishing Co.

Ulicny, G.R., & Jones, M.L. (1987). Consumer management of attendant services. In *Rehabilitation research review.* Lawrence: University of Kansas, Research and Training Center on Independent Living.

U.S. Department of Health and Human Services, Public Health Service, Health Resources and Services Administration, Maternal and Child Health Bureau. (1992, Summer). *Moving on: Transition from child-centered to adult health care for youth with disabilities*. Washington, DC: Author.

Valdes, K.A., Williamson, C.L., & Wagner, M.M. (1990). U.S. Department of Education, Office of Special Education Programs. *The National Longitudinal Transition Study of Special Education Students*, *10*(7).

Walker, B. (1989). Strategies for parent-teacher cooperation. In G.H.S. Singer & L.K. Irvin (Eds.), *Support for caregiving families: Enabling positive adaptation to disability* (pp. 103–119). Baltimore: Paul H. Brookes Publishing Co.

Ward, M.J., & Kohler, P.D. (1996). Teaching self-determination: Content and process. In L.E. Powers, G.H.S. Singer, & J. Sowers (Eds.), *On the road to autonomy: Promoting self-competence for children and youth with disabilities* (pp. 275–290). Baltimore: Paul H. Brookes Publishing Co.

Wehman, P. (1981). *Competitive employment: New horizons for severely disabled persons*. Baltimore: Paul H. Brookes Publishing Co.

Wehmeyer, M.L. (1992). Self-determination and the education of students with mental retardation. *Education and Training in Mental Retardation*, *27*, 302–314.

Williams, P., & Shoultz, B. (1984). *We can speak for ourselves*. Bloomington: Indiana University Press.

Williams, R., & Long, J. (1979). *Toward a self-managed life style*. New York: Houghton Mifflin.

Zeaman, D., & House, B.J. (1960). Approach and avoidance in the discrimination learning of retardates. In D. Zeaman (Ed.), *Learning and transfer in mental defectives* (Progress Report No. 2) National Institute on Mental Health, USPHS, Research Grant M-1099 to University of Connecticut.

Chapter 14

LEARNING WITH PURPOSE

A Lifelong Learning Approach Using Self-Determination Skills

Loretta A. Serna

SINCE THE EARLY 1980s, professional attention focused on youth who are at risk for failure in their schools and communities has increased (McWhirter, McWhirter, McWhirter, & McWhirter, 1993). Such attention has increased because of the many adolescents who are dropping out of school, using illegal drugs, engaging in sexual activities and violent acts (e.g., gangs), giving birth out of wedlock, and being physically and sexually abused (Dryfoos, 1990; Schorr, 1988). As the numbers of these youth increase, and more and more adolescents are unable to finish school and establish a secure work and family environment, the United States will, in the words of The National Commission on Excellence in Education (1983), become a *nation* at risk for failure. To combat this growing trend of failure, professionals need to 1) understand the behaviors of these youth, 2) be aware of past intervention programs that have benefitted youth who were at risk for failure, and 3) develop new and effective intervention programs that address the changing problems of today's youth. This chapter focuses on each of these three issues.

The development and refinement of the *Learning with PURPOSE* curriculum has spanned over a 4-year period and has involved the participation of many individuals in a team effort. I would like to thank the staff of the Office of Special Education and Rehabilitative Services for making funds available for 3 years of concentrated work in the self-determination area. In addition, the continued support of the Department of Special Education at the University of Hawaii and the Hawaii University Affiliated Program has enabled programs like this one to become realities.

UNDERSTANDING THE
BEHAVIOR OF YOUTH AT RISK FOR FAILURE

McWhirter et al. (1993) conducted a comprehensive review of the literature on adolescents who are at risk for failure. They compared behaviors exhibited by adolescents at risk with the behaviors of adolescents who were successful in their school and community activities. Their findings indicated that adolescents who were at risk for failure differed from their successful counterparts in several areas. For example, adolescents who were at risk had difficulty establishing effective school work habits and meaningful peer relationships, lacked survival skills, did not effectively communicate with others, and engaged in self-defeating behaviors to gain attention. These adolescents did not 1) self-evaluate their behavior, 2) problem-solve to overcome barriers or mishaps, or 3) exhibit decision-making skills to determine a productive course of action for their lives. At-risk adolescents were unable to deal with stressful situations in their lives and exhibited inappropriate stress-management skills (e.g., engaged in drug use).

In comparison, adolescents who seemed to be successful in their family and community activities did well in their academic course work, communicated appropriately with others, and gained positive attention from peers and authority figures. These adolescents usually exhibited reflective skills, self-evaluating their interactions with others and then improving their behavior based on their evaluations. They were future oriented and sought help and support to reach their goals. Most important, these students managed their stress in appropriate ways, used humor whenever possible, and learned from their mistakes.

With this understanding of youth behaviors and skills, researchers have developed effective interventions to meet the needs of youth who are at risk for failure. A review of these interventions will acquaint professionals with existing behavioral program options that are available as well as encourage researchers to develop new and more innovative interventions.

Adolescent- and Family-Focused Interventions

Behavioral researchers and clinicians have addressed the problems experienced by adolescents who are at risk for failure through school- and community-based interventions. These interventions have focused primarily either on the needs of the adolescent him- or herself or emphasized the family as a change agent for the adolescent. Some of the effective programs that focused principally on the adolescent have included 1) social skills training (e.g., Hazel, Schumaker, Sherman, & Sheldon-Wildgen, 1981, 1982), 2) learning strategies (e.g., Schumaker & Sheldon, 1985), 3) self-management strategies (e.g., Watson & Tharp, 1993), and 4) group home programs (e.g., Phillips, Phillips, Fixsen, & Wolf, 1974).

Although student-focused interventions have been effective in increasing adolescents' self-management, skill acquisition, and school attendance, many experimenters and clinicians have recognized that the adolescent's family must be involved if systemic change is to take place. For instance, research has long indicated that family members significantly influence the behavior of a child (Glueck & Glueck, 1951) and that adolescents usually do not overcome behavior problems unless family interventions are used (Robin, 1966). Because family members are usually the most important individuals in a person's life, the potential of the family to make productive changes in an adolescent's life is considerable. Consequently, family-focused interventions for students at risk for failure began to emerge in the 1970s. These interventions include 1) parent–adolescent communication training (e.g., Kifer, Lewis, Green, & Phillips, 1974; Serna, Hazel, Schumaker, & Sheldon, 1986), 2) parent–adolescent problem-solving training (e.g., Foster, Prinz, & O'Leary, 1983), 3) home and school behavioral contracting programs (e.g., Schumaker, Hovel, & Sherman, 1975), and 4) home-based family programs (e.g., Kinney, Haapala, & Booth, 1994; Serna, Schumaker, Sherman, & Sheldon, 1991).

Interventions that Focus on Self-Determination

In each of the interventions just mentioned, researchers and clinicians worked to teach skills that would *remediate* existing deficits like interactional problem behaviors, academic limitations, and communication problems between family members. Since 1990, however, researchers have become concerned with preventive interventions that will empower adolescents to become more independent and take greater control over their lives. Specifically, these interventions focus on skills related to self-determination.

Most professionals agree that self-evaluation, goal setting, goal planning, and decision making are among the major skills exhibited by a self-determined person (Serna & Lau-Smith, 1995b). For the purpose of this chapter, we have adopted the following definition:

> Self-determination refers to an individual's awareness of *strengths and weaknesses*, the ability to *set goals and make choices*, to be *assertive* at appropriate times, and to interact with others *in a socially competent manner*. A self-determined person is able to make independent decisions based on his or her ability to use resources, which includes *collaborating and networking* with others. The outcome for a self-determined person is the ability to realize his or her own potential, to become a productive member of a community, and to obtain his or her goals *without infringing on the rights, responsibilities, and goals of others*. (Serna & Lau-Smith, 1995b, p. 144)

The impetus for interventions that empower and enable adolescents to overcome barriers and difficulties arises from a federal initiative through the Office of Special Education and Rehabilitative Services (see Ward, 1995; Ward, Chapter 1). This initiative has prompted researchers to focus on proactive, rather than rehabilitative, skills for youth with disabilities and youth who are at risk for failure. The challenge within this focus is to engage students and teachers in planning for the future, a future in which students gain control over their lives. This initiative stresses that if adolescents believe that they have some control over their lives, they may be motivated to work toward goals that will prove to be successful. Additionally, if students experience success from their own initiatives, they may 1) feel better about themselves, 2) strive to overcome barriers, 3) become more independent, and 4) desire to contribute to their own lives and the lives of people in their family and community.

With funding from the U.S. Department of Education, through the OSERS self-determination initiative, we developed a comprehensive program called the *Learning with PURPOSE* program (Serna & Lau-Smith, 1995a). This program was specifically developed to teach self-determination skills to adolescents who are at risk for failure in their school and community. The curriculum includes two manuals—an instructor's guide for teaching self-determination skills to students at risk for failure (Serna & Lau-Smith, 1994) and lesson plans to accomplish this objective (Serna & Lau-Smith, 1995a). The following sections describe the *Learning with PURPOSE* curriculum, outline rationales for including parents and other family members in the teaching process, and describe a parent program to accompany the teacher-directed materials.

LEARNING WITH PURPOSE CURRICULUM

An extensive three-part study was conducted involving a literature review, a social validity study, and student interviews (Serna & Lau-Smith, 1995b). Following an analysis of findings from these study components and consultation with a community-based advisory team, seven domain areas were identified as being necessary skills for adolescents to become independent and proactive adults. These domains were as follows:

- Prerequisite social skills
- Self-evaluation skills
- Self-direction skills
- Networking skills
- Collaboration skills
- Persistence and risk-taking skills
- Dealing with stress skills and guidelines

Table 1 displays the seven domain areas of the *Learning with PURPOSE* curriculum along with the final set of skills under each domain. Specific skill areas require the attainment of specific prerequisite skills. Although it is preferrable that students demonstrate mastery on these prerequisites, they can be taught in conjunction with the target skills if necessary. For example, problem solving, giving negative feedback, and accepting negative feedback are prerequisite skills for the self-evaluation domain. If a student does not possess these skills, they can be taught prior to, or in conjunction with, the skills in the self-evaluation domain. Our experience indicated that simply focusing on the prerequisite skills enhanced

Table 1. *Learning with PURPOSE* program content reflecting seven skill domain areas related to self-determination

Prerequisite Social Skills

Giving Positive Feedback (BETTER THANKS)
Giving Criticism (BETTER RESOLVE)
Accepting Criticism (BETTER ADVICE)
Resisting Peer Pressure (BETTER RESIST)
Negotiation Skills (BETTER WIN–WIN)
Following Instructions (BETTER DO IT)
Conservation Skills (BETTER TALKING)
Problem Solving (ANSWERS)

Self-Evaluation Skills

Prerequisite Skills: Giving Positive Feedback, Giving Criticism, Accepting Criticism, and Problem Solving
Evaluating Present Skills
Evaluating Skills Needed for Future Goals

Self-Direction Skills

Action Planning for Accomplishing Life Achievements *(PYRAMID Strategy)*
Goal Setting
Goal Planning
Self-Management to Achieve Goals
Evaluating Outcomes

Networking Skills

Informal Networking

Prerequisite skills: Conversation and Rules for Keeping Friends Guidelines
Seeking Information
Seeking Advice
Initiating Activities
Joining Activities
Dealing with Rejection
Keeping Friends (Guidelines)

Formal Networking

Seeking Information from a Qualified Professional
Seeking Advice from a Qualified Professional
Seeking a Mentor
Seeking Peer Support
Proposing Collaborations

(continued)

Table 1. (continued)

Collaboration Skills

Prerequisite Skills: Negotiation, Problem Solving, Action Planning, Goal Setting, and Evaluating Outcomes
Determining Team Needs (Facilitator and Team Member Skills)
Teaming to Develop Goals (Facilitator and Team Member Skills)
Planning Strategies for Goal Achievement (Facilitator and Team Member Skills)
Group Problem Solving (Facilitator and Team Member Skills)

Persistence and Risk-Taking Skills

Prerequisite Skills: Problem Solving
Persistence Through Problem Solving
Risk Taking Through Decision Making

Dealing with Stress

Recognizing Feelings
Expressing Feelings Appropriately (all prerequisite skills are required for this skill)
Stress Reduction Guidelines
Anger Management Guidelines
Time Management Guidelines
Health-Related Guidelines

Adapted from Serna and Lau-Smith (1995b).

student skills in the various domains independent of specific instruction in that particular domain area. In the following sections, each domain is discussed by providing a definition of the domain; a rationale for including the domain in the curriculum; and, when appropriate or available, a brief history of the research that supports the use of the skills in each domain area.

Prerequisite Social Skills

Over the years, researchers (e.g., Bellack & Hersen, 1979; Libet & Lewinsohn, 1973; Wolpe, 1958) have put forth a number of definitions concerning social skills. For the purposes of this chapter, however, the definition of Phillips (1978) was adopted. According to this definition, social skills represent the interpersonal communication two people exchange in a mutually satisfying manner. Thus a socially skilled person is broadly defined as someone who can

> communicate with others in a manner that fulfills one's rights, requirements, satisfactions, or obligations to a reasonable degree without damaging the other person's similar rights, requirements, satisfactions, or obligations, and shares these rights, etc., with others in a free and open exchange. (Phillips, 1978, p. 13)

From the mid-1970s to the mid-1990s, behavioral researchers have worked toward the development of effective social skills programs to address delinquent behaviors (e.g., Braukmann, Maloney, Fixsen, Phillips, & Wolf, 1974; Hazel et al., 1981, 1982), family interaction problems (e.g., Alexander & Parsons, 1973;

Kifer et al., 1974; Serna et al., 1986; Serna et al., 1991), and communication problems (e.g., Fitzpatrick & Badzinski, 1985; Paul & Thelen, 1983; Seibold, Cantril, & Meyers, 1985). In each case, these researchers sought to teach specific social skills to adolescents (e.g., problem solving, volunteering information, conversation skills, negotiation skills, giving positive feedback, giving appropriate criticism, and nonverbal skills such as eye contact). In most cases where the skills were acquired, delinquent activity dropped, relationships improved, and increased interpersonal interactions were established. It was of some concern, however, that the generalization of the skills to a new environment or with other people was not achieved or reported. Serna et al. (1991) were among the few researchers who reported extensive work with the family and in the home environment and sought to achieve a consistent and appropriate use of communication skills among adolescents and their family members. The implications for curriculum development and the resulting research findings were twofold: First, we believed that teaching certain prerequisite social skills through the *Learning with PURPOSE* curriculum was a necessary component of a self-determination program. Second, we felt that significant others (e.g., parents, siblings, teachers) must be involved in order to promote the use of the skills in other environments.

Although there are countless social skills from which to choose, only eight skills were included in the *Learning with PURPOSE* curriculum. The selection of these skills was accomplished through a review of the social skills literature and with input from a group of 15 professionals and parents. These professionals and parents were asked to rank order, from a list of 64 social skills, those most necessary to teach adolescents to become independent young adults. Eight were selected from the original list of 64. The identification of these specific skills was further supported by Ford (1985), who proposed that in order for people to achieve the goals and desires of their personal and social lives, three components must exist: 1) self-perception, or an individual's ability to recognize and set goals; 2) behavioral repertoire, or a person's ability to effectively exhibit social skills, problem-solving skills, and communication skills; and 3) self-evaluation, or a person's ability to determine whether set goals and desires are achieved. The selected prerequisite social skills (see Table 1) were adapted from the ASSET program (Hazel et al., 1981) for adolescents and were presented in the form of mnemonics or acronyms that enabled students to remember the skill steps and perform the skill with greater ease.

Self-Evaluation Skills

Self-evaluation skills are assessment strategies that allow adolescents to systematically determine whether their behavior/performance is desirable, adequate, or needs improvement. When considering an achievement-related context such as self-determined behavior, most individuals produce outcomes that are evaluated by some internally or externally imposed criterion (Guilford, 1954). According to researchers in the area of self-evaluation (e.g., Hannover, 1988; Tesser & Campbell, 1982), judgments of self are achieved by a person's ability to use *reflective* and *comparison* skills. Self-evaluation strategies that employ reflective skills involve one's ability to evaluate his or her performances based on past experiences or with others who are closely related. Positive experiences with a particular situation or capable person who is close to one can result in a high self-evaluation of skills or performances.

Similarly, self-evaluation strategies that utilize comparison skills compare one's performance with the performances of others, often referred to as social comparison (Schunk, 1984). We are able to make judgments about ourselves by reflecting on past experiences and associations and determining whether they were positive or negative. If they were positive, we tend to evaluate ourselves and our skills highly. If we compare ourselves with others (e.g., classmates), evaluations will be influenced by whom we choose for the comparison. For example, if we compare ourselves with people who are able to perform skills in a similar manner (or with less proficiency) to ourselves, we will evaluate our skills highly because our skills are just as "good" as or better than their skills. If, however, we compare our skills with those whose performance is superior to ours, that evaluation may be somewhat negative.

According to Tesser and Campbell (1982), individuals are motivated to maintain a positive self-evaluation. If students develop an awareness of the skills they are able to perform well and those that need to be learned, they may be more motivated to set goals to attain the needed skills. At the time of this writing, few studies involving self-evaluation skills and adolescents who are at risk for failure can be found. One study (Serna & Lau-Smith, in preparation), however, did teach self-evaluation skills and other evaluation skills (i.e., problem solving, giving criticism and accepting criticism) to two groups of adolescents that included high achievers, average achievers, and at-risk achievers. Using a systematic instructional procedure, all students were able to learn the skills. Additionally, the effects of learning a problem-solving skill seemed to influence the performance of self-evaluation skills even prior to instruction in such skills. Thus, teaching problem-solving skills as well as self-evaluation skills can contribute to a student's ability to solve his or her own problems and develop goals needed for future success. Parents can contribute to the acquisition of these skills by facilitating problem-solving skills in the home and reinforcing reflective strategies by reminding adolescents of how well they performed specific activities.

The self-evaluation skills selected for the *Learning with PURPOSE* curriculum teach students how to evaluate their skills using a reflective process in which students ask themselves whether they have successfully performed a desired behavior or related behaviors. If students can recall positive experiences related to their performance, they will conclude that they are able to perform the skill. On the other hand, if they do not have any experiences upon which to draw or have had a negative experience, students are to determine that they *need to learn* the skill. Students involved in the *Learning with PURPOSE* process are encouraged to self-evaluate in a proactive manner ("I need to learn or develop the skill"), not in a self-defeating manner ("I am not good at that," or "I can't do that"). They are taught to make statements that motivate them to learn the skills they have identified. Additionally, through this process they recognize other skills they may already possess.

Self-Direction Skills

One of the most obvious characteristics of adolescents who are at risk for failure is their apparent lack of control over their lives and their environment. In an attempt to operationalize the concept of control, many theorists have focused on the implementation of self-directed skills (Rodin, 1990; Watson & Tharp, 1993), particularly goal-setting behaviors and the management of tasks to meet these goals.

Rodin (1990) suggested that every life transition or event provides new challenges for perceived and actual control. Adolescents must learn about adult commitments and responsibilities before they actually leave home. By learning to set a goal, develop a plan to meet that goal, and implement steps to achieve the designated plan, adolescents may perceive that they have established control in their lives. Learning to self-direct their behaviors allows adolescents to 1) become more independent, 2) increase on-task behavior, 3) decrease disruptive or off-task behaviors, and 4) monitor and regulate their own academic and community performances—providing them with more control over their environment (Graham, Harris, & Reid, 1992).

Numerous studies have examined self-direction, self-management, and goal setting in adolescents. For example, Hogan and Prater (1993) taught adolescents with disruptive behaviors to manage their on-task and academic behaviors in the classroom. Tollefson, Tracy, Johnsen, Farmer, and Buenning (1993) developed a goal-setting program for adolescents with learning disabilities. These researchers taught adolescents to 1) set goals, 2) work toward reaching the goals, and 3) accept personal responsibility for achieving the goals. Other researchers (e.g., Barbrack & Maher, 1984; Schunk, 1985; Schunk, 1990) have used goal-setting programs to increase appropriate behaviors, academic performances, and adolescents' reports of self-efficacy. To this date, however, studies examining long-term planning to accomplish a life achievement (e.g., graduating, going to college or business school, joining the army) have not been vigorously pursued. If adolescents and their families can agree on long-term plans of achievement and work toward those plans, familial support of adolescents' goals will be accomplished. In turn, adolescents will be able to accomplish more, experience success, and achieve a sense of control over their lives.

In the *Learning with PURPOSE* curriculum five self-directed skill areas are emphasized. The first such skill area, called the PYRAMID strategy, involves students in the acquisition of a long-term strategy to accomplish a life achievement (e.g., graduating from high school, getting a job, going to college). After this long-term strategy is acquired, adolescents are taught a set of specific skills to accomplish the identified life achievement. These include 1) goal-setting skills, 2) goal-planning skills, 3) self-management skills for staying focused on accomplishing each goal, and 4) skills to evaluate outcomes to judge whether the goal(s) and the identified life achievement have been accomplished.

Networking Skills

Successful functioning in the community requires that individuals actively seek information from a variety of resources including 1) television, 2) newspapers, 3) periodicals, 4) books, and 5) people. In reality, each such resource is a network or a system by which information is collected and stored. Networking skills, therefore, are those skills in which an adolescent must engage to obtain the information he or she needs from each resource.

The skills of networking were included in the *Learning with PURPOSE* curriculum on the recommendation of a diverse group of professionals and parents. This advisory board suggested that many adolescents who are at risk for failure do not know how to obtain needed information and were at a disadvantage when compared to more successful students. Additionally, the student interview study conducted at the onset of our project indicated that high-achieving students used informal and formal networking skills to gather needed information (Serna & Lau-Smith, 1995b). Anecdotal data from these students indicated that they relied heavily on these support systems to achieve their goals.

Positive peer relationships are important during adolescence. Unfortunately, many youth who are at risk for failure in the community and at school have few friends and experience difficulty with peer interactions. This situation is intensified once an adolescent leaves the school environment and tries to succeed as an adult in the community. Several researchers in the areas of social behavior and social networking have written about the informal networks that adolescents establish and from which they benefit (Argyle, Furnham, & Graham, 1981; Argyle & Henderson, 1985), the importance of friendship and networking when seeking acceptance and inclusion in the community (O'Donnell & Tharp, 1990; Parker & Asher, 1993), and the analysis of social networks of adolescents with and without disabilities (O'Donnell, 1992). For example, O'Donnell (1992) found that adolescents with similar disabilities (e.g., learning disabilities and behavior problems) seemed to seek out the company of each other rather than the company of students without disabilities. These friendships were formed in spite of the inclusive environment that the students experienced. Findings from these studies underscored the need for investigating social networks of adolescents so they can succeed in the community.

The networking skills outlined in the *Learning with PURPOSE* curriculum were identified to teach adolescents to obtain information from other people. The goal of these activities is to enable students to use knowledgeable people as their resources. Obtaining information from these individuals requires skills in two categories: 1) informal networking skills and 2) formal networking skills. Informal networking skills are those skills that are used to obtain information and help from friends, peers, and familiar or trusted adults (e.g., parents, teachers, ministers). Formal networking skills are those used to obtain information and secure assistance from adults in professional positions who have expertise in areas needed to accomplish a goal or make a decision. Formal networking skills are used within the curriculum to ask professionals whether they would consider being mentors as well as proposing collaborations with and requesting support from these individuals and qualified peers.

Unlike research related to informal networking, the number of investigations concerning formal networking skills is sparse. Some researchers have taught adolescents to seek out job opportunities by teaching interviewing skills (Matthews, Whang, & Fawcett, 1984), social skills for the workplace (O'Reilley & Chadsey-Rusch, 1992), and skills for initiating activities with friends (e.g., Kelley & Serna, in preparation). Few researchers have tried to teach students skills like seeking information from a qualified adult (Taylor & Harris, 1995) or skills related to identifying an appropriate mentor. These are areas that should be addressed if adolescents are to succeed in the community and as young adults.

Collaboration Skills

Collaboration skills are those related to managing, organizing, and cooperating. Such skills enable adolescents to work together to determine group needs, decide on a goal, develop a plan or a strategy to meet the goal, and implement the goal. Adolescents who learn collaboration skills in the *Learning with PURPOSE* curriculum choose group facilitators, share roles and responsibilities, determine their own needs and goals, and work to achieve goals identified in a cooperative decision-making process.

Research indicates that one outcome of cooperative learning strategies is more instances of positive social relationships for students (e.g., Johnson, Johnson, & Maruyama, 1983). This finding is extremely important because adolescents at risk for school failure do not resolve differences or work together in a socially appropriate manner. Collaborative skills are crucial because they enable adolescents to organize their learning (or activity) and determine their own goals, strategies, and outcomes. These skills prepare adolescents for the work world as well as enable them to work effectively within community- and family-oriented activities.

Most research on the effects of cooperative, competitive, and individualistic learning experiences on peer relationships has outlined the benefits of students learning to cooperate and participate in group work (e.g., Johnson et al., 1983; Pepitone, 1980; Slavin, 1977). Researchers like Gresham (1981) and Strain and Shores (1983) have emphasized that social skills must be taught in conjunction with cooperative learning strategies. Putnam, Rynders, Johnson, and Johnson (1989) report that students receiving collaborative skill instruction (i.e., instruction in management, reasoning strategies, and reconceptualization skills) inter-acted more positively with one another than those who did not receive such instruction. As of this date, however, research concerning the teaching of collab-oration skills for the determination of independent learning and activity out-comes have not been reported for adolescents who are at risk for failure.

The collaboration skills introduced in the *Learning with PURPOSE* curricu-lum are applicable for students who have learned and mastered certain prerequi-site skills. These necessary prerequisite skills are negotiation, problem solving, action planning, goal setting, and outcome evaluation. Once students learn these skills they are prepared to learn the collaborative skills for both the facilitator roles and team member roles within the curriculum. Students implement their collaboration skills during group or class meetings with the purpose of achieving an academic, social, or service-related goal.

Persistence and Risk Taking

The term *persistence* may be defined as the ability to continue despite interfer-ence. Effective goal attainment and task performance behaviors require that indi-viduals utilize strategies that will allow them to overcome barriers and difficul-ties. One strategy often employed by persistent people is effective problem solving. In addition to being persistent, however, successful individuals also make choices for themselves that benefit their future. These individuals are often referred to as "risk takers." Successful risk takers are not so by chance alone. They employ strategies and obtain information that allow them to take calculated risks that, if successful, prove to be financially, socially, personnally, or academ-ically beneficial. These individuals are able to make good decisions for them-selves. Thus, persistence through problem solving and risk taking through deci-sion making are two skills presented in the *Learning with PURPOSE* curriculum.

Problem-solving and decision-making skills are cognitive skills that require adolescents to engage in a sequence of carefully weighted steps. The student must do the following:

1. Evaluate outcomes or options
2. Weigh the consequences or response costs for making a given decision
3. Make decisions based on the value or merit of outcomes and options

McWhirter et al. (1993) suggested that students who are at risk for failure exhibit inappropriate problem-solving and decision-making skills. If all adolescents were able to effectively solve problems and make appropriate decisions for them-selves, we might find that greater numbers of them would stay in school, seek help, avoid violent activities, and choose to develop skills for a productive future.

An abundance of research has been conducted in the areas of problem solv-ing and decision making since the 1950s. This research has ranged from deter-mining models of problem solving and decision making (e.g., Janis & Mann,

1977; Mayer, 1992) to teaching problem-solving and decision-making skills to all populations of all ages (e.g., Nezu & D'Zurilla, 1979; Ross, 1982).

Dealing with Stress

Stress is a negative psychological state in which an individual has determined that a situation is too threatening or too pressured to respond in a normal or adequate manner (Hoffman, Levy-Shiff, Sohlberg, & Zarizki, 1992). In most cases, stress is associated with the immediate discomfort of a negative emotional response (e.g., fear, anxiety, frustration, or anger). Eventually, if not dealt with, stress can become the source of more physically debilitating conditions, such as heart attacks, high blood pressure, and/or weight loss or gain. Adolescents experience a great amount of stress and too often respond through overt activities such as truancy, delinquency, anxiety, depression, anger, or suicide.

The *Learning with PURPOSE* curriculum includes two specific skills that help adolescents identify their stressful feelings and express these feelings to alleviate the stress or find the support needed to do so. Included in the Dealing with Stress curricular domain are guidelines that teachers can use as discussion points during classroom instruction. These guidelines focus on types of anger management techniques, stress reduction tips, time management hints, and other health-related suggestions.

Anger (a form of stress) has had serious negative consequences for many adolescents (Kennedy, 1982; Schlichter & Horan, 1981). Intense anger can be overwhelming to the adolescent and has been directly linked to a decline in academic, family, and work-related activities (Feindler & Ecton, 1986). Students who are unable to manage stress and anger often experience related consequences. For example, if an adolescent does not show up to work because of feelings of depression due to stress, or if outbursts with other employees occur due to anger, the adolescent may lose his or her job. Additionally, family and peer relationships deteriorate under these circumstances. The lack of a support network common to youth at risk for failures increases the possibility that such adolescents will feel stressed. If adolescents are to be self-determined and want to achieve certain goals in their lives, they must learn to manage their stress.

Researchers have long worked to find strategies to counteract the effects of stress and enable people to cope with symptoms and stressful situations. Crowder (1983) suggested physical exercise, proper diet, relaxation, and meditation as potential stress-relieving activities. Other activities, like building positive self-esteem, improving time management and problem-solving skills (Young, 1991), and learning strategies to control anger (Coleman, Pfeiffer, & Oakland, 1992; Feindler, 1991; Glick & Goldstein, 1987) have been suggested as ways to help adolescents cope. When taught in conjunction with effective social and communication skills, adolescents can learn to seek out support from others. In this way, stress can be diminished or managed to a point where students are productive in their personal, social, and work lives.

PURPOSE: THE TEACHING MODEL

The teaching model, PURPOSE, is the primary method used to teach self-determination skills. The name of the model, PURPOSE, provides a mnemonic strategy to assist educators in its use (see Table 2). Following this acronym, teachers would

1. *P*repare students to learn a specific skill
2. Enable students to *U*nderstand the skill components
3. Have the students *R*ehearse the skill
4. Have the student *P*erform a self-check
5. Enable students to *O*vercome performance barriers
6. *S*elect and *E*valuate his or her performance (Serna & Lau-Smith, 1995b)

We also used two other teaching models, collaborative learning and problem-based learning; these three teaching models, used in combination, will facilitate students' acquisition and use of self-determination skills.

The length of time to teach a particular self-determination skill varies across students and teachers. While pilot-testing the curriculum, 45-minute blocks of time were allotted for instruction. Typically, an inclusive class of 18 students (i.e., high achievers, typical achievers, and at-risk achievers) could learn one skill during two 45-minute periods. We suggest that the materials be used across a

Table 2. The *Learning with PURPOSE* structured teaching model (the acronym *PURPOSE* summarizes the necessary steps to teaching a self-determination skill)

Did the instructor:
Prepare the student to learn the skill?
  Define the skill?
  Discuss the different situations where the skill could be used?
  Explain the different reasons for using the skill?
Have the student **U**nderstand and learn the skill steps?
  Read and define each skill step?
  Give rationales for each skill step?
  Give examples of how each skill step should be performed?
Have the students **R**ehearse the skill correctly?
  Model the skill for the students?
  Engage the students in the memorization of the skill?
  Have the students rehearse the skill in partners?
Have the students **P**erform a self-check of the skill?
  Have each partner check to see if the skill user performed all the skill
    steps and rehearse the skill until each student reaches a 100% criteria?
  Have the students perform a self-check of their skill performance?
Help the student **O**vercome any skill performance problems?
Have the students **S**elect other situations where the skill can be used?
Have the students **E**valuate any skill performances outside the teaching setting?

4-year period in order to adequately cover the entire curriculum. Students can be taught progressively more sophisticated skills across the secondary school years. For example, students entering middle school could begin learning the prerequisite social skills, followed by self-evalaution and self-direction skills. By the time these students become juniors and seniors in high school, they will be seeking mentors in the work or school communities. They will learn skills of collaboration so that larger learning experiences can be achieved. Finally, they will begin networking and learning the skills of persistence so they are able to go into the community and identify people who can aid with their transition into adult life.

Assessment

The *Learning with PURPOSE* curriculum includes three criterion-referenced assessment tools: 1) a teacher assessment form, 2) a student assessment form, and 3) a parent assessment form. The assessment tools can be used to identify general skill deficits so that curriculum domains may be targeted. Parents, teachers, and students, can also use the assessments as a tool for communication. For instance, planning meetings can be focused on discussing what skills the parents, student, and teacher have identified as needing emphasis. The commonly agreed upon skills can be used to begin further assessment procedures and, subsequently, instruction in the relevant self-determination skills.

Teaching Manuals

The teaching model of the *Learning with PURPOSE* curriculum is structured in two manuals: 1) the instructor's manual and 2) the lesson plan manual. The following sections outline the format and contents of each manual.

Instructor's Manual   The instructor's manual acquaints teachers with each skill in the curriculum. Skills are presented in a standard format that includes four separate divisions:

1. Preparing the student to learn
2. Student skill steps
3. Self-evaluation activities
4. Outcome or product

The first division provides the instructor with a format to prepare the student for learning the identified skill. This format includes the definition of the skill ("What Is It?" section) and information pertaining to where the skill is used (the "Where Is It Used?" section). The second division (called *"Your Skill"*) includes the verbal, nonverbal, and cognitive steps students need to learn to acquire the skill. This division also includes social rules that apply to the skill and things the student should consider before using the skill.

The third division of the skill format focuses on self-evaluation skills ("Check Yourself") and the fourth division is the Outcome or Product division. This division is included to remind instructors that a student must know what he or she can or should expect to happen after performing activities applying the various skills. Too often students are required to learn information without understanding how it will be of benefit to them or what might be the outcome of using the information.

Lesson Plan Manual   After reviewing several instructional models, we adopted a systematic instructional model (see Serna & Lau-Smith, 1995b) as the primary teaching format. Our experience with this format suggests that it is an effective instructional model for use with students who are at risk for failure and with students with moderate cognitive disabilities. As previously mentioned, we developed a mnemonic strategy to assist teachers, called PURPOSE, that summarizes the teaching format and outlines the steps that should be included while teaching a self-determination skill. Each letter of the mnemonic represents a section of the lesson. For example, the first letter, P, represents the "prepare" part of the lesson. The teacher is to define the skill, discuss the different situations in which the skill could be used, and explain the reasons for using the skill. Each section of the curriculum is scripted so that teachers have an idea of how the lesson should be conducted. See Table 2 for an outline of each section of the lesson plan.

PLANNING FOR PURPOSE: THE FAMILY COMPONENT

The family component of the *Learning with PURPOSE* curriculum involves the parents and/or the entire family in helping the student meet individual goals. This component was developed to enhance the generalization of self-determination skills. The program is titled—*PLANNING FOR PURPOSE: A family program for using self-determination skills in the home*. The program title reflects the incorporation of PURPOSE (the teaching model used to teach self-determination skills) and the parent component (describing how parents can help their children to acquire self-determined behavior). The *FOR* mnemonic (or family outreach resource for teachers and students working on self-determination skills) represents the philosophy of the family program. The *PLANNING* mnemonic of the program title is explained in Table 3.

The parent–student program consists of a 12- to 15-hour program that can be divided into weekly 2-hour meetings or Saturday meetings that are held for longer periods of time. The family component involves three separate phases:

1.   Developing an Action Plan
2.   Planning to Accomplish Goals
3.   Implementing the Action Plan

These three phases are described in the following sections.

Phase I: Developing an Action Plan

During the initial meeting sessions, students and parents meet in separate rooms. The students meet in one room to learn skills related to action planning, using the

Table 3. PLANNING FOR PURPOSE: An overview of what "PLANNING" represents and what parents will learn during the parent sessions of the program

In this program, parents are taught about mentoring, supporting, and motivating their child toward self-determined behavior. The parent portion of this program represents the acronym PLANNING:

Parents
Learning about
Action planning
Negotiation
Networking
Identifying strengths and needs
Nurturing independence by giving positive feedback
Giving rationales to motivate their children

PYRAMID strategy (see Table 4) and the accompanying PYRAMID worksheet (see Figure 1). The PYRAMID worksheet is completed when all the stepping stones and tasks/goals are delineated. This gives students a visual picture of all that is needed to accomplish the desired Life Achievement. The students also learn about goal setting (see Table 5), goal planning, and self-management so that they can begin developing their action plan. Simultaneously, the parents meet and begin to explore their role in action planning by identifying the strengths the family provides as well as the strengths the youth exhibits. The parents identify those areas where the family could provide more support for the adolescent as well as the skills the youth might need to acquire to reach a specific goal. At this point in time, the parents do not necessarily know what action plans or goals their adolescents are developing. The parents are, however, 1) developing a knowledge base of their child, 2) determining how their child's interest areas and skills may match his or her goals and desired life achievements, and 3) accumulating information concerning family and community resources.

Table 4. Action planning to accomplish life achievements (the PYRAMID strategy)

P	Produce a list of five Life Achievements you wish to accomplish during the next 5–10 years.
Y	Yield reasons for why each Life Achievement is important to you.
R	Rearrange your list of desired Life Achievements according to priority, importance, or preference.
A	Analyze your top priority Life Achievement according to the stepping stones that will help you accomplish your Life Achievement. Then, determine which stepping stone needs to be accomplished first, second, and so on.
M	Make a list of tasks needed to accomplish each stepping stone you outlined in the "A" step of the PYRAMID strategy.
I	Identify for which task each stepping stone must be accomplished first and put them, in order, on your Action Planning Worksheet #3 and your PYRAMID Worksheet.
D	Develop a "goal" statement for each stepping stone task outlined to accomplish your Life Achievement.

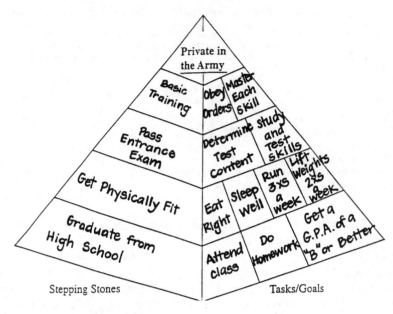

Figure 1. Example: PYRAMID Worksheet.

Because the parents do not know the specific plan their child is developing, they focus on providing positive feedback and exercising the skills they need to negotiate with their child. For example, parents are taught to praise their child for work and effort they have exhibited in developing an action plan and a goal. Parents are encouraged to negotiate when they are not in complete agreement with their son or daughter's action plan and goal, or when certain modifications of the action plan and goal must be discussed. During this initial phase, parents explore the issues of discouraging versus encouraging their child's efforts as they are learning skills for negotiating with their child. The focus when teaching these skills is to get parents to work *with* their child toward reaching mutual agreement concerning a chosen desired goal.

After approximately 4–6 hours of separate work, the parents and adolescents meet together to discuss the adolescent's action plan and related goals. The adolescent describes his or her action plan and the desired goal chosen to accomplish the action plan. In turn, the parents communicate ways in which they or other family members can support the student in actualizing the plan. Students and parents discuss the action plan, engage in negotiation when necessary, and come to agreement regarding the action plan and the goal.

Phase II: Planning to Accomplish Goals in the Action Plan

Once adolescents and parents come to a mutual agreement on the action plan and the goal to be accomplished as part of the action plan, they meet separately again.

Table 5. Goal-setting skill steps with student goal examples

Skill steps	Example
1. Identify the task(s) that needs to be accomplished. *Use your Goal Setting Worksheet.*	I need to get good grades.
2. Change each task into a goal statement by using an "I will . . ." statement. *Use your Goal Setting Worksheet.*	I will get good grades.
3. Determine the category of your goal statement:	
Ongoing/Daily Goals: Goals that must be done every day or with regularity in order to get complete benefits (e.g., eating healthy food).	I will attend school every day, without being late.
Short-Term Goals: Goals that can be completed within a few weeks or 1–3 months (e.g., getting certain tasks completed before leaving on a trip).	I will earn enough money to buy a new outfit for the school dance.
Long-Term Goals: Goals that can be completed within a few months (e.g., getting an "A" in your fall semester science class). *Use your Goal Setting Worksheet.*	I will complete my project for the science fair that is being held 5 months from now.
4. Clarify your goal statement by answering the following questions:	
a. What task do I want to accomplish?	What: Get an "A"
b. With whom will I accomplish this task?	With whom: By myself
c. Where will I accomplish this task?	Where: In my science class
d. When will the task be accomplished/completed? *Use your Clarifying Your Goal Statement Worksheet.*	When: By the end of the semester
5. Use the information in Step 4 to develop a clarified goal statement. *Use your Clarifying Your Goal Statement Worksheet.*	I will get an "A" in my science class by the end of the fall semester.

During this phase, the adolescents work toward the development of a plan to accomplish the goal in the action plan (utilizing their goal-planning and self-monitoring skills). They identify tasks that must be accomplished, how they will accomplish them, and a reward system for themselves. If their reward system involves other people, a behavioral contract is written so that they can commit to their plan with another person.

At the same time, the parents work on their contribution toward or participation in the accomplishment of the action plan. Guided by a parent group leader, they begin to gain knowledge about the self-management skills the adolescents are learning and developing. The parents then identify how family strengths can be utilized to ensure that the adolescent is able to accomplish each goal in the action plan. For example, if the adolescent wants a part-time job after school, parents might agree to drive their child to different work sites and help him or her fill out applications (if necessary). Finally, parents explore how to provide effective rationales for activities. This skill is a motivational skill and focused on with parents for the following reasons: 1) adolescents might experience failure and may not want to proceed with the goal attainment, 2) parents are key individuals for motivating their child to continue working toward his or her goal, and 3) parents are able to outline the positive consequences for continuing to work on the goal and the negative consequences for quitting. Adolescents often respond to such clear and realistic rationales. They do not always consider all the positive and negative consequences of their actions and can be motivated to continue toward their goal once these consequences are clear. Ultimately, however, it is the student's choice to continue working toward or to drop a goal.

The Phase II activities are accomplished after another period of 5–6 hours. After the adolescents have developed their plans and parents have been prepared to support these plans, the two groups meet together to discuss their work. Each adolescent presents his or her plan for accomplishing the goal and any self-monitoring procedures they developed. After this presentation, parents discuss how they will help the adolescent meet his or her goal. Self-monitoring procedures that include behavioral contracts are discussed at this time, modifications and contract negotiations are finalized, and the commitment to the contract is indicated by the signing of the contract document.

Phase III: Implementing the Action Plan to Accomplish the First Goal

The final stage of the family program (Phase III) is the implementation of the action plan to accomplish the first goal. This phase requires the family members to begin the tasks outlined for them to meet the goal. Each week, the members of the family training team (i.e., the parent group leader and the youth group leader) make individual telephone calls to each parent and adolescent. The parents and adolescents are asked about the weekly progress made toward the designated goal. If the progress is reported to be satisfactory, the group leader praises the family members for the work that was accomplished. If the parent and/or adolescent indicate that problems occurred or that tasks were not accomplished, the group leader helps the parent or adolescent problem-solve to overcome the barrier toward accomplishing the task or goal. The monitoring of the family progress continues for 6 weeks after the implementation of the action plan. If the family members achieve their goal during that time period, the group leaders always ask the family members if they wish to meet on their own to decide on the next goal and plan on the implementation of the tasks to accomplish the next goal. The family members may choose to work alone or with a group leader at this point. Their independence from the group leaders, however, is encouraged. When family members seem to be working toward goals on their own, they leave the program.

SUMMARY

The *Learning with PURPOSE* curriculum is a self-determination curriculum designed to teach skills to adolescents who are at risk for community and academic failure. The curriculum was piloted in inclusive settings with students who were high achievers, typical achievers, and at-risk achievers. Other pilot studies included teaching skills to young adults who have been diagnosed with mild and moderate cognitive disabilities. In each case, participants were able to learn the skills to a 100% accuracy. Informal monitoring of the generalization of the skills to the community or the classroom suggest that students are able to use the skills successfully. More formal studies on the generalization of the skills suggest that participants can use and teach the learned skills to their peers.

The *PLANNING FOR PURPOSE* program is a complementary component of the *Learning with PURPOSE* curriculum and involves teaching action planning procedures to the adolescents and their parents. The family program was designed to promote the generalization of self-determination skills among the adolescents as well as engage families to work together to achieve a mutually identified life objective. After this agreement is made, family members work together to decide on the goals needed to accomplish the life achievement. They delineate tasks and plan how each task will be accomplished. Finally, they develop a self-management or monitoring procedure to track their progress over time.

Collectively, focusing on student skill acquisition and involving families expands upon traditional intervention procedures and provides personal, family, and school supports for attaining future goals. Furthermore, the goal of these joint programs is to achieve a change in behavior through the use of proactive and preventive procedures. We believe that teaching adolescents and families to work and accomplish goals together may eventually outweigh the cost of and reduce the need for rehabilitative and crisis-related services. The ultimate desired outcome is appropriate independent behavior and productive self-determined young adults.

REFERENCES

Alexander, J.F., & Parsons, B.V. (1973). Short-term behavioral intervention with delinquent families: Impact on families process and recidivism. *Journal of Abnormal Psychology, 81*, 219–225.

Argyle, M., Furnham, A., & Graham, J.A. (1981). *Social situations.* Cambridge, England: Cambridge University Press.

Argyle, M., & Henderson, M. (1985). *The anatomy of friendships.* London: Heinemann.

Barbrack, C.R., & Maher, C.A. (1984). Effects of involving conduct problem adolescents in the setting of counseling goals. *Child and Family Behavior Therapy, 6*(2), 33–43.

Bellack, A.S., & Hersen, M. (1979). *Research and practice in social skills.* New York: Plenum.

Braukmann, C.J., Maloney, D.M., Fixsen, D.L., Phillips, E.L., & Wolf, M.M. (1974). Analysis of a selection interview training package. *Criminal Justice and Behavior, 1*, 30–42.

Coleman, M., Pfeiffer, S., & Oakland, T. (1992). Aggression replacement training with behaviorally disordered adolescents. *Behavioral Disorders, 18*(1), 54–66.

Crowder, W.W. (1983). Teaching about stress. *Clearing House, 57*(1), 36–38.

Dryfoos, J.G. (1990). *Adolescents at risk: Prevalence and prevention.* New York: Oxford University Press.

Feindler, E. (1991). Anger control for children and adolescents. In P.C. Kendall (Ed.), *Child and adolescent therapy: Cognitive-behavioral procedures* (pp. 206–222). New York: Guilford Press.

Feindler, E.L., & Ecton, R.B. (1986). *Adolescent anger control: Cognitive-behavioral techniques.* Elmsford, NY: Pergamon.

Fitzpatrick, M.A., & Badzinski, D.M. (1985). All in the family: Interpersonal communication in kin relationships. In M.L. Knapp & G.R. Miller (Eds.), *Handbook of interpersonal communication* (pp. 687–736). Beverly Hills, CA: Sage Publications.

Ford, M.E. (1985). The concept of competence: Themes and variations. In H.A. Marlow & R.B. Weinberg (Eds.), *Competence development: Theory and practice in special populations* (pp. 3–38). Springfield, IL: Charles C Thomas.

Foster, S.L., Prinz, R.J., & O'Leary, K.D. (1983). Impact of problem-solving communication training and generalization procedures on family conflict. *Child and Family Behavior Therapy, 5*, 1–23.

Glick, B., & Goldstein, A.P. (1987). Aggression replacement training. *Journal of Counseling and Development, 65*, 356–362.

Glueck, S., & Glueck, E. (1951). *Unraveling juvenile delinquency.* Cambridge, MA: Harvard University Press.

Graham, S., Harris, K.R., & Reid, R. (1992). Developing self-regulated learners. *Focus on Exceptional Children, 24*(6), 1–16.

Gresham, F.M. (1981). Social skills training with handicapped children: A review. *Review of Educational Research, 51*(1), 1–16.

Guilford, J.P. (1954). *Psychometric methods* (2nd ed.). New York: McGraw-Hill.

Hannover, B. (1988). *Evaluation of performance: A judgmental approach.* New York: Springer-Verlag.

Hazel, J.A., Schumaker, J.B., Sherman, J.A., & Sheldon-Wildgen, J.B. (1981). *ASSET: A social skills program for adolescents.* Champaign, IL: Research Press.

Hazel, J.S., Schumaker, J.B., Sherman, J.A., & Sheldon-Wildgen, J.B. (1982). Group training for social skills: A program for court adjudicated youths. *Criminal Justice and Behavior, 9*, 35–53.

Hoffman, M.A., Levy-Shiff, R., Sohlberg, S.C., & Zarizki, J. (1992). The impact of stress and coping: Developmental changes in the transition to adolescence. *Journal of Youth and Adolescence, 21*, 451–470.

Hogan, S., & Prater, M.A. (1993). The effects of peer tutoring and self management training on on-task, academic, and disruptive behaviors. *Behavior Disorders, 18*(2), 118–128.

Janis, I.L., & Mann, L. (1977). *Decision making: A psychological analysis of conflict, choice, and commitment.* New York: Free Press.

Johnson, D.W., Johnson, R.T., & Maruyama, M.G. (1983). Interdependence and interpersonal attraction among heterogeneous individuals: A theoretical formulation and a meta-analysis of the research. *Review of Education Research, 3*(1), 5–54.

Kelley, S.P., & Serna, L.A. (1995). *Preparing elementary students for the regular education setting: A study of the generalization of social skills across environments.* Manuscript in preparation.

Kennedy, R.E. (1982). Cognitive-behavioral approaches to the modification of aggressive behavior in children. *School Psychology Review, 11*(1), 47–55.

Kifer, R.E., Lewis, M.A., Green, D.R., & Phillips, E.L. (1974). Training predelinquent youths and their parents to negotiate conflict situations. *Journal of Applied Behavior Analysis, 7*, 357–364.

Kinney, J., Haapala, D., & Booth, C. (1994). *Keeping families together: The homebuilders model.* Chicago: Aldine.

Libet, J.M., & Lewinsohn, P.M. (1973). Concept of social skills with special reference to the behavior of the depressed person. *Journal of Consulting and Clinical Psychology, 40*, 304–312.

Matthews, R.M., Whang, P.L., & Fawcett, S.B. (1984). *Learning job-finding skills.* Lawrence: University of Kansas.

Mayer, R.E. (1992). *Thinking, problem solving, cognition* (2nd ed.). San Francisco: W.H. Freeman.

McWhirter, J.J., McWhirter, B.T., McWhirter, A.M., & McWhirter, E.H. (1993). *At-risk youth: A comprehensive response.* Pacific Grove, CA: Brooks/Cole.

The National Commission on Excellence in Education. (1983). *A nation at risk: The imperative for educational reform.* Washington, DC: U.S. Government Printing Office.

Nezu, A., & D'Zurrilla, T.J. (1979). An experimental evaluation on the decision-making process in social problem solving. *Cognitive Therapy and Research, 3*(3), 269–277.

O'Donnell, C.R. (1992). The interplay of theory and practice in delinquency prevention: From behavior modification to activity setting. In J. McCord & R. Tromblay (Eds.), *Preventing antisocial behavior: Interventions from birth through adolescence* (pp. 209–232). New York: Guildford Press.

O'Donnell, C.R., & Tharp, R.G. (1990). Community intervention guided by theoretical development. In A.S. Bellack, M. Hersen, & A.E. Kazdin (Eds.), *International handbook of behavior modification and therapy*, (2nd ed., pp. 126–151), New York: Plenum.

O'Reilley, M.F., & Chadsey-Rusch, J. (1992). Teaching a social skills problem-solving approach to workers with mental retardation: An analysis of generalization. *Education and Training in Mental Retardation, 27*, 324–334.

Parker, J.G., & Asher, S.R. (1993). Friendship and friendship quality in middle childhood: Links with peer group acceptance and feelings of loneliness and social dissatisfaction. *Developmental Psychology, 29*(4), 611–621.

Paul, S.C., & Thelen, M.H. (1983). The use of strategies and messages to alter aggressive interactions. *Aggressive Behavior, 9*, 183–193.

Pepitone, E.A. (1980). *Children in cooperation and competition.* Lexington, MA: Lexington Books.

Phillips, E.L. (1978). *The social skills basis of psychopathology: Alternative to abnormal psychology and psychiatry.* New York: Grune & Stratton.

Phillips, E.L., Phillips, E.A., Fixsen, D.L., & Wolf, M.M. (1974). *The teaching-family handbook.* Lawrence: University of Kansas.

Putnam, J.W., Rynders, J.E., Johnson, R.T., & Johnson, D.W. (1989). Collaborative skill instruction for promoting positive interactions between mentally handicapped and non-handicapped children, *Exceptional Children, 55*, 550–557.

Robin, L.N. (1966). *Deviant children grow up: A sociological and psychiatric study of sociopathic personality.* Baltimore: Williams & Wilkins.

Rodin, J. (1990). Control by any other name: Definitions, concepts, and processes. In J. Rodin, C. Schooler, & K.W. Schaie (Eds.), *Self-directedness: Cause and effects throughout the life course* (pp. 1–18). Hillsdale, NJ: Lawrence Erlbaum Associates.

Ross, J.A. (1982). *Adolescent decision making: Final R&D report* (Project No. 80-4033). Peterborough, Canada: Ontario Institute for Studies in Education.

Schlichter, K.J., & Horan, J.J. (1981). Effects of stress inoculation on the anger and aggression management skills of institutionalized juvenile delinquents. *Cognitive Therapy and Research, 5*(4), 359–365.

Schorr, L.B. (1988). *Within our reach: Breaking the cycle of disadvantage.* New York: Doubleday.

Schumaker, J.B., Hovel, M.F., & Sherman, J.A. (1975). *The progress program: A teaming technique.* Lawrence, KS: EXCELLENTerprises.

Schumaker, J.B., & Sheldon, J.B. (1985). *The sentence writing strategy: Instructor's manual.* Lawrence: University of Kansas.

Schunk, D.H. (1984, April). *Social comparison as a vicarious source of self-efficacy information.* Paper presented at the American Educational Research Association, New Orleans.

Schunk, D.H. (1985). Participation in goal setting: Effects of self-efficacy and skills of learning-disabled children. *Journal of Special Education, 19*, 307–317.

Schunk, D.H. (1990). Goal setting and self-efficacy during self-regulated learning. *Educational Psychologist, 25*(1), 71–86.

Seibold, D.R., Cantril, J.G., & Meyers, R.A. (1985). Communication and interpersonal influences. In M.L. Knapp & G.R. Miller (Eds.), *Handbook of interpersonal communication* (pp. 551–614). Beverly Hills, CA: Sage Publications.

Serna, L.A., Hazel, J.S., Schumaker, J.B., & Sheldon, J.B. (1986). Teaching reciprocal social skills to parents and their delinquent adolescents. *Journal of Clinical Child Psychology, 15*(1), 64–77.

Serna, L.A., & Lau-Smith, J.A. (1995). *Teaching self-evaluation skills for students who are at risk for school failure.* Manuscript in preparation.

Serna, L.A., & Lau-Smith, J.A. (1994). *Learning with PURPOSE: An instructor's manual for teaching self-determination skills to students who are at risk for failure* (field-test version). Unpublished curriculum materials.

Serna, L.A., & Lau-Smith, J.A. (1995a). *Learning with PURPOSE: Lesson plans for teaching self-determination skills to students who are at risk for failure* (field-test version). Unpublished curriculum materials.

Serna, L.A., & Lau-Smith, J.A. (1995b). Learning with PURPOSE: Self-determination skills for students who are at risk for school and community failure. *Intervention in School and Clinic, 30*, 142–146.

Serna, L.A., Schumaker, J.B., Sherman, J.A., & Sheldon, J.B. (1991). In-home generalization of social interactions in families of adolescents with behavior problems. *Journal of Applied Behavior Analysis, 24*, 733–746.

Slavin, R.E. (1977). Classroom reward structure: An analytic and practical review. *Review of Educational Research, 47*(4), 633–650.

Strain, P.S., & Shores, R.E. (1983). Reply to "Misguided Mainstreaming." *Exceptional Children, 50*, 271–273.

Taylor, B.A., & Harris, S.L. (1995). Teaching children with autism to seek information: Acquisition of novel information and generalization or responding. *Journal of Applied Behavior Analysis, 28*, 3–14.

Tesser, A., & Campbell, J. (1982). Self-evaluation maintenance and the perception of friends and strangers. *Journal of Personality, 50*, 261–279.

Tollefson, N., Tracy, D.B., Johnsen, E.P., Farmer, M., & Buenning, M. (1993). Goal setting and personal responsibility training for learning disabled adolescents. *Psychology in the Schools, 21*, 224–233.

Ward, M. (1995). OSERS effort to facilitate self-determination. *Intervention in School and Clinic, 30*, 132.

Watson, D.L., & Tharp, R.G. (1993). *Self-directed behavior: Self-modification for personal adjustment*. Pacific Grove, CA: Brooks/Cole.

Wolpe, J. (1958). *Psychotherapy by reciprocal inhibition*. Stanford, CA: Stanford University Press.

Young, B.B. (1991). *A stress management guide for young people*. Rolling Hills Estates, CA: B.L. Winch and Associates/Jalmar Press.

Chapter 15

PROMOTING SELF-DETERMINATION FOR INDIVIDUALS WITH SEVERE DISABILITIES IN EMPLOYMENT SERVICES

Michael D. West

THE IMPORTANCE OF choice and self-determination for youth and adults with disabilities has been recognized by educational programs, adult services providers, advocacy groups, and individuals with disabilities themselves (Kennedy & Killius, 1986; Martin, Marshall, & Maxson, 1993; Nirje, 1972; Perske, 1989; Williams, 1989). With the Rehabilitation Act Amendments of 1992, PL 102-569, self-determination has been transformed from a "good idea" to a legislative mandate for federal/state vocational rehabilitation (VR) programs. The U.S. Congress, in the "Findings and Purposes" section of the act, asserted that disability "does not diminish the right of individuals to enjoy self-determination or make choices" and mandated that all programs and activities funded under the Act "shall be consistent with the principles of individual dignity, personal responsibility, self-determination, and pursuit of meaningful careers based on informed choice" (29 U.S.C. 701 Sec. 2).

Public Law 102-569, like the Americans with Disabilities Act (ADA) of 1990, PL 101-336, signaled a new era for people with disabilities and the programs and support services available to them—an era of inclusion, equal protection, accommodation, consumerism, and empowerment. This chapter first describes key changes mandated by the amendments to the Rehabilitation Act of 1973, PL 93-112, that promote choice and self-determination for VR consumers and ways in which choice and self-determination can be enhanced or abrogated for VR consumers. Barriers within the rehabilitation service system are then reviewed. Finally, recommendations that enhance opportunities to promote self-determination in VR programs and services are proposed.

SELF-DETERMINATION AND PEOPLE WITH DISABILITIES

The essence of self-determination is flexibility in managing the interactions between oneself and one's environments (Deci & Ryan, 1985). In short, self-determined people make *choices* in their lives and have *control* over decision-making processes and outcomes (Deci & Ryan, 1985; Lovett, 1991; Nosek & Fuhrer, 1992; Price, 1990). Self-determination is evident when individuals are free to exercise control and experience the outcomes of their choices free from coercion, obligation, or artificial constraints. Stated differently, self-determination refers to "the abilities and attitudes required for one to act as the primary causal agent in one's life and to make choices regarding one's actions free from undue external influences or interference" (Wehmeyer, 1992, p. 305).

As children and adolescents are given greater responsibilities and freedom by their parents and teachers, they develop the skills and capacities necessary to act in a self-determined manner (e.g., Doll, Sands, Wehmeyer, & Palmer, Chapter 5). However, research with children and adults with disabilities indicates that they have fewer opportunities than their peers without disabilities to participate in decision-making activities and learn from positive and negative consequences and therefore have limited opportunities to acquire and develop these skills and capacities (Bannerman, Sheldon, Sherman, & Harchik, 1990; Guess & Siegel-Causey, 1985; Kishi, Teelucksingh, Zollers, Park-Lee, & Meyer, 1988; White et al., 1982). For example, Houghton, Bronicki, and Guess (1987) analyzed interactions of special education staff and students in instructional and noninstructional settings and found that staff generally failed to respond to students' indications of choice and preference.

Bannerman et al. (1990) suggested that limitations on choice in educational or habilitative programs may be due to multiple reasons. These included impositions on staff, regulatory and accountability pressures, and fear that the choices and decisions made by people with disabilities will hinder or conflict with habilitative efforts. For example, an individual working in a vocational program may choose to engage in nonproductive activities rather than vocational training or work tasks that are mandated by the program's funding agencies or its subcontractual obligations, or may choose to engage in aberrant or disruptive behavior. In such cases, professionals may feel that limiting personal freedom is necessary and in the client's best interests. The terms *learned helplessness* and *programmed dependence* have often been used to describe an all-too-frequent consequence of the absence of choice and control: Individuals with disabilities fail to develop a sense of self-direction and self-efficacy. Failure to promote individuality and autonomy for people with disabilities begins in early childhood and can continue through employment and other adult services (Dattilo & Rusch, 1985; Guess, Benson, & Siegel-Causey, 1985; Ward, 1993; West & Parent, 1992).

In recent years, choice making and self-directed behavior have been recognized as an expression of dignity and autonomy for people with disabilities and have become a focus of educational and habilitative programs (Guess et al., 1985; Shevin & Klein, 1984). A growing number of parents, professionals, and individuals with disabilities themselves are convinced that all people can and should be taught to express preferences, make choices, and exert greater control over the decisions that affect their lives. Research in education and rehabilitation has demonstrated methods for enabling these behaviors for people with even the most severe and multiple disabilities (Reid & Parsons, 1990, 1991; Wacker, Wiggins, Fowler, & Berg, 1988).

Benefits of Self-Determination

Since the mid-1970s, there have been a number of research studies conducted to examine the effects of enhanced choice and control, for people both with and without disabilities. The weight of evidence from this research suggests that individuals tend to participate more and receive greater benefit from activities in which they can experience some choice or control. Students with disabilities appear to perform better when they choose instructional tasks, methods, or materials (Amabile & Gitomer, 1984). For example, Dattilo and Rusch (1985) found that students with disabilities engaged in a leisure activity more often when given the choice of participation than when the choice was eliminated. Children with autism have been found to exhibit fewer antisocial or challenging behaviors when they are allowed choices from among activities (Dyer, Dunlap, & Winterling, 1990; Koegel, Dyer, & Bell, 1987), as have adults with cognitive disabilities (Ip, Szymanski, Johnston-Rodriguez, & Karls, 1994). For example, Parsons, Reid, and Baumgartner (1990) studied clients of a sheltered workshop and found that attendance improved when participants were allowed to choose their own jobs, rather than being assigned to a particular job by the workshop staff.

In addition to choice, environmental control has also been the subject of research for children with and without disabilities. Buyer, Berkson, Winnega, and Morton (1987) attempted to modify stereotypic rocking of children with autism through the introduction of rocking chairs and found that the children used the rocking chairs more often when they could control the rocking themselves. Peck (1985) was able to increase social and communicative interactions of students with autism and mental retardation by increasing their levels of control over learning situations. Taylor, Adelman, Nelson, Smith, and Phares (1989) were able to increase the levels of perceived control in school situations of students with learning disabilities through involvement in decisions regarding class rules, learning activities, and changes in routines, and through opportunities to express dissatisfaction with their educational programs.

In essence, then, the literature suggests that when individuals have opportunities for choice in learning and social interactions, they are more likely to participate and to perform better. These findings are applicable and important to the provision of employment services for individuals with disabilities.

SELF-DETERMINATION AND
THE 1992 AMENDMENTS TO THE REHABILITATION ACT

The 1992 Amendments (PL 102-569) to the Rehabilitation Act of 1973, PL 93-112, mandated profound changes in the relationship between VR service providers and consumers of VR services. To improve the likelihood that consumers will secure satisfying and successful jobs and careers, the Act shifts the role of arbiter of appropriate goals and services from staff of the VR agency or service providers to the consumer of services. Public Law 102-569 contains major statutory changes related to 1) the determination of eligibility for VR-funded services and 2) the degree of choice and control that the VR consumer is empowered to exert over the service delivery process.

Eligibility Determination

The first change in the statutory language affected the determination of eligibility for services funded through the Rehabilitation Act. Prior to the 1992 Amendments, the VR service system required prospective clients to undergo assessments for rehabilitation potential, employability, and feasibility for services. In many VR systems, this process prevented individuals with very severe disabilities from receiving services because VR counselors did not have a reasonable expectation that services would result in employment. Many individuals with severe disabilities who were accepted as VR clients found that their vocational service options were limited to sheltered employment or other segregated day services.

With protection from discrimination and mandates for reasonable accommodation under the ADA, along with the increased availability of assistive technology, job coaching, and personal assistance in the workplace, "severe disability" is no longer analogous with limited employment potential. Title I of the Rehabilitation Act states unequivocally that all individuals, regardless of the severity of their disabilities, are presumed to be capable of gainful employment in integrated settings, given the necessary services and supports (Sec. 121), and therefore are presumed to be eligible for VR services. Consequently, language regarding "rehabilitation potential" has been stricken from the Act in favor of a two-part process: 1) assessment of eligibility for services based on disability status and 2) assessment of rehabilitation needs. The VR agency has the burden of providing clear and unequivocal evidence that an individual *cannot* become employed in order to make a determination of noneligibility for VR services (Sec. 123[c][4][A]). For individuals with severe disabilities, these changes will improve access to VR-sponsored services and supports that enable them to pursue career goals of their own choosing.

1992 "Choice Amendments" to the Rehabilitation Act

Once deemed eligible for services, the Act contains language to empower the VR consumer to become a "full partner" in the rehabilitation process. The individualized written rehabilitation plan (IWRP), which defines employment goals and services required to meet them, must be developed jointly by the consumer and his or her VR counselor, focusing on the consumer's career goals and specific job preferences. The IWRP must be developed using the native language or mode of communication of the consumer, and the consumer must be provided a copy. The consumer also documents in the IWRP how he or she was informed about options and participated in choice making.

In developing the IWRP, the consumer has the opportunity to choose from among an array of service options for pursuing IWRP goals, service providers of a preferred option, and service methods (Sec. 105). For example, an individual may feel that a method of training or support used by his or her provider agency may be too intrusive or stigmatizing and opt for more natural methods (see West & Parent, 1992). This focus on the consumer, allowing individuals with disabilities to elect to change service providers or methods if they do not feel that their needs are being adequately or promptly addressed, will, it is hoped, serve as a quality assurance mechanism.

Perhaps most significantly, the consumer is allowed to directly secure his or her own services, including using family members, friends, or co-workers as support providers, as long as their functions are consistent with the IWRP. This change allows consumers to go outside of the established service delivery system if they feel it is in their best interests or increases their comfort levels, as well as to exercise greater levels of choice and independence in the VR process (Hanley-Maxwell & Millington, 1992). As an example, an individual who has a documented need for personal assistance on the job may elect to use a family member who provides assistance at home (and perhaps even pay him or her with VR funds) rather than utilizing professional personal assistants or soliciting co-workers to provide these functions.

Service Planning and Improvements

Consumer involvement in VR policy and system change is also a key component of the 1992 Rehabilitation Act Amendments. VR agencies are required to establish state rehabilitation advisory councils, with majority membership of people with disabilities who are not employed by the VR agency. This council is responsible for, among other things, assessing consumer satisfaction with services and increasing consumer input in strategic planning for expanding and improving services (Sec. 120).

Perhaps the issue of self-determination for VR consumers, particularly people with severe disabilities, is most critical in decisions regarding long-term employment service options, specifically between facility-based sheltered work or other segregated services and community-based competitive employment with necessary supports. The next section explores consumer choice from among segregated and integrated options.

CONSUMER SELF-DETERMINATION
IN THE DUAL SYSTEM OF SERVICES

Individuals with severe disabilities who are in need of long-term employment support face a dual system of vocational services in which segregated, facility-based employment services and integrated, community-based services compete for resources and participants (Mank, 1994; McGaughey, Kiernan, McNally, Gilmore, & Keith, 1994). This dual system survives, even flourishes, despite 1) public policy initiatives, such as the Rehabilitation Act and the ADA, which are designed to encourage integrated employment for all individuals with disabilities and 2) growing acceptance of people with disabilities in the workforce and other community environments (Rees, Spreen, & Harnadek, 1991).

For over a quarter century, sheltered workshops, work activity centers, and other segregated employment options have been under fire. In one of the earliest attacks, Gersuny and Lefton (1970) equated sheltered employment with servitude, citing such practices as intruding unnecessarily into clients' personal lives, controlling the services and alternatives made available to them, and subverting the interests of clients to those of contracting businesses. As critics of segregated facilities have pointed out over the years (e.g., Garner, Lacy, & Creasy, 1972; Gersuny & Lefton, 1970; Mallas, 1976; Schuster, 1990) many of the financial and ethical dilemmas facing segregated facilities are of their own doing because they have undertaken two incompatible goals: 1) providing employment services to individuals with disabilities to optimize their employment potential and 2) operating a business enterprise. Critics contend that the conflict between service to individuals with disabilities and economic survival of the operation results in low wages; lack of movement to less restrictive settings; disregard of client preferences and goals; and low expectations of client employability on the part of workshop staff, local business, and the community at large.

With the advent of supported employment (i.e., time-limited employment services funded by the VR agency with ongoing support services typically funded by state mental health, mental retardation, or developmental disability service systems), integrated employment has become a viable option for any individual with a disability, regardless of the severity of the person's impairment or his or her limitations. In fact, the 1992 Rehabilitation Act Amendments specify that this option is reserved for those with the "most severe disability." This and other specialized services (e.g., assistive technology, personal assistance, school-to-work transition), as well as workplace mandates and protection under the ADA (e.g., reasonable accommodation, freedom from discrimination), would seemingly make segregated employment obsolete, a vestige of an era when isolation and segregation were more acceptable to families, educational and rehabilitation professionals, and society.

Yet even today *segregated employment services remain the primary service options for most individuals receiving long-term employment services*, with perhaps as many as 90% of extended employment service consumers, primarily composed of individuals with significant mental retardation or other severe developmental disabilities, in segregated options (Davis, 1994; McGaughey et al., 1994; Temple University Developmental Disabilities Center, 1990). This situation is disheartening and ironic in that these are the individuals for whom the efficacy, need, and benefits of supported employment were first demonstrated in the 1980s.

Given the current circumstances and the increased emphasis on self-determination, this section proposes the following:

1. Based on research on the financial and social impacts of movement from segregated to integrated employment, competitive employment is unquestionably a more appropriate and desirable option for all individuals with disabilities.
2. Research notwithstanding, the deciding factor in planning and delivering extended employment services should be the choices and goals of the individual.
3. Genuine consumer choice is abrogated, not enhanced, by the current service system that discourages consumers and their families from pursuing community-based employment as well as service providers from offering the option to everyone who might potentially select it.

Segregated versus Supported Employment

After years of research, the evidence is overwhelming that individuals with disabilities who need relatively permanent employment services fare better in supported employment than in sheltered work (Noble & Conley, 1987). This research includes examinations of 1) group differences between people employed in sheltered workshops versus individuals working in supported employment and 2) the effects of movement from sheltered to supported employment on individuals' earnings, satisfaction, and quality of life.

Prominent within the first area of research was the *National Employment Survey for Adults with Developmental Disabilities* (Kiernan, McGaughey, & Schalock, 1986), which examined segregated and integrated services and outcomes for more than 85,000 individuals served by 1,119 agencies. Findings from this seminal study showed that average quarterly earnings of sheltered workshop clients were $402.75, compared to $786.01 for individuals in supported employment. People working in sheltered workshops had an average hourly wage of $1.31, and those in supported employment, $2.59.

Group comparisons have been made on nonmonetary variables as well. For example, Sinnott-Oswald, Gliner, and Spencer (1991) surveyed 10 individuals within each of three matched cohort groups—people with disabilities in sheltered employment, people with disabilities in supported employment, and a control group of individuals without disabilities. Results indicated that supported employment participation was positively related to a number of quality of life variables, including access to and involvement in leisure activities, self-esteem, mobility, and job skill perceptions.

One limitation of these descriptive studies is that there may be functional differences between individuals participating in sheltered and supported employment that influence not only placement decisions, but productivity, earnings, and quality of life as well. Thus, longitudinal analysis of people moving from sheltered to supported employment may be a more valid method of assessing program impacts. Early studies of movement from sheltered to supported employment in the states of Virginia (Hill & Wehman, 1983), Illinois (Lagomarcino, 1986), and Vermont (Vogelsberg, Ashe, & Williams, 1985) established that supported employment services benefited the consumer of services and taxpayers who paid for services. More recent evidence continues to affirm the monetary and nonmonetary benefits of movement from sheltered to supported employment. For example, Kregel, Wehman, and Banks (1989) followed 1,550 individuals, most of whom resided in Virginia, who moved from alternative services to supported employment. They found that weekly work hours, hourly salaries, and monthly earnings increased dramatically, from 280% to 576% across disability groups. Individuals with severe mental retardation were among those who benefited the most. Similar monetary gains were reported for supported employment programs in Michigan (Thompson, Powers, & Houchard, 1992) and Connecticut (Helms, Moore, & McSewyn, 1991).

Movement from sheltered to supported employment has been shown to bring nonmonetary rewards as well (Inge, Banks, Wehman, Hill, & Shafer, 1988). For example, Helms et al. (1991) found that movement resulted in significant increases in community presence and participation. Finally, Test, Hinson, Solow, and Keul (1993) surveyed 34 supported employment participants and found satisfaction with employment, co-worker and supervisor relations, supported employment services, and job coaches. Of the 28 who had previously received sheltered employment services, 26 (92.8%) indicated that they would rather have their present job than return to the sheltered workshop.

But what about the two participants in the Test et al. (1993) study who indicated that they would prefer to return to the sheltered workshop? Having experienced different options, shouldn't each individual have the opportunity to choose to work wherever they prefer, regardless of the economic and social ramifications? I believe that the answer must be an unequivocal yes; each individual has his or her own motivations for working and should be allowed to decide which environments best fulfill his or her needs. Indeed, supporters of sheltered employment and other segregated services would argue that making segregated options available enhances choice making for vocational service consumers and their families because many individuals with disabilities prefer the social relationships with other individuals with disabilities, feelings of safety and security, fewer expectations, limited risk, and other aspects of these types of programs.

However, a closer look at the current service system, in which segregated services absorb the overwhelming majority of consumers, resources, and programmatic emphasis, reveals that there are artificial constraints on the freedom of VR consumers to choose *integrated* employment. Thus, genuine consumer choice is abrogated, not enhanced, by the existing dual service system, as the following sections illustrate.

Abrogation of Consumer Choice

The existing employment service system abrogates choice in five interrelated ways, which are described in detail in this section:

1. Many states have instituted constraining rate structures and reimbursement methods for time-limited and extended services that discourage access to supported employment for all eligible participants.
2. Federal and state agencies continue to fund a dual system of competing employment services that discourages conversion of resources that would allow for increased community-based employment to more consumers.
3. Funding and attitudinal barriers limit access to supported employment for specific disability groups, like people with acquired disabilities and significant mental retardation.
4. Many potential supported employment consumers and their families face financial disincentives to competitive employment.
5. Many localities continue to have limited service access and shortages of qualified supported employment personnel.

Constrained Reimbursement Mechanisms   It is apparent that funding difficulties are inhibiting the growth of supported employment in many states. To some degree, insufficient case service funds to serve all eligible participants accounts for the declining growth of the program (Revell, Wehman, Kregel, West, & Rayfield, 1994). However, evidence is mounting that the *ways* in which state VR and extended service agencies fund supported employment also create barriers to program expansion, and thus the opportunity for VR consumers to choose this option.

As an example, many state VR agencies use a flat-rate method of funding time-limited services. Providers receive a fixed amount of money per placement or per week of service, often limiting the time and/or money allocated for each service consumer, regardless of individuals' employment goals or training and support needs (West, Revell, & Wehman, 1992). This reimbursement system discourages providers from offering competitive employment as a service option to a substantial number of their consumers, particularly people with extensive training and support needs due to the severity of their disabilities.

This barrier is perhaps most acute within the extended services system, predominantly state mental retardation, developmental disabilities, and mental health agencies. VR-funded time-limited services are driven by the IWRP (see earlier section, "1992 Choice Amendments") that specifies employment goals and services required to meet those goals. Yet the majority of extended service funding systems are "slot-based" systems that are driven by service capacity, regardless of the types or extent of services rendered. Findings from state surveys and technical assistance activities conducted by the Rehabilitation Research and Training Center on Supported Employment at Virginia Commonwealth University (VCU-RRTC) suggested that most extended service funding agencies have added supported employment service slots at identical (or in some cases, lower) daily or monthly rates as compared to alternative facility-based programs (Revell et al., 1994; West et al., 1992). For example, an adult services provider agency may receive a statewide predetermined amount per month for each of its service consumers, whether they are being maintained in competitive employment or simply engaging in unpaid prevocational work activities.

Because facility-based services and costs are more constant and predictable than extended supported employment services, and because of the long-term commitment required for extended services, provider agencies have little incentive to move individuals from work activity or sheltered employment into supported employment, or to hire additional job coaches to increase their extended service capacity. An all-too-common result is that providers are faced with an uncertain future cost for extended services that may or may not be met by the funding sources, and therefore have a financial disincentive for initiating or expanding the service to more consumers with severe disabilities who may require crisis management, extensive accommodations, or frequent replacement.

Conversion Disincentives   Despite a national policy of integration and employment for individuals with disabilities and 8 years of systems change funding across the nation, integrated and segregated service options continue to compete for service funds. The VCU-RRTC's national surveys have consistently found that the overwhelming majority of provider agencies have added supported employment as a service option without reducing resources for segregated services (Revell et al., 1994; West et al., 1992). As Mank (1994) writes, this situation is reinforced by conflicting national policies in the VR and disability service systems; that is, the same legislation and programs (i.e., the Rehabilitation Act and the Developmental Disabilities Assistance and Bill of Rights Act) that encourage and fund integrated employment training and placement also fund segregated services such as sheltered workshops and work activity centers. He further writes that programs that are not committed to initiation or expansion of integrated employment opportunities have little pressure or incentive to do so.

A related conversion issue is that of slot funding, as previously described in this chapter and practiced extensively by day service funding agencies. National surveys by the VCU-RRTC and others, such as the Institute for Community Integration in Boston, have found that, despite tremendous growth in the number of individuals receiving supported employment, this group has consistently represented only about 10%–12% of all individuals served in day services. This apparent contradiction has fueled speculation that in many areas of the nation, individuals who move from an alternative day service into supported employment have their prior service slot refilled, perhaps from agency waiting lists (McGaughey et al., 1994). Consequently, funds for extended services may not be available when needed by the individual receiving supported employment. As noted in a recent report by McGaughey et al. (1994), a large percentage of supported employment provider agencies do not have funds for extended services and therefore are absorbing the costs; asking consumers or employers to absorb the cost; or more frequently, not providing extended services. Again, the likely outcome is that service providers artificially limit the number of individuals who are given the option of choosing to enter supported employment.

Finally, rehabilitation facilities face financial disincentives to moving personnel, consumers, and resources from facility-based subcontract work to community-integrated employment services. The incompatible goals of sheltered employment mentioned previously, optimizing consumer employment opportunities and meeting the needs of subcontractors, can cause facilities to limit the number of individuals who are given the option of being employed elsewhere. To do otherwise could jeopardize the financial stability of the organization and the livelihood of most of its consumers.

Limited Access for Underserved Populations   Although the efficacy of supported employment has been demonstrated for individuals with many different types of disabilities, the VCU-RRTC's national surveys have found that nearly 90% of service consumers are individuals with mental retardation or mental illness (West et al., 1992). In large part, this is due to the availability of extended services funding from state mental retardation and mental health funding agencies. Individuals with acquired disabilities such as brain injuries or spinal cord injuries occurring after age 22, or even other developmental disabilities such as cerebral palsy, autism, and epilepsy, have traditionally been underserved in supported employment due to the absence of an identified public agency to fund extended services (West et al., 1992).

Provisions in the Rehabilitation Act Amendments of 1992 that allow the use of friends, family, co-workers, and other natural support agents as extended services providers may improve access for these underserved groups, but the impact will not be evident for some time. Meanwhile, limited access to extended service funding systems for these groups is an inhibiting factor in the continued growth of the program and the opportunity for individuals who would otherwise be eligible participants to have this option made available to them.

Another underserved group is individuals with pervasive support needs. This group currently represents only about 8% of all individuals with mental retardation in supported employment (Revell et al., 1994; West et al., 1992). As Kregel and Wehman (1989) showed in their analysis of supported employment participants' functional, social, and behavioral characteristics, only a small portion would qualify as having "the most severe disabilities." For individuals who have truly severe disabilities, the opportunity to choose supported employment may be abrogated by attitudinal barriers (i.e., the presumption of unemployability) on the part of parents, VR counselors, employers, and service providers.

Financial Disincentives   The financial disincentives of employment for individuals with severe disabilities have long been discussed in the rehabilitation and public policy literature (e.g., Bowe, 1993; Conley, Noble, & Elder, 1986; Hommerztheim & Schuermann, 1980; Kiernan & Brinkman, 1988; Walls, Masson, & Werner, 1977). Many individuals with severe disabilities have not been given opportunities to develop valued work skills or behaviors to become employed full time or in financially rewarding occupations and, consequently, the disincentives may be more acute.

In addition, those individuals who work part time (the majority of supported employment consumers) are often unable to receive employer-sponsored health insurance (West, Kregel, & Banks, 1990). This fringe benefit is important for many individuals with disabilities who have ongoing health concerns or who would lose Medicaid benefits after achieving gainful employment. Thus, employment even in part-time positions carries the risk of termination of financial and medical assistance and a net decrease in standard of living. For this reason, many individuals with severe disabilities and their families see no other option but to work at less than their full potential or in low-paying sheltered jobs.

Limited Service Access   Many areas of states have limited service access due to shortages of qualified supported employment agencies or personnel. This impediment to program expansion and service access must be viewed at several levels. First, in many areas of the nation, particularly rural areas but also mid-sized towns and cities, supported employment provider agencies have yet to be established. If a center-based program exists, its leadership may not believe that the local job market would support a competitive employment program such as supported employment or that such a program would be cost-effective. Thus, many individuals who would otherwise be eligible for supported employment do not have ready access to services.

Second, because of the funding limitations and economic disincentives described previously, many vocational service provider agencies maintain a small supported employment staff in relation to the agency as a whole. Staffing constraints necessarily translate into limited numbers of consumers who can 1) enter time-limited supported employment services and 2) be maintained in extended services.

On a final level, surveys of job coaches and provider agencies conducted by the VCU-RRTC and others have consistently found that program staff tend to enter the field inexperienced and untrained and to have limited participation in in-service training and staff development (Everson, 1991). In relation to comparable human services positions, salaries of front-line staff tend to be low, and many programs experience high job coach turnover (Winking, Trach, Rusch, &

Tines, 1989). These programmatic impediments can lead to ineffective or inefficient services, poor consumer outcomes, lack of service continuity, and reduced capacity for both time-limited and extended services.

BUILDING SELF-DETERMINATION INTO VR PROGRAMS AND SERVICES

Since its inception, the legislative intent and programmatic focus of the VR program has been to assist individuals who need time-limited interventions, such as specialized equipment purchase, short-term training, or physical restoration, to enter or return to the job market. Only since 1986, when supported employment became a VR service option, has the program as a whole begun to address the needs of individuals with severe lifelong disabilities who require extensive training, accommodation, and support in order to remain employed. This was a major policy shift for the program, one that has been difficult for many state VR systems and provider agencies to implement. The VR program again faces a major policy shift with the Rehabilitation Act Amendments of 1992, from a role as guardian and dispenser of funds and services for clients to a customer service paradigm where the consumer's goals, preferences, and choices are paramount (Campbell, 1991).

The U.S. Department of Education has begun to issue a number of proposed regulations for implementing the Rehabilitation Act Amendments of 1992. At this writing, the requirements and procedures that will be placed on state VR agencies in this critical area are pending. However, there is much that state VR and private provider agencies can and should do to promote self-determination of consumers with severe disabilities, including the following:

- Training VR counselors, program directors, and supervisors on new choice-making regulations and procedures
- Developing consumer and family orientation packages on consumers' rights to choice, workplace accommodations, and other mandates of the Rehabilitation Act Amendments of 1992 and the ADA
- Incorporating choice and self-determination assurance and monitoring standards and mechanisms in vendorship contracts with provider agencies (Schaller & Szymanski, 1992)
- Compiling outcome data on the effectiveness of service options and service providers that can be used by consumers and family members to make informed choices
- Developing new consumer assessment strategies that focus on consumers' values, goals, interests, and preferences (cf. Winking, O'Reilly, & Moon, 1993)
- Focusing job development and placement activities on consumers' career goals, motivations, and needs, particularly in regard to income and fringe benefit requirements

- Initiating work experience and career exploration programs that allow consumers to develop work and career preferences and goals from an array of options
- Building sufficient flexibility into service options to allow consumers incremental opportunities to learn more about their work values and goals, such as career exploration programs, extended job tryouts, and the freedom to choose to leave a job without jeopardizing VR funding status

Ultimately, however, achieving self-determination will be the responsibility of consumers themselves. As individuals with disabilities prepare for entry into the work world, they and their family members and advocates will require information regarding their rights to 1) obtain access to VR services and 2) participate fully in planning and choosing their vocational directions, VR-sponsored services and supports, and service providers. Training in self-advocacy will be essential for putting that information into action.

Ensuring self-determination for individuals with disabilities in VR services will require systemic changes as well. Constraints within the dual system of services artificially limit the number of individuals who are given the opportunity to try competitive employment, and the risk of financial loss restricts the freedom of many individuals to choose that route. Many states have already initiated sweeping changes in their VR and extended service funding mechanisms to provide incentives to provider agencies for expanding supported employment opportunities for more of their consumers, and for those with more severe disabilities. Successful efforts need to be replicated throughout the federal/state VR system, or the self-determination and integration mandates of the Rehabilitation Act Amendments of 1992 will never be fully realized.

Foremost among those reforms are service reimbursement methods in which *people* are funded rather than the slots they fill. In these types of systems, money follows the consumer as he or she moves from one service option to another, in some systems using vouchers that are then redeemed by the provider. While slot-based systems predetemine the number of people who can enter a particular option and therefore limit choice, service vouchers put more control in the hands of consumers and their families by allowing them to "vote with their feet" for the types of work environments and support methods they want. The market (i.e., vendored vocational services) will respond accordingly.

CONCLUSIONS

Expansion of supported employment capacity is a vital step in empowering VR consumers with severe disabilities to exercise true self-determination. Genuine, informed choice between segregated and integrated work cannot occur without experiencing both options. Too many people with disabilities are not given the opportunity to try and to choose integrated, community-based employment and are locked into a service system that talks of integration and self-determination, but sanctions exclusion and servitude.

REFERENCES

Amabile, T.M., & Gitomer, J. (1984). Children's artistic creativity: Effects of choice in task materials. *Personality and Social Psychology Bulletin, 10*, 209–215.

Americans with Disabilities Act (ADA) of 1990, PL 101-336. (July 26, 1990). Title 42, U.S.C. 12101 et seq: *U.S. Statutes at Large, 104*, 327–378.

Bannerman, D.J., Sheldon, J.B., Sherman, J.A., & Harchik, A.E. (1990). Balancing the right to habilitation with the right to personal liberties: The rights of people with developmental disabilities to eat too many doughnuts and take a nap. *Journal of Applied Behavior Analysis, 23*, 79–89.

Bowe, F.G. (1993). Statistics, politics, and employment of people with disabilities. *Journal of Disability Policy Studies, 4*(2), 83–91.

Buyer, L.S., Berkson, G., Winnega, M.A., & Morton, L. (1987). Stimulation and control as components of stereotypic body rocking. *American Journal of Mental Deficiency, 91*, 543–547.

Campbell, J.F. (1991). The consumer movement and implications for vocational rehabilitation services. *Journal of Vocational Rehabilitation, 1*(3), 67–75.

Conley, R., Noble, J., & Elder, J. (1986). Problems with the service system. In W. Kiernan & J. Stark (Eds.), *Pathways to employment for adults with developmental disabilities* (pp. 67–83). Baltimore: Paul H. Brookes Publishing Co.

Dattilo, J., & Rusch, F.R. (1985). Effects of choice on leisure participation for people with severe handicaps. *Journal of The Association for People with Severe Handicaps, 10*, 194–199.

Davis, S. (1994). A status report to the nation on inclusion in employment of people with mental retardation. *Journal of Vocational Rehabilitation, 4*, 243–254.

Deci, E.L., & Ryan, R.M. (1985). *Intrinsic motivation and self-determination in human behavior.* New York: Plenum.

Developmental Disabilities Assistance and Bill of Rights Act, PL 94-103. (October 4, 1978). Title 42, U.S.C. 6000 et seq: *U.S. Statutes at Large, 89*, 486–507.

Dyer, K., Dunlap, G., & Winterling, V. (1990). Effects of choice making on the serious problem behaviors of students with severe handicaps. *Journal of Applied Behavior Analysis, 23*, 515–524.

Everson, J.M. (1991). Supported employment personnel: An assessment of their self-reported training needs, educational backgrounds, and previous employment experiences. *Journal of The Association for People with Severe Handicaps, 16*, 140–145.

Garner, R.E., Lacy, G.H., & Creasy, R.F. (1972). Workshops—Why, what, whither? *Mental Retardation, 10*(3), 25–27.

Gersuny, C., & Lefton, M. (1970). Service and servitude in the sheltered workshop. *Social Work, 15*, 74–81.

Guess, D., Benson, H.A., & Siegel-Causey, E. (1985). Concepts and issues related to choice-making and autonomy among people with severe disabilities. *Journal of The Association for Persons with Severe Handicaps, 10*, 79–86.

Guess, D., & Siegel-Causey, E. (1985). Behavioral control and education of severely handicapped students: Who's doing what to whom and why? In D. Bricker & J. Filler (Eds.), *Severe mental retardation: From theory to practice* (pp. 241–255). Reston, VA: Council for Exceptional Children.

Hanley-Maxwell, C., & Millington, M. (1992). Enhancing independence in supported employment: Natural supports in business and industry. *Journal of Vocational Rehabilitation, 2*(4), 51–58.

Helms, B.J., Moore, S.C., & McSewyn, C.A. (1991). Supported employment in Connecticut: An examination of integration and wage outcomes. *Career Development of Exceptional Individuals, 14,* 159–166.

Hill, M., & Wehman, P. (1983). Cost benefit analysis of placing moderately and severely handicapped individuals into competitive employment. *Journal of The Association for People with Severe Handicaps, 8,* 30–38.

Hommerztheim, D.L., & Schuermann, A.C. (1980). Economic disincentives to rehabilitation. In R.A. Weisgerber, P.R. Dahl, & J.A. Appleby (Eds.), *Training the handicapped for productive employment* (pp. 365–375). Rockville, MD: Aspen Publishers.

Houghton, J., Bronicki, G.J., & Guess, D. (1987). Opportunities to express preferences and make choices among students with severe disabilities in classroom settings. *Journal of The Association for Persons with Severe Handicaps, 12,* 18–27.

Inge, K.J., Banks, P.D., Wehman, P., Hill, J.W., & Shafer, M.S. (1988). Quality of life for individuals who are labeled mentally retarded: Evaluating competitive employment versus sheltered workshop employment. *Education and Training in Mental Retardation, 23,* 97–104.

Ip, S.M.V., Szymanski, E.M., Johnston-Rodriguez, S., & Karls, S.F. (1994). Effects of staff implementation of a choice program on challenging behaviors in people with developmental disabilities. *Rehabilitation Counseling Bulletin, 37,* 347–357.

Kennedy, M., & Killius, P. (1986). Self-advocacy: Speaking for yourself. In B. Shoultz, M. Kennedy, & N. Erevelles (Eds.), *Materials on self-determination.* Syracuse, NY: Center on Human Policy.

Kiernan, W.E., & Brinkman, L. (1988). Disincentives and barriers to employment. In P. Wehman & M.S. Moon (Eds.), *Vocational rehabilitation and supported employment* (pp. 221–223). Baltimore: Paul H. Brookes Publishing Co.

Kiernan, W.E., McGaughey, M.J., & Schalock, R.C. (1986). *National employment survey for adults with developmental disabilities.* Boston: Children's Hospital, Developmental Evaluation Clinic.

Kishi, G., Teelucksingh, B., Zollers, N., Park-Lee, S., & Meyer, L. (1988). Daily decision-making in community residences: A social comparison of adults with and without mental retardation. *American Journal on Mental Retardation, 92,* 430–435.

Koegel, R.L., Dyer, K., & Bell, L.K. (1987). The influence of child-preferred activities on autistic children's social behavior. *Journal of Applied Behavior Analysis, 20,* 243–252.

Kregel, J., & Wehman, P. (1989). Supported employment: Promises deferred for people with severe disabilities. *Journal of The Association for Persons with Severe Handicaps, 14,* 293–303.

Kregel, J., Wehman, P., & Banks, P.D. (1989). The effects of consumer characteristics and type of employment model on individual outcomes in supported employment. *Journal of Applied Behavior Analysis, 22,* 407–415.

Lagomarcino, T.R. (1986). Community services: Using the supported work model with an adult service agency. In F.R. Rusch (Ed.), *Competitive employment: Issues and strategies* (pp. 65–75). Baltimore: Paul H. Brookes Publishing Co.

Lovett, H. (1991). Empowerment and choices. In L.H. Meyer, C.A. Peck, & L. Brown (Eds.), *Critical issues in the lives of people with severe disabilities* (pp. 625–626). Baltimore: Paul H. Brookes Publishing Co.

Mallas, A.A. (1976). Current workshop strengths and weaknesses. *Education and Training of the Mentally Retarded, 11,* 334–348.

Mank, D. (1994). The underachievement of supported employment: A call for reinvestment. *Journal of Disability Policy Studies, 5*(2), 1–24.

Martin, J.E., Marshall, L.H., & Maxson, L.L. (1993). Transition policy: Infusing self-determination and self-advocacy into transition programs. *Career Development of Exceptional Individuals, 16,* 53–61.

McGaughey, M.J., Kiernan, W.E., McNally, L.C., Gilmore, D.S., & Keith, G.R. (1994). *Beyond the workshop: National perspectives on integrated employment.* Boston: Children's Hospital, Institute for Community Inclusion.

Nirje, B. (1972). The right to self-determination. In W. Wolfensberger (Ed.), *Normalization* (pp. 176–193). Toronto: National Institute on Mental Retardation.

Noble, J., & Conley, R. (1987). Accumulating evidence on the benefits and costs of supported and transitional employment for people with severe disabilities. *Journal of The Association for Persons with Severe Handicaps, 12,* 163–174.

Nosek, M.A., & Fuhrer, M.J. (1992). Independence among people with disabilities: I. A heuristic model. *Rehabilitation Counseling Bulletin, 36,* 6–20.

Parsons, M.B., Reid, D.H., & Baumgartner, M. (1990). Effects of choice versus assigned jobs on the work performance of people with severe handicaps. *Journal of Applied Behavior Analysis, 23,* 253–260.

Peck, C.H. (1985). Increasing opportunities for social control by children with autism and severe handicaps: Effects on student behavior and perceived classroom climate. *Journal of The Association for Persons with Severe Handicaps, 10,* 183–193.

Perske, R. (Ed.). (1989). *Proceedings from the National Conference on Self-Determination.* Minneapolis: Institute on Community Integration, University of Minnesota.

Price, E.B. (1990). Independence and the individual with disabilities. *Journal of Rehabilitation, 56,* 15–18.

Reid, D.H., & Parsons, M.B. (1990). Assessing food preferences among people with profound mental retardation: Providing opportunities to make choices. *Journal of Applied Behavior Analysis, 23,* 183–195.

Reid, D.H., & Parsons, M.B. (1991). Making choice a routine part of mealtimes for people with profound mental retardation. *Behavioral Residential Treatment, 6,* 249–261.

Rees, L.M., Spreen, O., & Harnadek, M. (1991). Do attitudes towards people with handicaps really shift over time? Comparison between 1975 and 1988. *Mental Retardation, 29,* 81–86.

Rehabilitation Act Amendments of 1992, PL 102-569 (October 29, 1992). Title 29, U.S.C. 701 et seq: *U.S. Statutes at Large, 100,* 4344–4488.

Revell, W.G., Wehman, P., Kregel, J., West, M., & Rayfield, R. (1994). Supported employment for people with severe disabilities: Positive trends in wages, models, and funding. *Education and Training in Mental Retardation and Developmental Disabilities, 29,* 256–264.

Schaller, J.L., & Szymanski, E.M. (1992). Supported employment, consumer choice, and independence. *Journal of Vocational Rehabilitation, 2*(4), 45–50.

Schuster, J.W. (1990). Sheltered workshops: Financial and philosophical liabilities. *Mental Retardation, 28,* 233–239.

Shevin, M., & Klein, N. (1984). The importance of choice-making skills for students with severe disabilities. *Journal of The Association for Persons with Severe Handicaps, 9,* 159–166.

Sinnott-Oswald, M., Gliner, J.A., & Spencer, K.C. (1991). Supported and sheltered employment: Quality of life among workers with disabilities. *Education and Training in Mental Retardation, 26,* 388–397.

Taylor, L., Adelman, H.S., Nelson, P., Smith, D.C., & Phares, V. (1989). Perceptions of control at school among students in special education programs. *Journal of Learning Disabilities, 22,* 439–443.

Temple University Developmental Disabilities Center. (1990). *The final report on the 1990 National Consumer Survey of People with Developmental Disabilities and Their Families.* Philadelphia: Temple University.

Test, D.W., Hinson, K.B., Solow, J., & Keul, P. (1993). Job satisfaction of people in supported employment. *Education and Training in Mental Retardation, 28,* 38–46.

Thompson, L., Powers, G., & Houchard, B. (1992). The wage effects of supported employment. *Journal of The Association for Persons with Severe Handicaps, 17,* 87–94.

Vogelsberg, R.T., Ashe, W., & Williams, W. (1985). Community-based service delivery in a rural state: Issues for development and implementation. In R. Horner, L.M. Voeltz, & B. Fredericks (Eds.), *Education of learners with severe handicaps: Exemplary service strategies* (pp. 29–59). Baltimore: Paul H. Brookes Publishing Co.

Wacker, D.P., Wiggins, B., Fowler, M., & Berg, W. (1988). Training students with profound or multiple handicaps to make requests via microswitches. *Journal of Applied Behavior Analysis, 21,* 331–343.

Walls, R.T., Masson, C., & Werner, T.J. (1977). Negative incentives to vocational rehabilitation. *Rehabilitation Literature, 38*(5), 143–150.

Ward, M.J. (1993). Foreword. In P. Wehman (Ed.), *The ADA mandate for social change* (pp. xv–xix). Baltimore: Paul H. Brookes Publishing Co.

Wehmeyer, M.L. (1992). Self-determination and the education of students with mental retardation. *Education and Training in Mental Retardation, 27,* 303–314.

West, M., Kregel, J., & Banks, P.D. (1990). Fringe benefits available to supported employment participants. *Rehabilitation Counseling Bulletin, 34,* 126–138.

West, M.D., & Parent, W.S. (1992). Consumer choice and empowerment in supported employment services: Issues and strategies. *Journal of The Association for Persons with Severe Handicaps, 17,* 47–52.

West, M., Revell, W.G., & Wehman, P. (1992). Achievements and challenges: I. A five-year report on consumer and system outcomes from the supported employment initiative. *Journal of The Association for Persons with Severe Handicaps, 17,* 227–235.

White, W.J., Alley, G.R., Deshler, D.D., Schumaker, J.B., Warner, M.M., & Clark, F.L. (1982). Are there learning disabilities after high school? *Exceptional Children, 49,* 273–274.

Williams, R.R. (1989). Creating a new world of opportunity: Expanding choice and self-determination in the lives of Americans with severe disability by 1992 and beyond. In R. Perske (Ed.), *Proceedings from the National Conference on Self-Determination* (pp. 16–20). Minneapolis: Institute on Community Integration, University of Minnesota.

Winking, D.L., O'Reilly, B., & Moon, M.S. (1993). Preference: The missing link in the job match process for individuals without functional communication skills. *Journal of Vocational Rehabilitation, 3*(3), 27–42.

Winking, D.L., Trach, J.S., Rusch, F.R., & Tines, J. (1989). Profile of Illinois supported employment specialists: An analysis of educational background, experience, and related employment variables. *Journal of The Association for Persons with Severe Handicaps, 14,* 278–282.

Section III

SUMMARY

Chapter 16

FUTURE DIRECTIONS
IN SELF-DETERMINATION

Articulating Values and Policies, Reorganizing Organizational Structures, and Implementing Professional Practices

Deanna J. Sands and Michael L. Wehmeyer

AS ECHOED IN chapters throughout this volume, policy and practice in education, rehabilitation, and other disability-related fields increasingly emphasizes the importance of self-determination if individuals with disabilities are to succeed in school and fulfill roles associated with adulthood. These chapters have described the antecedents to the self-determination movement, argued for its importance and urgency, and highlighted practices to achieve this outcome. A thorough review of these individual contributions leads to three conclusions:

1. Self-determination is a highly valued and largely unrealized outcome to and for people with disabilities.
2. The systems to which people with disabilities must turn for support, educational, rehabilitational, and otherwise too frequently foster dependency and reliance and hinder personal control.
3. There is ample justification for professionals in disability services to support the development, acquisition, and use of self-determination skills.

The effort to support the development of skills and capacities for self-determination among youth with disabilities cannot, however, be seen as a single-track effort. First, it is clear that successful efforts to promote self-determination will involve multiple components, like peer and adult mentoring, community-based experiences, instruction in skills acquisition, environmental manipulations to promote choice, involvement in program decision making, and so forth, many of these occurring simultaneously (Wehmeyer, Martin, & Sands, in press). Second, the overall effort to support self-determination cannot occur outside of the many reform agendas ongoing in fields like special education and vocational rehabilitation.

In education, considerable attention has been directed toward both the organizational structure and delivery of special education services (Gartner & Lipsky, 1987; Skrtic, 1991) and to processes for including students with disabilities into their home schools and general education classrooms (Kozleski & Jackson, 1993; Salisbury, Palombaro, & Hollowood, 1993; York, Vandercook, MacDonald, Heise-Neff, & Caughey, 1992). The self-determination movement, and efforts to support this outcome, should not, and perhaps cannot, operate independent of the inclusion movement. Nor, we would suggest, should efforts to include children and youth with disabilities in typical classrooms exclude the important contributions offered by the self-determination movement.

Likewise, neither the self-determination nor the inclusion movement can or should operate outside of the broader school reform efforts currently under way. Sarason (1990) identified what he called the "predictable failure of educational reform" (p. 40) as stemming from the failure of reformers to adequately address and alter power relationships in the schools. He contends that unless schools move from a rigid, hierarchical power structure (administrator to teacher to student) to one in which all stakeholders, including students and their families, experience control in educational planning, decision making, and implementation, the underlying problems in education will not be resolved. So, once again, these movements—inclusion, self-determination, and school reform—are not serial activities occurring in a vacuum but are parallel and intertwined.

As West (Chapter 15) has argued, similar circumstances exist within the field of vocational rehabilitation. It is impossible to move forward with reforms like supported employment unless issues of consumer involvement, choice, and empowerment are resolved. This can be extended to other movements and recommended practices within disability services such as supported living and natural supports. Perhaps it is not just hyperbole when McFadden and Burke (1991) emphasize a "new paradigm" for human services in the 1990s—empowerment and choice.

COMPLEX ISSUES LEAD TO INACTION

The demands placed on schools and rehabilitation agencies during the social, political, and economic changes described previously are often unrelenting and overwhelming. Many expectations are placed on such organizations by government entitites, community members at large, families, and students or consumers. With each change, complex issues emerge that challenge professionals to examine and often modify their roles, functions, and practices. One can understand how it may be confusing for many professionals to organize and manage schools and classrooms or to proceed with vocational training and placement in light of such constantly evolving, complex, systemic changes.

There are multiple factors that moderate the ability of professionals to deal with such change and to utilize research in recommended practices, including 1) knowledge and learning, 2) attitudes and beliefs, and 3) contextual variables (Malouf & Schiller, 1995). Factors such as isolation, ambiguity of educational and vocational goals, heavy workloads and excessive regulations, lack of collegiality, and limited resources influence professionals' initiative and their ability to change their actions. However, some professionals may be too eager to adopt new technologies, often jumping on the latest bandwagon without taking adequate time to understand or fully question the validity or effectiveness of proposed changes. In their haste to adopt shifting innovations, many of these professionals misapply or insufficiently develop the technique (Bellamy, in Sands, in press; Fleming, 1988). After repeated cycles of difficulties or failures with recommended changes, they are often left feeling cynical, skeptical, and full of despair (Apple & Beane, 1995; Lortie, 1975).

Without in-depth discussions and responses that acknowledge the interplay of proposed changes on the purpose and conduct of schooling, rehabilitation, and other services, responses are often isolated, piecemeal, or nonexistent (Noddings, 1995). Consider that despite years of intense calls for educational reform, our schools operate in much the same fashion as they did some 50 years ago (Daggett, in O'Neil, 1995b; Goodlad, 1984).

ORGANIZING COMPLEXITY TO SUPPORT CRITICALLY RESPONSIVE ACTION

It is difficult to respond to changes, like the promotion of self-determination, with actions that are purposeful and effective without a systematic framework by which to sort, analyze, evaluate, and critically reflect upon issues important to the change process. Employing a systematic process allows one to organize thoughts and solve problems of practice by 1) reflecting upon the relative impact of varying perspectives, 2) considering and evaluating the sufficiency of the current knowledge base, 3) weighing the advantages and disadvantages of possible options, and 4) formulating and evaluating plans of action.

In this chapter, we apply a model proposed by Bellamy (in Sands, in press) to examine the values, policies and regulations, organizational structures, and professional behaviors and procedures necessary to create contexts that support self-determination as an educational outcome. Bellamy's formulation focuses on school reform. However, we believe that it is equally applicable to other disability services and that, unless practitioners and policy makers attend to these multiple variables, efforts to promote self-determination could fall to the wayside and become yet another unrealized educational or vocational reform initiative.

USING MULTIPLE VANTAGE
POINTS TO UNDERSTAND REFORM ISSUES

Bellamy (in Sands, in press) proposed a framework that described the interrelationship between four vantage points: 1) values and beliefs, 2) policy decisions, 3) organizational structures, and 4) procedural or programmatic practices. According to Bellamy, each of these four vantage points provides (a) a unique set of questions to ask about an issue, (b) one or more paradigms from which to access or develop a research and knowledge base, and (c) a particular set of action strategies to influence change. These four vantage points are discussed next.

Four Vantage Points

The *philosophical vantage point* addresses the underlying values or beliefs that serve as the foundation to a particular perspective or set of competing perspectives. For example, on the one hand, proponents of inclusive practices believe that children and youth with disabilities should be educated in their neighborhood schools in general education classes with their same-age peers (Sapon-Shevin, in O'Neil, 1995a). On the other hand, opponents to inclusive practices believe that children and youth with disabilities have unique needs that require specialized education programs separate from general education classrooms (Shanker, in O'Neil, 1995a). Beliefs serve as the basis for setting policy, organizing services, and implementing practices. Thus, when people operate from differing philosophical bases they often advocate for distinct, and sometimes competing, policies, organizational supports, and professional practices. Knowledge bases that undergird the philosophical vantage point include the fields of ethics, sociological data, opinion polls, and critical inquiry. Influencing change in philosophical views can be accomplished through persuasive communication, advocacy, sensitivity training, and use of the media.

　　Governing policies and regulations serve as the basis for inquiry at the *policy vantage point*. Policies and regulations convert values and beliefs into operating doctrine. For example, beliefs that all children had a right to education served to undergird the principal of "free and appropriate education" that guided initial and ongoing legislation applying to the education of students with disabilities. Policy analysis and evaluation, along with legal research, yield the knowledge base for this vantage point and lobbying, coalition building, and legal and political action support change at this level.

　　At the *organizational vantage point*, one questions if the goals of an organization's programs, structures, and assignment of personnel roles and responsibilities are consistent with adopted philosophy, meet policy and regulatory requirements, and are effective in achieving stated goals. Based on results of program demonstration and evaluation (i.e., the knowledge base at this level), organizational change, restructuring, and design can support change.

Finally, questions at the fourth level, the *professional/procedural vantage point*, query the effectiveness and controversies of the organization's strategies, tools, and procedures in achieving organizational, policy, and societal goals and values. In other words, do we have information that tells us if what we are doing works? Model demonstration projects and research can yield the information necessary to support staff development, peer support networks, and action research necessary to sustain change at this level.

The application of Bellamy's vantage points allows professionals to thoroughly analyze an issue by clarifying controversial questions and issues; identifying and reflecting on the existing knowledge base; determining the need for change; and then, if warranted, generating a set of strategies to support this change effort. In order to address an issue in a cogent and comprehensive manner, it is critical that factors specific to each vantage point be clearly delimited. For example, if teachers are called upon to implement a new curriculum (procedural), inadequate attention to their staff development needs (organizational) can thwart or undermine their abilities to adequately implement the program. This could then lead to a compromise in the achievement of the district's goals and objectives set forth through curriculum mandates (policy) that were established in order to achieve desired student outcomes (philosophical). Understanding the interrelationships between each of these perspectives allows us to track and target potential problems.

What becomes important, then, is to accurately identify the point at which problems arise. When people engage in conversations in which they discuss issues across vantage points, it tends to perpetuate and complicate their ability to adequately understand and respond to issues, to take a personal stand, and to define a set of actions that can be carried out to support change efforts. Elaborating upon the previous example, if two teachers are debating the use of a particular curriculum, the problem for one may stem from personal values and beliefs that are counter to that curriculum, and for the other, lack of knowledge regarding implementation procedures. Failure to address these concerns at their respective vantage points will impede efforts to resolve their respective needs.

APPLYING THE VANTAGE POINTS TO SELF-DETERMINATION

Adopting self-determination as a platform for reform and as a standard for educational and rehabilitative practices will require change in current school and rehabilitation service policies, organizational structures, and professional practices (Halloran, 1993). From literature on reform and research on systemic change we know that leadership in setting goals and providing resources, the sponsorship of incremental change, and participatory planning and decision making are essential ingredients for success (Janney, Snell, Beers, & Raynes, 1995; Sarason, 1990). To adequately accomplish each of these tasks, it is necessary to understand the underlying values and beliefs, current regulatory support, recommended organizational structures, and proposed recommended practices for self-determination. Furthermore, it is critical that we identify unanswered questions that remain and knowledge bases that have yet to be fully developed. Drawing heavily from information presented throughout this volume and applying Bellamy's vantage points, we summarize in this section the current knowledge base about self-determination and propose issues requiring future research or consideration.

Philosophical Vantage Point

Philosophically, the emergence of the self-determination movement requires us to question the goals and objectives of education and rehabilitation; the role of agencies and professionals in addressing the needs of individuals with disabilities; and, most fundamentally, the way in which society views disability and people with disabilities. As Ward (Chapter 1) and Wehmeyer (Chapter 2) emphasized, the self-determination movement is a result of the empowering civil rights movements of the preceding decades and the emergent voices of people with disabilities demanding greater control in their lives.

Throughout this volume, advocates of the self-determination movement proclaim a set of values and beliefs that undergird efforts to promote this outcome. First among these is the acceptance that disability is a part of the human experience and that people with disabilities "are people first, and have the right to be valued and experience dignity and respect independent of any qualifier or label others might place on them" (Wehmeyer, in press). A necessary corollary to this belief is that, as described in the Rehabilitation Act Amendments of 1992 (PL 102-569),

> the presence of a disability in no way diminishes the rights of individuals to live independently, enjoy self-determination, make choices, contribute to society, pursue meaningful careers and enjoy full inclusion and integration in the economic, political, social, cultural and educational mainstream of American society (Sec. 2 [a][3][A - F])

A second, and related, underlying belief is that self-determination is essential for and related to the empowerment of the individual. Like self-determination, *empowerment* is a term that lends itself to hyperbole and rhetoric. The Cornell Empowerment and Family Project (1990) defined empowerment as

> an intentional, ongoing process, centered in the local community, involving mutual respect, critical reflection, caring and group participation through which people who are lacking in an equal share of valued resources gain greater access to and control over those resources.

Based on this definition, Wehmeyer (1993) suggested that the term *empowerment* embodies the following basic values. Empowerment is

1. centered in the local community and encompasses integration and inclusion as implied outcomes;

2. an ongoing process that must take into consideration the individual, his or
   her environment, and others within that environment;
3. based on the philosophical assumption that all people are worthy of respect and dignity;
4. individualized, goal driven, and task oriented;
5. focused on a more equitable distribution of and access to valued resources,
   like money, jobs, education, power, or friends, [and] to individuals who
   lack an equal share of these resources. (Wehmeyer, 1993, p. 16)

Mithaug (Chapter 8) urged us to go one step further and acknowledge that self-determination is a right of all people and that there is a collective responsibility for improving the prospects for self-determination among the least well-situated groups of people. Those prospects involve a match between an individual's capacity for autonomous thought and action and improving opportunities for effective choice and action. Mithaug posited that the responsibility for improving prospects for self-determination among youth with disabilities is both a moral obligation as well as the fundamental purpose of the special education system.

Powers and colleagues (Chapter 13) and West (Chapter 15) emphasized a common set of beliefs, whether focused on youth (Powers et al.) or adults (West) with disabilities. Those beliefs are that individuals are their own best change agents and that such agency only emerges when there is shared responsibility for planning and decision making. These beliefs are inherent in most efforts to support self-determination, as emphasized by the emergence of practices like the self-directed IEP (individualized education program) described by Martin and Marshall (Chapter 11) or the Group Action Planning procedure introduced by Turnbull and colleagues (Chapter 12).

Turnbull and colleagues (Chapter 12) also remind us that values for self-determination may incite controversy among families from cultures that hold opposing beliefs and values for their offspring. This concern arises from the position that western values and beliefs serve as a basis for self-determination. While western values include both personal independence and social interdependence, there is a history of the struggle of Americans to achieve a balance between those two bases (Dennis, Williams, Giangreco, & Cloninger, 1993). This conflict is reflected in the historical overemphasis on individualism and independence rather than on interdependence and social relationships in the organization of schools and educational goals for people with disabilities (Haring, 1991; Noddings, 1984; Schlechty, 1990). Future study of the role of self-determination as an outcome for individuals with and without disabilities must consider the role of cultural contexts and associated variables of levels of acculturation, family composition, and community supports.

Governmental and Policy Vantage Point

Within the governmental and policy vantage point it is important to analyze laws, regulations, and policies to determine if they support and reflect the underlying beliefs or philosophies meant to govern our behaviors. It appears to be the case that it is efforts at this vantage point that are driving the current focus on self-determination, as illustrated by the aforementioned language in the Rehabilitation Act Amendments of 1992, as well as the passage of the Americans with Disabilities Act of 1990 (ADA) (PL 101-336). Legislation like the Carl D. Perkins Vocational and Applied Technology Act (PL 101-392) and the Individuals with Disabilities Education Act of 1990 (IDEA) (PL 94-142) require consumer involvement in planning for services (Wehmeyer & Ward, 1995), and laws like the Fair Housing Amendments Act of 1988 (PL 100-430) and Section 504 of the Rehabilitation Act (PL 102-569) protect basic civil rights that support integration, choice, and equal access, and thus, support self-determination (Brotherson, Cook, Cunconan-Lahr, & Wehmeyer, 1995).

Unfortunately, the presence of policy and legislation offering protections does not ensure either compliance or positive outcomes. West (Chapter 15) detailed how variables related to policy can negatively impact the implementation of otherwise progressive statutes. Of concern is whether the spirit of legislation and policy is carried out at the organizational and professional levels. As was indicated in Martin and Marshall (Chapter 11), although the value for active student participation was articulated in the earliest version of PL 94-142 back in 1975, research over the years has confirmed that student participation in the development of their IEPs is either nonexistent or passive. So, while language in newer regulations mandate student participation and decision making in the IEP and transition planning process, there remain concerns that implementation will reduce this intent to bureaucratic and nonresponsive practice. Similarly, choice and participatory planning procedures in the Rehabilitation Act Amendments do not mean that self-determination will follow without continued advocacy and vigilance.

It is incumbent upon professionals to be knowledgeable about the policies and regulations that govern and influence the goals, objectives, and procedures of their organizations and professional practices. Thorough analysis and careful interpretation at the governmental or policy vantage point allows human services professionals to take actions that improve the potential that laws and policies consistent with values and beliefs will be implemented and enforced or influence, through political, legal, or professional lobbying and advocacy, rules and regulations that are more consistent with the values of self-determination.

Organizational Vantage Point

Organizationally, the issue of self-determination is central to the manner in which services are designed and delivered in school buildings, vocational and living environments, and other community-based agencies. This includes the roles of professionals, support service staff, consumers (students), and family members. Organizational structures serve as the foundation for professional and procedural ways of behaving. Because many human services organizations grew from a belief that the condition of disability had to be remediated or "fixed," existing service and support mechanisms often place consumers and their families in passive, recipient roles that undermine self-intiative and self-respect (Ward, Chapter 1). For this reason, the organizational level poses perhaps the greatest challenge to efforts to facilitate self-determination among individuals with disabilities. Without extensive attention and responses to these organizational issues, professionals and consumers are at risk for continued relationships and practices that are counterproductive to self-determination.

From this volume we have learned much regarding how we should structure our organizational goals, service delivery mechanisms, and professional roles to foster or permit consumer development and expression of self-determination. First and foremost, the goal of organizations should be to create environments that maximize opportunities for individuals to enact choice in pursuit of self-determined needs and interests (Mithaug, Chapter 8). This goal is in keeping with the beliefs and values that undergird the movement for self-determination; the spirit of important legislative mandates; and proposals such as Wehmeyer's (Chapter 2) that self-determination become a recognized, valued outcome of our education and rehabilitation systems.

Because the manifestation of self determination is highly individualized (Kennedy, Chapter 3), organizations must seek operating structures and mechanisms that allow for individual expression of self-determination. The supports and services required for one individual may or may not be required by others. This demands great flexibility in organizational structures and operations. The personal stories of Brenda Doss and Bess Hatcher (Chapter 4) are poignant reminders of how, too often, our systems have difficulty responding to personal choice.

If personal choice is to drive the operation and structure of organizations, opportunities for exercising that choice must be provided throughout the planning, implementation, and evaluation of an organization's operating practices. For example, in schools, students should have a voice at the building level, as well as personnally, in decision-making matters such as curriculum content, course selection and scheduling, governance, and extracurricular activities (Abery & Stancliffe, Chapter 7; Powers et al., Chapter 13). Within a living context, consumers should have a clear and present voice in the selection of their living quarters, whether and with whom they might share their home, and the nature and type of support services they require in order to function in their home as independently as possible. Collaborative relationships with families and other agencies providing support services to individuals increase individual capacity to master and generalize self-determined behaviors across multiple contexts (Abery & Stancliffe, Chapter 7).

Changing the function and purpose of professional and consumer roles is perhaps the most fundamental shift that must occur if we are to support self-determination as an educational and rehabilitation outcome. Supporting self-directed learning requires that professionals facilitate rather than direct student skill acquisition and application (Doll et al., Chapter 5; Martin & Marshall, Chapter 11). Furthermore, as pointed out by Kennedy (Chapter 3) and Turnbull and colleagues (Chapter 12), professionals must become adept at establishing trusting relationships, listening, allowing for mistakes, and providing constructive feedback. At the same time, students and consumers must be prepared to assume active, directing roles in their educational, living, vocational, and community pursuits. These shifting roles will require intensive staff development and will be greatly influenced as preservice and in-service personnel preparation programs adopt the curriculum of self-determination (Powers et al., Chapter 13).

Professional/Procedural Vantage Point

The professional/procedural vantage point is often the element that is most pressing in the minds and hearts of practitioners. It is at this level that we deal with the day-to-day decisions and practices that support educational and rehabilitation outcomes. The self-determination initiative sponsored by OSERS (the Office of Special Education and Rehabilitative Services) has made a significant contribution to our ability to foster professional and procedural practices that facilitate self-determination. The latter portion of this volume addressed those knowledge bases and can be used to inform professional practice to support self-determination. There are several points of consensus related to practice that warrant identification:

• We must start early and address the developmental progression of skills and capacities of self-determination (Abery & Zajac, Chapter 9; Doll et al., Chapter 5).

• Various component elements require support and/or instruction: choice making, decision making, problem solving, goal setting and attainment, self-observation, internal locus of control, positive self-efficacy and outcome expectancy, and self-awareness and self-knowledge (Field & Hoffman, Chapter 10; Serna, Chapter 14; Wehmeyer, Chapter 2).

• Home and school environments must be structured physically and affectively to allow for maximum choice and self-direction, personal control, nurturance, privacy, socialization, and stimulation and manipulation (Abery & Zajac, Chapter 9; Cook, Brotherson, Weigel-Garrey, & Mize, Chapter 6; Doss & Hatcher, Chapter 4).

• Curricula now exist that allow us to teach students with and without disabilities the skills of self-determination and allow them to practice those skills across multiple contexts including home, school, and IEP planning (Martin & Marshall, Chapter 11; Field & Hoffman, Chapter 10; Serna, Chapter 14).

• Facilitation of the development of self-determination will require the provision of opportunities for choices, constructive feedback, guidance through goal setting and decision making, and support for frustration and positive coping (Doll et al., Chapter 5; Powers et al., Chapter 13; Serna, Chapter 14; West, Chapter 15).

- Participatory planning processes such as Group Action Planning create a responsive context by which to support individual and family self-determination (Turnbull et al., Chapter 12).

The efforts sparked by federal self-determination initiatives have provided us with a substantive amount of information and resources to support change initiatives. We must expand upon these tools and processes as we seek effective practices that 1) target younger children and at earlier grade levels, 2) complement other reform initiatives such as inclusive practices, and 3) support the necessary staff development.

The four vantage points—philosophical, governmental/policy, organizational, and professional/procedural—are useful in classifying the multiple variables that can support or impede our ability to respond to complicated educational innovations or controversies. Applying these vantage points to analyze self-determination suggests that there are multiple actions and issues that must be addressed to support and sustain systemic change over time to realize this outcome for individuals with disabilities. It should be apparent by now that these vantage points are interrelated. Typically, the goals and assumptions of one level are set by those above and the information base used to evaluate one level is supplied from the level below. Suppose, for example, that a school wants to implement a curriculum (procedure) for self-determination that requires participation from families and local community organizations. If a school does not have a mechanism by which to coordinate or manage this participation (organization), implementation of the curriculum could be compromised. If the curriculum effort were to fail, information from the procedural level could serve to inform us of ineffective structures at the organizational level such as lack of mechanisms to foster family and community participation.

SELF-DETERMINATION—MOVING INTO THE FUTURE

We have suggested previously that achieving the outcome that all students with disabilities leave school as self-determined young adults will be as difficult and complex to achieve as similar efforts to ensure that school graduates are employed and living in the community (Wehmeyer et al., in press). Achieving this outcome in adult systems, like vocational rehabilitation, will be equally difficult, as illustrated by West (Chapter 15) and Abery and Stancliffe (Chapter 7). There are no quick and easy fixes or magic formulas to help us carry forth the underlying values and beliefs that drive this movement. As we look at sources of controversy within each vantage point it is clear that the knowledge bases required to respond to the many questions are emerging, yet incomplete. If we are to achieve school communities and adult services that have the capacities and supports necessary to respond to individual consumer needs, it becomes important to respond to these questions and build knowledge bases that inform and direct our practice.

CONCLUSIONS

The primary purposes of this volume are to introduce the topic of self-determination to practitioners in the field of disability services, initiate a dialogue about this important construct, and provide practical applications for promoting this outcome. We believe that the complexity of this effort has been duly documented in the various chapters. However, there is a danger that this complexity will overshadow the paradoxical simplicity of the self-determination movement itself. Self-determination is, most basically, enabling and allowing control and choice for all people, including people with disabilities. The simplicity of this message belies the complexity of achieving this outcome, but illustrates the compelling nature of the call. As repeated by Ward (Chapter 1), Kennedy (Chapter 3), and Ruth Sienkiewicz-Mercer and Ray Gagne in Wehmeyer (Chapter 2), this is an outcome that is as important as virtually any other in the lives of people with disabilities, as illustrated by the following example.

Regina Demaresse (1989) lived for most of her early life in an institution for people with mental retardation. With the support of a circle of friends, she moved from the institution to the community and her reflections on the processes that both held her at the institution and moved her to the community make for both a chilling accusation of the past and a clarion call for the future. Demaresse came to the conclusion that the professionals who worked with her were worried more about creating false hope than allowing her to dream, and by focusing on avoiding false hope, they created a self-fulfilling prophesy of dependence. Demaresse responded by pondering the following:

> I've never heard these same professionals speak of "true hope", but it seems to me that [false hope] might be its opposite. Must hope be either true or false? Doesn't hope imply something that has not yet come to pass? Isn't there really something wrong with telling a despairing young person who wants to live independently out in the community that such ideas are ludicrous? Should you let bright, vibrant, sensitive or just plain feeling people, worthy of dignity and love, lose all hope rather then give them "false" hope, because you assume that if you've never seen it done before, it's not a possibility? (p. 9)

Despite seemingly insurmountable barriers, Demaresse, like Ward, Kennedy, Gagne, and Sienkiewicz-Mercer, achieved her goals and became an independent, self-determined person. She summarized her experience by saying:

> In the end, I did move out of the institution and into the community; I am living with the kind of roommates I had hoped for, in the kind of quiet country setting I dreamed about; I do have the kind of assistance and help I had hoped for; and my time is spent writing the book I have always dreamed of, without the institution dictating where and when I could do all kinds of things I like best. I am glad that a group of us got together to share some "false hope." (p. 9)

In the end, the real purpose of this volume is to encourage professionals in all fields to go beyond what we know and expect and create some "false hope" in the lives of people with disabilities by encouraging and supporting them to be self-determined individuals.

REFERENCES

Americans with Disabilities Act of 1990 (ADA), PL 101-336. (July 26, 1990). Title 42, U.S.C. 12101 et seq: *U.S. Statutes at Large, 104,* 327–378.

Apple, M.W., & Beane, J.A. (1995). The case for democratic schools. In M. Apple & J. Beane (Eds.), *Democratic schools* (pp. 1–25). Alexandria, VA: Association for Supervision and Curriculum Development.

Brotherson, M.J., Cook, C.C., Cunconan-Lahr, R., & Wehmeyer, M.L. (1995). Policy supporting self-determination in the environments of children with disabilities. *Education and Training in Mental Retardation and Developmental Disability, 30,* 3–14.

Carl D. Perkins Vocational and Applied Technology Education Act of 1990, PL 101-392. (September 25, 1990). Title 20, U.S.C. 2301 et seq: *U.S. Statutes at Large, 104,* 733–843.

Cornell Empowerment and Family Project. (1990). *Networking: A bulletin on empowerment and family support.* Ithaca, NY: Author.

Demaresse, R. (1989). On avoiding false hope. In D. Wetherow (Ed.), *Introduction to the Whole Community Catalog* (p. 9). Manchester, CT: Communitas.

Dennis, R.E., Williams, W., Giangreco, M.F., & Cloninger, C. (1993). Quality of life as context for planning and evaluation of services for people with disabilities. *Exceptional Children, 59,* 499–512.

Fair Housing Amendment Act of 1988, PL 101-430. (September 13, 1988). Title 42, U.S.C. 3601 et seq: *U.S. Statutes at Large, 102,* 1619–1636.

Gartner, A., & Lipsky, D. (1987). Beyond special education: Toward a quality system for all students. *Harvard Educational Review, 57,* 367–395.

Goodlad, J.I. (1984). *A place called school: Prospects for the future.* New York: McGraw-Hill.

Halloran, W.D. (1993). Transition services requirement: Issues, implications, challenge. In R.C. Eaves & P.J. McLaughlin (Eds.), *Recent advances in special education and rehabilitation* (pp. 210–224). Boston: Andover Medical.

Haring, T.G. (1991). Social relationships. In L.H. Meyer, C.A. Peck, & L. Brown (Eds.), *Critical issues in the lives of people with severe disabilities* (pp. 195–217). Baltimore: Paul H. Brookes Publishing Co.

Individuals with Disabilities Education Act of 1990 (IDEA), PL 101-476. (October 30, 1990). Title 20, U.S.C. 1400 et seq: *U.S. Statutes at Large, 104,* 1103–1151.

Janney, R.E., Snell, M.E., Beers, M.K., & Raynes, M. (1995). Integrating students with moderate and severe disabilities into general education classes. *Exceptional Children, 61,* 425–439.

Kozleski, E.B., & Jackson, L. (1993). Taylor's story: Full inclusion in her neighborhood elementary school. *Exceptionality, 4,* 153–175.

Lortie, D. (1975). *Schoolteacher: A sociological study.* Chicago: University of Chicago Press.

Malouf, D.B., & Schiller, E.P. (1995). Practice and research in special education. *Exceptional Children, 61,* 414–424.

McFadden, D.L., & Burke, E.P. (1991). Developmental disabilities and the new paradigm: Directions for the 1990s. *Mental Retardation, 29*(1), iii–vi.

Noddings, N. (January, 1995). A morally defensible mission for schools in the 21st century. *Phi Delta Kappan,* 365–368.

Noddings, N. (1984). *Caring: A feminine approach to ethics and moral education*. Los Angeles: University of California Press.

O'Neil, J. (1995a). Can inclusion work? A conversation with Jim Kauffman and Mara Sapon-Shevin. *Educational Leadership, 52*, 7–11.

O'Neil, J. (1995b). On preparing students for the world of work: A conversation with Willard Daggett. *Educational Leadership, 52*, 46–51.

Rehabilitation Act of 1973, PL 93-112. (September 26, 1973). Title 29, U.S.C. 701 et seq: *U.S. Statutes at Large, 87*, 355–394.

Rehabilitation Act Amendments of 1992, PL 102-569. (October 29, 1992). Title 29, U.S.C. 701 et seq: *U.S. Statutes at Large, 100*, 4344–4488.

Salisbury, C.L., Palombaro, M.M., & Hollowood, T.M. (1993). On the nature and change of an inclusive elementary school. *Journal of The Association for Persons with Severe Handicaps, 18*, 75–84.

Sands, D. (in press). Analyzing and responding to educational issues: Taking action to support communities of learners for the 21st century. In D. Sands, E. Kozleski, & N. French (Eds.), *Special education for the twenty-first century: Making schools inclusive communities*. Pacific Grove, CA: Brooks/Cole.

Sarason, S.B. (1990). *The predictable failure of educational reform*. San Francisco: Jossey-Bass.

Schlecty, P. (1990). *Schools for the twenty-first century*. San Francisco: Jossey-Bass.

Skrtic, T.M. (1991). The special education paradox: Equity as the way to excellence. *Harvard Educational Review, 61*, 148–206.

Wehmeyer, M.L. (1993). Sounding a certain trumpet: Case management as a catalyst for the empowerment of people with developmental disabilities. *Journal of Case Management, 2*, 14–18.

Wehmeyer, M.L. (in press). Self-directed learning and self-determination. In M. Agran (Ed.), *Student-directed learning: A handbook on self-management*. Pacific Grove, CA: Brooks/Cole.

Wehmeyer, M.L., Martin, J.E., & Sands, D.J. (in press). Self-determination for children and youth with developmental disabilities. In A. Hilton, D. Finn, & R. Ringlaben (Eds.), *Best practices in educating students with developmental disabilities*. Austin, TX: PRO-ED.

Wehmeyer, M.L., & Ward, M.J. (1995). Student involvement in transition planning: The spirit of the IDEA mandate. *The Journal for Vocational Special Needs Education, 17*, 108–111.

York, J., Vandercook, T., MacDonald, C., Heise-Neff, C., & Caughey, E. (1992). Feedback about integrating middle-school students with severe disabilities in general education classes. *Exceptional Children, 58*, 244–258.

INDEX

Page numbers followed by "f" or "t" indicate figures or tables, respectively.